JUST SATISFACTION UNDER THE EUROPEAN CONVENTION ON HUMAN RIGHTS

How effective is the European Court of Human Rights in dispensing justice? With over 17,000 judgments handed down, it is undoubtedly the most prolific international court, but is it the most efficient when compensating the victims of a violation? This crucial but often overlooked question is the focus of this important new monograph which gives a clear, comprehensive and convincing demonstration of the negative impact, in terms of unpredictability and legal uncertainty, of the discretion used by the Court when it comes to the regime of reparation. It reveals the adverse influence of such a high level of discretion on the quality of its rulings – ultimately on the coherence of the system and on the Court's authority – and makes suggestions for improvement.

OCTAVIAN ICHIM is a legal researcher with an inter-disciplinary background. He previously worked as a case lawyer at the Registry of the European Court of Human Rights. This book is a fully updated and revised version of his thesis, which won the 2013 René Cassin Thesis Prize from the International Institute of Human Rights, Strasbourg, France.

JUST SATISFACTION UNDER THE EUROPEAN CONVENTION ON HUMAN RIGHTS

OCTAVIAN ICHIM

CAMBRIDGE
UNIVERSITY PRESS

CAMBRIDGE
UNIVERSITY PRESS

Shaftesbury Road, Cambridge CB2 8EA, United Kingdom

One Liberty Plaza, 20th Floor, New York, NY 10006, USA

477 Williamstown Road, Port Melbourne, VIC 3207, Australia

314–321, 3rd Floor, Plot 3, Splendor Forum, Jasola District Centre, New Delhi – 110025, India

103 Penang Road, #05–06/07, Visioncrest Commercial, Singapore 238467

Cambridge University Press is part of Cambridge University Press & Assessment, a department of the University of Cambridge.

We share the University's mission to contribute to society through the pursuit of education, learning and research at the highest international levels of excellence.

www.cambridge.org
Information on this title: www.cambridge.org/9781107072367

First published 2015

A catalogue record for this publication is available from the British Library

Library of Congress Cataloging-in-Publication data
Ichim, Octavian, 1978– author.
Just satisfaction under the European Convention on Human Rights / Octavian Ichim.
pages cm
Revision of author's thesis (doctoral – Graduate Institute of International and Development Studies, Geneva, Switzerland), 2012.
ISBN 978-1-107-07236-7 (Hardback)
1. European Court of Human Rights. 2. Human rights – Europe. 3. Judgments – Europe. I. Title.
KJC5138.I24 2014
342.2408′5269–dc23
2014019428

ISBN 978-1-107-07236-7 Hardback

To my wife, Oana, and our son, Andrei

CONTENTS

ACKNOWLEDGMENTS

This book addresses a crucial issue which has been neglected by academics for far too long: the way in which the European Court of Human Rights allocates just satisfaction. The inspiration to write this study came shortly after I had started working as a case lawyer at the European Court. The book is a revised and updated version of my doctoral thesis, which I defended at Geneva's Graduate Institute of International and Development Studies in September 2012.

Being inspired, however, has little effect if that inspiration is not carefully channelled. Thankfully, I was wisely guided by my thesis supervisor, Professor Andrea Bianchi, and I would like to express my gratitude to him. He has had an enduring and decisive influence on my intellectual formation through his constant reshaping of my critical thinking and, at the same time, by incessantly pushing me beyond the limits. I am also deeply grateful to the other members of the thesis committee: to Professor Andrew Clapham for his valuable comments and advice since the very earliest stages of my research, which have definitely helped me to improve this final version, and to Professor Francesco Bestagno for his enriching commentaries and suggestions.

The original thesis was awarded the 2013 René Cassin Thesis Prize by the International Institute of Human Rights, Strasbourg. I would like to offer my heartfelt thanks to the members of the jury, formed by Professors Helen Keller, Olivier de Schutter and Gudmundur Alfredsson, and chaired by Professor Philip Alston, to whom I am especially grateful for his willingness to provide me with insightful comments.

My journey in the field of human rights has been initiated by Professor Lucius Caflisch, who was the supervisor of my masters thesis at the Graduate Institute and judge at the Court, and to whom I am most grateful. Particular thanks must also go to the Court's judges and Registry staff who kindly answered all my questions, especially Judge Egbert Myjer, Stanley Naismith, Section Registrar, Peter Kempees, the

Head of the Just Satisfaction Division, and Crina Kaufman, Head of Division.

I am further indebted to my good friend, Kevin Fray, for his professionalism and meticulous English revision of the whole manuscript. My sincere admiration also goes to the editorial team at Cambridge University Press, and in particular to the two anonymous reviewers who provided me with helpful comments on some parts of the original draft.

I would also like to thank my parents, Rodica and Traian, for never ceasing to encourage me.

But most of all, there are two people in my life who deserve my entire gratitude: my loving wife, Oana, who nurtures the same passion for human rights and whose patience, unconditional support and critical advice have been crucial during the long hours through which I have strived to complete my work, and our precious angel, Andrei, who brings an increased sense of meaning and purpose to our lives and to whom I now have the most wonderful of obligations: to make up for lost time. This book is dedicated to them.

TABLE OF CASES

European Court of Human Rights

European Commission of Human Rights

Resolutions by the Committee of Ministers

International Court of Justice

Permanent Court of International Justice

Inter-American Court of Human Rights

Iran–United States Claims Tribunal

International Tribunal for the Law of the Sea

Arbitration tribunals

TABLE OF TREATIES AND DECLARATIONS

1

Introduction

1.1 Scope of the study

The Convention for the Protection of Human Rights and Fundamental Freedoms[1] (the Convention) has created a unique international system for defence of human rights. The judgments delivered by the European Court of Human Rights (the Court) benefit from worldwide recognition and authority. They cover a vast area of manifestation of fundamental rights attributes, and further develop the human rights theory. But while those rulings are often innovative and highly influential in particular fields – and thus merit acclamations for expanding the scope of protection – the adjudication on victims' claims for reparation usually raises questions. The main problem is that the judges offer scant reasoning for their awards: typically, they are evasive. When comparing the just satisfaction levied in a case with previous judgments in similar disputes, it is sometimes difficult to understand the departure from the precedent. While the Court is not formally bound by its precedent, it is a matter of consistency to construe a harmonious practice. The circumstances of a case may call for a departure, but then again the absence of argument undermines the Court's authority. The judges rely heavily on the discretion conferred by the general language of the treaty provision on just satisfaction and put forward the principles of necessity and equity, which they still need to define. The result is a divergent case law on reparation and a lack of clear valuation principles.

The main objective of this study is to demonstrate that the broad discretion that the Strasbourg judges enjoy in the field of reparation, coupled with the absence of well-defined and consistent principles either in the Convention or in practice, leads to an inconsistent approach to the matter and ultimately limits the efforts of the victims of human rights

[1] European Convention for the Protection of Human Rights and Fundamental Freedoms, 4 November 1950, ETS 5, 213 UNTS 221.

violations to access effective reparation for the prejudice suffered. A further aim is to perform a thorough analysis of the system of reparation, in order to depict the origins of those shortcomings and to propose improvements. It will not be argued that reparation offered in Strasbourg is fully ineffective, but that it is frequently subjected to a discretionary interpretation and application. Using the extensive practice of the Court, the scrutiny will reveal that there is neither consistency nor predictability in the case law. The judges refrain from defining criteria for compensation and prefer to rule under the shield of absolute discretion on the matter. That has largely generated an incoherent approach to reparation. It is a central aim of the present study to raise awareness of the fact that the system needs to evolve towards effective reparation.

National and international courts and tribunals normally enjoy discretion when deciding the appropriate redress. Such discretion is inevitably higher in the context of compensation for non-pecuniary injury, in so far as that category of harm is inherently impossible to transform into money in an accurate manner. The problem with the Strasbourg system is that, for more than fifty years now, the judges have been reluctant to engage in interpretive exercises. They use principles of reparation without defining them. In particular, it is often hard to perceive the way in which redress for moral damage is established, let alone the existence of a method of calculation. Awards are rather made by approximation with previous rulings, the judges using the diversity of an ample – but fluctuating – precedent when deciding an amount, instead of arriving at a certain result on the basis of a clear set of principles.

What is more striking, though, is that, even if the Court has already started to use a sort of standardized approach in respect of compensation for non-pecuniary damage, the case law has definitely not gained the expected consistency. It is known that, for a limited number of violations, the judges rely on tables which fix the limits of compensation in specific cases. For the time being, the amounts established and the method of calculation are confidential, the Court preferring instead to maintain a large margin of discretion and manoeuvrability. It is, nonetheless, possible to make fairly accurate speculations based on the existing practice in respect of each type of damage. More beneficial to an understanding of the theory of reparation under the Convention would be to extract the logic, if any, used by the judges when deciding the necessity and then the appropriate form of redress. This exercise will put in evidence the shortcomings of the traditional discretionary ruling.

In all probability, the existence of a public standard of compensation would generate more awareness regarding the need to adopt a coherent approach. The problem is that the Court's judges come from different legal and cultural backgrounds, which may pose difficulties as to their motivation and perception of the need to secure consistency for their judgments. Still, it is hard to believe that a clear practice would leave them indifferent to their own precedent. For example, the well-established principles of what amounts to breaching conduct from the state, such as ineffective investigation or unlawful expropriation, are always referred to by the Court in subsequent practice and altered only through the intermediary of a Grand Chamber judgment.

Therefore, the study will argue for the beneficial impact which a more objective, standardized approach based on equitable criteria of application would have on the theory of reparation for moral damage, and even on some heads of material loss. Certainly, it is impossible to conceive of and realistically to implement a fully objective system of compensation, given that moral injury, in particular, depends on the individual attributes of the victim. It is not impossible, however, to keep the judges' discretion within acceptable limits by establishing both lower and upper thresholds for the level of compensation to be allocated within the context of each type of violation.

One may further wonder why the Court, although operating with a human rights philosophy, has sometimes awarded higher compensation for less serious violations. There are several cases where the judges have granted comparable or even higher amounts for the non-pecuniary prejudice caused by interference with the right to protection of property than for moral harm suffered from unlawful killings or inhuman or degrading treatment. Is not that a perversion of human rights? A transparent method of the calculation of monetary compensation and a clear theory of equity, which would allow the adjustment of the award to the specific circumstances of the case and to the victim's condition, should absolutely reflect that situation.

There are many authors who have revealed occasional deficiencies in the Court's rulings on just satisfaction, but no effective solution has been proposed or adopted. It is therefore the purpose of the present survey to suggest appropriate modifications to the Convention mechanisms. Reference will be made to principles, theories and practical examples found in general international law and in other particular regimes of human rights protection. Special attention is given to the similar regime of human rights protection created by the American Convention on

Human Rights (the American Convention),[2] without, however, transforming the analysis of the European Convention into an in-depth comparison between the two mechanisms of control, but using instead some references in order to highlight the shortcomings of the European system. In spite of its specialized analysis, the study is intended not only for the academic discourse on reparations, but also as a tool for judges and legal practitioners who apply the treaty, as well as prospective petitioners, who may find a better understanding of the regime of just satisfaction under the Convention. The Court's judges and the Registry lawyers will also become aware of the shortcomings in the system and hopefully seek to improve the current state of affairs.

1.2 Methodology

The analysis will proceed as follows. After an introductory presentation of the system of control, Chapter 2 considers the particular features of the methods and principles that govern the notion of just satisfaction, with a view to establishing the basis of inquiry. Often, the inconsistency in the Court's approach to the issue of reparation seems to originate in the way the judges make use of the existing principles. In fact, their manifest reluctance to develop those principles and to lay down clear standards and guidelines in the field ultimately interferes with the Court's credibility. It is precisely on account of inconsistent practice that it is difficult to maintain legitimacy.

After the review of the general principles of reparation under the Convention, the analysis will progressively become more specialized. Chapter 3 will address the theoretical and practical aspects of the specific conditions for the application of Article 41 on just satisfaction, with a special emphasis on the right of individual petition, which is the distinctive feature of the Strasbourg system. There are quite a few inter-state cases, even if the conditions of admissibility for the member parties are less strict than for individuals. In the end, however, it is the Court that decides on the necessity to afford redress if a violation is found.

Looking deeper into the practical application of the article on just satisfaction, Chapter 4 will explore the prevalent case law for each type of damage, i.e., pecuniary and non-pecuniary, as well as reimbursement of costs and expenses. Special attention is given to reparation for moral

[2] American Convention on Human Rights, 22 November 1969, OEA/ser.L/II.23, Doc. 21, rev. 6 (1979), OASTS No. 36.

prejudice, where the Court's discretion is the greatest. The aim is to decipher the underlying logic used by the judges when they decide on the necessity to make reparation, when they choose the appropriate form of redress and when they establish the amount of compensation. The method of analysis employed is a qualitative review of the Court's rulings, as opposed to a quantitative survey of the practice that would transform the study into elementary statistics. The purpose is to reveal trends in the judicial process, and to ascertain whether there is consistency in the case law.

The case law is fairly impressive, given that it is made up of thousands of judgments and decisions. When there is only one judgment departing from the precedent, there may be an exception, but when there are already several rulings, they denote acceptance. For that reason, when accounting for principles, standards or new orientations, reference will only be made to some limited practical examples. All those pronouncements are available on the Court's website, through the intermediary of the Hudoc database. The analysis will not cover all of them, because the cases are highly repetitive. A list of selective cases is provided in the annexes at the end of the study, with reference to compensation for non-pecuniary damage for different types of violation, with the purpose not only of illustrating the lack of consistency in the Court's awards, but also of facilitating identification of some patterns in the practice of reparations.

In Chapter 5, the examination will then focus on the procedural incidents that may either facilitate or encumber the availability of compensation for the victim. Equally important for securing effective reparation is the enforcement of the Court's judgments and the specific recommendations made by the judges in respect of execution. Thus, in addition to pecuniary redress, the victim may benefit from individual measures or have the moral satisfaction that the breaching state has been directed to introduce legal amendments so as to prevent further infringements of the rights of persons in a similar position.

In Chapter 6, the study will switch perspective from the past to the future. Having offered a detailed account of the state of affairs, it is time to suggest further developments. The most imperative need is for the judges to provide an explanation for their rulings on just satisfaction and to make an effort to produce consistent practice. Questions also arise as to whether the Court should embark on a constitutional mission and, if so, what would be the effects on individual reparation. Guarantees of non-repetition may also justify a place in the system of control. Finally, when everything has been considered, the question of the reform of the system of reparation should be brought to the fore.

1.3 Preliminary remarks about the Convention system

Before entering into an analysis of the system of reparation, a brief presentation of the control machinery is appropriate. The Council of Europe was created by ten states[3] after the end of the Second World War with the aim of enhancing co-operation in Europe and promoting human rights, democracy and the rule of law. It presently includes forty-seven member states with some 820 million citizens.[4] There are also six countries with observer status.[5] The headquarters are in Strasbourg. The Council of Europe has established a series of standards, charters and conventions, the most famous being the European Convention on Human Rights.[6] Signed in Rome on 4 November 1950 by the then members of the Council, the Convention came into force on 3 September 1953 following ratification by ten states.[7]

The Convention consecrated a series of fundamental rights, predominantly civil and political, but in a rather succinct language. It has been the role of the Court to interpret and give further meaning to those provisions. The special feature of the system is that rights and obligations are not provided on a reciprocal basis between the contracting states, as in the case of classical treaties. Instead, it has created a set of integral obligations, where states undertake commitments to the benefit of the private person. The Convention has been changed several times, the latest reforms being introduced by Protocol No. 14 or waiting for implementation by Protocols Nos. 15 and 16. Each amendment

[3] Belgium, Denmark, France, Ireland, Italy, Luxembourg, the Netherlands, Norway, Sweden and the United Kingdom.

[4] The only state located in Europe which is not a member as of 2014 is Belarus.

[5] The Holy See, the United States of America, Canada, Japan, Mexico and Israel.

[6] For an analysis of the evolution of the Convention system, see E. Bates, *The Evolution of the European Convention on Human Rights: From Its Inception to the Creation of a Permanent Court of Human Rights* (Oxford University Press, 2010).

[7] In chronological order of ratification: the United Kingdom (8 March 1951), Norway (15 January 1952), Sweden (4 February 1952), Germany (5 December 1952), Saarland (14 January 1953), Ireland (25 February 1953), Greece (28 March 1953), Denmark (13 April 1953), Iceland (29 June 1953) and Luxembourg (3 September 1953). Saarland became an integral part of Germany on 1 January 1957.

necessitates ratification by all the member parties, but then forms a part of the treaty. In essence, new protocols have either introduced additional rights,[8] or improved the mechanism of control,[9] or added some procedural rights.[10]

Initially, the control machinery was made up of three bodies: a part-time Court, the now abolished European Commission of Human Rights (the Commission) and the Committee of Ministers. The novelty of the system resided in the creation of a right of individual petition. It was at first optional, with the possibility of renewal, but was then gradually accepted by all the contracting states and eventually made compulsory. Any individual, including a legal person, now has the possibility of bringing an application to Strasbourg.

The drafters of the system had different views on the creation of a court. While the supporters considered that only courts may ensure observance of the law, that a judicial settlement of disputes on treaty interpretation should be accepted and that the notion of sovereignty should not constitute an obstacle, the opponents perceived a too ambitious aim in establishing an authority that would interfere in internal affairs, and rather preferred to bestow upon the Commission the task of solving legal questions, or were simply against the proliferation of international organizations.[11] The compromise solution was to set up a court, but with jurisdiction under an optional clause. The Court was thus established on 21 January 1959, when eight signatory states acknowledged its jurisdiction.

In the beginning, the Court's activity was fairly scant. The system was in its running-in phase; litigants had to become familiar with the supranational procedure. The judges delivered the first judgment on the merits of a case in 1961, in *Lawless v. Ireland*,[12] and then the next three rulings only in 1968.[13] The Court received only eleven cases in its first

[8] Protocols Nos. 1, 4, 6, 7, 12 and 13. [9] Protocols Nos. 3, 5, 8, 10, 11 and 14.

[10] Protocols Nos. 2 and 9.

[11] See discussions within the Conference of Senior Officials held at Strasbourg between 8 and 17 June 1950, in Council of Europe, *Collected Edition of the 'Travaux Préparatoires' of the European Convention on Human Rights* (8 vols., The Hague: Martinus Nijhoff Publishers, 1975–85), Vol. IV, at 114–16 and 128.

[12] *Lawless v. Ireland (no. 3)*, 1 July 1961, Series A no. 3.

[13] *Wemhoff v. Germany*, 27 June 1968, Series A no. 7; *Neumeister v. Austria*, 27 June 1968, Series A no. 8; and *Case 'relating to certain aspects of the laws on the use of languages in education in Belgium' v. Belgium* (merits), 23 July 1968, Series A no. 6 ('*Belgian linguistic*').

fifteen years of existence, but the situation changed in the late 1970s.[14] In addition to pronouncements on the merits, the Court also dealt with some incidental matters, such as preliminary objections, procedural questions and awards of just satisfaction. Progressively though, as more states joined the organization and accepted jurisdiction, disputes before the old Court increased in number and also diversified in respect of subject matter. The drafters of the system had not anticipated that the judges would need to work so hard; the initial text of the Convention merely specified that '[t]he members of the Court shall receive for each day of duty a compensation'.[15]

The new permanent, full-time Court came into being on 1 November 1998, following modifications introduced by Protocol No. 11. It comprises a number of judges equal to that of the members of the Council of Europe and it is assisted by a Registry in its daily work. The Registry is currently made up of some 640 staff members, which include lawyers and other administrative and technical staff and translators. The lawyers do not decide cases, but only examine and prepare applications for adjudication. They draft analytical notes for the judges, in one of the two official languages, advise judges in respect of national law, and correspond with the parties on procedural matters. In other words, they give an opinion on the facts and legal questions, but the judges may or may not endorse that view.

The Court functions in accordance with the Convention and with its own Rules.[16] Its role is to examine and decide both individual and inter-state applications. If found in violation of the rights or freedoms provided in the treaty, a state may be ordered to make reparation. The Court's judgments are binding on the states concerned and execution is supervised by the Committee of Ministers. But the role of the Committee was not always limited to the execution phase. Before entry into force of Protocol No. 11, it also had significant quasi-judicial powers. Former Article 32 of the treaty provided that an application declared admissible by the Commission and then transmitted to the Committee of Ministers, but not referred to the Court within three months, was to be decided by a two-thirds majority vote of the Committee.

[14] R. Bernhardt, 'Human Rights and Judicial Review: The European Court of Human Rights', in D. M. Beatty (ed.), *Human Rights and Judicial Review: A Comparative Perspective* (Dordrecht: Martinus Nijhoff Publishers, 1994), at 300.

[15] Former Article 42 of the Convention.

[16] See the latest Rules of Court which entered into force on 1 January 2014, available on the Court's website (www.echr.coe.int/Pages/home.aspx?p=basictexts/rules&c=).

In its capacity as a political organ, the Committee relied heavily on the specialist advice of the Commission's experts, without being officially bound by those views. It regularly used to endorse the Commission's opinion, and thus to endow it with a binding effect. The solution was laudable in so far as it conferred a judicial basis to their decisions. What was quite striking, though, was that the individual petitioner had no representation before the Committee, whereas the state accused of breaching the treaty even had a right to vote in respect of the solution to the case. Simply stated, the government concerned was defendant and judge at the same time.[17] In practice, however, the fact that the Committee used to endorse the Commission's reports limited to the maximum its political involvement in the mechanism of control. In the end, when Protocol No. 11 established a permanent Court, it also took away from the Committee its quasi-judicial powers. The result is that it has transformed the procedure into an entirely judicial process.

The Commission was a non-judicial body of independent experts, one from each state party. The first members were elected by the Committee of Ministers on 18 May 1954. Their role was to receive and examine applications from both states and individuals, reject those which were inadmissible and transmit to the Court or to the Committee those which raised important issues in respect of the Convention guarantees. At times, in its opinion on the merits of a case – the so-called 'Article 31 Report' – the Commission made propositions to the applicant's benefit even when it had not established a breach.[18] This was rightly considered a sort of humanitarian action, unjustifiable though because its task was to apply the treaty, not to launch into sympathetic activities.[19]

The Commission played an important role for the system in its capacity as a filtering body. It was 'the gatekeeper to the Convention's system of collective enforcement'.[20] Even if the drafters reserved for the Court the most intellectually challenging activity of deciding state responsibility, and left to the Commission the routine work, that task was very significant. As at present, more than 90 per cent of applications have been declared inadmissible. Basically, the Commission acted as a quality checker of what came to Strasbourg and sent upward only what

[17] P. Leuprecht, 'Article 32', in L.-E. Pettiti, E. Decaux and P.-H. Imbert (eds.), *La Convention européenne des droits de l'homme. Commentaire article par article* (Paris: Economica, 1999), at 705.

[18] *Austria v. Italy*, no. 788/60, Commission's report of 30 March 1963.

[19] S. Trechsel, 'Article 31', in Pettiti, Decaux and Imbert, note 17, at 695–6.

[20] Bates, note 6, at 120.

deserved particular attention. It used to suggest reparation in situations disclosing a breach of the treaty, but the Court was not bound by the Commission's findings on the merits or by the recommendations for recovery of damage. The judges sometimes used their power to give a more restrictive solution. Such has been the case when the Court has not upheld the Commission's findings and thus ruled for the inadmissibility of a claim.[21]

In the early years of the system of protection, there were few cases that reached the old Court for a review against the Convention standards. That situation occasionally generated tension between the two institutions, to the extent that some judges even questioned the future of the Court's role. In the mid-1960s, while the Court included 'some of the finest international judges in the world', they were prevented by 'this usurpation of authority by the Commission' from starting to create the Strasbourg jurisprudence.[22] However, one should not ignore that the control mechanism was in its incipient stage. Its subsequent evolution largely proves that the judges have had countless occasions to build and refine a solid case law, not only in respect of violations on the merits, but also in respect of reparation. Eventually, the Commission was abolished in 1998, when Protocol No. 11 entered into force.

1.4 Evolution of the system of compensation

The formula of an award of just satisfaction after the finding of a breach of treaty obligations is not an innovation of the Strasbourg system, but was transposed from traditional international law. During its first ruling on the matter in the *Vagrancy* cases, the Court mentioned that the provision on reparation had its origin in similar clauses which were present in classical treaties such as the 1921 German–Swiss Treaty on Arbitration and Conciliation and the 1928 Geneva General Act for the Pacific Settlement of International Disputes.[23] While those instruments dealt with inter-state remedies, the concept has been

[21] See, e.g., in the case of *Mellacher and Others v. Austria* (nos. 10522/83, 11011/84 and 11070/84), the Commission's decision of 11 July 1988 and the Court's judgment of 19 December 1989, Series A no. 169.

[22] Bates, note 6, at 214.

[23] *De Wilde, Ooms and Versyp v. Belgium* (Article 50), 10 March 1972, Series A no. 14, para. 16.

adjusted for application to individual complaints. It was thus the intention of the drafters to draw a parallel between the principles regulating typical inter-state relationships in international law and the norms applying to a system based on state obligations to the benefit of private persons. The judges have also developed the central principle of the Convention system of reparation – which is *restitutio in integrum* – by reference to the general principles of state responsibility.

The evolution of the concept goes back to the *travaux préparatoires*, when a proposed authority for the Court to annul internal legislation or judgments generated negative reaction. In the Draft Convention prepared by the European Movement and submitted to the Committee of Ministers on 12 July 1949, the Court's envisaged powers were not limited to making reparation, but extended further to the possibility of imposing on the state concerned a line of conduct, such as repealing or amending acts or punishing the perpetrators.[24] However, a Preliminary Draft Convention submitted to the Committee of Ministers by a Committee of Experts on 15 February 1950 did not include those wide-ranging attributes, confining the judges' powers to the present limitation of granting only just satisfaction.[25] In a subsequent report of 16 March 1950, the Experts declared that 'the Court will not have the power to declare null and void or amend Acts emanating from the public bodies of the signatory States'.[26]

Eventually, the drafters refrained from giving extensive powers to the judges in the final text of the Convention, apparently being concerned to draw up a system that would gain political support. The text of the present Article 41 on just satisfaction reads as follows:

> If the Court finds that there has been a violation of the Convention or the Protocols thereto, and if the internal law of the High Contracting Party concerned allows only partial reparation to be made, the Court shall, if necessary, afford just satisfaction to the injured party.

[24] See the text of Article 13(b) in the *Collected Edition of the 'Travaux Préparatoires'*, note 11, Vol. I, at 300–2. It provided as follows: 'The Court may either prescribe measures of reparation or it may require that the State concerned shall take penal or administrative action in regard to the persons responsible for the infringement, or it may demand the repeal, cancellation or amendment of the act.'

[25] See Article 36 in the *Collected Edition of the 'Travaux Préparatoires'*, note 11, Vol. III, at 246.

[26] Commentary to Article 39 (43) (new) in the *Collected Edition of the 'Travaux Préparatoires'*, note 11, Vol. IV, at 44.

That provision is not conceptually different from that of former Article 50.[27] Governments are traditionally reluctant to give away prerogatives of state sovereignty and to have an outside influence on their internal affairs. Such an entitlement for the Court would probably have had the effect of deterring the European states from being involved in a regional mechanism for human rights protection. In contrast, the Inter-American system is more revolutionary in that respect. The American Convention provides that, when the exercise of the rights protected is not ensured in domestic legislation, 'the States Parties undertake to adopt, in accordance with their constitutional processes and the provisions of this Convention, such legislative or other measures as may be necessary to give effect to those rights or freedoms'.[28] The Court of San José had no reservations in ordering a breaching state, in accordance with that provision and leaving for the state the choice of the means, to 'adopt in its domestic legislation, the legislative, administrative and any other measures that are necessary in order to adapt . . . legislation to . . . the Convention'.[29]

At first sight, from the perspective of an efficient protection of human rights, the European Convention may seem to suffer from a drawback by reference to its American counterpart. The Strasbourg system is more focused on a case-by-case examination of the concrete application of domestic provisions, rather than on providing a truly effective remedy for present and future collective risks posed by legislation in disagreement with treaty standards. The Convention machinery has nonetheless endeavoured to compensate for that deficit. While the treaty does not allow the Court to invalidate laws or other internal acts in a direct manner, the judges still have the power to proclaim that legal provisions are incompatible with the treaty and even to order the state to take general measures to remedy the situation. This gives not only the state involved, but also the other member states, a signal that amendments are

[27] 'If the Court finds that a decision or a measure taken by a legal authority or any other authority of a High Contracting Party, is completely or partially in conflict with the obligations arising from the present convention, and if the internal law of the said Party allows only partial reparation to be made for the consequences of this decision or measure, the decision of the Court shall, if necessary, afford just satisfaction to the injured party.'

[28] Article 2 of the American Convention.

[29] Point 5 of the operative part in the *Case of the 'Street Children' (Villagrán-Morales et al.) v. Guatemala* (reparations and costs), 26 May 2001, Series C no. 77.

needed so as to prevent recurrence. As aptly noted, the control system may thus reveal a deterrent effect.[30] In that sense, the judges have identified in Article 1 of the Convention a commitment on the part of the contracting states to ensure that their legislation is compatible with treaty standards.[31]

The Court and the Committee of Ministers were the two Convention organs that were originally given the power not only to deliver a final and binding decision on the merits of a case, but also to grant reparation. Their relationship was governed by the principle of subsidiarity, inasmuch as the Committee had to settle a case only when the Court had not been given notice. The official reason for giving the Committee a judicial role was the need for a body to decide on those cases that were not, or could not be, referred to the Court.[32]

The Court has the same prerogatives in respect of an award, which will be explained in detail in the following chapters. Some remarks are therefore in order as to the Committee's former quasi-judicial activity. In the event of wrongful conduct, the Committee imposed a time limit by which the breaching state had to take some measures, and supervised the enforcement. Even if not expressly mentioned, those measures included individual redress or general indications. When it had expressly specified the means which a state had to use to put an end to unlawful acts or omissions, the state had to carry out those means, not simply to produce a certain result.[33]

The Committee was well aware of the importance and different nature of its tasks, and therefore designed a set of specific rules.[34] In practice, it did not itself establish just satisfaction, even when a petition

[30] D. J. Harris et al., *Law of the European Convention on Human Rights* (Oxford University Press, 2009), at 32.

[31] *Maestri v. Italy* [GC], no. 39748/98, ECHR 2004-I, para. 47.

[32] A. Drzemczewski, 'Decision on the Merits: By the Committee of Ministers', in R. St. J. Macdonald, F. Matscher and H. Petzold (eds.), *The European System for the Protection of Human Rights* (Dordrecht: Martinus Nijhoff Publishers, 1993), at 737.

[33] J. Velu, 'Report on "Responsibilities for States Parties to the European Convention"', in *Proceedings of the Sixth International Colloquy about the European Convention on Human Rights (13–16 November 1985) = Actes du sixième Colloque international sur la Convention européenne des droits de l'homme (13–16 novembre 1985)* (Dordrecht: Martinus Nijhoff Publishers, 1988), at 606–14.

[34] Rules of procedure adopted by the Committee of Ministers relating to the application of Article 32 of the Convention, *Yearbook of the European Convention on Human Rights* 4 (1961), p. 14.

was similar to other cases where the Court had already afforded redress,[35] but used to recommend the reparation proposed by the Commission. Starting in 1987, those rules were amended for the purpose of giving the Committee competence for granting just satisfaction, because the treaty made no express reference to such a power.[36] The Committee was not ordering reparation *suo motu*, but only at the applicants' request. The opposing parties also had the possibility to reach a friendly settlement, and the case was to be closed if agreement was based on respect for human rights.

The Committee normally dealt with repetitive cases. In doing so, important aspects raised by the application of the Convention were reserved for judicial review by the Court, instead of political scrutiny. The decisions taken by the Committee did not represent judicial decisions, unlike the Court's rulings. Therefore, they did not enjoy the same authority, namely *res judicata* and *res interpretata*, but they did have a binding effect on states, which was secured by an enforcement mechanism. Even so, the quasi-judicial powers conferred on the Committee have rightly been criticized.[37]

In essence, the Committee acted as a forum for political solutions to judicial questions, and sometimes failed in fulfilling its role and in performing its treaty obligations. Those were the cases where the Committee was not taking any decision in respect of the alleged violation and, consequently, was not proposing any reparation. Such use of its powers was manifestly inconsistent with the express wording of the Convention, which called for a decision whether there had been a violation or not. As should have been anticipated, the main concern of the Committee was the promotion of good political relations between the

[35] J.-F. Flauss, 'La pratique du Comité des ministres du Conseil de l'Europe au titre de l'article 32 de la Convention européenne des droits de l'homme (1985–1987)', *Annuaire français de droit international* 33 (1987), at 742 and the cases cited.

[36] On 19 December 1991, the Committee decided to delete Rule 5, which provided that the recommendations made by the Committee in respect of the measures required from the respondent state were not binding because they were not decisions.

[37] See, e.g., F. W. Hondius, 'The Other Forum', in F. Matscher and H. Petzold (eds.), *Protecting Human Rights: The European Dimension – Studies in Honour of G. J. Wiarda = Protection des droits de l'homme: la dimension européenne – Mélanges en l'honneur de G. J. Wiarda* (Cologne: Carl Heymanns Verlag, 1988), at 647; P. Leuprecht, 'The Protection of Human Rights by Political Bodies: The Example of the Committee of Ministers of the Council of Europe = Der Schutz der Menschenrechte durch politische Organe: das Beispiel des Ministerkomitees des Europarates', in M. Nowak et al. (eds.), *Fortschritt im Bewusstsein der Grund- und Menschenrechte: Festschrift für Felix Ermacora = Progress in the Spirit of Human Rights* (Kehl: N. P. Engel, 1988), at 95.

member states, rather than the effective application of the treaty. It took almost forty years for the system to realize and finally redress such denials of justice.

Governments were generally very receptive to signs from Strasbourg as to the consequences of a violation. Based on the Commission's opinion or on previous judgments by the Court in similar disputes, they used to remedy the internal effects of a breach even before a decision by the Committee.[38] In those cases, the Committee was simply taking note of internal measures or payments, in the context of the reparation due for a violation,[39] without assessing the compatibility with the Convention of any legislative modifications.

When Protocol No. 11 abolished the powers of the other treaty organs involved in the examination of a case, it conferred exclusive power on the judges to award just satisfaction. The Court has also gained exclusivity in respect of friendly settlements. Thereafter, it has been solely competent to rule on alleged breaches of the Convention or its Protocols, and to procure redress. The Court has also become more proactive. Before those amendments, the judges used to confine themselves to pecuniary awards, but following the establishment of a permanent Court, they started to indicate individual and general measures.[40]

The present organization, with a sole judicial organ deciding the general policy of reparation, gives more consistency to its case law, because the views of the abolished Commission were not always in agreement with the Court's rulings. Thenceforward, the judges have only been concerned with synchronization between the different Sections of the Court. It is nonetheless of great assistance that the Committee was kept involved in monitoring the enforcement of the Court's rulings, owing to the fact that it has the requisite political leverage to induce states to abide by final judgments. Such supervision of execution by a political organ, which does not exist in the American system of protection of human rights, has, theoretically at least, proved its efficiency.

[38] Flauss, note 35, at 732.

[39] See, e.g., Resolution DH(83)8 of 22 April 1983 in *B. v. the United Kingdom*, and Resolution DH(83)9 of 23 June 1983 in *Andorfer Tonwerke, Walter Hannak and Co. i.L. v. Austria*.

[40] See below, Section 5.3 of Chapter 5.

2

Methods and principles of legal analysis

The aim of this chapter is to fix the basis of inquiry, with particular emphasis placed on the standards of reparation. First and foremost, it should be mentioned that the drafters of the Convention have been well aware that, in most cases, damage caused by human rights violations cannot be fully restored. For that reason, while the Court promotes the theoretical primacy of the principle of *restitutio in integrum*, the official standard of reparation is that of just, fair compensation. This does not mean that the state can discharge its obligation of reparation by a simple remuneration for its wrongful behaviour, especially when the breach is continuous. During execution of a Court judgment, and sometimes even at the moment of adjudication, states may be required, in virtue of that duty to make full reparation, to adopt individual or general measures in addition to a pecuniary award.

The judges have sometimes drawn inspiration from general international law when establishing broad or more specific guidelines on the conditions and limits of reparation. The Court has relied on the general rule when it has placed the principle of *restitutio in integrum* at the very foundation of reparation, or when it has decided to adjust compensation to the level of economic development in the respondent state, so as to avoid redress being out of all proportion for the wrongdoer. It also invokes the general principles of treaty interpretation, although in that field it may be suspected that it seeks only to give formal authority to its own interpretation. When the interpretation given by the judges to the treaty obligation to provide redress differs from the general consequences of wrongful conduct in international law, the Convention applies as *lex specialis*. However, it is open to debate whether it has transformed into a self-contained regime, given that it cannot be perceived that there is any intention in the system to totally exclude the application of the common framework of state responsibility.[41] It is a special regime that

[41] For a view that the Convention has created a self-contained regime, see B. Delzangles, *Activisme et Autolimitation de la Cour européenne des droits de l'homme*

applies its own rules, but which sometimes refers to the general rules of responsibility or to other rules of international law whenever the judges deem it necessary to give stronger justification to the interpretation of the internal norm.

The analysis that follows will therefore identify the standards of compensation, as developed by the Court, the principles associated with the identification of the proper reparation, as well as the methods used when making an award. This is not an easy task for all types of injury. In particular, the Court retains a large degree of flexibility in respect of rewards for moral damage and has no intention of renouncing such a wide power. The rulings on reparation denote some reluctance in defining and grounding the principles used in practice. The most evident illustration is the absence of a theory of equity. The judges make reference to equity on almost every occasion on which they make an award, yet without clarifying how they perceive it. Does that mean that they position themselves above the norm, and, by reducing that equity to no more than an ordinary tool through which they make reparation a much easier process, involuntarily damage the Court's legitimacy?

It is nothing extraordinary or blameworthy that the Strasbourg judges enjoy discretion as to awards for non-pecuniary harm, most judges in national or international courts do. What is striking though, is that the case law, in conjunction with either overt or indirect statements made by some practitioners, among which are judges and registrars of the Court, reveals the clear existence of parameters for compensation, which for the time being are not accessible to the public but only for internal use within the Court.[42] Instead, the judges prefer to rule in equity, without revealing the connotation they assign to equity and thus depriving the practice of any predictability. While the Court should enjoy some flexibility in having recourse to equity, the absence of any standard weakens the authority of the concept, particularly as the judges have generally defined the legal concepts they use in the process of adjudication: for instance, torture, fair trial, private life, unreasonable length of proceedings and so on. They have also provided interpretations for different aspects of the provision on just satisfaction, ever since the first judgment on reparation.

(Clermont-Ferrand: Fondation Varenne, 2009), at 134–8. However, the argument revolves around the fact that the treaty generally excludes other means of dispute settlement, and the author makes no reference to the Court's position, reflected in its practice, vis-à-vis the general international law.

42 See below, Subsection 4.2.2 of Chapter 4.

By contrast, they remain silent on equity, although they use it whenever they compensate moral damage. All these standards and principles merit further attention.

2.1 Just satisfaction versus full reparation

The notion of 'just satisfaction' found in the European Convention is relatively original. Both terms of that expression disclose different interpretations and implications. 'Satisfaction' in general international law represents merely one of the forms of reparation, and not even the most important. It covers non-pecuniary damage which is not financially assessable. Such an obligation does not even exist under the Convention, which leaves the impression that the drafters have ignored the original meaning of 'satisfaction' as a simple remedy in international law, rather preferring to use the term for reparation in general. While it is true that the European Convention preceded the codification of the basic rules of state responsibility by the International Law Commission in its Articles on State Responsibility for Internationally Wrongful Acts (the ILC Articles),[43] satisfaction as a form of redress was nonetheless, even at that time, a well-established principle of international law.[44] Therefore, it would not be unreasonable to accept that the drafters made a deliberate choice of that term, rather than an unfortunate mistake.

The Convention identifies the notion of 'just satisfaction' with the entire spectrum of reparation available to an injured party, for pecuniary and non-pecuniary damage, as well as reimbursement of costs and expenses. It normally takes the form of financial redress. Accordingly, and in contrast with the Inter-American Court,[45] the European Court never orders a state to express regret or to apologize for a violation of human rights, neither to the victim nor to the other contracting states for any potential legal prejudice. When in agreement that a claimant has suffered non-pecuniary harm, the judges may order the breaching state to pay an amount of money, but may also consider that the finding of a

[43] ILC Articles on the Responsibility of States for Internationally Wrongful Acts, UN Doc. A/56/10 (2001). For the text of the ILC Articles and commentary, see J. Crawford, *The International Law Commission's Articles on State Responsibility: Introduction, Text, and Commentaries* (Cambridge University Press, 2002).

[44] See the examples given in the Commentary to Article 37 of the ILC Articles, Crawford, note 43, at 232–4.

[45] See, e.g., *Tibi v. Ecuador* (preliminary objections, merits, reparations and costs), 7 September 2004, Series C no. 114, para. 261.

violation constitutes adequate just satisfaction. Would this last-mentioned solution amount to a sort of satisfaction within the meaning of general international law?

The answer seems to be in the negative. In the context of general international law, it has sometimes been assumed that 'unlike restitution and compensation, both of which require an express request by the injured State, it appears that every request for restitution or compensation implicitly entails a request for satisfaction ... since the form of reparation is chosen after the wrongful act has been established'.[46] At first sight, when transposing that statement into Convention practice, one may declare that every pronouncement of a violation automatically offers satisfaction to the victim, but more attentive examination reveals the unsuitability of that approach.

While it is true that the International Court of Justice held in *Corfu Channel* that a declaration of wrongfulness may represent in itself appropriate satisfaction, Albania expressly claimed satisfaction in that case.[47] In Strasbourg, the Court has so far used the 'appropriate satisfaction' formula only in respect of individual applicants. Individuals cannot be considered to have suffered so-called legal prejudice as a result of a breach of the treaty, simply because they are not party to the Convention. In their case, unlike for states, the general trend is to fix an amount of money corresponding to the moral damage. When the Court declines to do so, the main reason would rationally be that the severity of the victim's moral prejudice does not call for more than the very declaration of that violation. It is beyond doubt that the judges have no intention to offer a type of satisfaction within the meaning of general international law, for any affront suffered by private persons, otherwise they would have done so, most likely in the form of a supplementary declaration under the heading of just satisfaction.

A strong argument for the absence of satisfaction from Convention law is offered by comparison with the Inter-American system. That regime expressly provides for the possibility of awarding measures of satisfaction such as '(a) a public act to acknowledge international responsibility and amend the memory of the victims; (b) publication or dissemination of the Court's judgment; (c) measures to commemorate

[46] Y. Kerbrat, 'Interaction between the Forms of Reparation', in J. Crawford, A. Pellet and S. Olleson (eds.), *The Law of International Responsibility* (Oxford University Press, 2010), at 578.

[47] *Corfu Channel*, Merits, ICJ Reports 1949, p. 4, at 35.

the victims or the facts; (d) scholarships or commemorative grants, and (e) implementation of social programs'.[48] Within a judgment, the Inter-American Court examines under different headings the claims for non-pecuniary damage and the other forms of reparation, including measures of satisfaction.[49] There is no doubt that, when ruling on reparation, the Court of San José makes a clear distinction between satisfaction and compensation for pecuniary and non-pecuniary damage. In the absence of such a differentiation in the European system, it would be difficult to assume that the Strasbourg Court implicitly offers satisfaction to the victims. If satisfaction is naturally included in every pronouncement, what then is its relevance?

It has been suggested that the measures of satisfaction awarded by the Inter-American Court have the role of humanizing reparations in international human rights law, given that they go beyond a simple order to pay some monetary compensation.[50] Some judges from that court have also warned against the danger of mercantilization of reparations, in the sense of reducing their wide range to simple indemnifications.[51] Does the current European system encourage the process of 'monetizing' international human rights law remedies in the sense of focusing excessively on translating issues into a financial framework as opposed to alternatives? It seems that the Strasbourg judges have opted for a system that is the most convenient from a practical point of view and they are resistant to any influence from the practice of the Court of San José.

Theoretically, the European Court should indeed not transform into a calculating machine, because in that case 'the labour itself of an international tribunal of human rights would be irremediably devoid of all sense'.[52] But then comes the practical test. Can a system that delivered 18 judgments in 2011 and 21 judgments in 2012 (the Court of San José) be feasibly compared to another that delivered 1,157 and 1,093 judgments (the European Court), respectively? Also, it should not be ignored that there are important differences, in all societal aspects, between the

[48] Annual Report of the Inter-American Court of Human Rights, 2012, available on the Inter-American Court's website (www.corteidh.or.cr/index.php/en/court-today/publicaciones), at 18.

[49] See, e.g., *Case of the Mapiripán Massacre v. Colombia* (merits, reparations and costs), 15 September 2005, Series C no. 134.

[50] J. M. Pasqualucci, *The Practice and Procedure of the Inter-American Court of Human Rights* (Cambridge University Press, 2013), at 205.

[51] Para. 28 of the separate opinion of Judge Cançado Trindade in the *Case of the 'Street Children'* (reparations and costs), note 29.

[52] Ibid., para. 37.

member states that come under the jurisdiction of the two courts. Reasonable doubt is therefore justified.

As regards the choice of the epithet 'just' instead of 'full', one cannot but agree that this was done so as to allow the judges a wide margin of appreciation – and implicitly discretion – with respect to what would amount to appropriate redress in each particular case, not only as a type of reparation but also as an amount of compensation. It would have been both an exaggeration and too heavy a burden for the judges to claim that they can always fully restore the injury caused. It is beyond doubt that circumstances may prevent some form of damage from being recovered and that non-pecuniary harm cannot be precisely evaluated. Just satisfaction is not equivalent to full satisfaction. Most of the time it is less, at least from a victim's perspective, because, in the process of fixing redress, not only does the human factor intervene, that is, the judge or the arbitrator, but so too do objective elements such as the nature of the harm, in particular as regards the moral damage. It is therefore reasonable and judicious to permit certain leverage to the judges, be they national or international, because nothing would totally erase the consequences of a breach and then fully restore the situation which existed before. As will be explained below, *restitutio in integrum* does indeed represent the re-establishment of the *status quo ante*, but only to a certain extent and predominantly in theory.

Theory and practice adopt a slightly different perspective in respect of reparation. The ILC Articles on state responsibility have a pedagogical function, inasmuch as they articulate the generally accepted standards in the field. In Article 31, they proclaim the principle of full reparation, but the rule is not absolute. Article 34 and its Commentary reveal that the obligation to make full redress is limited by the inherent capabilities and restrictions existent in each form of reparation, which have to ensure the proportionality between harm and fault.[53] In other words, as a philosophy, the principle is always that of full reparation, but in practice no authority may affirm that it made 'full' redress. There is no difficulty in accepting that, as long as the ILC Articles themselves permit derogations by special rules.[54] The Strasbourg machinery is one such *lex specialis*.

In fact, the Convention has precisely opted for a system of 'just' reparation, being directly concerned with the practical and effective application of the concept by the Court. It was the most feasible

[53] Crawford, note 43, at 211–12. [54] Article 55 of the ILC Articles.

alternative in so far as, in the words of the former Commission, just satisfaction does not necessarily require 'complete satisfaction'.[55] The question is whether the Convention has implemented the principle in this fashion on purely practical grounds or in virtue of its subsidiarity vis-à-vis the domestic legal systems, or even to avoid engaging the judges or creating fierce debate on what would amount to 'full' reparation. The answer to all these inquiries should in all probability be in the affirmative. The Convention organs always insist on the secondary function of the Court in affording redress, leaving to the states the main duty to provide reparation in the event of a breach of the treaty. Even Article 41 makes awards by the Court dependent upon the impossibility to obtain full reparation at the domestic level.

Moreover, while accepting the conceptual primacy of *restitutio in integrum*, the margin of discretion conferred by the word 'just' allows the judges to put forward the rather equivocal principle of equity and to award not necessarily what it should be but rather what they consider to be appropriate redress in the specific circumstances. Such is the case when the judges find it difficult to distinguish between heads of damage or between pecuniary and non-pecuniary damage, and thus make an assessment on an equitable basis.[56] The problem still remains that in similar disputes they allocate different amounts of compensation, but without any further clarification as to why like cases are not treated alike. While not conceptually wrong, the lack of any judicial explanation affects the Court's credibility.

At the international level, the International Court of Justice continues to promote the traditional principle of reparation as established in *Factory at Chorzów*, that is, restoration when possible to the position existing before the illegal act, or else compensation and/or satisfaction.[57] The Inter-American Court also endorses the idea of *restitutio in integrum*, being nonetheless aware that it is not possible in all cases, and thus alternative measures are called for.[58] The text of Article 63(1) of the American Convention, like Article 41 of the European Convention, refrains from using the expression 'full reparation', instead making

[55] *Stran Greek Refineries and Stratis Andreadis v. Greece*, 9 December 1994, Series A no. 301-B, para. 79.

[56] See, e.g., *Perdigão v. Portugal* [GC], no. 24768/06, 16 November 2010, paras. 85–6.

[57] See, e.g., *Ahmadou Sadio Diallo (Republic of Guinea v. Democratic Republic of the Congo)*, Merits, Judgment, ICJ Reports 2010, p. 639, para. 161.

[58] See, e.g., *Acosta-Calderón v. Ecuador* (merits, reparations and costs), 24 June 2005, Series C no. 129, para. 147, and *Case of the Mapiripán Massacre* (merits, reparations and costs), note 49, para. 244.

reference to fair compensation as a form of redress. When referring to the principle of *restitutio in integrum*, some judges at the Court of San José have even considered that 'although it may be an ideal target for reparations, it does not correspond to a truly attainable goal ... [because] [f]ull restitution ... is conceptually and materially impossible'.[59] Still, that argument was simply illustrated with violations of the most personal attributes, such as the right to life, personal freedom, and physical integrity or destruction of an object, which are indeed irreversible, but human rights infringements are not limited to those actions.

Along similar lines, the Iran–United States Claims Tribunal considered in the case of *INA Corporation*, in the context of the standard of compensation in the presence of lawful expropriations, that 'international law has undergone a gradual re-appraisal, the effect of which may be to undermine the doctrinal value of any "full" or "adequate" (when used as identical to "full") compensation standard'.[60] *In casu*, having regard to the Treaty of Amity, which provided the standard of 'just compensation' in the form of 'the full equivalent of the property taken',[61] the Tribunal proposed compensation in an amount equal to the fair market value. In *Amoco*, the Tribunal further declared that '"[j]ust compensation" has generally been understood as a compensation equal to the full value of the expropriated assets', but admitted that there is no proper formula for determining the full equivalent.[62]

In sum, the theory of state responsibility is normally governed by the principle of full reparation, but human nature, both that of judge and victim, and the objective features of some breaches, make it impossible in practice to establish or agree on what is tantamount to complete redress. Even the ILC Articles do not classify full redress as an absolute standard, but they leave for the primary rule the choice of the level of compensation. Therefore, while international courts and tribunals acting within the confines of specific regimes accept the theoretical primacy of the principle of full reparation, they have no practical

[59] Concurring opinion of Judge García Ramírez in *Bámaca-Velásquez v. Guatemala* (reparations and costs), 22 February 2002, Series C no. 91.

[60] *INA Corporation v. Iran*, 12 August 1985, 8 Iran–US CTR 373, at 378.

[61] Article IV(2) of the Treaty of Amity, Economic Relations, and Consular Rights between the United States of America and Iran, 15 August 1955, 284 UNTS 93; 8 UST 899; TIAS No. 3853.

[62] *Amoco International Finance Corporation v. Iran*, 14 July 1987, 15 Iran–US CTR 189, para. 209.

possibility other than to award what they deem to be equitable in the circumstances of the case.

It is not ideologically wrong that the drafters of the Convention have preferred the standard of 'just satisfaction' over that of 'full reparation', because it would have been utopian to have suggested that the Court could restore the *status quo ante* in every single case. In practice, compensation is the most common form of redress, for the reason that it is generally more problematic to re-establish the *status quo ante* than to estimate financially assessable damage. It is beyond doubt that international judges and arbitrators generally exert discretion as to what represents appropriate redress. They are nonetheless bound by a professional obligation to convince the parties and public opinion of the fairness of their decision. In that sense, even if the application of the standard of just satisfaction depends on the circumstances of the case, the lack of a clear set of principles negatively affects the coherence of the system.

2.2 Causal link

The causal link represents the necessary connection between the illegal activity and the resulting harm.[63] In the absence of causality, the alleged injury is dissociated from the offending conduct and does not justify recovery. There is no express reference to causal link in the text of Article 41, obviously because the whole logic of reparation for unlawful conduct implies the existence of causality.[64] The Court will assign responsibility to a state either when the impugned illegality can be attributed to an official body or agent, or when the state had a positive obligation to take preventive measures to protect a right or to conduct an effective investigation into the circumstances of a violation, but remained passive. The problem with such an 'if . . . then . . .' hypothetical reasoning is that it does not offer certainty as to how the missing action would have prevented the damage and how the potential victim would have reacted.[65]

[63] For an analysis, see P. D'Argent, *Les réparations de guerre en droit international public: la responsabilité internationale des Etats à l'épreuve de la guerre* (Brussels: Bruylant, 2002), at 622–44.

[64] The same holds true for Article 63(1) of the American Convention. The ILC Articles address the causal relationship in Article 31.

[65] F. Rigaux, 'International Responsibility and the Principle of Causality', in M. Ragazzi (ed.), *International Responsibility Today: Essays in Memory of Oscar Schachter* (Leiden: Martinus Nijhoff Publishers, 2005), at 88.

After passing the test of responsibility, the applicants have an obligation to produce relevant evidence in order to establish a direct causal link between the breach and the alleged damage. It is the breach found by the Court to be a violation of the Convention that matters, not any other allegation.[66] The requirement is very strictly assessed by the judges, and the victims of certain violations are often deprived of any compensation or are left with nothing more than the recognition of the illegality. Such is the case, for instance, with pecuniary damage claimed by the victims of procedural irregularities. In particular, if one considers the great number of violations found in Strasbourg in respect of the length of internal proceedings, the Court does not usually perceive a causal connection between that breach and the alleged material harm,[67] apart from some exceptions.[68] A similar category concerns the loss actually suffered and loss, or diminished gain, to be expected in the future in cases regarding confiscation of property,[69] or non-enforcement or delayed execution of judgments which ordered the return of property.[70] In those cases, when deciding the claims for material damage, the Court had no other reasonable choice than to adopt a general formula that it could not speculate either as to what the outcome of the proceedings at issue might have been if the violation of the right to a fair trial had not occurred,[71] or as to the loss of profit or benefit.[72]

Now the question may arise: does the requirement of a causal link exist only in respect of material loss or also for moral damage? The Court obviously demands that condition for both,[73] although discussions and problems arise exclusively in the context of pecuniary damage. As for non-pecuniary harm, causality is more or less evident, and the Court does not even need an elaborate substantiation from the applicant in order to make an award. The judges have pointed to the necessity to

[66] See, e.g., *Mathew v. the Netherlands*, no. 24919/03, ECHR 2005, paras. 223–4.

[67] See, e.g., *Basoukos v. Greece*, no. 7544/04, 27 April 2006, para. 22, and *Bähnk v. Germany*, no. 10732/05, 9 October 2008, para. 54.

[68] See, e.g., *Lechner and Hess v. Austria*, 23 April 1987, Series A no. 118, para. 64; *Martins Moreira v. Portugal*, 26 October 1988, Series A no. 143, para. 65; and *Kambourov v. Bulgaria*, no. 55350/00, 14 February 2008, para. 87.

[69] See, e.g., *Merit v. Ukraine*, no. 66561/01, 30 March 2004, paras. 81 and 84.

[70] See, e.g., *Kemal Turhan v. Turkey*, no. 4397/08, 3 November 2011, paras. 16 and 19.

[71] See, among many others, *Stork v. Germany*, no. 38033/02, 13 July 2006, para. 50.

[72] See, e.g., *Seceleanu and Others v. Romania*, no. 2915/02, 12 January 2010, para. 58.

[73] See, e.g., *Andrejeva v. Latvia* [GC], no. 55707/00, 18 February 2009, para. 111.

have causal nexus for moral damage as a mere association with the indispensable character of that condition for making an award in respect of material damage.[74] Moral suffering comes as an inherent consequence of any violation, the only problem is how to quantify it. Certainly, when the victim claims reparation for a particular form of manifestation of the alleged moral harm, a causal link is necessarily required. As an illustration, in *Halford v. the United Kingdom*, the Court concluded that there was no evidence that the stress suffered by the victim was directly attributable to the interception of her calls, rather than to her other conflicts with the police.[75]

In respect of material damage, practice shows examples when the Court has accepted a chain of causation for loss of earnings following the death of the provider or change of career prospects,[76] and even for loss of private clients.[77] Notwithstanding their inherent speculative character, a direct causal link per se seems evident, and it is also uncontested that a family member offering financial support or a private clientele would have continued with their activity if not prevented by unlawful conduct. But at the same time, the extent to which those persons would have done so is pure speculation, likewise the corresponding reparation. Nothing would allow judges to assume that incapacity for work, or death, or loss of clients may not, in any case, have occurred. For instance, they rightly refused to accept a causal nexus between unlawful detention and alleged opportunity to earn a living,[78] between confinement in a clinic and a prospective career,[79] or for loss of income during unemployment.[80] Hence, the Court reserves the prerogative to hypothesize in the circumstances of each case.

[74] See, in particular, *Kadiķis v. Latvia (no. 2)*, no. 62393/00, 4 May 2006, para. 67.

[75] *Halford v. the United Kingdom*, 25 June 1997, *Reports of Judgments and Decisions* 1997-III, para. 76.

[76] *Barberà, Messegué and Jabardo v. Spain* (Article 50), 13 June 1994, Series A no. 285-C, paras. 16–20; *Çakıcı v. Turkey* [GC], no. 23657/94, ECHR 1999-IV, para. 127; *Salman v. Turkey* [GC], no. 21986/93, ECHR 2000-VII, para. 137; and *Ertak v. Turkey*, no. 20764/92, ECHR 2000-V, para. 150.

[77] *Doustaly v. France*, 23 April 1998, *Reports of Judgments and Decisions* 1998-II, para. 54 *in fine*, and *Georgiadis v. Cyprus*, no. 50516/99, 14 May 2002, para. 53.

[78] *Richert v. Poland*, no. 54809/07, 25 October 2011, paras. 63 and 65, and *Andreyev v. Estonia*, no. 48132/07, 22 November 2011, paras. 85 and 88.

[79] *Storck v. Germany*, no. 61603/00, ECHR 2005-V, para. 176.

[80] *Atanasov v. the former Yugoslav Republic of Macedonia*, no. 22745/06, 17 February 2011, paras. 36 and 38.

However, similar to the notion of equity examined below, where the most judicial discretion can be found, the need for a connection between breach and injury may also lead to inconsistent rulings in the absence of clear standards. This has happened in the context of procedural violations, where the Court has usually refused to see a causal link.[81] It may be logical, given that, but for such a deficiency, accepting causation between the breach of a procedural right and certain damage would account for the presumption that municipal proceedings would have ended differently. Yet the judges, having declared that a plaintiff had suffered loss of opportunities, have often made an award for material damage.[82] In other cases, even if accepting a loss of opportunity warranting monetary compensation, in addition to non-pecuniary damage, the Court has concluded that the applicant suffered only some non-pecuniary damage.[83] Therefore, by omitting any argument, and generally by eluding formulation of guiding principles, the Court sometimes defends its margin of discretion in a way that evades any scholastic scrutiny of the reasoning.

One of the recent cases provides a very good illustration from this point of view. In *Sabeh El Leil*, where the applicant's employment contract at the Kuwaiti embassy in Paris was terminated following reorganization, the Grand Chamber found a violation of his right of access to a court. The ruling on just satisfaction is open to discussion, because it raises the question of the Court's rationale in offering compensation for pecuniary damage when only a procedural right has been violated. Thus, in Strasbourg, the applicant recovered an important percentage of the unemployment benefits awarded by the national first-instance court in a set of proceedings that had eventually been dismissed.[84] As is well known by practitioners, claims

[81] See, e.g., *Ekbatani v. Sweden*, 26 May 1988, Series A no. 134, para. 35 *in fine*; *Mežnarić v. Croatia*, no. 71615/01, 15 July 2005, para. 43; and *A.L. v. Finland*, no. 23220/04, 27 January 2009, para. 49.

[82] E.g., in *F.E. v. France*, 30 October 1998, *Reports of Judgments and Decisions* 1998-VIII, para. 63.

[83] *Elsholz v. Germany* [GC], no. 25735/94, ECHR 2000-VIII, paras. 70–1. The relevant text reads as follows: '[H]e may therefore have suffered a real loss of opportunity warranting monetary compensation. *In addition*, the applicant certainly suffered non-pecuniary damage through anxiety and distress . . . [t]he Court thus concludes that the applicant suffered some non-pecuniary damage' (emphasis added). A similar ruling was made by the Grand Chamber in *T.P. and K.M. v. the United Kingdom* [GC], no. 28945/95, ECHR 2001-V, paras. 115–16.

[84] *Sabeh El Leil v. France* [GC], no. 34869/05, 29 June 2011, paras. 70 and 72. The applicant claimed EUR 82,224.60 in respect of pecuniary damage, covering the total amount awarded by the employment tribunal, and EUR 2,000 for moral damage. The Court awarded him EUR 60,000 for all heads of damage combined.

brought under the Convention for financial rights are linked to the protection of property, not to the right to a fair trial, which was the only violation invoked and upheld by the Court in that case. The artifice resorted to by the Grand Chamber was the formula of 'loss of real opportunities', a vague notion that is still to be defined.

The Court has created some ambiguity because it has not stated exactly whether the loss of opportunity belongs to the category of material damage or to that of moral damage. That ambiguity further persisted because the Court has made reference to cases which also have not made such a distinction.[85] The judges have nonetheless acknowledged, after accepting a loss of opportunity, that '[i]n addition, the applicant has sustained non-pecuniary damage'.[86] In other words, they have included loss of opportunity in the sphere of material damage, which is not conceptually wrong, as will be shown in a subsequent chapter.[87] The problem is that, in doing so, they have allowed the applicant to recover an important proportion of the salary rights that a domestic court awarded in a vitiated procedure, because it is evident that the amount agreed by the Grand Chamber mainly covers the pecuniary damage.[88] Moreover, as a consequence of that judgment, it is France, the respondent state, that has to reimburse the damages claimed by the plaintiff against a third state.

From the perspective of a causal link, that ruling is inconsistent with the Court's case law from at least two points of view. First, the causal link between salary rights and the procedural right to a fair trial is rather weak, given that it is well established that such rights should be claimed and recognized in the context of protection of property. Second, while the Strasbourg judges strictly affirm on every occasion that they do not speculate as to the outcome of the domestic proceedings if conducted properly, that seems to be what they did in the present case. They assumed that, if the applicant had been given a fair trial, he would have had a big chance of winning.[89] It is somewhat unfortunate that none of them have expressed a dissenting or even a concurring opinion to explain the grounds for that decision. The reasons may be questionable for an outsider, a situation that may affect the Court's credibility.

[85] See para. 72. [86] Ibid. [87] See below, Subsection 4.1.4 of Chapter 4.

[88] Compare with a similar case, *Cudak v. Lithuania* ([GC], no. 15869/02, ECHR 2010), where, in the absence of any domestic judgment as to the applicant's claims for pecuniary damage, the Grand Chamber awarded the victim EUR 10,000 for all heads of damage combined and considered that she should benefit from a retrial.

[89] They did the same in *Ramanauskas v. Lithuania* ([GC], no. 74420/01, ECHR 2008, para. 87).

It follows that the Court has created a precedent and thus opened the path for giving substantial compensation for the material damage that was at stake in domestic proceedings that have not been handled in accordance with the exigencies of a fair trial. That chain of causation is rather overshadowed by a high degree of speculation. However revolutionary that approach may be – and indeed to the victim's benefit – it seems unlikely that the contracting states would routinely permit such an authoritative interference in internal business, all the more so because they have already adopted legislation that allows the reopening of domestic proceedings as a consequence of a judgment by the Court, which means that when finding violations of a procedural right, the judges should only direct the state to reopen proceedings and give full effect to the right previously ignored.

In conclusion, the Court needs to develop principles whereby it can explain in more detail when and why a causal link is denied. In particular, if the judges so easily refute any causation in procedural violations, the offending state has no interest in amending the legislation, because it would cost it more than a finding of a violation. Certainly, if disparate incidents become routine, the state risks a pilot judgment imposing general measures to rectify that structural failure. The Court should therefore put in balance the influence of the procedural right over the final outcome in order to decide whether domestic proceedings should be reopened or whether compensation for moral harm would be enough. However, the causal link is not the only notion diverted on occasion from its natural course. The principle of *restitutio in integrum* may experience the same effects.

2.3 *Restitutio in integrum*

2.3.1 Notion

The Court has from the beginning considered *restitutio in integrum* as one of its guiding principles,[90] although it was only at a much later time, in *Papamichalopoulos and Others v. Greece*,[91] that it declared its supremacy, in the context of an arbitrary deprivation of property. It made

[90] *De Wilde, Ooms and Versyp* (Article 50), note 23, para. 20; *Ringeisen v. Austria* (Article 50), 22 June 1972, Series A no. 15, para. 21; and *Neumeister v. Austria* (Article 50), 7 May 1974, Series A no. 17, para. 40.

[91] *Papamichalopoulos and Others v. Greece* (Article 50), 31 October 1995, Series A no. 330-B, paras. 34 and 36.

express reference to the *Factory at Chorzów* case, where the Permanent Court of International Justice enunciated that fundamental principle as follows: 'reparation must, as far as possible, wipe out all the consequences of the illegal act and re-establish the situation which would, in all probability, have existed if that act had not been committed'.[92]

In general, at least in theory, international courts and tribunals give priority to that standard, whether codified or applied as a customary rule. For example, Article 63(1) of the American Convention confers full entitlement on the judges to impose specific measures for reinstallation of the *status quo ante.*[93] That treaty does not distinguish between the different forms of reparation, referring to *restitutio in integrum* as merely one of them, whereas the European agreement confirms the primacy of restitution.[94] However, this has not prevented the Inter-American Court from taking every opportunity to enjoin the states parties to take all the necessary steps so as to make restitution.[95] Those measures differ fundamentally from those ordered in Strasbourg, inasmuch as they refer to actions such as nullification of a conviction,[96] finding the remains of a victim and delivery to his or her family,[97] or investigation and punishment of the perpetrators of human rights violations.[98] Yet, the Court of San José is well aware that the rule of restitution is not absolute, because

[92] *Factory at Chorzów (Merits)*, 1928, PCIJ, Series A, No. 17, at 47.

[93] The principle emerges only implicitly from Article 27 of the Protocol to the African Charter on Human and Peoples' Rights: see the Protocol to the African Charter on Human and Peoples' Rights on the Establishment of an African Court on Human and Peoples' Rights, 9 June 1998, OAU Doc. OAU/LEG/EXP/AFCHPR/PROT (III).

[94] C. Gassama, 'Le principe de *restitutio in integrum* dans le contentieux international des droits de l'homme', *Mediterranean Journal of Human Rights* 9 (2005), at 126–8.

[95] In that respect, it frequently holds that '[t]he responsible State may not invoke provisions of domestic law to modify or fail to comply with its obligation to provide reparation, all aspects of which (scope, nature, methods and determination of the beneficiaries) [are] regulated by international law'; see, e.g., *Case of the Ituango Massacres v. Colombia* (preliminary objections, merits, reparations and costs), 1 July 2006, Series C no. 148, para. 347, and *Claude-Reyes et al. v. Chile* (merits, reparations and costs), 19 September 2006, Series C no. 151, para. 151.

[96] *Cantoral-Benavides v. Peru* (reparations and costs), 3 December 2001, Series C no. 88, para. 77.

[97] See, e.g., *Molina-Theissen v. Guatemala* (reparations and costs), 3 July 2004, Series C no. 108, para. 85.

[98] See, e.g., *Loayza-Tamayo v. Peru* (reparations and costs), 27 November 1998, Series C no. 42, para. 171, and *Vargas-Areco v. Paraguay* (merits, reparations and costs), 26 September 2006, Series C no. 155, para. 155.

there are cases where it may not be possible, sufficient or appropriate.[99] Although it delivered the first judgment on reparations in 1989, the first occasion when it was able to order *restitutio in integrum* in the form of the release of the applicant came only in 1997 in *Loayza-Tamayo v. Peru* given that, unlike the previous cases, the victim was still alive.[100]

Within the Strasbourg system, the legal basis for the obligation to make *restitutio in integrum* resides in the fact that the Court pronounces on state responsibility and that states have a treaty obligation to comply with the final judgments, while Article 41 on just satisfaction appears to be a fall-back provision for cases where restitution is impossible.[101] In virtue of the principle of subsidiarity, and in view of the fact that the Court's judgments are essentially declaratory, the responsibility and manner of performing *restitutio* belong to the state. The judges held in *Papamichalopoulos* – and have confirmed in subsequent practice – that '[i]f the nature of the breach allows of *restitutio in integrum*, it is for the respondent State to effect it, the Court having neither the power nor the practical possibility of doing so itself'.[102] They can only indicate measures by which a state may restore the position existing before a violation.

The original condition is normally re-established by way of some actions with retrospective effects rather than by payment of a sum of money. In practice, however, it is often more difficult than in theory to return to the previous state of affairs. In a case in which a state refuses or is unable to reinstate the *status quo ante*, nothing prevents the Court from reactivating its competence under Article 41, even if not for ordering restitution, but in order to offer compensation. When the unlawful activity continues, *restitutio in integrum* makes necessary the end of the interference in the first place. The Court may further recommend provisional measures when another infringement is imminent, in order to prevent not only a violation but also the impossibility of restoring the original condition.

[99] *Aloeboetoe et al. v. Suriname* (reparations and costs), 10 September 1993, Series C no. 15, para. 49.

[100] I. Piacentini de Andrade, 'L'affaire *Loayza Tamayo c/Pérou* et ses suites', in E. Lambert Abdelgawad and K. Martin-Chenut (eds.), *Réparer les violations graves et massives des droits de l'homme: la Cour interaméricaine, pionnière et modèle?* (Paris: Société de législation comparée, 2010), at 114.

[101] L. G. Loucaides, 'Reparation for Violations of Human Rights under the European Convention and *Restitutio in Integrum*', *European Human Rights Law Review*, no. 2 (2008), at 188.

[102] *Papamichalopoulos* (Article 50), note 91, paras. 34 and 36.

The judges have started timidly, particularly with cases involving claims for the restitution of property expropriated by the state, as in *Hentrich v. France*, where they said that 'the best form of redress would in principle be for the State to return the land'.[103] But the latest practice of pointing to individual and general measures denotes more involvement in supporting the theory of *restitutio in integrum*. It is no longer exceptional for the Court to indicate a course of action in disputes revealing unlawful detention or unfairness of criminal proceedings, or when the violation is the result of a shortcoming in the legal system itself, notwithstanding the absence from the Convention of a power to impose a particular conduct on a breaching state.

However, the *status quo ante* may not be re-established for the majority of human rights violations, including loss of life or liberty, ill-treatment, deprivation of family life or suppression of free speech. In those cases, monetary compensation remains the sole alternative and *restitutio in integrum* becomes a guiding principle for determination of an appropriate redress.[104] Even the heading of Article 41, as aptly noted, which is 'just satisfaction', seems to refer to the pecuniary aspect of reparation, rather than to its more important principle of *restitutio in integrum*.[105]

As to the effective application of the standard, when a dispute in Strasbourg is discontinued as a result of a friendly settlement or unilateral declaration by the defendant government, the Court does not make any pronouncement as to the responsibility of the state. So, logically, there is no obligation to provide *restitutio in integrum*, but the judges pay special attention to any discrepancy in the terms of an agreement or declaration, more than to the amount or form of reparation per se. Friendly settlements in particular may be used to restore the *status quo ante*. The parties may agree, for instance, on the reopening of internal

[103] *Hentrich v. France*, 22 September 1994, Series A no. 296-A, para. 71.

[104] The Court has sometimes reversed the logical order of making an award for pecuniary compensation only when *restitutio in integrum* is not possible: see M. De Salvia, 'Le principe de l'octroi subsidiaire des dommages-intérêts: d'une morale des droits de l'homme à une morale simplement indemnitaire?', in J.-F. Flauss and E. Lambert Abdelgawad (eds.), *La pratique d'indemnisation par la Cour européenne des droits de l'homme* (Brussels: Bruylant, 2011), at 18.

[105] M. De Salvia, 'La satisfaction équitable au titre des mesures individuelles et la pratique des organes de la Convention européenne des droits de l'homme: qu'en est-il du principe de sécurité juridique?', in H. Hartig (ed.), *Trente ans de droit européen des droits de l'homme: études à la mémoire de Wolfgang Strasser* (Brussels: Bruylant, 2007), at 46.

proceedings, reversal of an administrative decision, or on the quashing or pardoning of a prison sentence, although restoration to the original condition may be subject to certain limitations.

The Committee of Ministers also applies the standard of *restitutio in integrum* during the supervision of execution. While the Court may not give priority in its ruling to the obligation to restore the original condition, the Committee usually insists on that at the moment of enforcement. As an illustration, in a banal case where the judges found a violation in respect of the length of proceedings, but did not award just satisfaction because the applicant had not claimed any,[106] the Committee routinely invited the state to provide it with information about the adoption of individual measures which would put an end to the breach and erase the consequences so as to achieve as far as possible *restitutio in integrum*, as well as of general measures for the prevention of similar violations.[107] Given that the domestic proceedings were still pending when the Court delivered its judgment, in the process of execution, the state accelerated and eventually closed those proceedings almost two years later.[108] It may therefore be assumed that the offender made a real effort to re-establish the *status quo ante*.

It should be noticed that unlike the Court – and not only in this example, but in all cases as a rule – the Committee does not impose on states a time limit for making reparation. Certainly, it cannot disregard the intervals already fixed by the judges for payment or for implementation of individual or general measures. The reason is more political than judicial, given that the Committee avails itself of political pressure in order to secure execution. Even if the formula is widely accepted in so far as it is innovative and normally successful in the end, the method may lose its efficiency if the prorogation maintains a person in a state of injustice.

In essence, applicants are entitled to benefit from the remedies offered by the Convention mechanism in its entirety, therefore not only from the Court, but also from the Committee in the form of individual measures requested from the state. While accepting that delays are inevitable for the accomplishment of a condition close to full redress, leaving full discretion to the breaching state may lead to further abuse. As a well-known legal maxim affirms, justice delayed is justice denied. It follows that, *de lege ferenda*, the Committee should amend its rules for the

[106] *Nicolas v. France*, no. 2021/03, 27 June 2006, paras. 20 and 25.

[107] Resolution DH(2009)58 of 2 April 2009 in *Nicolas v. France*.

[108] Ibid.

supervision of the execution of judgments by introducing the possibility to fix time limits in accordance with the circumstances of each particular case. A general deadline seems to be unrealistic, but threshold limits may be fairly reasonable. The Committee would adjust them accordingly at each meeting.

The just-mentioned example also reveals that the Committee may award redress even when the Court does not do so. Unless a regrettable anomaly, this raises a further question: has the Committee of Ministers the power to award *ultra petita* or are there two different regimes of reparation, one judicial and the other political? In fact, 'the Nicolas case' illustrates very well all the consequences of a breach of treaty by a contracting state. First and foremost, the Court often reiterates in the context of reparation that 'a judgment in which it finds a breach imposes on the respondent State a legal obligation to put an end to the breach and make reparation for its consequences in such a way as to restore as far as possible the situation existing before the breach'.[109] Thus, the wrong-doing state has a legal obligation to restore the *status quo ante*, not only considered from a victim's perspective, but also in virtue of the fact that a violation represents per se a breach of the treaty.

In other words, the Court examines and decides whether the personal interest has been affected, while the Committee of Ministers basically defends the general interest. While the former comes necessarily under judicial scrutiny, the latter has been entrusted to a political forum made up of representatives of all the member states. In abstract terms, states will themselves decide the effect of a breach in their respect. This is the reason why the Committee, whenever confronted with an infringement and irrespective of whatever reparation is granted by the Court, requests the state, as a consequence of the very act of violation and in defence of the general interest, to make *restitutio in integrum*. It is a sort of reparation for legal prejudice, a satisfaction within the meaning of general international law offered to the contracting parties. The Strasbourg machinery relies therefore on a single system of reparation, but with two components: the prevailing and most evident judicial element, which secures protection of the personal interest, and a less manifest political element, which guarantees the effective realization of the first, but also defends the general interest of the regional organization.

[109] *Iatridis v. Greece* (just satisfaction) [GC], no. 31107/96, ECHR 2000-XI, para. 32.

2.3.2 Limitations

In spite of its theoretical pre-eminence, the standard of full reparation may be totally or partially hindered in practice, either on objective or on subjective grounds. The Court admitted in *Papamichalopoulos* that not only the nature of the breach, but also the internal law of the respondent party may exclude *restitutio in integrum.*[110] It should be noticed that the problem of restitution arises only in connection with redress for material damage, because on the one hand the theory of legal injury does not find support in Convention law, and on the other hand, the concept of moral damage is in itself an abstract notion, not as to the existence of such harm in most cases, but in respect of its materialization. By the same token, the possibility of *restitutio* is always examined by the Court in the part of the judgment which relates to reparation for pecuniary damage. Similarly, the ILC Articles also regard satisfaction as a substitute for restitution, not as a constitutive element.

The impossibility of *restitutio in integrum* may therefore derive from legal or from material reasons. Legal grounds may refer not only to the codification in the breaching state, but also to the Convention itself. For instance, it may be that *res judicata* prevents restitution, although the contracting parties have generally introduced the possibility of reviewing a case following a judgment from Strasbourg. When a violation stemmed directly from the provisions of a law, the Court declared that it had no power to repeal domestic legislation. Hence, the state's obligation to make *restitutio in integrum* does not require a commitment to reinstate the *status quo* that would have existed in the absence of such provisions.[111] The fact that the treaty has not bestowed upon the judges a right to order changes in domestic law corresponds to the second aspect of the legal reasons that may render *restitutio* impossible, that is, the provisions of the Convention itself. What is the effective protection that individuals enjoy when a violation emerges from the law? Compared with its Inter-American counterpart, the Court exerts significantly less leverage as to the modification of internal legislation, though one has to admit that it has an indirect influence, coupled with a rational interest of the state in preventing future condemnations.

When confronted with deprivation of property, the Court has accepted that '[l]egitimate objectives of "public interest", such as pursued in

[110] *Papamichalopoulos* (Article 50), note 91, para. 34 *in fine.*

[111] *Marckx v. Belgium*, 13 June 1979, Series A no. 31, para. 58.

measures of economic reform or measures designed to achieve greater social justice, may call for less than reimbursement of the full market value'.[112] In other words, the state is logically discharged from making restitution if it proves that the general interest was at stake, yet without being exempted from offering appropriate compensation. And this is the part where states usually fail. In *Papamichalopoulos*, the Court made a distinction between the pecuniary consequences of lawful expropriation and those of unlawful dispossession, based on decisions by other international courts and arbitration tribunals.[113] The standard of compensation was set lower in the event of legal seizure, but still there have been many cases where the breach resided in the insufficiency of compensation.[114] Certainly, even when the expropriation has been found lawful, the state may return the property of its own motion.

As far as the material grounds are concerned, the impossibility of *restitutio* may originate in the nature of the breach and in the type of damage. The two are interconnected. It is of the essence of the most serious human rights violations that they translate into irreversible acts and effects. The consequences of unlawful killing, torture, inhuman or degrading treatment, or illegal detention can never be fully erased. For example, the judges ruled in *Ringeisen*, one of their early cases, that while it is appropriate to deduct from a sentence the time spent in unlawful pre-trial detention, 'it does not in any way thus acquire the character of *restitutio in integrum*, for no freedom is given in place of the freedom unlawfully taken away'.[115] But then in *König* they have considered that 'when proceedings are continued beyond the "reasonable time" . . ., the intrinsic nature of the wrong prevents complete reparation (*restitutio in integrum*)'.[116] Hence, the Court is disposed to expand the standard of *restitutio* to all the rights and freedoms guaranteed by the Convention. In doing so, it implicitly acknowledges that the internal law cannot restore the *status quo ante*, because it is the very nature of the breach that prevents it, and therefore the Court assumes itself the role of granting

[112] *James and Others v. the United Kingdom*, 21 February 1986, Series A no. 98, para. 54 *in fine*.

[113] *Papamichalopoulos* (Article 50), note 91, para. 36. Regrettably though, that distinction has been eliminated by the Grand Chamber in *Guiso-Gallisay v. Italy*: see below, Subsection 4.1.2.1 of Chapter 4.

[114] E.g., *Former King of Greece and Others v. Greece* [GC] (just satisfaction), no. 25701/94, 28 November 2002, para. 75.

[115] *Ringeisen* (Article 50), note 90, ibid.

[116] *König v. Germany* (Article 50), 10 March 1980, Series A no. 36, para. 15. Also see *Eckle v. Germany* (Article 50), 21 June 1983, Series A no. 65, para. 13.

reparation. Applicants to Strasbourg have thus the benefit of full international protection, not only for the rights agreed by the parties, but also for the remedies entailed by infringement.

There are, however, situations where a violation that would normally produce reversible consequences generates *in casu* irreversible harm. There is therefore a practical impossibility of restitution. The most obvious example is that of a taking by the state of property, which in the meantime has been lost or destroyed, or even acquired by third parties in good faith.[117] Another illustration would be that of an illegally detained person who has been released during the Convention proceedings. In such cases, while the Court will logically find a violation, financial compensation remains the only possible redress. If a plaintiff is partly to blame for the injury sustained, the judges may adjust the compensation accordingly.[118]

In general international law, the impossibility of restitution ought to be entirely material, not merely legal or practical. A breaching state may not invoke domestic legislation for the failure to provide *restitutio in integrum*, but has to overcome political or administrative obstacles, provided that the property to be restored had not been lost, destroyed or has wholly deteriorated.[119] The European Court has opted for a more flexible approach, undoubtedly in view of the recurrent claims in that respect and conceivably because the recipient is usually an individual. It does accept a practical impossibility of restitution, which gives states relatively unrestricted freedom to choose the most convenient form of reparation. Objectionable as it may be, that position is in line with the traditional interpretation of the Convention as not conferring on the judges a right to make consequential orders or declaratory statements in connection with states' obligation to comply with the Court's judgments.[120] It is therefore laudable that the Strasbourg system has recently initiated, with the approval of the member states, a practice of

[117] See, e.g., *Nistorescu v. Romania*, no. 15517/03, 17 June 2008, para. 24, and *Tamir and Others v. Romania*, no. 42194/05, 15 September 2009, para. 38.

[118] See, e.g., *Johnson v. the United Kingdom*, 24 October 1997, *Reports of Judgments and Decisions* 1997-VII, para. 77, and *Beyeler v. Italy* (just satisfaction) [GC], no. 33202/96, 28 May 2002, paras. 23, 28 and 29.

[119] Crawford, note 43, at 216.

[120] See, e.g., *Akdivar and Others v. Turkey* (Article 50), 1 April 1998, *Reports of Judgments and Decisions* 1998-II, para. 47. There were, however, exceptions even in the past; see, e.g., *Piersack v. Belgium* (Article 50), 26 October 1984, Series A no. 85, point 1 of the operative part.

giving directions to the governments concerned in respect of remedies for systemic deficiencies.

An apparent need for reinforcement of the principle of *restitutio in integrum* has led the Court not only to specify the required individual or general measures, but also lately to include them in the operative part of a judgment. This would seem to warrant the conclusion that the judges, confronted with an increasing number of violations, have finally adopted a firmer stance and begun to issue specific injunctions as to restitution. However, what seems to emerge from the relevant practice so far is that such indications are rather exceptional and are usually associated with certain types of infringements. After all, the judges may not assume more powers than those conferred by the treaty.

The Court has always affirmed its subsidiarity, and the member states have even agreed to introduce that principle into the treaty.[121] It is a logical restraint, based on a limited assessment of domestic affairs by an international court and on lack of direct effect of its judgments. Hence, when deemed feasible, the responsible state has broad discretion as to the choice of the means for complying with a judgment and for restoring the situation existing before the breach. The Committee of Ministers has the authority to impose certain actions or even legislative adjustments, but the Court may simply give some directions at the time of its ruling. While, at the level of the organization, the Court's power deficit is somewhat compensated by that political body, it would be more efficient for human rights protection, and even more helpful for the state, to reinforce the principle of *restitutio in integrum* by allowing the judges, instead of a political organ, to specify in each dispute the necessary measures that would reinstate the *status quo ante*. It is commendable that the Inter-American system permits the judges to order the appropriate course of action.

2.3.3 *Appropriate or rather defective application by the Court?*

The answer to this question lies most likely in between the two alternatives. *Restitutio in integrum* is indeed the most appropriate form of reparation, although no more than in theory at times. It has an innate capacity to annihilate the consequences of a violation and to restore the previously existing situation. Notwithstanding its logical authority, practice shows that the Court gives priority to pecuniary compensation

[121] Protocol No. 15, adopted in 2013, but not yet in force.

over *restitutio*, and even when it appears that the latter would be possible. In other words, it is not only the Convention that may limit the efficiency of the principle, but also the judges at the moment of its application.

The most illustrative examples in that sense come from breaches of peaceful enjoyment of possessions, when the Court usually makes available pecuniary compensation as an alternative to the principal injunction to return the property. Cases where the judges assume that there are no obstacles to restitution and thus leave no further alternative to the offender are fairly rare.[122] The problem is that the respondent state may conveniently prefer compensation over restitution, given that it is not required to prove the alleged impossibility. Although this is clearly done as a precaution against the unfeasibility of restitution at the municipal level, as in the context of a legal transfer of property, some remarks are in order with regard to the legal justification and potential effects of this method.

That position is at variance with general international law. The international practice preceding the Convention made express reference to the traditional principles of reparation. When the Permanent Court of International Justice declared the primacy of *restitutio in integrum* in *Factory at Chorzów*, it also held that only if that remedy was not feasible would the payment of a sum be an option.[123] In that case, the Permanent Court officially noted that the parties had agreed that restitution was impossible.[124] The Inter-American Court at least considered that 'the State must take all legislative, administrative, and any other measures necessary', including expropriation,[125] and also made the alternative redress dependent upon objective and well-founded reasons for which restitution is not possible.[126]

The Strasbourg Court's approach is fairly questionable. As an illustration, in *Carbonara and Ventura v. Italy*, a case of unlawful dispossession where the question of just satisfaction had been reserved – hence, the state had the possibility to propose effective reparation based on the findings on the merits – the government alleged that restitution was not feasible because it would have

[122] E.g., *Gladysheva v. Russia*, no. 7097/10, 6 December 2011, para. 106.

[123] *Factory at Chorzów (Merits)*, note 92, at 47. [124] Ibid., at 48.

[125] *Xákmok Kásek Indigenous Community v. Paraguay* (merits, reparations and costs), 24 August 2010, Series C no. 214, paras. 281 and 284.

[126] *Yakye Axa Indigenous Community v. Paraguay* (merits, reparations and costs), 17 June 2005, Series C no. 125, para. 217.

involved the partial demolition of a school built on the applicants' land, but the judges proposed compensation as an alternative to restitution without any further inquiry into those allegations.[127] The question then arises: why does the Court from the beginning make pecuniary compensation available in the event of a failure to restore the *status quo ante* within a fixed time limit, without requiring the state to prove the impossibility of restitution, either *de facto* or *de jure*? Does the principle of *restitutio in integrum* enjoy an effective application under the Convention in such cases?

Moreover, the formula may give rise to some inconsistencies when extended to other types of damage. Emphasis has already been placed by one of the Court's judges on two rather discordant judgments as regards the alternative obligation of payment of moral damages.[128] The Court held in the operative part of *Claes and Others v. Belgium*, where it had found a violation of some of the applicants' right to a fair trial, that only if they do not request a retrial is the state to pay them compensation for moral harm and for the costs of proceedings.[129] One of the judges in that Chamber's composition has even expressed an opinion on that point,[130] which means that all the judges were aware of a possible contradiction at the moment of their deliberations. While they may have in all probability considered that *restitutio in integrum* would have wiped out all the consequences of the breaching act, it has already been explained that moral harm may never be totally erased, but only compensated. That was the solution rightly adopted in the second judgment. In *Lungoci v. Romania*, where it again found interference with the fair trial guarantees, the Court awarded reparation for moral damage, but this time in addition to the possibility for the applicant to have the proceedings reopened.[131] What is striking, however, is that the conflicting operative provisions of the two judgments have subsequently been cited in some dissenting or concurring opinions, but as a positive

[127] *Carbonara and Ventura v. Italy* (just satisfaction), no. 24638/94, 11 December 2003, paras. 29 and 39.

[128] C. Birsan, 'Les aspects nouveaux de l'application des articles 41 et 46 de la Convention dans la jurisprudence de la Cour européenne des droits de l'homme', in Hartig, note 105, at 31–3.

[129] *Claes and Others v. Belgium*, nos. 46825/99, 47132/99, 47502/99, 49010/99, 49104/99, 49195/99 and 49716/99, 2 June 2005, point 5(a) of the operative part.

[130] Partly concurring opinion of Judge Rozakis.

[131] *Lungoci v. Romania*, no. 62710/00, 26 January 2006, point 3(a) of the operative part.

example where the Court had ordered a retrial, not as contradictory rulings in respect of an award for moral damages.[132]

It is further inferred by some authors that an option for the breaching state to choose between restitution and compensation confers efficacy on the system,[133] whereas some of the Court's judges are well aware that such provision for alternative payment undermines the application of the principle of *restitutio in integrum*, thus giving a wrongdoer the possibility to 'buy off' treaty violations and to keep the benefits of illegal conduct.[134] For example, in the claims brought against former communist countries in respect of properties unlawfully nationalized in the past, the Court often makes a formal order to the state to return those assets in the first place, and some properties have indeed been returned.[135] Normally, however, claimants are compensated with the substitute amount established by the Court for the current market value of the assets, without touching upon any reimbursement for the years in which the government had used their properties and obtained profit.[136] If one was running a business at the moment of the taking, reimbursement of the profit made by the state should be possible.[137] The solution occasionally advanced by the Court is to take the loss of profit into account when fixing the amount for moral harm.[138]

It may well be true that an award of reparation is more efficiently complied with when the respondent has an alternative, but a defective application of the standard of *restitutio in integrum* may further open the way to illegal expropriations in the public interest.[139] In so far as states are not firmly required, when acting against the law, to return lands, buildings or movable property, the mere existence of the principle has no deterrent effect whatsoever. Governments would rationally prefer to pay

[132] Para. 11 of the joint concurring opinion of Judges Rozakis, Spielmann, Ziemele and Lazarova Trajkovska in *Salduz v. Turkey* [GC], no. 36391/02, ECHR 2008, and para. 6 of the partly dissenting opinion of Judges Spielmann and Malinverni in *Popovitsi v. Greece*, no. 53451/07, 14 January 2010.

[133] Gassama, note 94, at 146. [134] Loucaides, note 101, at 186.

[135] See, e.g., Resolution DH(2007)90 of 20 June 2007 in the case of *Brumărescu and 30 other cases against Romania*.

[136] See, among many others, *Străin and Others v. Romania*, no. 57001/00, ECHR 2005-VII, paras. 80–3, and *Olimpia-Maria Teodorescu v. Romania*, no. 43774/02, 4 November 2008, paras. 34–6.

[137] See, e.g., *Khamidov v. Russia*, no. 72118/01, 15 November 2007, para. 192.

[138] See, e.g., *Radu v. Romania*, no. 13309/03, 20 July 2006, para. 49, and *Rusu and Others v. Romania*, no. 4198/04, 19 July 2007, para. 36.

[139] Loucaides, note 101, at 188.

the price and to keep the assets, if strategic purposes so demand. On the contrary, an order coming from Strasbourg to restore the original situation and to compensate the loss of profit, as well as the moral damage, would realistically generate some more domestic concern before authorizing any seizure of property. It would therefore be advisable for the Court to abandon the practice of fixing an alternative monetary award in case the state does not make restitution within a certain time. Departure from that approach in the field of personal liberty, where release has been promptly ordered, has been welcomed by some judges[140] because it fully concords with the purpose of the principle.

The efficacy of the system could thus be further enhanced if the judges, when considering restitution to be the most appropriate redress, required states to submit reasonable evidence that *restitutio in integrum* was impossible. Otherwise, when the Court specifies that remedy alternatively with payment of compensation, the effects of a ruling for just satisfaction may be perverted by the breaching state, which in addition to being responsible for the violation, has also the possibility of choosing, and thus deciding, the most convenient form of reparation. To that extent, there is no effective protection of human rights. In that respect, the European Court differs from the Inter-American Court, which appears to be less appreciative of the internal capabilities of restoring the *status quo ante.*[141]

Nonetheless, besides solitary exceptions, the cause for concern is presently limited to property cases. A sporadic abandonment of theoretical formalism in favour of empirical proficiency may even be accepted. On the one hand, the strict application of the principle should not become an obsession, because the Convention is a regional treaty deemed to respond to practical necessities. On the other hand, the Court is composed of law experts who employ largely accepted judicial notions. Hence, they cannot discredit the content of the law. The principle of *restitutio in integrum* must preserve its original form and function, and must transcend a regional treaty.

[140] Para. 10 of the partly concurring opinion of Judge Costa in *Assanidze v. Georgia* [GC], no. 71503/01, ECHR 2004-II.

[141] See, e.g., *Sawhoyamaxa Indigenous Community v. Paraguay* (merits, reparations and costs), 29 March 2006, Series C no. 146, paras. 210–15. Also, the Inter-American Commission on Human Rights has a power to recommend a state to repeal or amend legislation: see *International Responsibility for the Promulgation and Enforcement of Laws in Violation of the Convention (Arts. 1 and 2 of the American Convention on Human Rights)*, Advisory Opinion OC-14/94 of 9 December 1994, Series A no. 14, para. 39.

The member states are fully aware of the relevance of a system of effective reparation. To that end, they have admitted the need to provide in their legal systems the necessary prospects for achieving *restitutio in integrum*, especially by offering the possibility of reopening cases following judgments by the Court.[142] In fact, along with the obligation to abide by the Court's judgments and with the supervision by the Committee of Ministers, they have created a mechanism for the reinforcement of the principle. Yet, it would be difficult to believe that they will always act in good faith and in the interest of the victim of their own unlawful conduct. Certainly, a negative preconception is also detrimental to the system. The Strasbourg judges must therefore create a balance between interests and obligations, between theory and reality, but they must also give consistency to international law principles. Theory must be supported by practice. While successful in theory, the practical operation of the standard leaves the door open for further improvements.

International courts and tribunals do not contest the primacy of *restitutio in integrum*. In the absence of a so-called universal recipe for re-establishing the *status quo ante*, the methods differ for each particular case. There is nonetheless more or less enthusiasm on the part of the international judge, usually based on treaty provisions, to become involved in the effective application of the principle. As for the European Court, while accepting that impossibility of *restitutio in integrum* is often objective, the case law stands for a positive evolution from a traditional minimal implication towards a progressively active role. Based on the growing orders for individual and general measures, an aspect that will be considered in a subsequent chapter, there is reason to surmise that the Court has assuredly embarked on an irreversible process to create a system of reparation that may ensure an effective application of the theory of full reparation. There are only some fine, though important, adjustments to be made.

2.4 Equity

In the field of reparations, equity is a valuable tool at the hand of the judges. Most often in the context of reparation for moral prejudice, they

[142] Recommendation R(2000)2 of 19 January 2000 on the re-examination or reopening of certain cases at domestic level following judgments of the European Court of Human Rights, available on the Council of Europe's website (https://wcd.coe.int/ViewDoc.jsp?id=334147).

determine the compensation in equity. As already explained, the system of reparation under the Convention has been designed to secure a *just* satisfaction in the sense of a fair rather than a full redress. On 28 March 2007, the then President of the Court issued a Practice Direction for just satisfaction claims, in which he declared that the Court 'may find reasons of equity to award less than the value of the actual damage sustained or the costs and expenses actually incurred, or even not to make any award at all'.[143] The situation of the amount of damage or the level of the costs being the result of the applicant's own fault is given as an example. Now some questions may arise from that statement. What does 'equity' mean and what are its connotations? Who defines equity and on what basis? And when does the so-called equity justify a total lack of compensation?

2.4.1 Notion

Equity has been widely used in the process of decision making by international courts and tribunals. Authors usually cite the individual opinion of Judge Hudson in the case of *Diversion of Water from the River Meuse* as being the most famous dictum with reference to equity. He assumed that 'principles of equity have long been considered to constitute a part of international law'.[144] In particular, the International Court of Justice has had an important role in conferring a certain meaning to this rather abstract notion. It did so especially when confronted with disputes brought by states in respect of maritime delimitations, although it missed the opportunity to develop it further in the specific context of human rights violations, in its recent judgment in *Diallo*.[145]

In the *North Sea Continental Shelf* case, the International Court stated that 'it is not a question of applying equity simply as a matter of abstract justice, but of applying a rule of law which itself requires the application of equitable principles'.[146] In other words, '[i]t is not a matter of finding simply an equitable solution, but an equitable solution derived from the

[143] Para. 2 of the Practice Direction in respect of just satisfaction claims, available on the Court's website (www.echr.coe.int/Pages/home.aspx?p=basictexts/rules&c=).

[144] *Diversion of Water from the River Meuse (Netherlands v. Belgium)*, 1937, PCIJ, Series A/B, No. 70, p. 4, at 76.

[145] *Ahmadou Sadio Diallo (Republic of Guinea v. Democratic Republic of the Congo)*, Compensation, Judgment, ICJ Reports 2012, p. 324.

[146] *North Sea Continental Shelf*, Judgment, ICJ Reports 1969, p. 3, para. 85.

applicable law'.[147] It appears that equity is not a judge's subjective conviction of what is reasonable, because it amounts to absolute discretion and may transform into arbitrariness. The use of equity must be based on legal norms, because 'when mention is made of a court dispensing justice or declaring the law, what is meant is that the decision finds its objective justification in considerations lying not outside but within the rules, and in this field it is precisely a rule of law that calls for the application of equitable principles'.[148]

The use of equity in international law raises the question whether the European Court operates within the same boundaries of the concept or whether at least it makes some reference that would reveal its source of inspiration. In the *Continental Shelf* case, the International Court equated justice based on equity with justice according to the rule of law and further declared that application of equity should display consistency and a degree of predictability.[149] Does the use of equity by the Strasbourg judges in awards of reparation conform to that theory, so as to avoid arbitrariness? As largely demonstrated in the present study, it is certain that the Court's practice on reparation is neither consistent nor predictable. What is then the legal basis for the equity invoked by the European judges and what is the connotation assigned to it by the Court? How does it fit with the understanding of equity under general international law?

First and foremost, the present scrutiny focuses on equity as used by the Court's judges when allocating reparation to victims. They may also refer to equitable principles when they decide the merits of a dispute, for example when they assess the fairness of domestic proceedings. In respect of reparation, the Court has extracted the equity from the wording of Article 41. As the heading of that article denotes – the equivalent in French being 'satisfaction équitable' – the standard of reparation in Strasbourg is that of just satisfaction, in the sense of fair compensation. Moreover, the Court is entitled to make redress only 'if necessary', that is, only when it considers that it is equitable to remedy the consequences of a violation. The Court thus assumes that the principle of equity has been imposed by the treaty clause on 'just satisfaction'.[150] The problem is that the judges have been reluctant to engage in interpretive exercises as to

147 *Fisheries Jurisdiction (Federal Republic of Germany v. Iceland)*, Merits, Judgment, ICJ Reports 1974, p. 175, para. 69.

148 *North Sea Continental Shelf*, note 146, para. 88.

149 *Continental Shelf (Libyan Arab Jamahiriya/Malta)*, Judgment, ICJ Reports 1985, p. 13, para. 45.

150 *König* (Article 50), note 116, para. 19.

the connotations and conditions of application of that principle under the Convention law. They have never developed a theory in that sense, nor have they made any reference to some general principles advanced in international law.

Absence of a theory of equity is one of the causes of the lack of consistency in the Court's rulings on reparation. The judges have still to assign a clear connotation for the equity they use, and not simply to infer entitlement to resort to that notion from the text of the Convention. By and large, equity has different connotations, depending on who is using it. As rightly emphasized, the usage of equity invoked by moralists and philosophers is not always the same as that pleaded by diplomats and politicians.[151] What is then the connotation of equity as invoked by the Court? It should be conceded that it depends on the judges' personal background, given that they are coming from different cultures and legal systems.

The concept of being 'just' means something that is fair, equitable, rightly given. When the judges are certain that a victim has sustained prejudice, but it is impossible for them to assess the exact extent of damage, they use the principle of equity as a tool to provide redress. For example, they may indicate a lump sum for loss of profits or earnings. Compensation for non-pecuniary injury is always made in equity, because the inner nature of that harm does not lend itself to precise estimation. The Inter-American Court also admitted in its first judgment on reparations in *Velásquez-Rodríguez* that indemnification for emotional harm must be based on the principles of equity.[152] The reverse of the medal is that the method entitles the judges to a high degree of discretion.

2.4.2 Practical use by the Court

The text of the Court's Practice Direction, after that vague reference to 'reasons of equity', further provides that, when setting the amount of an award, judges may consider the applicant's position as an injured party and that of the breaching state as responsible for the public interest, and will also normally take into account the local economic

[151] C. R. Rossi, *Equity and International Law: A Legal Realist Approach to International Decisionmaking* (New York: Transnational Publishers, 1993), at 3.

[152] *Velásquez-Rodríguez v. Honduras* (reparations and costs), 21 July 1989, Series C no. 7, para. 27.

circumstances.[153] Thus, the Court finds it reasonable to differentiate between victims in accordance with the level of economic development in the respondent state. While such a distinction may prima facie raise questions as to an apparent discrimination promoted even by the Court,[154] it would make little sense to grant similar amounts for the same violation regardless of whether the applicant lives in a richer or poorer country – provided that the offending state is the victim's country of residence – because the value of the money is different and does indeed depend on local economic development and purchasing power. As the International Court declared in the *North Sea Continental Shelf* case, '[e]quity does not necessarily imply equality'.[155] It is therefore reasonable to adapt a sum, because it is the concrete benefit secured to the victims that must be commensurate, not the amount per se.

The reverse of the effect of adjusting compensation to the local economic situation is that the state does not suffer an exceptional economic burden as a result of the breaches it has committed. While it is arguable whether such concerns should matter in the presence of human rights violations, it is nonetheless a principle of international law. Article 35(b) of the ILC Articles gives preference to compensation over restitution when the latter would involve a burden out of all proportion. Thus, when deciding the form of reparation, the economic stability of the wrongdoer is important.[156] Likewise, the Convention system reassures the member states that their economy is not put at risk by subscribing voluntarily to a control of their responsibility.

The Court is very careful to fix such compensation for non-pecuniary harm so as to 'reflect in the broadest of terms the severity of the damage; they are not, nor should they be, intended to give financial comfort or sympathetic enrichment at the expense of the Contracting Party concerned'.[157] It follows that the Court strives for a balance between the interests of both parties in a dispute, without necessarily favouring the victim of a violation. While sparse awards would probably not have any noticeable effect, a constant policy in that respect would indeed have negative consequences for the economic situation.

153 Para. 2 of the Practice Direction, note 143.
154 See below, Subsection 4.4.2.2 of Chapter 4.
155 *North Sea Continental Shelf*, note 146, para. 91.
156 Crawford, note 43, at 216–17.
157 *Varnava and Others v. Turkey* [GC], nos. 16064/90, 16065/90, 16066/90, 16068/90, 16069/90, 16070/90, 16071/90, 16072/90 and 16073/90, 18 September 2009, para. 224.

The International Court of Justice also held in the *North Sea Continental Shelf* case that, in order to arrive at an equitable result, different considerations should be put in balance, certainly with a relative weight to be given to some of them, but without relying on one consideration to the exclusion of all others.[158] Then, in *Tunisia/Libya*, it stated that '[w]hile it is clear that no rigid rules exist as to the exact weight to be attached to each element in the case, this is very far from being an exercise of discretion or conciliation; nor is it an operation of distributive justice'.[159] The prevalent form of equity in international law is therefore equity *infra legem*, 'which constitutes a method of interpretation of the law in force, and is one of its attributes'.[160]

The European Court does not refer to any circumstance when deciding in equity. While the Court's intention may reasonably aim at offering just satisfaction as it deems appropriate, it makes a rather arbitrary use of the concept, given that in reality it reaches its conclusions on the basis of standard amounts provided in some tables for exclusive internal use, but in theory it ventilates the principle of equity. The Court has therefore the means, but not the willingness, to prescribe some particular equitable criteria. In the absence of a set of clear principles, the adoption of a standardized approach generates further discretion, which eventually interferes with the consistency of the practice.

Officially, equity is a guiding principle 'which above all involves flexibility and an objective consideration of what is just, fair and reasonable in all the circumstances of the case, including not only the position of the applicant but the overall context in which the breach occurred'.[161] The Court may find it equitable to award loss of profits or earnings, to limit the standard of *restitutio in integrum* when a property had been legally expropriated or to adjust compensation when the victim had also been at fault in producing the prejudice. In practice, however, in the absence of any legal basis for its reasoning, it appears that the Court normally makes use of the principle to substantially reduce the amounts sought by complainants, especially in respect of non-pecuniary damage.

[158] *North Sea Continental Shelf*, note 146, para. 93.

[159] *Continental Shelf (Tunisia/Libyan Arab Jamahiriya)*, Judgment, ICJ Reports 1982, p. 18, para. 71.

[160] *Frontier Dispute (Burkina Faso/Republic of Mali)*, Judgment, ICJ Reports 1986, p. 554, para. 28.

[161] *Varnava*, note 157, para. 185.

Even if moral prejudice does not lend itself to accurate calculation, the judges may at least give some grounds for their estimation or, better, reveal their internal criteria and standardized approach. In doing so, they would ensure predictability and consistency to the case law. In some cases the victims do not even claim a certain amount, but leave the matter to the Court's appreciation. In the absence of further arguments, how can one perceive that equity was the ground for the award? Jennings rightly emphasized that '[n]o reasonable litigant expects the decision of a court to be predictable; but the range of considerations used for a decision and the procedures for their application should certainly be predictable'.[162]

It is somewhat unfortunate that the Strasbourg judges come up with a sum in compensation and they declare that it is established in equity, without further judicial arguments, and all the more that the victims do not ask for any decision *ex aequo et bono*, but strive for a legal ruling based on Convention law. The International Court of Justice did the same in *Diallo*. It is debatable whether equity really exists in the absence of consistency, reasoning or foreseeability. As Franck aptly put it, '[t]o be effective, the system must be *seen* to be effective' in the sense that 'decisions must be arrived at discursively in accordance with what is accepted by the parties as *right process*'.[163]

Often, when reading the just satisfaction part in a Court's judgment, especially the award for non-pecuniary damage, it is difficult to understand when, where and how the principle of equity has been applied. It may even be speculated that the judges establish an amount and then justify it by equity, instead of fixing the sum in equity. Certainly, one cannot deny them recourse to equitable considerations in the absence of specific provisions in the law, but equity should not be used as a shield for discretion on the matter. The Court's practice, especially in the context of compensation for non-pecuniary damage, shows that the judges frequently limit their reasoning to the fact that they apply equity instead of revealing to the parties and to the wider public on what basis the decision has been taken.

The Court has decided compensation in equity not only for moral harm, but also for the material damage sustained by deprivation of

[162] R. Y. Jennings, 'Equity and Equitable Principles', *Annuaire suisse de droit international* 42 (1986), at 38.

[163] T. M. Franck, *Fairness in International Law and Institutions* (Oxford: Clarendon Press, 1995), at 7 (emphasis in original).

property.[164] Nonetheless, it seems rather inappropriate to justify on equitable grounds the material loss actually sustained.[165] The principle of *restitutio in integrum*, which is expressly promoted by the Court, should guarantee full reparation. The consequence would be that pecuniary prejudice should be at least estimated, if not precisely calculated, on the basis of evidence submitted by the parties for proving its very existence. When the parties have not substantiated their allegations, the Court should have recourse to experts, as it did in *Papamichalopoulos*. It is again regrettable that the Court prefers to substitute an objective legal reasoning with a rather speculative ruling which does not allow ascertainment of whether the judges have based their ruling on a realist, not hypothetic, economic value and if they have thus offered full redress. As one dissenting judge correctly asserted in *Hentrich*, 'the Court should not shelter behind "equity" but rule on the legal issues and invite experts to provide it with the data which would enable it to assess the value of the land, if need be in equity. Deciding in equity, like any other judicial decision, requires a clear and reliable view of the facts.'[166]

Yet, the Court has continued that practice of ruling in equity when evidence to determine the material damage was lacking in the file. For example, in *Selçuk and Asker v. Turkey*, where the victims had not substantiated their claims as to the quantity and value of their lost property, the judges declared that 'the Court's assessment of the amounts to be awarded must, by necessity, be speculative and based on principles of equity'.[167] What is completely striking, though, is that in a case decided the following year, which did not concern a simple dispossession but a serious breach of the right to life in so far as the authorities killed the applicant's son, the Grand Chamber decided that, in the absence of further information, it could not allow compensation for the income that would have been provided by the victim.[168] It is indeed an obvious inconsistency that has been properly emphasized by one of the judges sitting in that Grand Chamber formation, who questioned 'why the

[164] See, e.g., *Loizidou v. Turkey* (Article 50), 29 July 1998, *Reports of Judgments and Decisions* 1998-IV, para. 34, and *Xenides-Arestis v. Turkey* (just satisfaction), no. 46347/99, 7 December 2006, para. 42.

[165] In *Diallo* (note 145), the International Court of Justice also awarded redress for material damage in equity; for a criticism, see the separate opinion of Judge *ad hoc* Mampuya.

[166] Dissenting opinion of Judge Martens in *Hentrich v. France* (Article 50), 3 July 1995, Series A no. 320-A.

[167] *Selçuk and Asker v. Turkey*, 24 April 1998, *Reports of Judgments and Decisions* 1998-II, para. 106.

[168] *Oğur v. Turkey* [GC], no. 21594/93, ECHR 1999-III, para. 98.

"principles of equity" should be enlisted when they favour some and be scrapped when they favour others'.[169] When the use of equity by the Strasbourg judges is compared with the understanding of the concept under general international law, it is sometimes difficult to discern the elements of consistency and predictability assigned to equity by the International Court of Justice in the case of the *Continental Shelf*. It is rather an exercise of discretion that the same Court has clearly disapproved of in *Tunisia/Libya*.

To conclude, in the absence of a theory of equity, the European Court appears to employ the principle in a fairly discretionary way. It is unfortunate that the judges have not elaborated upon a legal theory of equity, based on their internal standards for compensation of moral prejudice, or at least drawn inspiration from rulings of other international courts. The International Court of Justice seems to disclose a similar reticence in defining some equitable criteria, preferring instead to keep a margin of appreciation that excludes any predictability from its rulings.[170]

The Convention has indeed entitled the judges to rule on the necessity of reparation, but flexibility should not transform into arbitrariness. Equity should rely on more objective legal principles, rather than on conscience, sympathy, personal perception and reaction as to what is right and wrong. A court should apply legal rules, not some concepts transcending those rules, with the purpose of facilitating its tasks. Even if it uses equity, it should frame it in a legal reasoning, given that '[a] reference to a specific equitable rule [such as abuse of right, estoppel or proportionality] may raise less alarm or criticism than a general reference to the vast notion of equity'.[171]

Therefore, the Court's judges should establish limits for the use of equity, otherwise it would transform into an extra-judicial exercise. They should not be subjective, but strive for a legal reasoning in applying and interpreting the law. Otherwise stated, they should discharge their legal functions. Equity is not above the law, so 'the judge or arbitrator who is to decide in accordance with equity should not disengage himself too

[169] Partly dissenting opinion of Judge Bonello.

[170] M. Virally, 'L'équité dans le droit. A propos des problèmes de délimitation maritime', in *International Law at the Time of Its Codification: Essays in Honour of Roberto Ago*, Vol. II (Milan: Giuffrè, 1987), at 533.

[171] R. Lapidoth, 'Equity in International Law', *Proceedings of the Annual Meeting (American Society of International Law)* 81 (1987), at 144.

much from the legal rules'.[172] This is the test which the Strasbourg judges will have to pass if they wish to enforce the authority of the system.

2.5 Different judges with different perspectives

The Strasbourg judges are fully aware of the importance of human rights protection and of the fact that their findings transcend the circumstances of a case, inasmuch as they may be used as legal guidance by judges of municipal courts in their interpretation and promotion of the Convention standards. Therefore, they must adopt an objective position in a dispute, without favouring the victim or the breaching state.[173] Cases of a victim-oriented approach supported by *ultra petita* awards of reparation are relatively scant, and the Court has assumed an active role in achieving effective protection. It has repeatedly declared since the early cases that its role 'requires it to determine proprio motu' whether a state has fulfilled its treaty commitments in a certain case.[174] The Court may thus invoke other infringements arising prima facie from the same facts and has always considered itself to be the master of the characterization to be given in law to the facts submitted to its examination.[175] Its declared intention is to review efficiently the state conduct against treaty obligations, because the Convention aims at a protection of human rights which is practical and effective, not theoretical or illusory.[176]

However, while in theory a judgment ought to be as objective as possible, it is doubtful that the judges' reasoning can be estranged from their subjective perception of things. A judge will normally see the problem through the lenses of his or her own intellectual and cultural formation. At the same time, the fact that the Strasbourg judges, and especially the Registry lawyers, are not required to be specialists in international law makes it more difficult to have the occasional recourse to rules from outside the special regime. All that Article 21 of the Convention requires for the selection of judges is that they '[be] of high moral character and must either possess the qualifications required

[172] Ibid., at 147.

[173] For a study of the Court's activism and self-restraint from the perspective of its relationship with the member states, see Delzangles, note 41.

[174] *Lawless*, note 12, para. 40.

[175] See, e.g., *Handyside v. the United Kingdom*, 7 December 1976, Series A no. 24, para. 41, and *Powell and Rayner v. the United Kingdom*, 21 February 1990, Series A no. 172, para. 29.

[176] *Airey v. Ireland*, 9 October 1979, Series A no. 32, para. 24.

for appointment to high judicial office or be jurisconsults of recognised competence'. A survey of their CVs reveals that less than half of them have strong expertise in international law. As for the Registry lawyers, only 'knowledge' of international law is required.[177] It is therefore of some significance that during the recent discussions for the reform of the Court, the Interlaken Declaration urged the contracting parties to improve the quality of the selection procedure by including a requirement for 'knowledge of public international law',[178] while the Brighton Declaration held that '[t]he authority and credibility of the Court depend in large part on the quality of its judges and the judgments they deliver'.[179]

The Strasbourg rulings express general trends as to the interpretation of the Convention, and those trends reflect the Court's role in the protection of human rights. For example, the judges have extensively interpreted the pilot-judgment procedure and have not only started to advise the respondent state that it should take action, but also suggested the particular measures that would be necessary. Another valuable source of the judges' position vis-à-vis the efficiency of the system of protection is their dissenting and concurring opinions attached to the rulings, especially those expressed in Grand Chamber decisions, where they usually establish principles of fundamental importance.[180] It is fairly rare for seventeen judges to share the same view.

An attentive reading of separate opinions reveals the judges' conception of their role and further denotes that some of them may be more inclined to find and emphasize the wrongfulness in the state's conduct, while others are more prepared to accept and defend the state's margin of appreciation.[181] Judges also challenge the Court's position in particular

[177] See the job advertisements on the Council of Europe's website (www.coe-recruitment.com/index.aspx#).

[178] Para. 8(a) of the Interlaken Declaration of 19 February 2010, available on the Court's website (www.echr.coe.int/Pages/home.aspx?p=court/reform&c=).

[179] Para. 21 of the Brighton Declaration of 20 April 2012, available on the Court's website (www.echr.coe.int/Pages/home.aspx?p=court/reform&c=).

[180] For a comprehensive study of separate opinions at the Court, see F. Rivière, *Les opinions séparées des juges à la Cour européenne des droits de l'homme* (Brussels: Bruylant, 2004). Also see R. C. A. White and I. Boussiakou, 'Separate Opinions in the European Court of Human Rights', *Human Rights Law Review* 9, no. 1 (2009).

[181] M.-E. Baudoin, 'Consonances et dissonances dans le discours européen des droits de l'homme – Violationnistes et étatistes: la définition du rôle du juge européen', in S. Hennette-Vauchez and J.-M. Sorel (eds.), *Les droits de l'homme ont-ils constitutionnalisé le monde?* (Brussels: Bruylant, 2011).

matters, such as the question of jurisdiction.[182] The case law is evolving in line with the transformations in society and the Court is confronted with new fields which call for an application of the Convention guarantees, such as bioethics, environmental questions and social rights.[183]

Oscar Schachter assumed some two decades ago, with reference to the International Court of Justice, that it would be difficult to deny that judges are generally influenced by the views of their governments, let alone those who are nationals of the state party to the dispute.[184] Is that also true for the Court's judges? The record proves the contrary. The infrequency of dissenting opinions by national judges indicates that 'the Strasbourg Court is not the place where national judges routinely seek to defend the interests of the country in respect of whom they are elected, or serving as an ad hoc judge'.[185] But it may be simplistic to assume that the 'interests' of the national country can only be defended through the medium of a theoretical dissent, which may be rather ineffective in practice. Other more effective and insidious methods may be used if a judge were to be tempted to adopt a protective attitude towards the national government.

Thus, one may imagine that a favourable state-oriented approach in respect of the amount of reparation given to the victims would bring more tangible advantages to the state. It is well known that the Court works in Sections and that the President of the Section designates a judge to act as Judge Rapporteur in a case.[186] The Rapporteur can request the parties to submit relevant information, 'decide whether the application is to be considered by a single-judge formation, by a Committee or by a Chamber', and also 'submit such reports, drafts and other documents as may assist the Chamber or the Committee or the respective President in carrying out their functions'.[187] In all this work, the Rapporteurs are assisted by the Registry lawyers, and their propositions in respect of the effective compensation may indeed denote a state-oriented or a victim-oriented approach.

[182] See the two concurring opinions of Judge Rozakis and Judge Bonello in *Al-Skeini and Others v. the United Kingdom* [GC], no. 55721/07, 7 July 2011.

[183] On this topic, see E. Dubout, 'Les "nouvelles" frontières des droits de l'homme et la définition du rôle de juge européen', in Hennette-Vauchez and Sorel, note 181.

[184] O. Schachter, *International Law in Theory and Practice* (Dordrecht: Martinus Nijhoff Publishers, 1991), at 43.

[185] White and Boussiakou, note 180, at 52–3.

[186] Rules 48–50 of the Rules of Court.

[187] Rule 49(3) of the Rules of Court.

For example, at the moment of deliberation for a case of ill-treatment where in similar cases the Court has normally awarded against the same state amounts of between 10,000 and 12,000 euros (EUR) in respect of non-pecuniary damage, the Rapporteur may very well propose 10,000 or 12,000, arguing admittedly that the violation was more or less serious than previous examples. It is therefore a matter of judicial discretion that comes from the margin of appreciation that judges enjoy when deciding on reparation, but which may nonetheless have its roots in the personal opinion and attitude of each judge. Taking into account that the Court's caseload is made up of thousands of cases, even if insignificant on a case-by-case basis, such variations in the sums given in compensation may bring more benefit to the economic interest of a state than a dissenting opinion. Certainly, that is a theoretical exercise, but what if it in fact happens? What would prevent judges from so acting? The selection of judges is a political process. Evidently, when a dispute reveals important far-reaching effects, their decisions may be politically, instead of judicially, motivated.[188] That reverberates on the Court's prestige.

Questionable results may also originate in efforts to adapt the system to the general principles of international law, an exercise which is not always an easy task for the Court. The Convention regime, in view of the *lex specialis* status of the treaty and of the particular scope and object of the rights protected, applies some principles which are different from the general norm in international law. This does not prevent the judges from using international law, albeit in a selective manner: either to give authority to their judgment, or as a counter-example to justify departure.[189] Yet, if taking international law as a source for the authority of their rulings, the condition of being specialists in international law appears to be essential not only for the Court's judges, but also for its lawyers, because '[i]n a large measure the standard of the Court's work, and its effectiveness, depend on the quality of its registry'.[190] This is all the more so given that an interpretation delivered by the Court is not necessarily confined to the special regime, but may have wider implications.

[188] On this subject, see E. Voeten, 'Politics, Judicial Behaviour, and Institutional Design', in J. Christoffersen and M. R. Madsen (eds.), *The European Court of Human Rights between Law and Politics* (Oxford University Press, 2011).

[189] In this sense, see Delzangles, note 41, at 343–7.

[190] R. White and C. Ovey, *The European Convention on Human Rights* (Oxford University Press, 2010), at 23.

It is therefore important for the Court to have a staff that can persuasively employ methods and concepts that go beyond a mechanical application of the treaty. In this way, they can seize the opportunity offered by the absence of a clear theory of reparations in international law and, taking advantage of an ample case law, further develop new concepts. In so doing, those from outside the Convention regime would praise the quality of the regional system of reparation.

3

Conditions for the application of Article 41

3.1 Novelty of the system: the right of individual petition

3.1.1 Notion

The originality of the Strasbourg system for human rights protection comes from the prerogative bestowed upon individual applicants to bring their complaints directly before an international court and, if successful, to obtain reparation. In other words, states have agreed that private persons may denounce breaches of their international obligations. By conferring such a fundamental right, the Convention has made the individual a subject of international law, evidently within its limits of application. While not a condition per se for the concrete application of Article 41, the right of petition is undoubtedly a prerequisite element which entitles individuals to seek reparation before the Court.

The right of individual petition before an international court is not a creation of the European Convention,[191] but the European model is quite unique in international law. The Strasbourg Court is the only international court where private persons have direct access to defend their rights. While in international law it is the state that usually defends the rights of its nationals by reason of the principle of diplomatic protection, petitioners under the Convention generally complain against their own state. That entitlement has proved to be a lot more effective than the alternative of requesting from states themselves periodic reports on compliance with treaty obligations, which is used by other universal and regional organizations equipped with agreements protecting individuals' rights. Claims to Strasbourg are reviewed by a control machinery of an entirely judicial nature. The ILC Articles specify expressly that they are without prejudice to any right conferred directly

[191] Early developments have been traced back to 1907: see F. Orrego-Vicuña, 'Individuals and Non-State Entities before International Courts and Tribunals', *Max Planck Yearbook of United Nations Law* 5 (2001), at 54–5.

on an individual or entity other than a state,[192] without however establishing rules in that respect. It was therefore the task of conventional law to generate specific criteria for the exercise of such a right.

The most similar system is that created by the American Convention. The drafters relied on the European Convention and thus created a dual mechanism with a Commission and a Court. Private persons have also been conferred a right of petition, but within the limits of the original European system, when they had access to the Commission alone, not to the Court. Thus, persons, group of persons or non-governmental entities may lodge petitions with the Inter-American Commission, whereas only the contracting states and the Commission have a right to submit a case to the Court of San José.[193] Laudably though, in absolute contrast to the twofold original European design with a Commission and a Court, the individual's right of application to the Inter-American Commission is not hindered by any condition of a state's acceptance of jurisdiction, whereas communications by states are indeed dependent upon such a recognition of competence by the allegedly wrongdoing state.[194]

3.1.2 Evolution

The idea of empowering individuals with a right to seize the Court was put forward even at the time of the creation of the Convention mechanism. Although mentioned at the Congress of Europe in May 1948, and then in the Draft Convention proposed by the European Movement in 1949,[195] the initiative was rejected by the member states during treaty negotiations. The majority expected that an individual's interests would be secured either by the Commission or by the state party whose national is considered to have been a victim or which has referred the case to the Commission.[196] Apparently, the drafters took extreme care to avoid overburdening the system with a surfeit of petitions, as well as to prevent abuses and politically inspired applications.[197] They nonetheless accepted an individual right of access to the Commission.

[192] Article 33(2) of the ILC Articles. [193] Article 61(1) of the American Convention.

[194] Article 45(2) of the American Convention.

[195] Article 12(c) of the Draft Convention provided that proceedings before the Court may be initiated by '[a]ny affected party, with the authorization of the Commission which shall be entitled to withhold such authorization without stating any reason': see the *Collected Edition of the 'Travaux préparatoires'*, note 11, Vol. I, at 300.

[196] Ibid., Vol. IV, at 44. [197] Ibid., Vol. II, at 188–200, and Vol. IV, at 132–40.

Discussions about an individual's *locus standi* before the Court were revived at the beginning of the 1970s. The old Commission and the Court upheld such a proposal, but the governments were less favourable.[198] Still, the right of individual petition was among the reforms put forward for the improvement of the Convention system. In 1990, the final text of a draft protocol was submitted for adoption to the Committee of Ministers.

Protocol No. 9 was thus opened for signature on 6 November 1990 and entered into force on 1 October 1994. It brought only limited improvements to the individual's capacity to introduce applications. The Protocol empowered private persons to have recourse to the Court, as long as the Commission had not declared their application inadmissible, but preserved the system of optional jurisdiction. The prospects for individuals to argue their case before the judges, and possibly receive just satisfaction, depended heavily on the defendant state's willingness to accept the Court's jurisdiction. In practice, however, the likely negative influence of states on the right of application was not as great as it seemed in theory, because all the contracting states had already accepted not only the competence of the Commission to receive petitions, but also the Court's compulsory jurisdiction.[199] It was accordingly quite natural to adopt that Protocol.

Yet, its role has been limited. The Protocol was merely optional, instead of being an instrument to amend the treaty. It conferred though a better procedural position on the individual petitioner, correcting at the same time a system which itself did not respect the rights that it defended and promoted. Intrinsic principles of the right to a fair trial laid down in Article 6 of the Convention, such as access to a court, participation in proceedings and equality of arms, were obviously ignored, given that states alone had a right to seize the Court. Those inconsistencies could not have persisted. They were finally rectified by a subsequent protocol, after forty years of existence of the European Convention, it having been quite an anomaly for a treaty defending human rights not to permit individuals the right to participate fully in the proceedings initiated by them.

Therefore, Protocol No. 9 was repealed by Protocol No. 11, which reformed the entire control machinery and introduced the Court's

[198] Paras. 2–11 of the Explanatory Report to Protocol No. 9, ETS No. 140 (also available at http://conventions.coe.int/Treaty/EN/Reports/Html/140.htm).

[199] Ibid., para. 12.

compulsory jurisdiction. At the same time, it conferred *locus standi* on the private person. The Protocol was opened for signature on 11 May 1994, was ratified by all the members of the Council of Europe, and entered into force on 1 November 1998. The right of individual application, which was previously optional, became compulsory upon ratification of the treaty by acceding countries.[200]

However, while the right of individual petition is the greatest achievement of the Convention system, it has been so successful that it even risks ruining the whole structure. The decision makers of the Council of Europe have therefore been searching for new solutions that would ensure a proper functioning of a court already overburdened with individual applications. One of them has been the new admissibility criterion introduced by Protocol No. 14, according to which an application would be declared inadmissible if the plaintiff had not suffered a significant disadvantage.

That condition has been highly criticized, even by some of the Court's judges, in so far as it practically reduces the efficiency of the right of individual petition, giving more discretion to the judges in the appreciation of the situations which deserve an examination on the merits. As rightly emphasized, it was a debate involving 'constitutionalists versus petitioners', where proponents of the Court's constitutional mission, who argued that it should concentrate on cases of principle, opposed those who defended its task to provide individual relief.[201] In any event, the provision may be perceived as a consequence of the increasing number of judgments where the Court declares that its findings constitute in themselves sufficient reparation, which denotes acceptance of the fact that some violations produce insignificant prejudice.

The notion of significant disadvantage is itself open to interpretation. Apparently, it was the intention of the drafters to introduce an element of flexibility for the further establishment by the Court of objective criteria of interpretation.[202] Obviously, there are some types of violations

[200] There is still one exception, which concerns separate declarations by states in respect of territories for whose international relations they are responsible: see Article 56 of the Convention.

[201] F. Vanneste, 'A New Inadmissibility Ground', in P. Lemmens and W. Vandenhole (eds.), *Protocol No. 14 and the Reform of the European Court of Human Rights* (Antwerp: Intersentia, 2005), at 70–3.

[202] Para. 80 of the Explanatory Report to Protocol No. 14, CETS No. 194 (also available at http://conventions.coe.int/Treaty/EN/Reports/Html/194.htm).

where it is beyond doubt that what is at stake is significant, such as cases in respect of torture, ill-treatment, the right to life, deprivation of liberty, non-retroactivity of criminal law or lack of domestic remedies.

At the theoretical level of human rights, there is no doubt that the new condition restricts the full right of individual petition, even if to a limited extent. But when changing the focus of discussion from theory to practice, what is sometimes at stake in those cases is indeed insignificant and does not deserve attention from an international court. The judges are thus facilitated in their task of dismissing those complaints. Given that the Court is the sole authority that decides what constitutes a significant disadvantage, the judges enjoy a considerable margin of appreciation, as in the context of moral damages, albeit that it is not unlimited. It is a matter of common sense that they cannot fix some absurd limits. At the same time, they should not disregard the fact that some of the important judgments where the Court had the opportunity to establish notions of principle were given in cases which would certainly not go beyond the threshold fixed by the significant disadvantage.[203] However, the judges are still attentive to serious challenges to human rights protection and there is reason to surmise that this will remain the case.

3.1.3 Effective use

The Court has classified the right of individual petition as one of the fundamental guarantees of the effectiveness of the system of protection.[204] While the exercise of the right per se is unlimited, Articles 34 and 35 of the Convention impose some restrictions on its effective use. Individual applicants must claim to be victims of a violation of a treaty right by one of the contracting parties and to have suffered a significant disadvantage. They may bring a complaint only after the exhaustion of all domestic remedies and within a period of six months from the final internal decision.[205] Further admissibility criteria may also render a petition inadmissible. Claimants should be aware that they cannot lodge an application which is anonymous, substantially the same as one previously examined by the Court or already submitted to another international procedure, incompatible with the Convention

[203] For example, *Adolf v. Austria*, 26 March 1982, Series A no. 49.

[204] See, e.g., *Mamatkulov and Askarov v. Turkey* [GC], nos. 46827/99 and 46951/99, ECHR 2005-I, para. 100.

[205] When Protocol No. 15 enters into force, the new delay will be four months.

or manifestly ill-founded, or which stands for abuse of the right of application.[206]

The right of individual petition is naturally linked to a state's obligation laid down in Article 34 not to obstruct in any way its effective use. There are no exceptions, it is an absolute right. In addition, whenever the Court deems it necessary to carry out an investigation, the states have a duty to furnish all necessary facilities.[207] There is no doubt that states may dispose of various and often hardly detectable forms of pressure, such as indirect acts to dissuade or discourage the victims from initiating or carrying forward Convention proceedings. For instance, states may implement some administrative procedures that make contact between lawyers and would-be applicants difficult, such as restricting access to migrant centres.[208] Having regard to the significance of the right of petition for the system of control, the Court may also raise *ex officio* the question of compliance with that obligation.[209]

In general, hindrances can be directed against the claimant, against his lawyer or representative or even against another contracting state.[210] Examples may thus include acts of intimidation, interrogatories, disciplinary sanctions or institution or threat of criminal proceedings against petitioners, members of their family or their legal representative, prohibition or other interference with the right to communicate with the Court, as well as pressure to withdraw an application or refusal to provide the Court with the requested information or facilities. While

[206] On the conditions of admissibility see, in general, S. Trechsel, 'Article 27', in Pettiti, Decaux and Imbert, note 17; K. Reid, *A Practitioner's Guide to the European Convention on Human Rights* (London: Sweet & Maxwell, 2011), at 26–56; P. Leach, *Taking a Case to the European Court of Human Rights* (Oxford University Press, 2011), at 107–58; White and Ovey, note 190, at 30–41; and M. L. Padelletti, 'Les nouvelles conditions de recevabilité matérielles d'une requête individuelle: l'entité du préjudice invoqué par la victime', in F. Salerno (ed.), *La nouvelle procédure devant la Cour européenne des droits de l'homme après le Protocole n° 14: actes du colloque tenu à Ferrara les 29 et 30 avril 2005* (Brussels: Bruylant, 2007).

[207] Article 38 of the Convention.

[208] E. Becue et al., 'The Administrative, Tax, Financial and Cost Hindrances against NGOs and Lawyers', in E. Lambert Abdelgawad (ed.), *Preventing and Sanctioning Hindrances to the Right of Individual Petition before the European Court of Human Rights* (Cambridge: Intersentia, 2011), at 137–9.

[209] See, e.g., *Drozdowski v. Poland*, no. 20841/02, 6 December 2005, para. 19, and *Maksym v. Poland*, no. 14450/02, 19 December 2006, para. 20.

[210] Russia exerted pressure over Moldova in the case of *Ilaşcu and Others v. Moldova and Russia* ([GC], no. 48787/99, ECHR 2004-VII, para. 481).

the state's activity must be of certain gravity, account should also be taken of the vulnerability of a plaintiff.[211]

A point of controversy as regards states' duty not to hinder the effective exercise of the right of petition was occasioned by the effect to be given to the power of the Convention organs to indicate interim measures. Were those measures mandatory in virtue of that obligation? The Court's case law reveals a radical evolution of the views on the matter. The question first arose in *Cruz Varas and Others v. Sweden*, where the government disregarded a request by the former Commission not to expel the applicants. By a flimsy majority of ten votes to nine, the Plenary Court admitted that a power to order interim measures would be necessary for a practical and effective protection of human rights, but concluded that unlike in other international instruments, such a power was neither contained in the Convention nor to be derived from the right of application.[212]

In the context of the evolution of international law since delivery of that ruling, the Court has changed its jurisprudence. In *Mamatkulov and Askarov v. Turkey*, where the applicants had been extradited in spite of indications to the contrary by the Court, the issue was raised again in respect of the binding effects of interim measures and their role in securing the right of petition. The Grand Chamber took note of recent decisions and orders on the matter by international courts and institutions, and declared that a failure to comply with those specific measures hindered the effective use of the right of individual petition.[213] Five months after delivery of that ruling, the Plenary Court inserted Rule 39 on interim measures in the Rules of Court. It should be mentioned that the American Convention, in the same article on reparation, empowers the Court of San José to adopt provisional measures '[i]n cases of extreme gravity and urgency, and when necessary to avoid irreparable damage to persons'.[214]

[211] For an analysis of different aspects regarding hindrances to the right of individual petition, see the essays published in Lambert Abdelgawad, note 208.

[212] *Cruz Varas and Others v. Sweden*, 20 March 1991, Series A no. 201, paras. 94 and 102. That judgment was confirmed in *Čonka v. Belgium* (dec.), no. 51564/99, 13 March 2001. For a criticism of the former non-binding character of the interim measures, see O. De Schutter, 'La protection juridictionnelle provisoire devant la Cour européenne des droits de l'homme', in H. Ruiz Fabri and J.-M. Sorel (eds.), *Le contentieux de l'urgence et l'urgence dans le contentieux devant les juridictions internationales: regards croisés* (Paris: Pedone, 2003).

[213] *Mamatkulov and Askarov*, note 204, paras. 113–17 and 128.

[214] Article 63(2) of the American Convention and Article 27(1) of the Rules of Procedure (available at http://www.corteidh.or.cr/index.php/en/about-us/reglamento/reglamento-vigente).

In *Mamatkulov and Askarov*, the Court also compensated the victims' moral injury suffered as a result of interference with their right of petition.[215] The fact that no other violation was found in that case clearly indicates that a breach of the right of petition is not conditioned on the favourable outcome of the claim. Having a right is not equivalent to being right. Applicants have a right to make their allegations, without being constrained by any requirement of precision or accuracy. And, given that the right of petition is autonomous, plaintiffs are generally entitled to redress for a breach.[216] In that context, only financial compensation would be appropriate, because the principle of *restitutio in integrum* would make no sense in so far as the victim has nonetheless succeeded in presenting a petition before the Court, in spite of interference to the contrary from a state.

Turning to the underlying desideratum of guaranteeing an effective right of petition, one may wonder whether the admissibility criterion of exhaustion of domestic remedies also applies in the context of allegations of violations of that right. In answering that question, one should take into account the judges' assertion that a state's obligation not to interfere with the right of petition confers upon an applicant a right of a procedural nature.[217] As it is not a substantive right, claimants have no obligation to initiate domestic proceedings before coming to Strasbourg. The Court itself declared that allegations of infringement of that right 'do not give rise to any issue of admissibility, including exhaustion of domestic remedies'.[218] Thus, it has wisely reserved exclusivity in assessing the veracity of allegations of abuse by state authorities, in order to confer proficiency on the effective use of the right of petition.

3.2 When does the Court award compensation?

The Court considered for the first time the question of an award of just satisfaction in the *Vagrancy* cases,[219] which concerned certain aspects of

[215] See para. 134.

[216] Other examples of compensation for breach of the right of petition include *Ilaşcu*, note 210, para. 489; *Aoulmi v. France*, no. 50278/99, ECHR 2006-I (extracts), para. 118; *Olaechea Cahuas v. Spain*, no. 24668/03, 10 August 2006, paras. 89 and 90; and *Nurmagomedov v. Russia*, no. 30138/02, 7 June 2007, para. 66.

[217] See, e.g., *Shamayev and Others v. Georgia and Russia*, no. 36378/02, ECHR 2005-III, para. 470.

[218] *Davydov and Others v. Ukraine*, nos. 17674/02 and 39081/02, 1 July 2010, para. 332.

[219] *De Wilde, Ooms and Versyp* (Article 50), note 23.

Belgian legislation on vagrancy and its application to the complainants. The plaintiffs alleged several violations, including arbitrary detention, ill-treatment and slavery. By nine votes to seven, the Court found only a breach of Article 5(4) in that the applicants had no remedy open to them before a court against the decisions ordering their detention, and reserved for the victims the right to apply for just satisfaction.[220] Then it decided, in a separate judgment, that the claims for damages were not well founded.

The absence of reparation in the particular circumstances of the *Vagrancy* cases has not prevented the judges from establishing a series of important principles emerging out of the interpretation of the notion of just satisfaction. They extracted from the text of the Convention four general conditions for an award: a decision or measure taken by an authority of a contracting state in conflict with its obligations under the treaty; the consequences of the violation are only capable of being wiped out partially at the internal level; the existence of an injured party; and an estimation by the Court that it is necessary to afford just satisfaction.[221] The first two requirements can be classified as conditions for admission of a claim for reparation, while the other two are conditions for a grant of compensation.[222]

3.2.1 *The finding of a violation*

The Court first has to declare that the facts submitted by a petitioner denote a treaty violation. Only when it has done that will it examine any claims for just satisfaction. When the case is inadmissible or does not confirm the existence of any infringement, claims for reparation are not taken into account. An applicant may invoke several violations, but in that case the judges must hold that at least one of them is founded in order to award compensation.[223] It does not matter if the internal decision or measure taken by an authority is completely or partially in conflict with the Convention, if it was an act or an omission, or to which branch of state power that authority belongs. What is important is that a member state is held responsible for a breach of the treaty.

[220] *De Wilde, Ooms and Versyp v. Belgium* (merits), 18 June 1971, Series A no. 12.

[221] *De Wilde, Ooms and Versyp* (Article 50), note 23, para. 21.

[222] M. Enrich Mas, 'Right to Compensation under Article 50', in Macdonald, Matscher, and Petzold, note 32, at 779–84.

[223] *Enea v. Italy* [GC], no. 74912/01, 17 September 2009, para. 159.

A relevant point has been raised by two of the Court's judges in relation to the occasional practice with respect to the requirement of the existence of a violation as a precondition for an award. In three cases decided on the same day, where the applicants' prison sentences were suspended on medical grounds, the Court declared that the state would be in breach of Article 3 if it returned them to prison in spite of a lack of significant improvement in their medical fitness to withstand such a measure.[224] The majority of that Chamber's judges allowed the plaintiffs to recover a certain amount of money for moral damage.

The two dissenting judges rightly emphasized that the exact wording of Article 41 is that 'there has been a violation of the Convention', which means that the contracting parties have agreed to empower the Court to make reparation only when an effective breach of the treaty had already occurred, and not in the presence of a simple risk of violation.[225] Indeed, as aptly noted, that condition for state responsibility had already been codified in the ILC Articles. It would be of great interest for an outsider to know the reasons for departure from the text of the Convention and from the general rule, all the more so given that the Court still continues to award damages in the absence of an effective breach.[226] However, the common practice in cases revealing a potential violation of Article 3 or Article 8 is to proclaim that the official confirmation of such a possibility provides sufficient redress for any non-pecuniary damage sustained. Leaving aside the fact that even a mere threat of unlawful activity may cause more or less moral suffering to a person, it is nonetheless the right solution from a legal point of view, because the defendant state would not be ordered to make reparation for a breach of treaty that it had not already committed.

3.2.2 The internal law of the respondent state allows only partial reparation

After the finding of a violation, the Court awards just satisfaction only if the internal law of the breaching state allows no more than partial reparation. Even in the absence of real *restitutio in integrum*, the Court accepted that in such situations it would at least suffice for redress to be

[224] *Gürbüz v. Turkey*, no. 26050/04, 10 November 2005; *Kuruçay v. Turkey*, no. 24040/04, 10 November 2005; and *Uyan v. Turkey*, no. 7454/04, 10 November 2005.

[225] Partly dissenting opinion of Judges Caflisch and Türmen in *Gürbüz*.

[226] See, e.g., *Butt v. Norway*, no. 47017/09, 4 December 2012, para. 95.

provided that came close to it. This was considered the case, for example, when the time spent by the applicant in detention on remand was reckoned as part of his sentence and he was then granted remission of the remainder.[227]

Within the general law of state responsibility, the internal provisions do not have relevance in international litigation,[228] but within the Convention, this condition is an expression of the principle of subsidiarity, the judges having first to inquire into what is available domestically. In this regard, the Inter-American regime of reparation is quite in opposition to the Strasbourg one, in so far as it does not depend on the internal legislation's capacity to make restitution, but comes fully within the confines of the supranational judicial power. Relying on the applicable principles of international law, in its very first judgment on reparation, the Court of San José confirmed the autonomy of the system of compensation vis-à-vis the means of redress available in domestic law.[229]

In Strasbourg, this condition for an award appears to be in conflict with the present practice of the Court. In order for the judges to consider whether domestic law permits any reparation, they should give the state the occasion to prove it. That was facilitated in the past by the practice of delivering a first judgment on the merits and then a subsequent judgment on just satisfaction. States had an opportunity to provide redress after the finding of a violation, and the judges had the chance to assess whether that reparation complied with the principle of *restitutio in integrum*. Such was the case, for instance, in *Piersack v. Belgium*, where the Court found that the impartiality of the tribunal which sentenced the plaintiff was open to doubt. Having adjourned the question of just satisfaction, the victim received a new trial with all the guarantees laid down by the Convention. That made the Court admit in its subsequent judgment that 'those proceedings brought about a result as close to *restitutio in integrum* as was possible in the nature of things', even if the petitioner had been given the same sentence.[230] But in the present circumstances, where the Court, as a rule, decides both merits and reparation, what kind of assessment does it deliver? Productivity coupled

227 *Neumeister* (Article 50), note 90, para. 41. For stances to the contrary, see *De Cubber v. Belgium* (Article 50), 14 September 1987, Series A no. 124-B, para. 21, and *Hauschildt v. Denmark*, 24 May 1989, Series A no. 154, para. 56.

228 Articles 3 and 32 of the ILC Articles.

229 *Velásquez-Rodríguez* (reparations and costs), note 152, paras. 30–1.

230 *Piersack* (Article 50), note 120, para. 11.

with an ever increasing workload inevitably discourages the practice of dealing with reparation separately from the merits.

Some of the judges still believe that the Court should explore the prospects of domestic law to allow full *restitutio*, because such impossibility is a strict legal precondition for an award of just satisfaction.[231] Nonetheless, it must be conceded that there can be no realistic expectations that the system will adopt a standard two-phase procedure, whereby, following a finding of a violation, a separate judgment on just satisfaction would first assess the incapacity of the internal law to provide full restitution and then, if necessary, provide redress. The only reasonable alternative for the judges is to take for granted that the Court is better situated than the domestic courts for making reparation in a case of a breach of the treaty.

In the presence of violations where *restitutio in integrum* is clearly impossible owing to the very nature of the injury, the possibility offered by the internal law to recover a part of the damage does not represent an impediment for the applicants to bring their claims directly to Strasbourg. Notwithstanding the origins of the provision on just satisfaction in treaties which took the view that the nature of the injury permitted restoration of the *status quo ante*, when assessing if domestic legislation permits the wiping out entirely of the consequences of a violation, the majority of judges held in the *Vagrancy* cases that it was irrelevant whether or not it was the very nature of the injury that had made restitution impossible. They concluded that even if it was possible to bring a claim for damage, the effects of the applicants' unlawful detention would not be removed.[232]

That interpretation was very extensive, and although it may seem defective, it was the right option. It was considered flawed by the dissenting judges, who discerned an absolute obligation for states to offer *restitutio in integrum*, which was contrary to the maxim *impossibilium nulla obligatio est.*[233] But even if the argument of the majority may not have been wholly coherent, the Court could not have declined jurisdiction whenever restitution was, either *de facto* or *de jure*, impossible. Such a restrictive approach, in the context of a fairly large spectrum

[231] Partly concurring opinion of Judge Zupančič in *Lucà v. Italy*, no. 33354/96, ECHR 2001-II.

[232] *De Wilde, Ooms and Versyp* (Article 50), note 23, para. 20.

[233] Joint separate opinion of Judges Holmbäck, Ross and Wold. They preferred the option of redress before the national courts, arguing that in any event the consequences of a violation can never be wiped out entirely.

of violations irreversibly affecting the human person, would have instituted a procedural hurdle for a large number of petitioners seeking redress in Strasbourg. The judges themselves have subsequently admitted that the Convention is a law-making instrument that has to be interpreted so as to realize the aim and achieve the object of the treaty, not to restrict to the greatest possible degree the obligations undertaken by the contracting states.[234]

The Court usually takes into account any partial reparation already received by the complainant at domestic level[235] or a change in legislation as a result of a finding of a continuous violation on the merits.[236] It may also dismiss or adjourn examination of a claim for compensation when the internal proceedings are still pending. In the absence of an outcome to the case before the domestic courts, the judges cannot assess, for instance, whether the internal law is capable of granting full redress for any financial consequences of the length of proceedings.[237] The Court, however, may verify the outcome of the national proceedings.[238] It may even order the state to conclude the proceedings and to offer compensation to the victims.[239]

At first glance, this condition of partial reparation may look similar to one of the admissibility criteria provided for in Article 35, namely the exhaustion of domestic remedies. The Court has already delivered an interpretation in the *Vagrancy* cases. The Belgian government raised two pleas of inadmissibility in the context of just satisfaction, submitting that the plaintiffs had not exhausted domestic remedies and, accordingly, had not established that the internal law allowed incomplete reparation. The judges dismissed those arguments, considering that exhaustion of domestic remedies, as an admissibility requirement, related only to the institution of the Strasbourg proceedings. The introduction of an application came under a different section of the Convention from the award of just satisfaction, which was the final phase. If a petitioner were

234 *Wemhoff*, note 13, para. 8.

235 *O'Keeffe v. Ireland* [GC], no. 35810/09, 28 January 2014, paras. 202–3.

236 *Dudgeon v. the United Kingdom* (Article 50), 24 February 1983, Series A no. 59, paras. 13–14.

237 *Zanghì v. Italy*, 19 February 1991, Series A no. 194-C, para. 25, and *A.J. Hadjihanna Bros. (Tourist Enterprises) Ltd & Hadjihannas v. Cyprus*, no. 34579/05, 18 January 2007, para. 44.

238 See, e.g., *Pressos Compania Naviera S.A. and Others v. Belgium* (Article 50), 3 July 1997, *Reports of Judgments and Decisions* 1997-IV, paras. 10 and 14.

239 See point 6 of the operative part in *Nihayet Arıcı and Others v. Turkey*, nos. 24604/04 and 16855/05, 23 October 2012.

obliged to exhaust twice the internal remedies before obtaining compensation, the total length of the Convention proceedings would go against the idea of effective protection of human rights. In conclusion, such a requirement was deemed incompatible with the aim and object of the treaty.[240]

3.2.3 *An injured party*

The Court does not entertain a claim for compensation if an applicant is not an injured party. The plaintiff must establish the existence of a direct causal link between the breach and the alleged damage. The notion of 'injured party' resembles the 'victim' requirement for introduction of individual petitions.[241] The two terms are not defined in the Convention. The classical explanation given by the Court in the *Vagrancy* cases, and also repeatedly endorsed in subsequent case law, was that the two terms were synonymous only in the context of just satisfaction, although they both denoted a person directly affected by an act or omission.[242] In the context of the victim requirement for lodging an application, there was a difference between those notions, given that the existence of a violation was conceivable even in the absence of prejudice, which was relevant only when damage flowing from the breach was to be established.[243] Harm was not seen as a prerequisite for a finding of a violation, while an injured party was a victim of an infringement who had suffered prejudice. The absence of prejudice is also a particular feature of state responsibility under general international law.[244]

240 *De Wilde, Ooms and Versyp* (Article 50), note 23, paras. 15–16. Also see, among other authorities, *Barberà, Messegué and Jabardo* (Article 50), note 76, para. 17.

241 For a presentation of the victim requirement, see P. van Dijk et al., *Theory and Practice of the European Convention on Human Rights* (Antwerp: Intersentia, 2006), at 55–78, and J. A. Frowein, 'La notion de victime dans la Convention européenne des droits de l'homme', in *Studi in onore di Giuseppe Sperduti* (Milan: Giuffrè, 1984), at 587–99.

242 *De Wilde, Ooms and Versyp* (Article 50), note 23, para. 23.

243 See, e.g., *Lüdi v. Switzerland*, 15 June 1992, Series A no. 238, para. 34, and *İlhan v. Turkey* [GC], no. 22277/93, ECHR 2000-VII, para. 52. For an opinion that the victim requirement for lodging an application also requires a grievance, see K. Rogge, 'The "Victim" Requirement in Article 25 of the European Convention on Human Rights', in Matscher and Petzold, note 37, at 539–45.

244 It has been argued that '[i]t is . . . self-evident that any violation of a legal obligation entails in itself a damage, irrespective of the occurrence of a "visible" injury as a distinct condition for the wrongfulness of such violation': see A. Tanzi, 'Is Damage a Distinct Condition for the Existence of an Internationally Wrongful Act?', in M. Spinedi and B. Simma (eds.), *United Nations Codification of State Responsibility* (New York: Oceana, 1987), at 10.

That slight difference between the two notions has been rendered ineffective as a consequence of the entry into force of Protocol No. 14 in 2010, which has introduced the admissibility requirement of the significant disadvantage. The French version of the treaty, which is equally authentic, employs the expression 'préjudice important'. It clearly follows from the French text that the notion of 'disadvantage' is equivalent to that of 'injury', as opposed to a merely unfavourable condition or circumstance. As rightly noted, the new condition does not formally alter the victim requirement for lodging an application, but it does modify the classical theory that the existence of a violation of the Convention is conceivable even in the absence of prejudice.[245] Minimum damage has thus become a condition for the existence of a treaty violation. What is more, the alleged injury must be significant in order to surpass the threshold of admissibility.

At this point, and especially in view of the changes that the significant disadvantage requirement will instigate in the Court's future jurisprudence, a few remarks may be apt as to the notion of 'victim'. Before Protocol No. 14, when initiating the Strasbourg proceedings petitioners had only to claim to be victims of an infringement, not also to prove that they were indeed victims. Now the applicants have also to prove that they had in fact suffered a significant disadvantage in order to pass the new admissibility test, because mere allegations would not suffice. Moreover, if the facts submitted do not meet the other admissibility criteria provided for in Article 35, the Court will dismiss the request without further inquiries into the circumstances of the case. The only exception to the victim requirement concerns inter-state applications.

The Court has further developed in its case law the notions of direct, indirect and potential victim. Despite sporadic instances to the contrary, the overwhelming majority of plaintiffs claim to be direct victims. Indeed, the Court has established that the person claiming to be a victim must be directly affected by the impugned measures.[246] Unlike applications brought by the contracting states, and also unlike the system of

[245] V. Berger, 'Le "préjudice important" selon le Protocole n° 14 à la Convention européenne des droits de l'homme: questions et réflexions', in M. G. Kohen (ed.), *Promoting Justice, Human Rights and Conflict Resolution through International Law = La promotion de la justice, des droits de l'homme et du règlement des conflits par le droit international: Liber Amicorum Lucius Caflisch* (Leiden: Martinus Nijhoff Publishers, 2007), at 85.

[246] *Klass and Others v. Germany*, 6 September 1978, Series A no. 28, para. 33.

individual petition under the American Convention,[247] the European Convention does not allow private persons to introduce an *actio popularis*, namely to request interpretation or review of internal legislation without having been directly affected by it.

The Court has then admitted in enforced disappearance cases that an applicant may be an indirect victim, given the close link with the direct victim of a violation. In other words, a family member of a person who had disappeared may claim to have been exposed to treatment contrary to Article 3.[248] Thus, in *Kurt v. Turkey*, which concerned the disappearance of the applicant's son during an unacknowledged detention, the Court held that the applicant also suffered inhuman and degrading treatment, in her quality as the mother of the direct victim, and also as herself a victim of the authorities' attitude towards her agony.[249] It awarded non-pecuniary damages, both to the applicant and to her son.

The following year, in a dispute where the person concerned had not only disappeared, but, after the establishment of the facts, was also presumed dead by the Strasbourg organs, the Grand Chamber decided the principles for recognizing family members as indirect victims. Accordingly, a family member is not by definition a victim of inhuman treatment contrary to Article 3, because emotional distress is inevitable for a relative of a direct victim of a serious violation. Special factors are required, which give the suffering of the indirect victim a dimension and character distinct from the predictable hardship. The Court will assess that suffering on the basis of relevant elements, which include how close the family tie is, the particular circumstances of the relationship, the extent to which the family member witnessed the events and then attempted to obtain information about the victim, as well as the response of the authorities.[250] In the case at hand, although the applicant was the

[247] Article 44 of the American Convention does not provide for a victim requirement for individual applications.

[248] When the person taken into custody has later been found dead, the Court will consider the issue only under Article 2 (right to life). However, a long period of initial disappearance may raise issues under Article 3 (prohibition of torture): see in this respect *Gongadze v. Ukraine*, no. 34056/02, ECHR 2005-XI, paras. 184–6, and *Luluyev and Others v. Russia*, no. 69480/01, ECHR 2006-XIII (extracts), para. 114.

[249] *Kurt v. Turkey*, 25 May 1998, *Reports of Judgments and Decisions* 1998-III, paras. 130–4.

[250] *Çakıcı*, note 76, para. 98. Also see the partly dissenting opinion of Judge Thomassen joined by Judges Jungwiert and Fischbach. For a criticism of the *Çakıcı* test, see T. Feldman, 'Indirect Victims, Direct Injury: Recognising Relatives as Victims under the European Human Rights System', *European Human Rights Law Review*, no. 1 (2009).

brother of the direct victim, he was found not to have suffered treatment contrary to Article 3, on the grounds that he was not present when the security forces took his brother, and also that he was not the principal initiator of petitions and inquiries to the authorities. However, the Court awarded him reparation for moral damage, considering that he was an injured party and had undoubtedly suffered damage in respect of the violations found.[251]

The Inter-American Court, after initially adopting a classical approach in respect of redress, which was to allow direct victims exclusively to participate in the proceedings, subsequently changed that attitude and further permitted closely related family to be awarded compensation.[252] In fact, it seems to be more permissive with the standard of proof for the moral harm experienced by the victim's family members. For example, in the case of the next of kin of two victims of unlawful and arbitrary detention, torture and death, the Court of San José declared that no evidence was required as to the alleged moral damage, in so far as 'it is reasonable to reach the conclusion that the affliction suffered by the victims extends to the closest members of the family, especially those who were in close emotional contact with them'.[253]

The difference in the position of the two courts as regards the moral injury suffered by the close relatives of victims of serious violations becomes fairly evident. While the Inter-American Court has adopted a subjective and more humane vision of that moral harm, normally taking it for granted, the European Court has preferred a more objective approach, considering that 'the essence of such a violation does not so much lie in the fact of the "disappearance" of the family member but rather concerns the authorities' reactions and attitudes to the situation when it is brought to their attention'.[254] The Court of San José even applies '[a] presumption . . . that human rights violations and impunity in connection with them cause suffering' to very close relatives of the victims or of other persons linked to them.[255]

251 *Çakıcı*, note 76, para. 130.

252 L. Burgorgue-Larsen and A. Úbeda de Torres, *The Inter-American Court of Human Rights: Case Law and Commentary* (Oxford University Press, 2011), at 225–7.

253 *Gómez-Paquiyauri Brothers v. Peru* (merits, reparations and costs), 8 July 2004, Series C no. 110, para. 218. Also see *Bámaca-Velásquez* (reparations and costs), note 59, para. 63.

254 *Çakıcı*, note 76, para. 98.

255 *Las Palmeras v. Colombia* (reparations and costs), 26 November 2002, Series C no. 96, para. 55.

The Strasbourg Court has also accepted the notion of potential victim, in the following situations: when it was impossible for the applicants to show that the legislation they complained of had actually been applied to them because of the secret nature of the measures it authorized;[256] when a law by itself violated the rights of the petitioner, in the absence of any specific measure of implementation, and the petitioner also ran the risk of being directly affected by it;[257] as well as where the authorities had decided, but had not yet carried out, the forced removal of aliens, and where enforcement of that measure would have exposed the complainant, on arrival in the receiving country, to the risk of treatment contrary to Article 3,[258] or would have infringed the right to respect for family life.[259] When alleging to be a potential victim, plaintiffs must produce reasonable and convincing evidence in respect of the possibility that a violation affecting them personally will indeed occur, because mere suspicion or conjecture is insufficient.[260]

In any event, as rightly noted, the Court should reconsider the notion of potential victim in the light of the latest changes to the admissibility criteria,[261] because now a case will be declared inadmissible if the claimant has not suffered a significant disadvantage. The use of the present perfect tense means that the applicant should have already suffered a prejudice. On the contrary, in the context of potential victim, the prejudice is likely to occur at some moment in the future. The Court will have to clarify that issue, either by abandoning the notion of potential victim, or by arguing that even a potential victim in the situations just mentioned has suffered a prejudice, most probably a moral one. And yet, that prejudice would have to be significant.

256 See, e.g., *Klass*, note 246; *Malone v. the United Kingdom*, 2 August 1984, Series A no. 82; and *Weber and Saravia v. Germany* (dec.), no. 54934/00, ECHR 2006-XI.

257 For example, legislation punishing homosexual acts in *Dudgeon v. the United Kingdom*, 22 October 1981, Series A no. 45; *Norris v. Ireland*, 26 October 1988, Series A no. 142; and *Modinos v. Cyprus*, 22 April 1993, Series A no. 259; certain legislation relating to education in *Belgian linguistic* (merits), note 13, and *Kjeldsen, Busk Madsen and Pedersen v. Denmark*, 7 December 1976, Series A no. 23; or legislation concerning family relationships outside marriage in *Marckx*, note 111, and *Johnston and Others v. Ireland*, 18 December 1986, Series A no. 112.

258 *Soering v. the United Kingdom*, 7 July 1989, Series A no. 161.

259 *Beldjoudi v. France*, 26 March 1992, Series A no. 234.

260 *Tauira and Others v. France*, no. 28204/95, Commission's decision of 4 December 1995, *Decisions and Reports* (DR) 83-B.

261 Berger, note 245, at 85.

A petitioner is deprived of victim status only if the domestic authorities have acknowledged the violation, expressly or in substance, and then afforded redress. The Court is very strict in this respect. In general, a simple decision or measure favourable to the applicant is not sufficient.[262] For example, a deduction from a sentence equal to the time spent in custody on remand, in the absence of an acknowledgment of a breach of the Convention, does not deprive the plaintiff of victim status, although it will be taken into account by the judges for assessing the extent of any prejudice.[263]

3.2.4 Necessity to afford just satisfaction – is there a right to compensation?

Recent developments in international law, and further affirmation of specialized regimes such as human rights, humanitarian law and international criminal law, could not have confined the individual to traditional diplomatic protection by the state. The individual may now be directly conferred rights and also obligations under international law. The European Convention, in virtue of its scope, provides exclusively for a set of rights to the benefit of private persons, without any duty on their part. Does it also guarantee a corresponding right to reparation in the event of a violation?

Under the general international law of state responsibility, the obligation of reparation is formulated 'as an obligation of the responsible State resulting from the breach, rather than as a right of an injured State or States'.[264] Nor is there any express right under the Convention for a victim to obtain redress. Article 41 authorizes the Court to afford just satisfaction to an injured party only 'if necessary'. It does not specify when an award is necessary and, despite some views to the contrary,[265]

[262] See, e.g., *Lüdi*, note 243, para. 34.

[263] *De Jong, Baljet and Van den Brink v. the Netherlands*, 22 May 1984, Series A no. 77, para. 41.

[264] Crawford, note 43, at 202.

[265] G. Ress, 'Reflections on the Protection of Property under the European Convention on Human Rights', in S. Breitenmoser et al. (eds.), *Human Rights, Democracy and the Rule of Law = Menschenrechte, Demokratie und Rechtsstaat = Droits de l'homme, démocratie et état de droit: Liber Amicorum Luzius Wildhaber* (Zurich: Dike, 2007), at 633, and P. Tavernier, 'La contribution de la jurisprudence de la Cour européenne des droits de l'homme relative au droit de la responsabilité internationale en matière de réparation – Une remise en cause nécessaire', *Revue trimestrielle des droits de l'homme* 72 (2007), at 955.

what seems to emerge from the Court's interpretation and relevant case law is that a victim is not entitled to just satisfaction as a 'true subjective right',[266] but only as a possibility. The matter comes under the Court's entire discretion. The treaty itself introduced that unrestricted power. The judges continue to make use of it when deciding whether the conditions for reparation are met, as well as what type of compensation is called for, especially in the context of non-pecuniary damage, when they frequently consider that the finding of a violation is sufficient in itself. That authority is preserved at the risk of giving rise to inconsistency. The Court should nonetheless define some clear and more objective guidelines for the application of the necessity principle.

In its second case where it examined the question of just satisfaction, the Court declared that such necessity existed when a respondent government had refused to award an applicant the reparation to which he considered himself entitled.[267] Then, in *The Sunday Times*, when the plaintiffs claimed costs and expenses in accordance with the general English rule that 'costs follow the event', the Plenary Court refused to apply domestic rules and concluded that the injured party was not entitled to costs as of right, therefore the matter was at its discretion.[268] Later on, in *McCann and Others v. the United Kingdom*, where a breach of the right to life was at stake, the Grand Chamber refused compensation for any pecuniary or non-pecuniary damage on the grounds that the applicants' relatives, who were killed by the security forces, were actually suspected of terrorist acts.[269] It seems evident that the judges have traditionally preferred to assess the necessity of just satisfaction on a case-by-case basis.

It should be further mentioned that the necessity to order compensation does not bear the same weight as the necessity to pursue a case in the public interest. Unlike *ex officio* consideration of the necessity to examine an application when the complainant withdraws it or no longer shows any interest in the case, the Court does not take into account, in

[266] C. Tomuschat, 'Just Satisfaction under Article 50 of the European Convention on Human Rights', in P. Mahoney et al. (eds.), *Protection des droits de l'homme: la perspective européenne, mélanges à la mémoire de Rolv Ryssdal = Protecting Human Rights: The European Perspective, Studies in Memory of Rolv Ryssdal* (Cologne: Carl Heymanns Verlag, 2000), at 1426–8.

[267] *Ringeisen* (Article 50), note 90, para. 22.

[268] *The Sunday Times v. the United Kingdom* (Article 50), 6 November 1980, Series A no. 38, para. 15.

[269] *McCann and Others v. the United Kingdom* [GC], 27 September 1995, Series A no. 324, para. 219.

those cases, any necessity to afford just satisfaction. It will only look to the items actually claimed, and will not examine of its own motion whether the applicant has been otherwise prejudiced, because no question of public policy is involved.[270] This clearly shows that, unlike protection of human rights, compensation is not a matter of public interest.

Moreover, the Court refrains not only from making *ex officio* awards, but also from ruling *ultra petita*. As a matter of principle, applicants may not receive more than they claimed, or what they did not claim. In the words of its Inter-American counterpart, '[r]eparations should not make the victims or their successors either richer or poorer'.[271] Nevertheless, examples that may amount to *ultra petita* adjudication are present in the European Court's case law.[272] In *Apostol v. Georgia*, the Court ordered the state to secure enforcement of a domestic judgment even if the plaintiff had not sought any form of reparation.[273] Then, in *Chember v. Russia*, the applicant did not submit any claim for just satisfaction, but the Court considered that it was 'exceptionally possible' to award the victim compensation for non-pecuniary damage, given that he had been subjected to inhuman punishment.[274] A similar position has been adopted in some cases where the petitioner had not lodged a claim in due form.[275] In other words, the Court ordered what it had not been asked for.

It is somewhat unfortunate that the Strasbourg judges make full use of their discretion on the matter, generally advancing the words 'if necessary' and 'equity' as the sole argument, without further elucidating on their ruling on reparation in order to confer transparency, clarity or consistency on their pronouncements. So the question is: why have the judges been unwilling to engage in interpretive exercises and to elaborate a test of necessity? The situation is similar to that created by the use of the principle of equity, when they refer to an abstract notion without any attempt to define it. Is this justified? What would be the consequences of further developing the test of necessity?

270 *The Sunday Times* (Article 50), note 268, para. 14.

271 *Case of the Ituango Massacres* (preliminary objections, merits, reparations and costs), note 95, para. 348.

272 Tavernier, note 265, at 958.

273 *Apostol v. Georgia*, no. 40765/02, ECHR 2006-XIV, paras. 70–3.

274 *Chember v. Russia*, no. 7188/03, ECHR 2008, paras. 75–7. Also see *X v. Croatia*, no. 11223/04, 17 July 2008, paras. 61–3.

275 *Davtian v. Georgia*, no. 73241/01, 27 July 2006, paras. 68–71, and *Gorodnitchev v. Russia*, no. 52058/99, 24 May 2007, paras. 140–3.

According to the judges, it is the express language of Article 41 which gives them authority to have recourse to necessity. Some of them have criticized that practice on the grounds that the principle of necessity comes into play only when the previous conditions of the finding of a violation and of availability of partial reparation in internal law are concurrently met.[276] When domestic law does not provide for any redress, 'the "if necessary" condition becomes irrelevant and the Convention leaves the Court no discretion at all as to whether to award compensation or not'.[277] However, the Court has not embarked upon such a restrictive interpretation of Article 41. Therefore, why are the judges reluctant to define necessity?

A reasonable argument would be that the drafters of the system did not anticipate its extraordinary development into what has ultimately become an overburden. Being confronted with different proposals to give the Court more or less restrictive powers in respect of granting just satisfaction, they have reached a compromise. In so far as they could not have predicted the evolution of the regime of reparation, the drafters have inserted an element of flexibility that has secured the judges a large margin of manoeuvrability in deciding whether reparation is necessary in the circumstances of the case. In their turn, the judges make full use of that entitlement. In doing so, they may put in balance the interests of the parties and also take into account similar precedents. What is striking, though, is that even when the case law has witnessed an exponential increase and, unavoidably, has sometimes revealed a lack of clarity and coherence, the Court has still been evasive as to the principle of necessity.

It must be conceded that, as with the use of equity, the absence of a clear test of necessity creates inconsistency in the case law and eventually impedes the Court's legitimacy. The two concepts are closely related, in so far as the judges should first decide the necessity of reparation and then apply the principles of equity in order to identify the specific redress. While not an easy exercise, it is not impossible for the Court to elaborate a theory of necessity, particularly as a pattern may be extracted from the existent case law. Yet the judges seem to lack enthusiasm for making accessible the reasoning used at the moment of

[276] Partly dissenting opinion of Judge Bonello joined by Judge Maruste in *Nikolova v. Bulgaria* [GC], no. 31195/96, ECHR 1999-II. The same dissenting opinion was submitted by Judge Bonello in *Aquilina v. Malta* [GC], no. 25642/94, ECHR 1999-III.

[277] Ibid.

deliberations, which would confer security and transparency on the system of reparation.

3.3 Who may claim compensation?

Anyone who may lodge an application may also request compensation for the alleged violation. Member states as well as persons, non-governmental organizations (NGOs) or groups of individuals, irrespective of their nationality, may seek redress for a violation by one of the contracting parties of the rights set forth in the Convention. For individual applicants, the Convention established only the general requirement of victim status, without differentiating between natural and legal persons. There is also no requirement of nationality, citizenship or residence. Aliens, refugees and stateless persons may therefore apply. Also, unlike national systems, the respondent party will always be a contracting state. Given that they assumed the obligation to secure protection of the rights included in the Convention, they are the ultimate debtors of just satisfaction.

3.3.1 Persons or groups of individuals

According to the French version of the treaty, an application may be lodged by 'toute personne physique, toute organisation non gouvernementale ou tout groupe de particuliers'. Therefore, the term 'persons' in the English text refers only to individuals, as opposed to legal persons, which are included under the heading of NGOs. As for a group of individuals, it simply designates several individual applicants acting before the Strasbourg organs without an organizational structure.[278] Individuals have had *locus standi* before the Court only since 1 January 1983. Before that date, any claim for just satisfaction had to be made through the old Commission or through a member state.

As opposed to the European mechanism, the Inter-American system does not include legal persons in its area of protection. Article 1 of the American Convention extends the states' obligation to protect human rights to all persons under their jurisdiction, but proclaims at the same time that the word 'person' refers to 'every human being'. Accordingly, the Inter-American Court, after pointing to the express recognition of

[278] See, e.g., *Guerra and Others v. Italy*, 19 February 1998, *Reports of Judgments and Decisions* 1998-I.

protection for legal persons by the European regime, interpreted that provision as generally excluding legal entities from the scope of the treaty. However, it conceded that, in special circumstances, individuals may resort to the system of protection in order to enforce their rights 'when they are encompassed in a legal figure or fiction created by the same system of law', such as complaints by individuals as shareholders.[279]

Another particularity of the Inter-American regime is that complaints by groups of individuals seem to carry more weight than those within the European system. Practice shows that, unlike the Strasbourg Court, the Court of San José is normally confronted with grave violations of human rights in Latin America, including massacres. Under those conditions, the judges have had no other feasible solution but to adopt a victim-oriented approach, given that massacres involve a large number of victims and it is often difficult to identify them. Therefore, the Inter-American Court has sought to overcome those shortcomings by requesting the Commission or the states concerned to identify the alleged victims. The judges themselves have examined the evidence presented by the parties and assumed the authority to treat individuals so identified as 'possible victims' who would be entitled to reparation.[280] At the same time, they reserved a right to determine other forms of reparation in favour of all the members of the villages affected by the facts of a case,[281] thus ordering community-based reparations or even measures to compensate society as a whole.[282]

While accepting that the European Court also carries out some form of investigation into the facts of serious violations, it seems excessive to claim that it has adopted a similar proactive attitude to its American counterpart. For example, when seised by five applicants alleging that their relatives had been unlawfully killed by state agents, even if official documents submitted by the government revealed that at stake was a massacre involving more than fifty victims, the Court limited its findings and awards of compensation to the five plaintiffs.[283] In contrast, when the state responsible for a massacre admitted that some forty-nine victims had been executed or had disappeared, the Inter-American

[279] *Cantos v. Argentina* (preliminary objections), 7 September 2001, Series C no. 85, para. 29.

[280] *Case of the Ituango Massacres* (preliminary objections, merits, reparations and costs), note 95, para. 94.

[281] Ibid., para. 354. Also see *Yakye Axa Indigenous Community* (merits, reparations and costs), note 126, para. 188.

[282] Pasqualucci, note 50, at 209–12.

[283] *Musayev and Others v. Russia*, nos. 57941/00, 58699/00 and 60403/00, 26 July 2007.

Court ordered reparation for all of them, whether individually identified or not, and also directed the state 'to search and individually identify the victims and their next of kin and to ensure effective payment . . . of the compensation and indemnification owed to the next of kin of victims as they are identified'.[284] Certainly, the Court of San José needed to adapt to the specificity of its cases in order to avoid impunity for grave violations, but nevertheless, with regard to what amounts to effective protection of human rights, the above illustrations clearly indicate a different approach by the two regional courts.

In Strasbourg, private persons may claim, in their own name, pecuniary and non-pecuniary damage, as well as reimbursement of costs and expenses incurred before the national courts and before the European Court. Any person concerned who has been invited by the Court to submit comments or participate in hearings has third-party and not applicant status, and thus cannot claim reparation.[285] Individuals may also act as lawyers or representatives for other applicants, but only when there is a power of attorney.

A further principle is that applications can only be introduced by, or in the name of, individuals who are alive. If a complainant dies after the petition has been lodged, and while the proceedings are pending before the Court, the heirs may express their intention to continue the application. In that case, they may claim the pecuniary damage suffered by the plaintiff, as well as costs and expenses,[286] but not injury that has a purely personal nature and was suffered only by the applicant.[287] Moral damage qualifies under this head. However, if the alleged victim of a violation has died before the introduction of the application, in circumstances giving rise to issues under Article 2 in respect of the right to life, individuals who are next of kin may bring an application in their own right, raising complaints related to the death.[288] In this capacity, they

[284] *Case of the Mapiripán Massacre* (merits, reparations and costs), note 49, para. 311(iii).

[285] See, e.g., *Koua Poirrez v. France*, no. 40892/98, ECHR 2003-X, para. 69.

[286] As opposed to the present Court, the possibility to continue an application has been treated slightly differently by the former Commission and the old Court: see, e.g., *X v. France*, 31 March 1992, Series A no. 234-C, para. 26. Also see G. B. Reffi and A. Bultrini, 'Le décès de la partie requérante dans la procédure devant les organes de la Convention européenne des droits de l'homme', in M. De Salvia and M. Villiger (eds.), *The Birth of European Human Rights Law = L'éclosion du droit européen des droits de l'homme: Liber Amicorum Carl Aage Norgaard* (Baden-Baden: Nomos, 1998).

[287] See, e.g., *X v. the United Kingdom* (Article 50), 18 October 1982, Series A no. 55, para. 19, and *Silver and Others v. the United Kingdom* (Article 50), 24 October 1983, Series A no. 67, para. 12.

[288] *Varnava*, note 157, para. 111.

may claim moral reparation for themselves. The heirs in these two distinct situations are not indirect victims. Confusion should also be avoided in cases where victims are not able to introduce a petition on their own, for different reasons such as detention, mental illness or very young age, and therefore act through a representative.

Within the Inter-American system, in contrast to the European one, it is worth noting that close relatives may receive compensation even if they have not participated in the proceedings before the Inter-American Court, personally or through a representative.[289] An equally distinctive feature of the Inter-American mechanism is that the reparation owed by the state to the direct victim is 'totally transferable'.[290] The Court of San José proclaimed in *Aloeboetoe* that '[t]he damages suffered by the victims up to the time of their death entitle them to compensation. That right to compensation is transmitted to their heirs by succession.'[291]

In Strasbourg, when only some of the applicant's heirs manifest their willingness to pursue the case, the Court either awards them the corresponding part of prejudice, on the basis of an established quota, or the whole damage, bearing in mind that the other heirs have at their disposal the means offered by the internal law to settle any potential dispute between them.[292] Distinction should also be made between the relatives and the heirs of a complainant, as a relative is not automatically an inheritor. Such was the case in *Malhous* where, following the applicant's death, the Court accepted that his nephew could continue the proceedings. The applicant also had two adult children, but they were disinherited. The Court therefore took into account the victim's will, in which he designated his nephew as his universal heir, and concluded that the nephew had a legitimate interest in pursuing the application, even though he was not the applicant's next of kin, and was also not confirmed as the applicant's heir according to the provisions of the national law.[293]

Children may also lodge applications, together with claims for just satisfaction.[294] They may do so by themselves, or through their legal

[289] See, e.g., *Myrna Mack-Chang v. Guatemala* (merits, reparations and costs), 25 November 2003, Series C no. 101, para. 245.

[290] Burgorgue-Larsen and Úbeda de Torres, note 252, at 226.

[291] *Aloeboetoe* (reparations and costs), note 99, para. 54.

[292] See, e.g., *Tamir*, note 117, para. 40.

[293] *Malhous v. the Czech Republic* (dec.) [GC], no. 33071/96, ECHR 2000-XII.

[294] For an extensive analysis of issues concerning children and their rights under the Convention, see U. Kilkelly, *The Child and the European Convention on Human Rights* (Aldershot: Ashgate, 1999).

representatives. In practice they are hardly ever able to properly lodge a complaint by themselves, because of either age or lack of resources or legal education. Cases are usually brought on their behalf by parents or other close relatives, which raises questions as to legal standing. Domestic rules in respect of child representation do not necessarily apply before the Court. The capacity of a natural parent to act on his child's behalf is dependent on whether the party who opposes the natural parent – and is entitled to represent the child under domestic law – can be deemed to protect efficiently the child's right under the Convention.[295] The Court held that even though a parent has been deprived of parental rights, his or her standing as the natural parent suffices to afford that parent the necessary power to apply to the Court on the child's behalf.[296] On the contrary, in a dispute between parents, the position as natural parent is not sufficient for introducing an application, given that it is the parent who has custody who is entrusted with safeguarding the child's interests.[297] The Strasbourg organs have already declared that claims by parents who no longer have custody of their children as a result of divorce or care proceedings, or who no longer enjoy parental rights, are inadmissible.[298]

A particular problem emerged in the context of complaints brought by persons acting as servants of the state in respect of their conditions of service. In *Pellegrin*, the Grand Chamber adopted a functional criterion based on the nature of the employee's duties and responsibilities. Employment disputes brought by public servants who occupied posts involving participation in the exercise of powers conferred by public law were not to be regarded as 'civil' within the meaning of Article 6(1) of the Convention, and thus fell outside the Court's competence *ratione materiae*. That was the case, for instance, with activities performed by the police and armed forces, and was justified by the fact that the state had a legitimate interest in requiring 'a special bond of trust and loyalty' from the holders of a portion of its sovereign power.[299] However, the Grand

295 *Siebert v. Germany* (dec.), no. 59008/00, 9 June 2005.

296 *Scozzari and Giunta v. Italy* [GC], nos. 39221/98 and 41963/98, ECHR 2000-VIII, para. 138.

297 See, e.g., *Eberhard and M.v. Slovenia*, nos. 8673/05 and 9733/05, 1 December 2009, para. 88, and *Wildgruber v. Germany* (dec.), no. 32817/02, 16 October 2006.

298 On some aspects of applications brought by children, see K. Reid, 'Article 25 of the Convention: Application by Children', in De Salvia and Villiger, note 286, at 301–7.

299 *Pellegrin v. France* [GC], no. 28541/95, ECHR 1999-VIII, paras. 64–7. On this topic, see L. Caflisch, 'The *Pellegrin* Ruling: Origins and Consequences', in L. C. Vohrah et al. (eds.), *Man's Inhumanity to Man: Essays on International Law in Honour of Antonio Cassese* (The Hague: Kluwer Law International, 2003).

Chamber reversed the strict approach of the *Pellegrin* test in a later case, *Vilho Eskelinen*, and has introduced new criteria for the applicability of the civil guarantees of the right to a fair trial. It concluded that the protection of the right to a fair trial should cover all disputes involving civil servants, unless the national law itself, expressly and on objective grounds in the state's interest, excludes access to a court for the post or category of staff in question.[300] The Court has thus opened the way for civil servants to bring to Strasbourg their claims for compensation.

3.3.2 Non-governmental organizations

The notion of 'NGO' generally covers legal persons, as opposed to natural persons. The legal entities that may submit applications and thus seek redress for alleged breaches of their rights must be private organizations, such as companies, political parties, churches or newspapers.[301] Their capacity to claim to be victims is interpreted independently from domestic law. Governmental organizations, be they central organs of the state or decentralized authorities, including legal entities participating in the exercise of governmental powers or running a public service under government control, do not have standing. The good reason given by the Court is that a member state cannot act as both applicant and respondent party.[302] In order for a public-law corporation to be considered an NGO, it should not have been established for public-administration purposes or hold governmental powers, and must be completely independent of the state.[303]

As to associations, the former Commission declared that they could not themselves claim to be victims of measures which affect their members but not themselves.[304] Likewise, an association with a social aim,

300 *Vilho Eskelinen and Others v. Finland* [GC], no. 63235/00, ECHR 2007-IV, para. 62.

301 See, e.g., C. Schwaighofer, 'Legal Persons, Organisations, Shareholders as Applicants: Article 25 of the Convention', in De Salvia and Villiger, note 286, and O. De Schutter, 'L'accès des personnes morales à la Cour européenne des droits de l'homme', in *Avancées et confins actuels des droits de l'homme aux niveaux international, européen et national: mélanges offerts à Silvio Marcus Helmons* (Brussels: Bruylant, 2003).

302 *Islamic Republic of Iran Shipping Lines v. Turkey*, no. 40998/98, ECHR 2007-V, para. 81.

303 *The Holy Monasteries v. Greece*, 9 December 1994, Series A no. 301-A, para. 49, and *Radio France and Others v. France* (dec.), no. 53984/00, ECHR 2003-X (extracts), para. 26.

304 *Association des amis de Saint-Raphaël et de Fréjus and Others v. France*, no. 38192/97, Commission's decision of 1 July 1998, *Decisions and Reports* (DR) 94-B. For a call to the contrary, see M. A. Nowicki, 'Non-Governmental Organisations (NGOs) before the European Commission of Human Rights', in De Salvia and Villiger, note 286.

such as the promotion of human rights, may not itself allege victim status for acts which affect only those persons whose interests it defends.[305] The right to submit an application, even if its members were not identified, was recognized.[306] If an association acts on behalf of its members, it has to identify them and provide evidence as to the power of representation.[307]

There is no difficulty in accepting the right of legal persons to claim material damage, including loss of income, reduced value of goodwill, loss of reputation, inflation, and decline in customers and business clientele.[308] They have also successfully sought reimbursement of costs and expenses. The same may not be said about non-pecuniary injury.[309] The issue of compensation for non-pecuniary damage claimed by commercial companies was settled by the Grand Chamber in *Comingersoll S.A. v. Portugal*. The judges accepted that commercial companies may suffer non-pecuniary harm, although claims in that respect may be more or less 'objective' or 'subjective'. When assessing such damage, the Court will take into account the company's reputation, uncertainty in decision-planning, disruption within the management of the company, as well as the anxiety and inconvenience caused to its managers.[310] Even before *Comingersoll*, the Court had permitted legal persons to recover non-pecuniary damage. Such was the case first with an association which suffered violation of freedom of expression and of the right to an effective remedy,[311] and then with a political party for frustration suffered as a result of infringement of freedom of assembly and association.[312]

Companies may also face difficulties when claiming profit, especially when it concerns future loss. The Court will incontestably decline to

[305] *19 Chilean Nationals and the S. Association v. Sweden*, nos. 9959/82 and 10357/83, Commission's decision of 14 March 1984, *Decisions and Reports* (DR) 37.

[306] See, e.g., *Church of Scientology Moscow v. Russia*, no. 18147/02, 5 April 2007.

[307] *Scientology Kirche Deutschland e.V. v. Germany*, no. 34614/97, Commission's decision of 7 April 1997.

[308] See, e.g., M. Emberland, 'Compensating Companies for Non-Pecuniary Damage: *Comingersoll S.A. v. Portugal* and the Ambivalent Expansion of the ECHR Scope', *British Yearbook of International Law* 74, no. 1 (2003), at 412 and the cases cited.

[309] On this topic see, e.g., M. Emberland, *The Human Rights of Companies: Exploring the Structure of ECHR Protection* (Oxford University Press, 2006).

[310] *Comingersoll S.A. v. Portugal* [GC], no. 35382/97, ECHR 2000-IV, para. 35.

[311] *Vereinigung demokratischer Soldaten Österreichs and Gubi v. Austria*, 19 December 1994, Series A no. 302, para. 62.

[312] *Freedom and Democracy Party (ÖZDEP) v. Turkey* [GC], no. 23885/94, ECHR 1999-VIII, para. 57.

make speculations and, in the absence of evidence for a direct link between the violation and the damage alleged, no award would be made. However, it may very well consider that the company has suffered non-pecuniary damage, and make an award under that head.

In principle, a company must lodge a petition through its statutory bodies or, in the event of liquidation, through its liquidators. A claim for just satisfaction cannot be filed by its shareholders.[313] Yet, there are some exceptions. An applicant who is the sole shareholder of a company may claim to have a victim status in respect of acts directed against the company, because there are no competing interests or differences of opinion among shareholders, or between shareholders and a board of directors.[314] Conversely, when the company itself was a party to the domestic proceedings, the executive director or a minority shareholder cannot bring a complaint in their own name and invoke victim status.[315]

Another exception is the piercing of the 'corporate veil'. In that case, a petition may be lodged on behalf of a company by other persons, for instance by its shareholders. The Court has declared that only exceptional circumstances may justify disregarding an applicant company's legal personality. Such examples include a clearly established impossibility for the company to introduce an application through its statutory bodies or, in the event of liquidation or bankruptcy, through its liquidators or trustees in bankruptcy.[316] The nature of the complaint and the conflict of interests between the parties involved play an important role in assessing those circumstances.

The just satisfaction sought by NGOs is further subject to some limitations coming from the very nature of some of the rights protected by the Convention. For example, an NGO cannot claim to be a victim of torture or deprivation of liberty. According to their scope and function, some types of NGOs will usually seek redress in connection with violation of rights corresponding to their very existence and

[313] The position of the former Commission, which accepted an automatic infringement of the shareholders' rights when a violation of the company's property rights resulted in a fall in the value of its shares, was not upheld by the Court: see *Agrotexim and Others v. Greece*, 24 October 1995, Series A no. 330-A, paras. 63–71.

[314] *Ankarcrona v. Sweden* (dec.), no. 35178/97, 27 June 2000.

[315] *Rahimov v. Azerbaijan* (dec.), no. 22759/04, 3 January 2008.

[316] See, e.g., *Agrotexim*, note 313, para. 66, and *Capital Bank AD v. Bulgaria* (dec.), no. 49429/99, 9 September 2004.

organization. Thus, churches and religious associations are typically, but not necessarily, linked to breaches of freedom of thought, conscience and religion or freedom of assembly and association, while newspapers and political parties are in a similar position regarding freedom of expression, and, likewise, commercial companies regarding protection of property. Undoubtedly, the right to a fair trial is almost always part of NGOs' claims, given that they have generally raised their complaints at the internal level before coming to Strasbourg. However, practice shows that there is no established pattern of classification.

3.3.3 *States*

Article 33 entitles any contracting party or group of states to refer to the Court any alleged breach of the Convention by another contracting party.[317] States taking part in this procedure must have ratified the treaty, but unlike the corresponding procedure under the American Convention, there is no condition of a declaration of competence.[318] There is also no requirement to claim victim status, as in the context of individual applications, because, for states, the prejudice is normally of a legal nature, in the form of a breach of an international treaty. This makes inter-state applications, at least in theory, a useful tool for bringing offenders to the fore.

3.3.3.1 Procedure

The admissibility criteria for the inter-state procedure are not as restrictive as in the case of individual applications. There are two conditions

[317] Formerly Article 24. For a general survey of the inter-state procedure see, among others, S. Leckie, 'The Inter-State Complaint Procedure in International Human Rights Law: Hopeful Prospects or Wishful Thinking?', *Human Rights Quarterly* 10, no. 2 (1988). For inter-state applications under the European Convention see, e.g., L.-E. Pettiti, 'Le système de Strasbourg. Les recours interétatiques dans le système de la Convention européenne des droits de l'homme', in D. Bardonnet (ed.), *The Peaceful Settlement of International Disputes in Europe: Future Prospects* (Dordrecht: Martinus Nijhoff Publishers, 1991); S. C. Prebensen, 'Inter-State Complaints under Treaty Provisions – The Experience under the European Convention on Human Rights', in G. Alfredsson et al. (eds.), *International Human Rights Monitoring Mechanisms: Essays in Honour of Jakob Th. Möller* (The Hague: Martinus Nijhoff Publishers, 2001), at 533–59; van Dijk et al., note 241, at 47–51; K. Rogge, 'Inter-State Cases under Article 33 of the European Convention on Human Rights', in Hartig, note 105; and Harris et al., note 30, at 821–3.

[318] Article 45 of the American Convention. The European Convention also contained such a provision before 1 November 1998, when Protocol No. 11 entered into force and gave the Court compulsory jurisdiction.

which apply – exhaustion of domestic remedies and the six-month time limit – but only when states invoke punctual violations and act for the alleged victim. These conditions are not relevant to complaints about administrative practice or legislative measures,[319] when states allege a violation *in abstracto*, not the concrete examples of application. In that context, if not requesting assessment of the prejudice in each particular case given as illustration, the state usually seeks to prevent continuation or recurrence of that practice or measure.[320] In the absence of a specific ruling so far, the Court would presumably propose – or even order – a change in practice or legislation, which would also provide appropriate redress for that kind of violation.

Another particularity of inter-state applications is that they are communicated immediately to the state concerned, without any preliminary examination, whereas individual complaints may be declared inadmissible or struck out of the Court's list at the admissibility stage, without further examination. In addition, while the admissibility and merits of individual applications are usually considered together in the same judgment, in inter-state cases they are examined separately. Such derogations are necessary in view of the particular weight that accusations between states carry with them. However, as has been observed, the fact that inter-state complaints are examined by a Chamber, instead of being brought directly before the Grand Chamber, may unnecessarily extend the procedure, because it is not unreasonable to assume that the losing state would in most cases disagree with the Chamber decision and also that the panel of five judges of the Grand Chamber would not refuse a referral.[321]

States may also seek reparation for the alleged violation. The Rules of Court invite states to give an indication of any claims for just satisfaction.[322] In *Ireland v. the United Kingdom* the applicant government expressly declined to claim monetary compensation, and consequently

[319] See, e.g., Prebensen, note 317, at 540, and van Dijk et al., note 241, at 128–9. An administrative practice consists of repetition of acts incompatible with the Convention and official tolerance by the state authorities, even if only at a subordinate level, and despite occasional reactions from the authorities: see *France, Norway, Denmark, Sweden and the Netherlands v. Turkey*, nos. 9940–9944/82, Commission's decision of 6 December 1983, *Decisions and Reports* (DR) 35.

[320] *Ireland v. the United Kingdom*, 18 January 1978, Series A no. 25, para. 159.

[321] A. Drzemczewski, 'The European Human Rights Convention: Protocol No. 11 – Entry into Force and First Year of Application', *Human Rights Law Journal* 21, nos. 1–3 (2000), at 2.

[322] Rule 46(e) of the Rules of Court.

the Court considered that it was not necessary to deal with the question.[323] This has created some disagreement in the past as to the possibility of a claim for compensation in inter-state applications.[324] However, after keeping the issue on the agenda for thirteen years, the Grand Chamber eventually decided in *Cyprus v. Turkey* that Article 41 applies to inter-state disputes.[325] In that case, the Court made a distinction between the types and purposes of complaints made by a state. Thus, while complaints about general issues aim at securing the public order of Europe and may not be compatible with an award of just satisfaction, specific victims' rights violations may warrant reparation. In fact, the judges were very clear that 'if just satisfaction is afforded in an inter-State case, it should always be done for the benefit of individual victims', for the simple reason that 'it is the individual, and not the State, who is directly or indirectly harmed and primarily "injured" by a violation of one or several Convention rights'.[326] But unlike diplomatic protection under general international law, where states are entitled to defend their own interest, as well as to take action on behalf of their citizens, a state under the Convention regime may also complain about violations committed against individuals or entities regardless of any nationality link.

State interest is usually absent when a collective guarantee of human rights prevails. These are pure acts of *actio popularis*.[327] Such expansion of state action, although at first glance it may be seen as interfering with internal affairs, aims at a collective enforcement of human rights among the European countries, and was proclaimed in the preamble of the Convention and also confirmed by subsequent case law.[328] When they ratified the Convention, the contracting parties vested in the treaty bodies the power to decide upon inter-state complaints. However, political and economic considerations play an important role in having recourse to this procedure, encouraging or rather deterring states from

323 *Ireland v. the United Kingdom*, note 320, paras. 244–5.

324 Van Dijk et al., note 241, at 172. For a view to the contrary, see Enrich Mas, note 222, at 777, and J.-P. Costa, 'The Provision of Compensation under Article 41 of the European Convention on Human Rights', in D. Fairgrieve, M. Andenas and J. Bell (eds.), *Tort Liability of Public Authorities in Comparative Perspective* (London: British Institute of International and Comparative Law, 2002), at 6.

325 *Cyprus v. Turkey* (just satisfaction) [GC], no. 25781/94, 12 May 2014, paras. 39–47.

326 Ibid., para. 46.

327 J. E. S. Fawcett, *The Application of the European Convention on Human Rights* (Oxford: Clarendon Press, 1987), at 343.

328 *Ireland v. the United Kingdom*, note 320, para. 239.

lodging an application,[329] although the old Commission made reference to the objective character of the inter-state action and also stressed that a state 'is not to be regarded as exercising a right of action for the purpose of enforcing its own rights, but rather as bringing before the Commission an alleged violation of the public order of Europe'.[330]

3.3.3.2 Cases brought so far

By the beginning of 2014, states had brought twenty-four complaints in seventeen cases pertaining to nine separate disputes. The first application was introduced in 1956 by Greece against the United Kingdom, in respect of alleged breaches by the British colonial regime in Cyprus. Next year, a second application was lodged by Greece against the United Kingdom, in respect of forty-nine cases of alleged ill-treatment of individuals by the police, security or military forces in Cyprus.[331] The Commission declared both applications admissible,[332] but the Committee of Ministers took note that the 1959 London and Zurich Agreements on the independence of Cyprus had settled the Cyprus question, and decided that no further action was called for.[333]

Then Austria lodged an application against Italy in 1960 for the reason that several breaches of the right to a fair trial and of the prohibition of discrimination had occurred during a murder case in the Italian courts against six young men from the village of Fundres/Pfunders. Both the Commission and the Committee of Ministers concluded that there had been no violation.[334]

The so-called 'Greek Case' was a reaction by Denmark, Norway and Sweden in 1967 and of the Netherlands in 1968 to the constitutional transformations in Greece following the *coup d'état* of April 1967. The Commission found several violations;[335] hence the Committee of

[329] For instances of political and economic implications of the inter-state complaint procedure, see Leckie, note 317, at 293–8.

[330] Commission's decision on the admissibility of application no. 788/60, *Austria v. Italy*, 11 January 1961, *Yearbook of the European Convention on Human Rights* 4 (1961), p. 116.

[331] Applications nos. 176/56 of 7 May 1956 and 299/57 of 17 July 1957.

[332] The Commission declared the applications admissible on 2 June 1956 and 12 October 1957, and then prepared two reports on 26 September 1958 and 8 July 1959.

[333] Resolutions DH(59)12 and 32 of 20 April and 14 December 1959.

[334] Application no. 788/60. The Commission adopted its report on 30 March 1963, and the Committee of Ministers issued Resolution DH(63)3 on 23 October 1963.

[335] *Denmark, Norway, Sweden and the Netherlands v. Greece*, nos. 3321/67, 3322/67, 3323/67 and 3344/67, Commission's report of 5 November 1969, *Yearbook of the European Convention on Human Rights* 12 (1969), p. 186.

Ministers became determined to propose the suspension of Greece from the Council of Europe. That intention never materialized because Greece left the organization in 1969 and also denounced the Convention, before the adoption of any resolution. Such reaction did not prevent the Committee from establishing the international responsibility of Greece for several violations committed before the date by which the denunciation became effective. However, it obstructed its power to take further action. The Committee urged the government concerned to restore human rights without delay and, in particular, to abolish torture and other ill-treatment of prisoners, as well as to release persons detained under administrative order.[336]

The 'Second Greek Case' was introduced in 1970 by the same countries against Greece, in respect of criminal proceedings against thirty-four persons accused of subversive activities. The Commission declared the application admissible, but then took note that Greece rejoined the Council of Europe in 1974, and given that it had received information about reparation offered to the victims of the dictatorship, it closed the proceedings at the parties' concordant requests.[337]

In 1971, Ireland brought a first application against the United Kingdom, alleging abuse by the British authorities in Northern Ireland. It was the first inter-state case which reached the Court. The judges concluded that the use of some interrogation techniques constituted a practice of inhuman and degrading treatment, and that a practice of inhuman treatment existed at a certain place of detention. As just mentioned, they did not consider the question of just satisfaction because the complaining state had expressly declined to request compensation for any individual person. A second application was introduced by Ireland in 1972, but was eventually discontinued by the Commission.

Cyprus brought four applications against Turkey. The first two were lodged in 1974 and 1975, as a reaction to the Turkish military operations in Northern Cyprus in July and August 1974. The Commission joined

[336] Resolution DH(70)1, adopted on 15 April 1970. Also see Resolution DH(74)2 of 26 November 1974. For a criticism of the solution, see M. Sørensen, 'Lost Opportunity: When Human Rights Were Sacrificed', reproduced in English by the Consultative Assembly on 26 January 1970 (AS/Inf (70) 10, Strasbourg: Council of Europe). The original article was published in the Danish newspaper *Politiken* on 5 January 1970.

[337] *Denmark, Norway and Sweden v. Greece*, no. 4448/70, Commission's report of 4 October 1976, *Decisions and Reports* (DR) 6.

them and found several violations.[338] The Committee of Ministers also considered that the events which had occurred in Cyprus constituted violations, but simply urged the parties to resume intercommunal talks. As expected in the absence of a bold stand on the matter, discussions were not relaunched, and the Committee eventually contented itself with insisting on the need to re-establish dialogue, proclaiming at the same time that this decision was completing its consideration of the case.[339]

The third application was brought by Cyprus in 1977, denouncing continuous violations by Turkey. In 1983, the Commission identified several violations, but in 1992 the Committee limited itself to making public the Commission's report, without any further consideration of the case.[340] Therefore, in 1994 Cyprus brought fresh proceedings against Turkey in respect of alleged violations of the rights of Greek-Cypriot missing persons and their relatives, of the home and property rights of displaced persons, of the rights of enclaved Greek Cypriots in northern Cyprus, and of the rights of Turkish Cypriots and the Gypsy community in northern Cyprus. In 2001, the Grand Chamber endorsed several violations, but considered that the possible application of the question of just satisfaction was not ready for a decision. In the absence of agreement between the parties in dispute, the court awarded an exceptional amount of EUR 90 million for non-pecuniary damage, to be distributed by the Cypriot government to the individual victims of violations.[341]

The so-called 'Turkish Case' originated in five applications lodged in 1982 by Denmark, France, the Netherlands, Norway and Sweden against Turkey, following a seizure of power by the Turkish army in September 1980. The Commission declared the case admissible, but in 1985 approved a friendly settlement between the parties.[342]

[338] *Cyprus v. Turkey*, nos. 6780/74 and 6950/75, Commission's report of 10 July 1976, unpublished.

[339] Resolution DH(79)1 of 20 January 1979, which made reference to an earlier decision of 21 October 1977, unpublished.

[340] *Cyprus v. Turkey*, no. 8007/77, Commission's decision of 10 July 1978, *Decisions and Reports* (DR) 13, and Commission's report of 4 October 1983, *Decisions and Reports* (DR) 72, as well as Resolution DH(92)12 adopted by the Committee of Ministers on 2 April 1992.

[341] For the judgment on the merits, see *Cyprus v. Turkey* [GC], no. 25781/94, ECHR 2001-IV. For the judgment on just satisfaction, see note 325.

[342] See the Commission's decision in *France, Norway, Denmark, Sweden and the Netherlands v. Turkey*, note 319, and Commission's report of 7 December 1985, *Decisions and Reports* (DR) 44. In this respect, see L. F. Zwaak, 'The Five Inter-State Complaints versus Turkey under the European Convention on Human Rights', *SIM*

An application brought by Denmark against Turkey in 1997 concerned the ill-treatment of a Danish national in police custody in Turkey. Denmark also requested the Commission to examine whether the interrogation techniques applied to that person were applied in Turkey as a widespread practice designed to extract under severe pain and suffering confessions and other statements. The case was declared admissible, but ended in a friendly settlement before the Court. Turkey paid compensation to the Danish citizen, admitted deficiencies in interrogation techniques, and expressed regret for the occurrence of occasional and individual cases of torture and ill-treatment. It also reported the measures already taken, and promised to make further improvements.[343]

Georgia brought three applications against Russia, emerging from the political tensions between the two states. The first petition was lodged in 2007 and concerned the alleged harassment of the Georgian immigrant population in the Russian Federation following the arrest in Tbilisi, in 2006, of four Russian service personnel on suspicion of espionage against Georgia. The four service personnel were eventually released. The applicant state denounced several violations on the grounds that Russia had permitted or caused the existence of an administrative practice involving, in particular, the arrest, detention and collective expulsion of Georgian nationals. The Grand Chamber attested to the existence of such practice,[344] but the question of reparation is still pending.

Georgia brought a second application against Russia in 2008, alleging an administrative practice of serious violations through indiscriminate and disproportionate attacks against civilians and their property in Abkhazia and South Ossetia by the Russian army and/or the separatist forces placed under their control.[345] The application was declared admissible and then jurisdiction was relinquished to the Grand Chamber, where the case is still pending. The following year, the government of Georgia requested the Court to demand that the Russian Federation ensure the prompt and unconditional release of four Georgian minors in the custody of the proxy regime in Tskhinvali Region/South Ossetia. Following their release one month later, Georgia

Newsletter 6 (1984), at 14–22, and, by the same author, 'A Friendly Settlement in the European Inter-State Complaints against Turkey', *SIM Newsletter* 13 (1986), at 44–8.

343 *Denmark v. Turkey*, no. 34382/97, ECHR 2000-IV.

344 *Georgia v. Russia (I)* [GC], no. 13255/07, 3 July 2014.

345 *Georgia v. Russia (II)* (dec.), no. 38263/08, 13 December 2011.

declared that it no longer wished to maintain the application. The Court struck the case out.[346]

Finally, in March 2014, Ukraine also lodged an application against the Russian Federation, given the military tension between the two countries. In view of the urgency of the situation, the Court has granted Ukraine's request for interim measures and urged the two states to refrain from taking any measures – military actions, in particular – that may cause breaches of the Convention rights of the civilian population. It is too early to predict compliance with those measures or the conduct of the proceedings before the Court.

3.3.3.3 Concluding remarks

States, as applicants, have a privileged position in the Convention system, because fewer requirements apply to them when lodging a petition. The purpose of the drafters was to encourage the member parties to take a stance and have an active role in defining and defending human rights principles within their territory. While the intention is laudable, the practice is rather disappointing, although such a reaction may have been anticipated and even accepted in the context of inter-state relations based mainly on political interests.

There are very few cases lodged by states. Of those that have ever reached the Court, only two have so far established state responsibility for breaches of the Convention.[347] However, even though the majority were terminated by friendly settlements, they did bring some reparation in the form of individual or general redress for the violations alleged.

States have usually introduced applications in their own name or in the name of their citizens, very rarely on behalf of the collectivity of the contracting parties. For instance, in the first three applications against Turkey, Cyprus denounced the Turkish military operations. The fourth petition, in which Cyprus alleged violations of the rights of some different categories of persons, or the application introduced by Denmark against Turkey in respect of the ill-treatment of a Danish national, had a different nature. Other cases involved a special link with the citizens of the respondent state, albeit not nationals of the complaining state: for example, the reaction by Greece to the alleged breaches by the British colonial regime in Cyprus; the case brought by Austria against Italy to defend the right to a fair trial of six young men who belonged to the

[346] *Georgia v. Russia* (dec.), no. 61186/09, 16 March 2010.

[347] *Ireland v. the United Kingdom*, note 320, and *Cyprus v. Turkey* (merits), note 341.

German-speaking community of South Tyrol; or the application lodged by Ireland in respect of abuse by the British authorities in Northern Ireland.[348]

Only the Greek and Turkish Cases are illustrations of *actio popularis*, when several states reacted to human rights breaches by military regimes.[349] However commendable that action may be, which has, after all, been taken only by a minority of the member states, it is regrettable that the Committee of Ministers preferred political responses instead of the expected judicial reaction. The same holds true for the first two applications brought by Cyprus against Turkey. The Committee accepted that the alleged events constituted violations, and further deemed necessary some measures to put an end to such violations and to prevent repetition, but nonetheless it did not perform its role to establish Turkey's responsibility for those infringements, as required by the former Article 32 of the Convention.[350] The Committee took no action other than merely urging the parties to resume dialogue. Moreover, as aptly noted, the handling of the third application by Cyprus against Turkey was even more disappointing, because the only solution that the Committee found appropriate was simply to publish the report adopted by the Commission.[351] The very few examples of *actio popularis* reveal that, in the absence of any direct or indirect interest, states do not usually take initiative aimed at general protection of human rights.

The way the Committee of Ministers handled those cases stands as evidence for past failures of the system to protect efficiently human rights and to secure effective redress. It seemed impossible for a political body vested with significant judicial powers to turn away from politics and perform objectively a judicial function. It was thus a great

[348] See, e.g., L. F. Zwaak, 'The Interstate Complaint under the European Convention on Human Rights and Fundamental Freedoms: The Five Complaints against Turkey', *SIM Newsletter* 0 (1982), at 14, and Prebensen, note 317, at 543–5.

[349] The Greek Case originated in a call by the Standing Committee of the Consultative Assembly of the Council of Europe in 1967 for the contracting parties to react to the suspension of a number of Convention guarantees by the military regime in Greece. See Leckie, note 317, at 289–93.

[350] See, e.g., V. Coufoudakis, 'Cyprus and the European Convention on Human Rights: The Law and Politics of *Cyprus v. Turkey*, Applications 6780/74 and 6950/75', *Human Rights Quarterly* 4, no. 4 (1982), and C. Tomuschat, '*Quo Vadis, Argentoratum*? The Success Story of the European Convention on Human Rights – and a Few Dark Stains', *Human Rights Law Journal* 13, nos. 11–12 (1992), at 402–3.

[351] Tomuschat, note 350, at 402–3.

achievement for the system that Protocol No. 11 removed from the Committee all prerogatives in respect of material violations of the treaty, and entrusted it only with the supervision of the execution of the Court's judgments. Even so, the scant presence of inter-state applications makes it difficult to assume that the Court would decide such complaints on exclusively legal grounds.

One may wonder what is at stake in inter-state cases, the finding of a violation or the compensation. What seems to emerge from the extremely low number of inter-state cases is that the members of the Council of Europe are not willing to point the finger too easily at each other in a quest for human rights observance, although they have legal tools and examples of a wide range of practical infringements, as attested by the hundreds of violations revealed by the Court in each recent year. Undoubtedly, human rights violations found by the Strasbourg Court are not of the same type and, most often, of the same gravity as those considered by the Court of San José. Leaving aside political motivations that may deter states from taking action, a reason for that scarcity of inter-state applications may be that contracting parties concede that state intervention is necessary only in situations of gross and widespread violations of human rights. That was the case with the reaction by several states to human rights breaches by military regimes in Greece and Turkey. However, examination of the few inter-state cases cannot show if there is any difference between compensation claimed by a state in its own name or for its own citizens, and compensation claimed for other nationals. Only Denmark, Georgia and Cyprus secured redress for their nationals.

At this point, it may also be worth wondering what the practical effects of the existence of an inter-state complaints procedure for the members of the Council of Europe may be. Obviously, the procedure was theoretically designed to secure 'the special character of the Convention as an instrument of European public order (*ordre public*) for the protection of individual human beings'.[352] An analogy may be drawn with the obligations *erga omnes*, owed to the international community as a whole, in respect of which the International Court of Justice declared in the *Barcelona Traction* case that 'all States can be held to have a legal interest in their protection'.[353] Yet, the Strasbourg practice shows that states

[352] *Cyprus v. Turkey* (merits), note 341, para. 78.

[353] *Barcelona Traction, Light and Power Company, Limited*, Second Phase, ICJ Reports, 1970, p. 3, para. 33.

would rather prefer informal diplomatic avenues instead of judicial action for the purpose of establishing responsibility, keeping the inter-state application as an option of last resort if diplomacy fails. The inter-state complaints procedure has thus not attained the great scope envisaged by the founders of the system, who thought of it as the main wheel in the Convention machinery.[354]

[354] L.-E. Pettiti, 'Réflexions sur les principes et les mécanismes de la Convention. De l'idéal de 1950 à l'humble réalité d'aujourd'hui', in Pettiti, Decaux and Imbert, note 17, at 27.

4

Types of damage: understanding the Court's logic in determining the necessity of an award and in quantifying it in monetary terms

The present chapter proceeds from the practice of the Court and seeks to decipher the grounds on which the judges decide to compensate a particular damage, and especially the basis for their calculations. The problem is that a simple reading of most awards, above all those for moral harm, inevitably raises fundamental questions such as 'why were they given?' and 'how were they assessed?'. The rationale is more evident in the context of material loss, as well as for costs and expenses, but hardly perceptible in the case of redress for moral damage, where the judges use equity in order to agree on a monetary or frequently non-pecuniary award. Further difficulties arise when a dispute reveals several violations, because they establish an amount for the whole moral prejudice, making it hard to discern the attitude towards a plurality of violations vis-à-vis the same victim. Assuming they exist, it is therefore appropriate to extract from the extensive case law the criteria used, but scarcely revealed, by the Strasbourg judges.

4.1 Reparation for material damage

4.1.1 Notion

Material damage is naturally linked to the right to protection of property guaranteed by Article 1 of Protocol No. 1 to the Convention. Does the Court award reparation for material damage only in the presence of a claim for property damage or loss? The answer is in the negative, otherwise plaintiffs would always have to invoke it, in addition to and in connection with the main violation. Petitioners may recover pecuniary loss whenever it is a direct consequence of the authorities' illegal actions, as in the case of pecuniary sanctions imposed on journalists in breach of freedom of expression. It matters little if the plaintiff is the direct or indirect victim of a violation, because only entitlement to the alleged pecuniary harm may justify an award. Moreover, pecuniary damages are transmissible to the heirs, by reason of their exclusively financial characteristic.[355]

The scope of the obligation to restore the original position extends not merely to the loss actually sustained (*damnum emergens*), but also to the loss, or diminished gain, to be expected in the future (*lucrum cessans*). In so far as the Court does not usually make redress of its own motion, it is an applicant's duty to adduce evidence as to the admissibility and merits of a claim. The former relates to the existence of a causal link between the material loss and the breach, whereas the latter concerns documentation pertaining to the quantum. If a request is not supported by evidence,[356] or not associated with the violation found, but with an allegation which has been dismissed,[357] the judges will reject it.

The higher the amount being claimed, the higher also is the standard of proof demanded by the Court. Given that no special issue would normally arise in respect of an amount agreed in a contract or awarded by an arbitral decision, the discussion is particularly relevant in the context of property unlawfully taken, when the passing of time alters the economic value. It is therefore in the petitioners' best interest to produce relevant evidence so as to demonstrate entitlement and facilitate evaluation. The most important awards are undoubtedly made in property cases, where the equivalent of the assets may even be in the order of millions of euros.[358]

Often the Court does not explain how it arrives at a figure, preferring to keep its discretionary margin of appreciation. The judges do not engage in detailed calculations, but merely examine whether the evidence is convincing. When damage proves difficult to estimate or if both parties have submitted pertinent documentation, the judges amalgamate the compensation with that for moral damage and order a lump sum in equity.[359] It may be that the recent inflow of cases is making it difficult to assess damage in detail. However, it should not be difficult for an observer to speculate about the amounts assigned to pecuniary and to

[355] See, e.g., *Deweer v. Belgium*, 27 February 1980, Series A no. 35, para. 37, and *X v. the United Kingdom* (Article 50), note 287, para. 12.

[356] See, e.g., *Deumeland v. Germany*, 29 May 1986, Series A no. 100, para. 96.

[357] See, e.g., *Kingsley v. the United Kingdom* [GC], no. 35605/97, ECHR 2002-IV, para. 40 *in fine*.

[358] See, e.g., the recent cases of *Lordos and Others v. Turkey* (just satisfaction), no. 15973/90, 10 January 2012, and *Agrokompleks v. Ukraine* (just satisfaction), no. 23465/03, 25 July 2013.

[359] See, e.g., *López Ostra v. Spain*, 9 December 1994, Series A no. 303-C, paras. 62–5.

non-pecuniary injury, on the basis of other awards for moral damage in similar cases. In any case, the Court comprises not only forty-seven judges, but also some 640 staff members of the Registry. Moreover, there has already been established a Just Satisfaction Division within the Registry. At least theoretically, the Court seems to have the necessary organizational tools to perform accurate calculations.

4.1.2 *Damnum emergens*

4.1.2.1 Property cases

The issue of the recovery of *damnum emergens* normally arises in property cases, where it represents the loss sustained, that is, the value of the taken property. Petitioners usually seek restitution or alternative compensation for their assets. Diligent applicants frequently submit expert reports which have evaluated the claimed property. Otherwise, the Court would base its calculation on the evidence produced by the defendant government, which is hardly likely to be in the plaintiff's best interest.[360] Rationally, a government would be inclined to submit reports in which a property would be valued at the lowest possible price. If complainants aim at higher amounts, they must validly challenge those allegations by stronger counter-evidence. Formally, such reports are not compulsory, but they represent a useful tool for the judges. When the Court anticipates difficulties in assessment, it may even order an expert report to be prepared by specialists agreed by the parties.[361]

Applicants often seek restitution of their property in the first place. The Court has always accepted the primacy of the principle of *restitutio in integrum*, although it has declared that it has 'neither the power nor the possibility of doing so itself'.[362] That is the official position, intended to reassure the contracting states that it has not assumed more powers than those conferred by the treaty, i.e., to order a course of action. In fact,

[360] For example, in *Maria Violeta Lăzărescu v. Romania* (no. 10636/06, 23 February 2010, paras. 29–30 and 34), the applicant valued her property at EUR 251,266, without submitting an expert report, and thus the Court awarded only EUR 104,229, which was the sum established by the report produced by the government.

[361] See, e.g., *Papamichalopoulos* (Article 50), note 91, para. 3; *Belvedere Alberghiera S.r.l. v. Italy* (just satisfaction), no. 31524/96, 30 October 2003, para. 6; and *Avellar Cordeiro Zagallo v. Portugal* (just satisfaction), no. 30844/05, 8 June 2010, para. 6. For a general view on the topic, see S. Turgis, 'Le recours aux expertises', in Flauss and Lambert Abdelgawad, note 104.

[362] *Papamichalopoulos* (Article 50), note 91, para. 34.

when the circumstances of the case allow it, the judges merely *indicate* to the respondent government that the return of the property would restore the *status quo ante*, although they are more determined in the operative part to *impose* a certain level of conduct.[363] For petitioners, it matters little if the Court's authority to offer *restitutio* is direct or rather indirect, their priority is to recover their property.

Moreover, in exceptional circumstances, the Court may also offer an equivalent item in compensation.[364] Such was the case in *Dumbravă v. Romania*, where it found a violation of the property right on the grounds that, in spite of a legal obligation under a domestic court's decision to sell to the applicant – at a special preferential price – the apartment where he had been living as a tenant, the state sold it to a third party. The Court ordered the performance of the sale, but at the same time it was aware of the possible difficulties at the internal level. As an alternative, it directed the state to offer for sale an apartment of equivalent surface area and value and, if the complainant considered that the offer was unacceptable, to pay him a sum equivalent to the loss which would have resulted from having that sale performed:[365] the so-called 'loss of opportunity' examined below. That approach seems innovative, because it left an alternative to the state to pay compensation only after making an effort to secure *restitutio*, and only if the victim did not agree. The state's margin of discretion was also considerably reduced by specifying the conditions of that sale.

As far as financial compensation is concerned, one vital question would be this: at what moment is the valuation made, at the time of dispossession or at the time of delivery of the Court's judgment? The judges have drawn inspiration from other international courts and tribunals and differentiated between the legal and illegal character of

[363] The typical formulae used by the judges in the reasoning, respectively, in the operative parts of a judgment are: 'The Court *considers*, in the circumstances of the case, that the return of the property in issue … would put the applicants as far as possible in a situation equivalent to the one in which they would have been if there had not been a breach of Article 1 of Protocol No. 1' (emphasis added), and '*Holds* that the respondent State is to return … ' (emphasis added). See, as illustrations, *Papamichalopoulos* (Article 50), note 91, para. 38 and point 2 of the operative part, and *Străin*, note 136, para. 80 and point 4(a) of the operative part.

[364] For example, the Court accepted equivalent land offered by the authorities in *Sabin Popescu v. Romania* (no. 48102/99, 2 March 2004, para. 91) and *Cloșcă v. Romania* (no. 6106/04, 30 September 2008, para. 29), or made a suggestion in that respect in *Humbatov v. Azerbaijan* (no. 13652/06, 3 December 2009, para. 38).

[365] *Dumbravă v. Romania*, no. 25234/03, 17 February 2009, para. 42.

dispossession. In the cases of *Papamichalopoulos*, *Former King of Greece* and *Guiso-Gallisay*, in particular, the Court invoked the precedent rulings of the Permanent Court in *Factory at Chorzów*, of the Iran–United States Claims Tribunal in *Amoco*, as well as the *Texaco* arbitration, which made a distinction between lawful and unlawful expropriation with a view to establishing the appropriate criteria to be used for determining the corresponding reparation in those two situations.[366]

On the one hand, when deprivation had been arbitrary, *de facto* or *de jure*, the Court declared in *Papamichalopoulos* that the nature of the breach entailed full reparation, that is, either the return of the property in issue or payment of the current market value.[367] In that particular dispute, it considered that the government should return the land and also the existing buildings for loss of enjoyment. In the alternative, it decided to award 'the current value of the land, increased by the appreciation brought about by the existence of the buildings, and the construction costs of the latter'.[368]

On the other hand, in the event of a lawful expropriation, the Grand Chamber held in the *Former King of Greece* that, in the case of non-restitution, the compensation 'need not . . . reflect the idea of wiping out all the consequences of the interference in question'.[369] In other words, the principle of *restitutio in integrum* loses primacy in that context. The reason is that in those cases the state's unlawful conduct under the Convention comes from the lack of any compensation, not from an inherent illegality of expropriation.[370] Therefore, the victim is entitled to full compensation at the level of the market value of the property at the moment when the property was taken. There are, however, exceptions which may call for less than reimbursement of the full market value, such as expropriations based on measures of economic reform or measures designed to achieve greater social justice, or even when a country's constitutional system suffers fundamental changes such as transition from monarchy to republic.[371] The amount obtained must be converted to the current value to offset the effects of inflation, in addition to simple statutory interest which would offset, at least in part, the long period of dispossession.[372]

[366] *Papamichalopoulos* (Article 50), note 91, para. 36; *Former King of Greece* (just satisfaction), note 114, para. 75; and *Guiso-Gallisay v. Italy* (just satisfaction) [GC], no. 58858/00, 22 December 2009, paras. 49–52.

[367] *Papamichalopoulos* (Article 50), note 91, paras. 36–9. [368] Ibid., para. 39.

[369] *Former King of Greece* (just satisfaction), note 114, para. 78. [370] Ibid. [371] Ibid.

[372] *Scordino v. Italy (no. 1)* [GC], no. 36813/97, ECHR 2006-V, para. 258.

Yet, although plausibly related to the circumstances of the moment when the property was taken, that distinction between legal and illegal deprivation has been questioned by the judges. After being confronted with a series of cases against Italy in respect of constructive expropriations,[373] the Grand Chamber eventually decided in *Guiso-Gallisay* to change the *Papamichalopoulos* case law as to the evaluation of property that was not being returned. It confined the compensation for the land to its value at the time of deprivation, when the victim lost the right of ownership, not at the moment when the Court made its judgment, and also refused to automatically award, for loss of use, the price of the buildings erected by the state.[374]

The justifications given by the judges were that the applicants in *Guiso-Gallisay*, unlike in *Papamichalopoulos*, had not sought restitution of their land in domestic proceedings and that the state had nonetheless occupied the plot in issue on the basis of a public-interest declaration.[375] While that argument appears rather unconvincing, they aptly noted that compensation for the constructions built by the state would lead to disparities in the treatment of plaintiffs, in so far as it depends on the works undertaken by the authorities, not on the land's original potential, and would also bear some punitive role for the state, instead of a compensatory purpose for victims.[376] It would indeed be speculative to establish what owners would have made of their land, or what kind of constructions they would have erected, in the same way as it would be difficult to try to predict what the outcome of a trial would have been were it not to have been deprived of the fair-trial guarantees.

Even with a more restrictive method of assessment, the Court still awarded compensation of some EUR 2 million for material damage in *Guiso-Gallisay*. The problem of constructive expropriation is well known to the Italian legal system, because a number of local authorities took possession of land in the 1970s without an expropriation order.[377] What would have happened if all those people had come to Strasbourg and obtained the current value of their land and also of the appurtenant buildings? The ruling in *Guiso-Gallisay* is highly questionable, in so far as it values

[373] For the elements of constructive expropriation, see the Chamber judgment on the merits, *Guiso-Gallisay v. Italy*, no. 58858/00, 8 December 2005, paras. 87–91. For a summary of the case law, see the judgment on just satisfaction in *Guiso-Gallisay*, note 366, paras. 98–101.

[374] *Guiso-Gallisay* (just satisfaction), note 366, para. 103.

[375] Ibid., para. 102.

[376] Ibid., para. 103 *in fine*.

[377] *Belvedere Alberghiera S.r.l. v. Italy*, no. 31524/96, ECHR 2000-VI, para. 21.

the effective loss in the same manner for either lawful or unlawful dispossession. One may even ask whether political reasons have not interfered with legal analysis. Nonetheless, it may be welcomed for declining routinely to equate the existing constructions with loss of profit.

The most important consequence is therefore that when it is impossible to return a property, and the victim must be compensated, the Court has practically removed the distinction between lawful and unlawful expropriations. Thus, in both situations, in order to offset the effects of inflation, it awards compensation based on the property's value at the moment when it was taken and then converts it to its current value. Is that fair? It is certainly not in agreement with the decision of the Permanent Court in the *Factory at Chorzów* case, which the Court itself has invoked, and which does make that differentiation between 'lawful liquidation and unlawful dispossession', with the effect that the payment of the value at the time of indemnification 'is designed to take the place of restitution which has become impossible'.[378] Here again, political motivation may have played a role. Ultimately, the Court is 'owned' by a political organization. States certainly agree to that approach, because they will go 'unpunished' no matter what they do in that respect.

As to the fairness of that approach, from the victim's point of view, it may be reasonably assumed that someone who has been served an official document for expropriation, then proved to be legal, would not suffer the same prejudice as someone abusively deprived of his or her property. From the perspective of both material and moral injury, a legal expropriation puts an end to ownership, there are no profits associated with that property, only with the amount received in compensation. It may also be argued that the victim performed its civic duty to contribute to the public interest and may be expected to share the costs. The Court will therefore assess the propriety of the sum.

As for unlawful deprivation, it is certain that victims suffer a higher degree of frustration knowing that they are the legal owners of their possessions but that they cannot enjoy their use. And when they finally obtain recognition of their right, when the Court delivers its judgment, they do not receive their property back or receive compensation equal to its value, but only compensation based on what it had been worth in the past, sometimes tens of years ago. In spite of all its apparent argumentation, the Court has still to provide an acceptable explanation as to why such an approach provides justice to the victims.

[378] *Factory at Chorzów (Merits)*, note 92, at 47–8.

What is striking, though, is that even after the change introduced by *Guiso-Gallisay*, the Court has continued to apply the previous approach of compensation at the level of the current market value in cases brought by the victims of expropriations by the former communist regimes in Eastern Europe.[379] In those kinds of disputes, the domestic authorities acknowledged that the deprivation had been illegal, but failed to compensate the victims. The victims eventually found redress in Strasbourg, in the form of the current market value of their properties. And yet, applying the *Guiso-Gallisay* formula, compensation should be lower. It may be that the Court sought to avoid the discrimination in treatment of the preceding similar cases, but, at the same time, it generated some discrimination between victims at the level of the member states, in so far as only some of them received the actual value of their properties. In any event, the judges issued a pilot judgment in respect of those cases, temporarily deferring consideration of similar applications.[380] It should therefore be expected that they will extend the above-mentioned standard in order to ensure consistency of the case law.

4.1.2.2 Other cases

While *damnum emergens* is predominantly claimed and granted in property disputes, that type of litigation does not have exclusivity. Other violations may also directly produce monetary loss, such as medical expenses associated with physical harm. The judges have reimbursed medical expenses incurred as a result of torture,[381] or costs sustained by the applicant and his family in their attempt to mitigate the unacceptable conditions of the applicant's detention and their negative consequences for his health,[382] as well as medical treatment required after being shot during a security operation,[383] or even the cost of a funeral.[384]

Another category of cases comprises those where the authorities imposed pecuniary sanctions on journalists in breach of their freedom

379 See, e.g., *Seceleanu*, note 72, para. 57.

380 *Maria Atanasiu and Others v. Romania*, nos. 30767/05 and 33800/06, 12 October 2010, para. 241.

381 See, e.g., *Aksoy v. Turkey*, 18 December 1996, *Reports of Judgments and Decisions* 1996-VI, paras. 111 and 113, and *İlhan*, note 243, paras. 107–9.

382 *Nevmerzhitsky v. Ukraine*, no. 54825/00, ECHR 2005-II (extracts), para. 142.

383 *Makhauri v. Russia*, no. 58701/00, 4 October 2007, paras. 135–9.

384 *Abdurrahman Orak v. Turkey*, no. 31889/96, 14 February 2002, para. 106, and *Mansuroğlu v. Turkey*, no. 43443/98, 26 February 2008, para. 126.

of expression. If the Court finds that their conduct was illegal, it usually orders the reimbursement of the fine or of other amounts that the victim had to pay.[385] The Court adopted the same approach in a case in which the applicants had been arrested and fined for taking part in demonstrations, because it was an interference with their freedom of assembly and association;[386] also in a case in which the application of a tax law had constituted interference in the applicant association's right to respect for its freedom of religion.[387] Similarly, it reimbursed the fees incurred in guardianship and custody proceedings, when the very provisions of the internal law, which allowed the applicant's child to be placed for adoption shortly after her birth without his knowledge or consent, violated the plaintiff's right to respect for family life.[388]

The judges have also reimbursed an estate agent's fees on the sale of a house and the fees for the survey of that house in a case of interference with the plaintiffs' exercise of their right to respect for their home, when it was caused by the authorities' refusal to grant them permanent and temporary licences to occupy their house.[389] In another case where it found a violation of the applicant's effective enjoyment of her right to respect for her home and her private and family life, on account of the nuisance caused by the vicinity of a waste-treatment plant, the Court provided redress, without quantifying it, for material prejudice.[390]

4.1.3 *Lucrum cessans*

Lucrum cessans is more difficult to evaluate than *damnum emergens*, because it contains an intrinsic element of speculation. The applicants must submit pertinent evidence in that respect, such as expert reports[391]

385 See, e.g., *Jersild v. Denmark*, 23 September 1994, Series A no. 298, paras. 40–1; *Öztürk v. Turkey* [GC], no. 22479/93, ECHR 1999-VI, para. 80; *Wizerkaniuk v. Poland*, no. 18990/05, 5 July 2011, para. 92; and *Lahtonen v. Finland*, no. 29576/09, 17 January 2012, paras. 86–8.

386 *Hyde Park and Others v. Moldova (nos. 5 and 6)*, nos. 6991/08 and 15084/08, 14 September 2010, para. 58. Also see *Satılmış and Others v. Turkey*, nos. 74611/01, 26876/02 and 27628/02, 17 July 2007, para. 78.

387 *Association Les Témoins de Jéhovah v. France* (just satisfaction), no. 8916/05, 5 July 2012, para. 19.

388 *Keegan v. Ireland*, 26 May 1994, Series A no. 290, paras. 64–5.

389 *Gillow v. the United Kingdom* (Article 50), 14 September 1987, Series A no. 124-C, para. 11.

390 *López Ostra*, note 359, para. 65.

391 See, e.g., *Zvolský and Zvolská v. the Czech Republic*, no. 46129/99, ECHR 2002-IX, para. 81.

or court decisions.[392] It may include profits or benefits, loss of earnings, salaries, pensions, interest, fines and, questionably though, even loss of income for a non-profit-making company.[393] When difficult to assess, the Court may order a lump sum for the whole material damage, or even for the whole prejudice, without revealing what it deemed to be appropriate for the loss sustained. When differences exist between the reports produced by the opposing parties, the Court makes its own assessment and it awards what it considers to be fair.[394] The judges may even speculate on the matter, invoking equity, when the extent of the prejudice, not its existence, is not proved.[395] However, in so far as it is compensated in some cases but not in other similar disputes, it seems to be a matter of discretion rather than equity.

4.1.3.1 Loss of profit or interest

Recovery of loss of profits is specifically permitted under general international law.[396] The Permanent Court upheld in *Factory at Chorzów*, as a matter of principle, the obligation to restore an undertaking or, if not possible, to pay its value, but further continued that '[t]o this obligation, in virtue of the general principles of international law, must be added that of compensating loss sustained as the result of the seizure'.[397] Another rule concerns the interest for a capital sum. In that specific case, the profit from that amount is the interest, so they cannot be granted simultaneously, but interest may normally be due for the profits that may have been earned.[398] The Strasbourg Court has integrated those principles, awarding interest on a sum established, for example, for the loss of earnings[399] or as an invalidity pension.[400] On occasion, it has preferred to fix an amount, instead of interest, for the loss of availability

392 See, e.g., *Ceachir v. Moldova*, no. 11712/04, 15 January 2008, paras. 53–5.

393 *Open Door and Dublin Well Woman v. Ireland*, 29 October 1992, Series A no. 246-A, paras. 85–7. See para. 5 of the partly dissenting opinion of Judge Matscher.

394 See, e.g., *Zlínsat, spol. s r.o. v. Bulgaria* (just satisfaction), no. 57785/00, 10 January 2008, paras. 42–5, and *Dichev v. Bulgaria*, no. 1355/04, 27 January 2011, para. 43.

395 See, e.g., *Buzescu v. Romania*, no. 61302/00, 24 May 2005, paras. 88 and 107.

396 Article 36(2) of the ILC Articles. See the Commentary in Crawford, note 43, at 228–30.

397 *Factory at Chorzów (Merits)*, note 92, at 48.

398 Crawford, note 43, at 230 and 239.

399 *Lustig-Prean and Beckett v. the United Kingdom* (just satisfaction), nos. 31417/96 and 32377/96, 25 July 2000, paras. 23–8.

400 *Schuler-Zgraggen v. Switzerland* (Article 50), 31 January 1995, Series A no. 305-A, para. 15.

of a sum ordered by a municipal court.[401] Loss of profit or interest should not be confused with the operation of updating an amount, in order to reflect inflation, which is *damnum emergens*, not *lucrum cessans*.

When in *Guiso-Gallisay* the Grand Chamber reconsidered the practice of awarding compensation for loss of profit or benefit, it awarded only simple statutory interest on the amount established for *damnum emergens*, instead of further allowing victims to recover the value of the buildings erected by the state on their lands. As already explained, although the deprivation was illegal, the method seems reasonable in light of the speculative element of the previous approach. Even the opponents of that ruling have not clarified on what basis plaintiffs would have been entitled to compensation against the loss of use of their land to the exact value of those structures built by the state. However, one may accept their argument claiming that offering only the interest for the main sum may have set aside the distinction between lawful and unlawful dispossession, and thus generally encourages states to take advantage of their unlawful acts.[402]

That approach in respect of the loss of profit seems to be in agreement with general international law, where the loss of profit may indeed be replaced with interest. Payment of interest does not raise any particular difficulty. If the judges agree that the complainant is entitled to interest, they have only to decide the starting point and the rate. The Strasbourg Court, like other international courts and tribunals,[403] determines without restriction the appropriate interest rate. Although plaintiffs may seek compound interest, the judges normally adopt the rate of statutory interest or even the inflation rate, depending on which is more favourable to the applicant.[404] They are attentive to the national economic

[401] *Guillemin v. France* (Article 50), 2 September 1998, *Reports of Judgments and Decisions* 1998-VI, para. 25.

[402] Dissenting opinion of Judge Tulkens in the Chamber judgment on just satisfaction (*Guiso-Gallisay v. Italy*, no. 58858/00, 21 October 2008), and partly dissenting opinion of Judge Spielmann in the Grand Chamber judgment (note 366). Also see M. van Brustem and E. van Brustem, 'Les hésitations de la Cour européenne des droits de l'homme: à propos du revirement de jurisprudence en matière de satisfaction équitable applicable aux expropriations illicites: note sous CEDH, 21 octobre 2008, *Guiso-Gallisay c. Italie*, req. no. 58858/00', *Revue française de droit administratif* 2 (2009).

[403] See, e.g., the Iran–United States Claims Tribunal in *Foremost Tehran, Inc. v. Islamic Republic of Iran*, 10 April 1986, 10 Iran–US CTR 228, at 252, and the International Tribunal for the Law of the Sea in *M/V 'Saiga' (No. 2) (Saint Vincent and the Grenadines v. Guinea)*, Judgment, ITLOS Reports 1999, p. 65, para. 173.

[404] See, e.g., *Beyeler* (just satisfaction), note 118, para. 23 *in fine*.

conditions, such as levels of inflation and rates of interest available to investors nationally during the relevant period.[405] In any event, the Court is not bound by any provisions of the domestic law, nonetheless having the possibility to take into account any pertinent domestic interest rates, in so far as they are reasonable.[406]

The Court reserves the right, more exactly the discretion, to afford or refuse compensation even when a loss of profit is fairly evident, such as in property cases. In those cases, it may choose to compensate that loss or it may refuse to speculate in the absence of evidence.[407] Certainly, evidence for what a victim would have gained is normally difficult to produce. The problem is not that the judges speculate in respect of the equivalent for loss of profit, because the valuation inevitably involves a degree of estimation, but that they seem to operate on a pick-and-choose basis as to when or not to award it. Such a method does not guarantee that the system of reparation is effective.

As a matter of principle, the existence of a certain loss of profit should be accepted, at least in a case of interference with the use of immovable property. Its calculation should be a secondary concern, because the Court may challenge it anyway at the moment of assessment, even in the absence of counter-arguments from the defendant government. This happened in *Loizidou v. Turkey*, where the applicant claimed and submitted an evaluation for the loss of profit from nine plots of land, but the government did not comment on the method of calculation. The Court instinctively admitted that interference with her property had generated losses. It nonetheless questioned her estimation and proposed instead 'the general approach to assessing the loss suffered by the applicant with reference to the annual ground rent, calculated as a percentage of the market value of the property that could have been earned on the properties during the relevant period'.[408] The system of compensation suggested by the judges appears to be reasonable. So, what prevents them from applying comparable standards in similar circumstances? It would

405 See, e.g., *Prodan v. Moldova*, no. 49806/99, ECHR 2004-III (extracts), para. 73, and *Runkee and White v. the United Kingdom*, nos. 42949/98 and 53134/99, 10 May 2007, para. 52.

406 See, e.g., *Efendiyeva v. Azerbaijan*, no. 31556/03, 25 October 2007, para. 21 *in fine*.

407 For example, when confronted with non-execution of municipal judgments ordering return of arable land, the Court, notwithstanding the lack of evidence, made an award in equity in *Sabin Popescu v. Romania* (note 364, para. 92), but refused to speculate in *Hîrgău and Arsinte v. Romania* (no. 252/04, 20 January 2009, paras. 43–4), in the absence of such evidence, nonetheless after making reference to *Sabin Popescu*.

408 *Loizidou* (Article 50), note 164, para. 33.

certainly offer effective and foreseeable reparation in the field. Here again, instead of producing some general guidelines as to the cases where loss of profit may be accepted, the judges prefer to have a margin of appreciation as to the recognition, and further demonstration, of the very existence of that loss.

4.1.3.2 Loss of earnings

Calculation of loss of earnings is a difficult operation, because it depends on a series of variables, particularly when the victim has died. In 1923, the Mixed Claims Commission delivered a decision in the case of the *Lusitania*, a British vessel sunk by a German submarine in 1915. The formula proposed for the wrong done to the victims' relatives took into account the contribution that the deceased would have made to the claimant, the pecuniary value of the victim's personal services in the claimant's care, education or supervision, as well as reasonable compensation for the moral suffering.[409] The pertinent factors for fixing an amount would include the personal attributes of both victim and claimant, such as age, sex, health, condition and probable life expectancy, as well as the victim's earning capacity and a reasonable probability of increasing or decreasing it, and personal expenditures.[410] It is therefore evident that such an assessment is not only complex, but also hypothetical.

The European system of reparation does not employ a standardized approach. Hence, the evaluation of loss of earnings is inherently speculative, even when causation is evident, because there is no precise factor for determining the evolution of the victim's career. Although it may refer to past earnings and pension rights,[411] it often represents a projection into the future of the effects of a violation, which departs from the classic theory of reparation as making redress for the prejudice already suffered. For that reason, claims for loss of future earnings have no connection with breaches of the property right under Article 1 of Protocol No. 1, but are linked directly to the violation. The judges adopt a different perspective when fixing reparation for the two types of prejudice. They will look backward in order to concretely assess the damage already caused by deprivation of possessions. Quite on the

[409] *Lusitania (United States v. Germany)* (1923), 7 RIAA 32, at 35. [410] Ibid.

[411] See, e.g., *Young, James and Webster v. the United Kingdom* (Article 50), 18 October 1982, Series A no. 55, paras. 10–11.

contrary, they will also look forward and speculate on what the gain would have become if the victim's professional development had not been curtailed.

The Court may draw inspiration from the amount that the complainant would have earned if not hindered by the state's infringement. The degree of speculation is consequently higher or lower. Theoretically, it should be easier to take into account a forfeiture of parliamentary seats following the dissolution of the applicants' party,[412] than to approximate how long a victim would have worked if not killed by the security forces or what would have been earned if the victim had been only at the educational stage at the moment of the killing. If the petitioner has been employed in another post during the period in which he or she had lost the initial job, and does not demonstrate that his or her salary was lower than the original one, the Court does not make any award.[413]

The most common situation is represented by claims for loss of future earnings suffered by family members as a result of the killing of the provider by the authorities of the respondent state. In particular, the Turkish cases concerning killings by security forces offer a broad area of illustration. Monetary compensation for the financial support that the victim would have secured to the dependants is inevitably speculative. For example, in *Aktaş v. Turkey*, where the deceased victim had been the owner of a shop that sold food products, the Court acknowledged the inherently uncertain character of the damage, but upheld the applicant's calculations based on the assumption that the victim, aged twenty-four at his death, would have worked until the age of sixty-five, and thus allocated EUR 226,065 for his widow and daughter for the loss of future income.[414] Still, nothing would guarantee that the victim would have lived or worked until that age, but those approximations are inherent in the nature of that prejudice. As noted in the dissenting opinion to that judgment, that sum may appear to be rather exorbitant. Given the extreme gravity of the violation, the judges make awards even if claims

[412] *Selim Sadak and Others v. Turkey (no. 2)*, nos. 25144/94, 26149/95 to 26154/95, 27100/95 and 27101/95, ECHR 2002-IV, para. 56.

[413] *Thlimmenos v. Greece* [GC], no. 34369/97, ECHR 2000-IV, para. 67. For an example where the Court accepted that the alternative income was lower, see *Doğan and Others v. Turkey* (just satisfaction), nos. 8803–8811/02, 8813/02 and 8815–8819/02, 13 July 2006, para. 54 *in fine*.

[414] *Aktaş v. Turkey*, no. 24351/94, ECHR 2003-V (extracts), paras. 349–55. Also see *Imakayeva v. Russia*, no. 7615/02, ECHR 2006-XIII (extracts), paras. 209–13.

are not properly substantiated, based on previous case law.[415] Those stances may amount to a tacit form of sanction for the state's reprobate conduct.

A similarly difficult assessment arises in the context of breaches affecting the victim's personal situation in the future, where approximation of damage flowing from infringement is also practically unfeasible. The solution left again to the judges is to avail themselves of discretion and equity. For example, in a situation in which the applicant had been tortured and suffered complete disability, being in need of constant medical treatment, they admitted that 'he will undeniably suffer significant material losses', and awarded him EUR 130,000.[416] As a drafting strategy in such cases, apparently to avoid any insinuation of abuse in the field, the Court provides a detailed account of both parties' views on the existence and extent of prejudice, followed by its own evaluation of those statements.[417] In doing so, it also makes an effort to give some assurance to an observer that such a decision is not only complex, but also complete.

At this point it should be mentioned that future loss produced by the effects of a violation on the victim's personal condition is different from the notion of loss of opportunity, which is examined in the next section. It all depends on whether the accent is put on personal life or assets. Reparation for the former seeks to redress what the victim has become as a result of the breach, whereas for the latter it compensates what the applicant has lost or was unable to gain. Based on the victim's potential and life expectancy, estimation of future loss requires special care for the prospects of career and personal fulfilment, including prospective salaries and pension. Such was the case, for instance, when assessing the extent to which suspension from school affected future employment,[418] or with persons discharged from the armed forces on the ground of their homosexuality, in pursuance of an official policy of the Ministry of Defence against homosexuals in the armed forces, where the Court

[415] See, e.g., *Gül v. Turkey*, no. 22676/93, 14 December 2000, para. 107; *Akdeniz and Others v. Turkey*, no. 23954/94, 31 May 2001, para. 130; and *Avşar v. Turkey*, no. 25657/94, ECHR 2001-VII (extracts), para. 442.

[416] *Mikheyev v. Russia*, no. 77617/01, 26 January 2006, para. 162.

[417] See, e.g., *Lustig-Prean and Beckett* (just satisfaction), note 399, paras. 13–29, and *Z and Others v. the United Kingdom* [GC], no. 29392/95, ECHR 2001-V, paras. 113–27.

[418] *Campbell and Cosans v. the United Kingdom* (Article 50), 22 March 1983, Series A no. 60, para. 26.

weighed their career forecast in the army against their civilian career prospects after discharge.[419]

The Inter-American Court also takes into account the victim's age and life expectancy, and the base salary, but also the personal expenses, as suggested in the above-mentioned *Lusitania* decision.[420] For the Court of San José, 'loss of earnings, calculated on the basis of probable life-span, indicates that the *restitutio in integrum* concept is linked to the possibility of maintaining the real value of the damages stable over a relatively long period of time'.[421] In addition, the Inter-American Court did once have a different and more innovative approach to those future losses. When the victim of a violation was still alive – and apart from material and moral damage, and thus presumably not included in either of them – the Inter-American Court had introduced the notion of 'life plan' or 'life project'.[422] It did so for the first time in *Loayza-Tamayo*, where it held that '[t]his notion is different from the notions of special damages and loss of earnings', being 'akin to the concept of personal fulfilment, which in turn is based on the options that an individual may have for leading his life and achieving the goal that he sets for himself'.[423]

In casu, the Inter-American Court found that the applicant, a university professor suspected of being a collaborator of the subversive group 'Shining Path', was unlawfully detained and suffered cruel, inhuman and degrading treatment. Disappointingly though, it refrained from quantifying that harm on the grounds that 'neither case law nor doctrine has evolved to the point where acknowledgment of damage to a life plan can be translated into economic terms', and thus declared that the judgment represented satisfaction by itself.[424] As pointed out by a dissenting judge, it would have been feasible to have agreed on an amount,[425] approximately and on an equitable basis, such as that in the traditional case of moral damage.

419 *Lustig-Prean and Beckett* (just satisfaction), note 399, paras. 22–9, and *Smith and Grady v. the United Kingdom* (Article 41), nos. 33985/96 and 33986/96, ECHR 2000, paras. 18–25.

420 See, e.g., *El Amparo v. Venezuela* (reparations and costs), 14 September 1996, Series C no. 28, para. 28.

421 *Velásquez-Rodríguez v. Honduras* (interpretation of the judgment of reparations and costs), 17 August 1990, Series C no. 9, para. 29.

422 See L. Burgorgue-Larsen and A. Úbeda de Torres, *Les grandes décisions de la Cour interaméricaine des droits de l'homme* (Brussels: Bruylant, 2008), at 257–60, and Piacentini de Andrade, note 100, at 118–21.

423 *Loayza-Tamayo* (reparations and costs), note 98, paras. 147–8.

424 Ibid., paras. 153–4.

425 Partially dissenting opinion of Judge de Roux-Rengifo.

The Court of San José was undecided as to the path to follow in order to remedy the interferences with a life project. It either ordered the breaching state to cover all the victim's costs for a degree preparing him for the profession of his choosing,[426] or included that particular harm in the monetary award for the non-pecuniary damages,[427] or even considered that no form of redress could return to the victim the personal fulfilment options or provide him with new opportunities.[428] Eventually, it seems to have abandoned that path and no longer awards compensation for that particular form of injury.[429]

Therefore, damage to the 'life plan' has yet to gain a place in international law. The Inter-American Court has adopted a more human rights-based approach, whereas the European Court has preferred a more pragmatic perspective. Even the very idea of a 'life project' is by no means unfamiliar to the Strasbourg Court, but the judges have not developed it further.[430] Certainly, the quest for new methods to cope with the ever-increasing number of cases does not incite them to philosophize.

4.1.4 Loss of opportunity

In some cases, when victims had been denied a fair trial before the municipal courts, the Court offered compensation for loss of opportunity. In essence, it refused to speculate on the possible outcome of internal litigation if fair-trial guarantees had been observed, but conceded that the complainants suffered some prejudice by the simple fact that they had not been allowed to properly present and defend their case. However, not all aspects of fairness in domestic proceedings, be they examined under Article 5 or Article 6 of the Convention, may justify an award in that respect. For example, the Court has deemed it inappropriate to compensate such a prejudice in the context of breaches of procedural rules caused by a lack of objective or structural independence and impartiality of internal courts,[431] or when the authorities had not appointed a lawyer to assist the applicant at the moment when his

[426] *Cantoral-Benavides* (reparations and costs), note 96, para. 80.

[427] *Tibi* (preliminary objections, merits, reparations and costs), note 45, paras. 245–6.

[428] *Gutiérrez-Soler v. Colombia* (merits, reparations and costs), 12 September 2005, Series C no. 132, para. 89.

[429] Pasqualucci, note 50, at 245–6.

[430] *Muminov v. Russia* (just satisfaction), no. 42502/06, 4 November 2010, para. 12, and *Kamaliyevy v. Russia* (just satisfaction), no. 52812/07, 28 June 2011, para. 8.

[431] See, in particular, *Kingsley*, note 357, para. 43 and the cases cited.

possible release from detention in a psychiatric institution was being examined.[432] Given that the Court does not normally accede to such a demand, it may be worth speculating that, when it does, it perceives a reasonable possibility that the outcome for the victim would have been different.[433] Otherwise stated, when the causal link between violation and alleged prejudice is open to discussion, the notion of causal link may facilitate the proof of causation.[434]

As a drafting technique, the issue has frequently been examined after the assessment of material loss, but before estimation of the moral harm, without a clear distinction as to which category of damage it has been adjoined. Therefore, what kind of injury is loss of opportunity, material or moral? Is it applicable exclusively in the context of procedural infringements or is it relevant to other breaches as well? Given that the Court usually offers reparation only if expressly claimed, it would be erroneous to suppose that in similar cases such a prejudice is not covered simply because it is not mentioned in the just satisfaction part of a judgment. Nonetheless, it has to be admitted that the judges often make redress in that respect in the absence of an express claim for loss of opportunity, though in the presence of a more general plea for damage.

Some authors have improperly associated loss of opportunity with moral damage,[435] supposedly in view of the fact that the case law itself is not consistent, notwithstanding a pattern that may be assumed to have been largely accepted. Thus, even in older cases where it found exclusively breaches of different aspects of the right to a fair trial, and which serve as exemplification for subsequent rulings, the Court compensated the loss of opportunities *in addition* to moral harm.[436] It hesitated, though, to categorize it precisely. In fact, the notion of loss of opportunity is in between the two principal types of damage, because a victim

[432] *Megyeri v. Germany*, 12 May 1992, Series A no. 237-A, para. 30.

[433] See, e.g., *Weeks v. the United Kingdom* (Article 50), 5 October 1988, Series A no. 145-A, para. 13, and *Barberà, Messegué and Jabardo* (Article 50), note 76, para. 16.

[434] A. Garin, 'La perte de chance, un préjudice indemnisable: contribution à une problématique de l'indemnisation du dommage par la Cour européenne des droits de l'homme', in Flauss and Lambert Abdelgawad, note 104, at 172–8.

[435] Harris et al., note 30, at 860.

[436] See, e.g., *Goddi v. Italy*, 9 April 1984, Series A no. 76, para. 35; *Colozza v. Italy*, 12 February 1985, Series A no. 89, para. 38; *Bönisch v. Austria* (Article 50), 2 June 1986, Series A no. 103, para. 11; *Pélissier and Sassi v. France* [GC], no. 25444/94, ECHR 1999-II, para. 80; and *Dulaurans v. France*, no. 34553/97, 21 March 2000, para. 43. For a recent judgment, see *Sabeh El Leil*, note 84, para. 72.

loses both money and confidence, but the material aspect seems to be predominant in so far as that particular moral harm dissolves in the larger moral injury suffered as a result of the violation.

The Court has sometimes suggested that loss of chance would rather amount to financial prejudice, for example when the claimant sought pecuniary damage, but the judges awarded a sum in respect of loss of opportunity.[437] On occasion, the Court considered that the victim 'sustained a loss of opportunities and undeniable non-pecuniary damage'.[438] In other judgments, however, it was expressly included in pecuniary[439] or in non-pecuniary damage.[440]

Yet, in the presence of a widely accepted possibility to reopen proceedings as a result of a judgment from Strasbourg, both litigants and the Court may lose interest in the notion of loss of opportunity on account of unfair domestic proceedings. But is that approach confined to procedural violations, i.e., when the victim was denied the benefits of the guarantees of a fair trial? The answer is definitely in the negative. The Court has derived its existence from a series of breaches with clear monetary implications; for example, when it had been impossible for the applicants to participate in any scheme for the redevelopment of their properties[441] or to use property,[442] when the authorities unlawfully refused to honour their obligation to sell property at a special preferential price,[443] when the claimants lost alleged business opportunities[444] or the control of a company's activity.[445] Such cases are also illustrations of the claim for loss of opportunity being examined under the heading of pecuniary damage.

[437] For example, *De Geouffre de la Pradelle v. France*, 16 December 1992, Series A no. 253-B, para. 39.

[438] *Bellet v. France*, 4 December 1995, Series A no. 333-B, para. 43, and *F.E.*, note 82, para. 63.

[439] See, e.g., *Lechner and Hess*, note 68, para. 64; *Weeks* (Article 50), note 433, para. 13; and *Megyeri*, note 432, para. 30.

[440] See, e.g., *McMichael v. the United Kingdom*, 24 February 1995, Series A no. 307-B, paras. 101–3; *Kingsley*, note 357, paras. 36–44; and *Varnava*, note 157, para. 224.

[441] *Sporrong and Lönnroth v. Sweden* (Article 50), 18 December 1984, Series A no. 88, para. 25.

[442] *Guiso-Gallisay* (just satisfaction), note 366, para. 107.

[443] *Basarba OOD v. Bulgaria* (just satisfaction), no. 77660/01, 20 January 2011, paras. 21–2, and *Popnikolov v. Bulgaria* (just satisfaction), no. 30388/02, 11 October 2011, para. 9.

[444] *Gawęda v. Poland*, no. 26229/95, 14 March 2002, para. 54, and *Sildedzis v. Poland*, no. 45214/99, 24 May 2005, para. 58.

[445] *Sovtransavto Holding v. Ukraine* (just satisfaction), no. 48553/99, 2 October 2003, para. 72.

In sum, the theory of loss of opportunity is still a vague notion, and the Court has not shown a real interest in defining it, which has sometimes led to questionable results.[446] The practice, however, would seem to warrant the conclusion that such a loss is ultimately assimilated to material damage. In fact, the pecuniary consequences of a deprivation of a real chance appear to weigh more than any moral hardship occasioned by the same act. Given that an award for moral injury would logically be made for the entire non-pecuniary harm, it follows that the Court does not consider the loss of opportunity as a part of it when it examines that question separately. Moreover, loss of chance is no longer compensated predominantly in the context of the unfairness of the internal proceedings, but rather in connection with evident material harm. It is therefore laudable that the Court has judiciously adapted its approach and was disposed to assimilate the loss of opportunity to the sphere of pecuniary damage.

4.2 The Court's discretion in respect of reparation for non-pecuniary damage

4.2.1 Notion

Reparation for non-pecuniary damage has not always been admitted by national and international courts and tribunals, but was accepted only at the beginning of the twentieth century.[447] In *Lusitania*, Grotius's saying that 'money is the common measure of valuable things' was used as a ground for declaring that the appropriate remedy should be measured by pecuniary standards.[448] The principle was later codified by the ILC,[449] but with the distinction that reparation may consist in compensation or satisfaction, depending on whether that injury is financially assessable.

[446] See, e.g., Garin, note 434, at 175. The author gives the example of the judgment in *Traore v. France* (no. 48954/99, 17 December 2002), which concerned an excessive length of proceedings, where the Court on the one hand admitted the absence of a causal link between the violation found and the damage alleged, but on the other hand declared that the victim had suffered a loss of opportunity which justified an award of EUR 10,000 (para. 31).

[447] P. Dailler, M. Forteau and A. Pellet, *Droit international public* (Paris: LGDJ, 2009), at 881. The majority of authors consider *Lusitania* to be the first case in which it was admitted, but some assert that it had already been established a few years earlier: see C. Barthe-Gay, 'Réflexions sur la satisfaction en droit international', *Annuaire français de droit international* 49 (2003), footnote 38 at 114.

[448] *Lusitania*, note 409, at 35.

[449] Article 31(2) of the ILC Articles.

Certainly, the ILC Articles focus on the secondary rules of state responsibility, and therefore put the emphasis on the non-pecuniary prejudice experienced by a state. Some authors have aptly questioned that distinction in the general theory of international law in respect of the non-pecuniary damage suffered by an individual, which is always quantifiable in money, and that sustained by a state, which may not be at all times financially assessable, and in which case the remedy of 'satisfaction' would be appropriate.[450]

The European Convention, in virtue of its status as *lex specialis*, has departed from that dual approach. The system of reparation has not adopted the notion of 'satisfaction' for prejudice which is not financially assessable. As a rule, the Court makes a monetary estimation for all non-pecuniary damage, with the particularity that it may award a sum of money or declare that the finding of a violation constitutes in itself sufficient reparation. In the latter case, it is not that the nature of the prejudice is not financially assessable, but that the moral damage sustained is not considered to be so important as to warrant pecuniary reparation. In other words, the impact of the violation depends on its gravity and, according to the specific circumstances, it may or may not have generated a significant prejudice. It is a matter of degree. Moreover, Article 41 on just satisfaction does not make a distinction as to whether the victim is a state or an individual person.

Non-pecuniary damage is an open-ended notion. The spectrum of human emotions is so broad that it may not be exhaustively quantified. Each individual's condition and personality exert a great influence. The Court compensated moral prejudice for the first time in 1972, in *Ringeisen v. Austria*,[451] but has admitted the principle since its very first judgment on just satisfaction in the *Vagrancy* cases.[452] For the purpose of reparation, non-pecuniary injury generally refers to mental and physical trauma, such as severe physical pain, sorrow, anxiety, distress, anguish, humiliation, prolonged uncertainty, frustration or feelings of injustice. Hence, a case-by-case approach is best suited for assessing compensation in that respect.

The Court has admitted that not only natural persons, but also companies and other legal persons may suffer non-pecuniary damage. Obviously, it has a different specification and amplitude. The judges held in *Comingersoll* that the non-pecuniary prejudice affecting companies

[450] Barthe-Gay, note 447, at 114. [451] *Ringeisen* (Article 50), note 90, para. 26.
[452] *De Wilde, Ooms and Versyp* (Article 50), note 23, para. 24 *in fine*.

may be more or less subjective or objective, and would include adverse effects on the company's reputation, uncertainty in decision-planning, disruption to management and anxiety and inconvenience caused to the members of the management team.[453]

From a semantic point of view, the expression 'non-pecuniary damage' is generally used interchangeably with that of 'moral damage'. It may be that 'non-pecuniary' is deemed to better reflect the idea that physical harm may be added to moral prejudice.[454] Some authors further add a legal injury, but the Convention system has not adopted that view. However, even a bodily injury, such as that caused by torture or ill-treatment, translates into pain and suffering, which is a psychological response. The financial consequences, such as medical expenses, may be claimed as pecuniary damage. For example, in *Z and Others v. the United Kingdom*, the Grand Chamber declared that the neglect and abuse suffered by the four applicant children for four and a half years constituted inhuman and degrading treatment. It thus compensated the pecuniary damage for future psychotherapeutic care, as well as the non-pecuniary harm originating in the traumatic effects of the violation.[455]

Any breach of the rights and freedoms protected by the Convention may cause moral prejudice, but not all breaches cause physical harm. Moral damage is the predominant form of non-pecuniary injury, and even when an infringement has generated bodily harm, it is ultimately the moral reflection of damage that matters for that purpose. The French equivalent used by the Court is 'dommage moral'. It is not therefore conceptually wrong to use 'moral' instead of 'non-pecuniary', but from a rigidly correct perspective, the term 'non-pecuniary' is more inclusive and also better suited to the cases in which the victim is a state or legal person.

Claims for moral prejudice are often patently excessive, even if there are also cases when plaintiffs seek a symbolic award. A subjective perception of their personal hardship presumably makes victims exaggerate, all the more so because, unlike in the strict context of material loss, no documentary evidence is required. Given their indubitable

[453] *Comingersoll*, note 310, para. 35.

[454] For example, in the case of *Selmouni*, the Court concluded that 'the applicant [had] sustained personal injury in addition to non-pecuniary damage' (*Selmouni v. France* [GC], no. 25803/94, ECHR 1999-V, para. 123).

[455] *Z and Others*, note 417, paras. 124 and 130.

existence, such damages are considerably easier to grant, even when they are not quantified, albeit only in the presence of a causal link between the breach found and the alleged suffering. Assessment of claims is a matter of appreciation, and given its impressive caseload, the Court does not individualize the moral damage, such as in its early cases,[456] but has recourse to standard formulae such as '[h]aving regard to the violations found above, the Court considers that an award of compensation for non-pecuniary damage is justified in this case' or '[t]he Court considers that the applicant must have suffered distress and anxiety on account of the violations found'.

The Court confines redress for moral prejudice to either monetary or simply declaratory awards. It may allocate a sum or declare that its judgment stands for sufficient reparation of any non-pecuniary harm. In sharp contrast with that limitative approach, the Inter-American Court has further extended the possibility of redress for non-pecuniary damage to 'assignment of goods or services that can be assessed monetarily', and even to 'execution of acts or works of a public nature or repercussion, which have effects such as recovering the memory of the victims, re-establishing their reputation, consoling their next of kin or transmitting a message of official condemnation of the human rights violations in question and commitment to the efforts to ensure that they do not happen again'.[457]

Thus, in the presence of serious rights abuse, the Inter-American system provides for extra types of reparation, such as the wider measure of satisfaction, which includes orders to the state to perform well-publicized acts such as acknowledgment of responsibility or an official apology, as well as to publish and disseminate the judgment, to commemorate the victims or the events, to locate and identify the victims, to cover educational expenses or to make collective reparations in cases involving large-scale violations and massacres.[458] No comparable actions are permitted to the Strasbourg judges, the drafters of the Convention having opposed such activist powers. Even on a practical level, and in view of the number of violations found in Strasbourg, such a system of measures of satisfaction would hardly be workable in Europe. How many monuments or how many streets should Russia or Turkey

[456] See, e.g., *König* (Article 50), note 116, para. 19, and *Artico v. Italy*, 13 May 1980, Series A no. 37, para. 47.

[457] *Case of the 'Street Children'* (reparations and costs), note 29, para. 84 *in fine*.

[458] Pasqualucci, note 50, at 204–12.

build or name in order to commemorate the victims of Article 2 violations? Despite some views to the contrary,[459] the replication of the Inter-American model is open to reasonable doubt.

4.2.2 *Method of calculation*

Redress for non-pecuniary damage is the field in which the Court has the largest room for discretion. That may nonetheless be accepted, because it is incontestable that the very nature of such harm does not allow for accurate calculations. Hence, the estimation is highly subjective. In general, courts and tribunals, whether national or international, naturally make use of subjective appreciation when compensating moral injury, deriving assessment from the principle of equity. In the same way, the Strasbourg Court decides an amount on an equitable basis, using the discretion conferred by Article 41, but nonetheless taking into account its previous awards. The problem is that in some cases the judges use standards of compensation for moral damage which are not revealed to the public.

It is no longer a secret – some judges and registras have clearly admitted – that the Court resorts to specific tables with different pecuniary rates for groups of countries in respect of some repetitive violations, such as those regarding the excessive length of municipal proceedings.[460] The Grand Chamber itself declared in that specific field that it has established 'scales on equitable principles for awards in respect of non-pecuniary damage under Article 41, in order to arrive at equivalent results in similar cases'.[461] That statement is quite important, as it clearly indicates that in applying those standards, the subjective and hypothetical element of the

[459] See, e.g., T. M. Antkowiak, 'An Emerging Mandate for International Courts: Victim-Centered Remedies and Restorative Justice', *Stanford Journal of International Law* 47 (2011).

[460] Costa, note 324, at 9 (J.-P. Costa was judge at the Court from 1998 to 2011 and President of the Court from 2007 to 2011); Harris et al., note 30, at 819 (M. O'Boyle, one of the authors, is the Court's Deputy Registrar); and E. Myjer and P. Kempees, 'Notes on Reparations under the European Human Rights System', *Inter-American and European Human Rights Journal* 2, nos. 1–2 (2009), at 91 (E. Myjer was judge at the Court from 2004 to 2012 and P. Kempees is the Head of the Just Satisfaction Division of the Registry of the Court). Also see G. Cohen-Jonathan and J.-F. Flauss, 'Cour européenne des droits de l'homme et droit international général', *Annuaire français de droit international* 48 (2002), footnote 57 at 692, and H. Keller, M. Forowicz and L. Engi, *Friendly Settlements before the European Court of Human Rights: Theory and Practice* (Oxford University Press, 2010), at 78.

[461] *Scordino*, note 372, para. 176.

moral prejudice was attenuated by an objective approach. The initiative is commendable in so far as it is more in line with the definition given to equity by the International Court of Justice in the *Continental Shelf* case, that 'its application should display consistency and a degree of predictability'.[462]

However, while the judges do indeed seem concerned with the consistency of the case law, they evade any further explanation for their lack of transparency. Implementation of a standardized approach to value moral harm is laudable, even if it has a limited application for the moment; what is regrettable is that the Court refuses to make public those criteria and methods of calculation, preferring instead to use them at its discretion. Even a recent high-level conference on the future of the Court, organized by the Committee of Ministers, has invited the judges to '[e]stablish and make public rules foreseeable for all the parties concerning the application of Article 41 of the Convention, including the level of just satisfaction which might be expected in different circumstances'.[463] For the time being, the levels of compensation may only be deduced with some degree of approximation by comparing them with awards in similar cases brought against the same state in a certain period of time.

It would be simplistic to believe that a one-size-fits-all standard of reparation for moral harm is workable, even when emerging from comparable situations. The Court has therefore adopted a flexible approach, and the practice denotes certain criteria. The elements taken into account when calculating the compensation for non-pecuniary injury pertain to the nature of the right protected by the Convention, to the gravity of the violation and to the victim's personality, and evidently the judges will award a higher sum in the presence of several breaches or even the full amount sought by the plaintiff.[464] They may also allocate a lower amount than usual when the complainant has already obtained a finding of a violation at domestic level and compensation by using a domestic remedy.[465]

On the one hand, the Court has often justified awards on the basis of the effects of state interference, either referring to the seriousness of a

[462] *North Sea Continental Shelf*, note 146, para. 88.

[463] Point F.2(d) of the Izmir Declaration of 27 April 2011, available on the Court's website (www.echr.coe.int/Pages/home.aspx?p=court/reform&c=).

[464] See, e.g., *Imakayeva*, note 414, paras. 214–16.

[465] *Ernestina Zullo v. Italy* [GC], no. 64897/01, 29 March 2006, para. 141.

violation, especially when the right to life or corporeal integrity was affected,[466] or merely considering that the victim has undeniably suffered non-pecuniary damage.[467] Even when not claimed, the judges have made exceptional awards based on 'the fundamental importance' of the rights guaranteed, in cases where they found violations of the right to life,[468] of the right not to be subjected to inhuman[469] or degrading[470] treatment, or of the procedural aspect of that right,[471] as well as of the applicant's right to liberty.[472] Such fairly recent and rather unexpected humane impulses on the part of the Court, however welcome they would be to some, have no legal basis. It is striking that the majority of those rulings were delivered against Russia; it may denote a target-oriented approach against the greatest violator of the Convention. Conceptually though, the Court should refrain from ruling *ultra petita*, because the provisions of the treaty must be applied equally to all petitioners. *In casu*, the judges have not exercised their normal discretion in assessing the amount of compensation, but have rather disregarded the objective conditions for having access to the European system of reparation.

On the other hand, the applicant's personal condition may further contribute towards increasing the amount. Such is the case when victims are children, when the judges may deem it appropriate to make a 'substantial award'.[473] There were even a few exceptions, when the victim's demeanour was perceived as immoral and thus not justifying reparation, which may nonetheless denote a punitive character for the

[466] See, e.g., *Selmouni*, note 454, para. 123, and *Jasinskis v. Latvia*, no. 45744/08, 21 December 2010, para. 88.

[467] See, e.g., *Hunt v. Ukraine*, no. 31111/04, 7 December 2006, para. 70, and *Ashot Harutyunyan v. Armenia*, no. 34334/04, 15 June 2010, para. 155.

[468] See, among others, *Kats and Others v. Ukraine*, no. 29971/04, 18 December 2008, para. 149.

[469] See, e.g., *Igor Ivanov v. Russia*, no. 34000/02, 7 June 2007, paras. 48–50; *Chember*, note 274, paras. 76–7; *Vladimir Fedorov v. Russia*, no. 19223/04, 30 July 2009, paras. 86–7; *Dorogaykin v. Russia*, no. 1066/05, 10 February 2011, paras. 48–9; and *Chudun v. Russia*, no. 20641/04, 21 June 2011, paras. 128–9.

[470] See, e.g., *Mayzit v. Russia*, no. 63378/00, 20 January 2005, paras. 87–8; *Babushkin v. Russia*, no. 67253/01, 18 October 2007, paras. 61–2; and *Nadrosov v. Russia*, no. 9297/02, 31 July 2008, paras. 53–4.

[471] See, e.g., *Denisenko and Bogdanchikov v. Russia*, no. 3811/02, 12 February 2009, paras. 141–2; *Alibekov v. Russia*, no. 8413/02, 14 May 2009, paras. 72–3; and *Maksimov v. Russia*, no. 43233/02, 18 March 2010, paras. 97–8.

[472] See, e.g., *Rusu v. Austria*, no. 34082/02, 2 October 2008, para. 62; *Khudyakova v. Russia*, no. 13476/04, 8 January 2009, paras. 106–7; and *Crabtree v. the Czech Republic*, no. 41116/04, 25 February 2010, para. 60.

[473] *Z and Others*, note 417, para. 130.

plaintiff.[474] Attributes of the victim's personality may indeed be taken into account in order to adjust the amount of compensation, but should be left outside the decisional process when establishing whether a petitioner is entitled to reparation. As rightly noted, damage should be based on the objective nature of the breach, the personal condition being merely a complementary element.[475]

The judges have further developed specific rules, but only for a limited type of repetitive violations. The most common illustration is the breach of the reasonable time requirement for the length of domestic proceedings. The Court has established a set of criteria to decide if the duration is excessive. While those standards have been specifically developed for the examination of the merits of a dispute, they will definitely influence an award for reparation. The Court will first determine the period in question and the levels of jurisdiction, and occasionally the number of courts which examined the case. In cases in which litigation had started before the ratification of the Convention by the contracting party, the judges will take into account the state of proceedings when deciding the reasonableness of the time that elapsed after that date.[476] The assessment will be based on the circumstances of the case, taking into account its complexity, the conduct of the applicant and of the relevant authorities, as well as what was at stake for the victim.[477] In addition, a plurality of plaintiffs before the Court may influence the award of just satisfaction.[478]

The Court may further consider the nature of the internal dispute, whether the proceedings are civil or criminal. As would be expected, the evaluation of a delay is stricter when the authorities have left the victim in excessive uncertainty pending criminal accusations, including during the phase of pre-trial investigations. However, the Court will not regard the internal litigation as 'criminal' when the complainant acted as a party claiming damages in criminal proceedings. Then the judges examine the procedural failures, observing the complexity of each case, in order to

474 See below, Subsection 4.4.4.2 of the present chapter.

475 Tomuschat, note 266, at 1426.

476 See, among many others, *Baglay v. Ukraine*, no. 22431/02, 8 November 2005, para. 27, and *Kozlica v. Croatia*, no. 29182/03, 2 November 2006, para. 16.

477 The cases usually cited by the Court when mentioning those principles, and depending on the civil or criminal character of the internal proceedings, are *Frydlender v. France* ([GC], no. 30979/96, ECHR 2000-VII, para. 43) and *Pélissier and Sassi* (note 436, para. 67), respectively.

478 See, in particular, *Arvanitaki-Roboti and Others v. Greece* [GC], no. 27278/03, 15 February 2008, paras. 27–36, and *Kakamoukas and Others v. Greece* [GC], no. 38311/02, 15 February 2008, paras. 39–48.

decide whether the plaintiff or the municipal courts were responsible for protraction. They may find relevant the periods of court inactivity, whether judgments had been quashed by higher courts as a result of errors committed by lower courts or whether the case was progressing, the number of hearings and amount of evidence produced, or the failure to summon different parties in the proceedings.[479]

The specific type of dispute is another important factor when determining whether the duration is or is not unreasonable, and ultimately for securing reparation. Particular diligence on the part of the domestic courts is due when the applicants have been affected by an incurable disease which will reduce their life expectancy,[480] when their health is quickly deteriorating,[481] for disputes related to compensation for damage to health[482] or for illegal detention,[483] when the victims are kept in detention pending the determination of a criminal charge against them,[484] for disputes in respect of family rights,[485] as well as for those concerning civil status and capacity or employment disputes.[486] Accordingly, the Court found that a length of three years and almost five months was excessive not only in the circumstances of litigation for compensation for physical injury caused by a car accident which involved the applicant, a five-year-old child, who suffered total paralysis of her lower limbs,[487] but also for a dispute regarding payment of arrears of an old-age pension, which constituted the principal source of income for the plaintiff.[488]

A practical illustration of the calculation method has been offered even by the Court. In the Chamber judgment in *Apicella v. Italy*, which has been subsequently endorsed by the Grand Chamber, the judges

[479] See, among others, *Ciută v. Romania*, no. 35527/04, 18 May 2010, paras. 28–30.

[480] See, e.g., *X v. France*, note 286, para. 47, and *Vallée v. France*, 26 April 1994, Series A no. 289-A, para. 47.

[481] *Nichitaylov v. Ukraine*, no. 36024/03, 15 October 2009, para. 39.

[482] See, e.g., *Marchenko v. Russia*, no. 29510/04, 5 October 2006, para. 40, and *Păunoiu v. Romania*, no. 32700/04, 16 September 2008, para. 27.

[483] See, e.g., *Marinică Tițian Popovici v. Romania*, no. 34071/06, 27 October 2009, para. 27.

[484] See, e.g., *Abdoella v. the Netherlands*, 25 November 1992, Series A no. 248-A, para. 24, and *Smirnova v. Russia*, nos. 46133/99 and 48183/99, ECHR 2003-IX, para. 83.

[485] See, e.g., *Lubina v. Slovakia*, no. 77688/01, 19 September 2006, para. 56.

[486] See, e.g., *Bock v. Germany*, 29 March 1989, Series A no. 150, para. 49, and *Ruotolo v. Italy*, 27 February 1992, Series A no. 230-D, para. 17.

[487] *Gheorghe and Maria Mihaela Dumitrescu v. Romania*, no. 6373/03, 29 July 2008.

[488] *Lelik v. Russia*, no. 20441/02, 3 June 2010.

indicated some criteria used for assessment of non-pecuniary damage sustained as a result of the length of proceedings. Thus, they take as a reference point a sum of between EUR 1,000 and EUR 1,500 for each year's duration of the whole proceedings, and they increase it by EUR 2,000 when what was at stake was particularly important, or decrease it if the victim has already received some compensation or in accordance with the number of courts dealing with the case, the applicant's conduct and the object of the internal dispute, as well as with the standard of living in the country concerned.[489] The merit of that approach is that it highlights that the judges indeed use a standardized method for establishing an amount. But while accepting that it has revealed some practical information, it seems that its value is limited. While the Court has clearly mentioned the amount by which a sum may be increased, it has provided more reasons for decreasing that sum but no further detail as to the extent.

In conclusion, the judges have offered an appearance of transparency, but in fact they continue to keep full discretion as to compensation, because in practice there are more circumstances that may justify a decrease than an increase. In the context of the unceasing number of repetitive cases coming to Strasbourg, it would be worth making an effort to fix the amounts by which a sum may be reduced as a result of a fault by a victim in the protraction of the delay. In addition, the approach should be adapted for the other groups of violations, because the classification in repetitive cases is not limited to the banal categories of length of proceedings or non-enforcement of domestic judgments, but practically includes a larger class of violations which follow a certain pattern, such as conditions of detention, or more country-specific breaches such as lack of investigation in unlawful killings or expropriation of property in Turkey or torture and ill-treatment in Russia. A standardized framework of compensation would generally prevent the Strasbourg judges from exercising their power to make reparation in a discretionary way.

4.2.3 *Monetary awards*

Financial awards vary not only in accordance with the different types of violation, but also within the same category and between different countries. In assessing the amount, the Court has admitted that it may derive some assistance from domestic practices, while not being bound by them.[490] It

[489] *Apicella v. Italy*, no. 64890/01, 10 November 2004, para. 26.
[490] *Z v. Finland*, 25 February 1997, *Reports of Judgments and Decisions* 1997-I, para. 122.

normally takes into account its own case law, although it has sometimes been criticized by its own judges for inexplicably failing to do that.[491] In any event, it does not offer interest on the sum allocated for non-pecuniary prejudice, as is the case with other international courts and tribunals, for example the International Tribunal for the Law of the Sea.[492]

The aim of this section is not to provide numbers, but to assess the Court's approach and to find out whether there is consistency in the legal reasoning, and thus to determine whether the system may offer effective reparation or if it is rather discretionary. In doing so, reference will be made to recent practice, which is relevant in so far as the Court may have adjusted its awards in light of the current global economic crisis. It may be worth speculating that for each type of violation the judges use a reference sum, which they increase or decrease according to circumstances. It should be logical to operate with round sums, such as EUR 15,000 or EUR 20,000. However, by allocating to victims amounts such as EUR 4,900,[493] EUR 5,850,[494] EUR 6,250[495] or EUR 9,750[496] without any explanation whatsoever, it unfortunately denotes that the Court has recently transformed into what Judge Cançado Trindade warned against, that is, a calculating machine.[497]

It is even possible that the Court uses a computer program to fix compensation and then exploits those figures, sometimes without at least adjusting them in equity. As argued in this study, standardization is good, but only as long as it is based on the application of some equitable criteria. It should not be confined to an exclusively mechanical calculation, devoid of any implication of the human factor, as should also be the case with obvious discrepancies in a given category of violations in the absence of any supporting argument.[498]

[491] Partly dissenting opinion of Judge Zagrebelsky joined by Judge Sajó in *Eryılmaz v. Turkey*, no. 32322/02, 27 October 2009.

[492] *M/V 'Saiga' (No. 2)*, note 403, para. 173.

[493] *Budaca v. Romania*, no. 57260/10, 17 July 2012, para. 55.

[494] *Soltész v. Slovakia*, no. 11867/09, 22 October 2013, para. 67.

[495] *Ivakhnenko v. Russia*, no. 12622/04, 4 April 2013, para. 56.

[496] *Ferhat Kaya v. Turkey*, no. 12673/05, 25 September 2012, para. 51; *Salih Salman Kılıç v. Turkey*, no. 22077/10, 5 March 2013, para. 36; and *Mimtaş v. Turkey*, no. 23698/07, 19 March 2013, para. 65.

[497] Para. 37 of the separate opinion of Judge Cançado Trindade in the *Case of the 'Street Children'*, note 29.

[498] In Annex 3, compare the sum claimed and awarded in full, without any explanation, in *Van der Velden v. the Netherlands* (no. 21203/10, 31 July 2012), with the other amounts normally allocated for Article 5 violations.

Even in the past some authors revealed inconsistencies in the case law.[499] Unfortunately, such situations still persist. They stand as evidence for the Court's wide discretion. It is therefore appropriate to provide some selective examples. They are supported with an annex of selected cases in respect of compensation awarded for non-pecuniary prejudice when different violations have been found. The purpose of those examples is to demonstrate that in the absence of a theory, the practice lacks coherence.

4.2.3.1 Deprivation of life

The right to life provided in Article 2 is incontestably the most important human right. The Convention avoids categorization of the rights, but it admits that implicitly because it is the first right in the list. Indeed, the rights are listed according to their importance even if, again, officially there should be no hierarchy.[500] The Court itself has admitted the gravity of the interference with the right to life, and that is further reflected in the level of compensation. However, there are some exceptions, inexplicable at least for an outsider, where the judges have awarded comparable sums for the moral prejudice suffered as a result of deprivation of property or where they have even considered that the finding of a violation of the right to life was sufficient. Such unfortunate deviations denote a distortion of the whole idea of human rights.

The majority of violations under Article 2 are found in respect of Turkey and Russia. According to Annex 1, the highest awards are given for the substantive aspect of the right, that is, when the state is responsible for the victim's death or disappearance. As expected, the substantive element is normally accompanied by the procedural one, namely the lack of effective investigation. The median sum is around EUR 20,000–30,000, but may vary depending on the number of violations and complainants, how many relatives were found dead, and also on the kinship tie. *In concreto*, in a case in which a plaintiff had lost her husband, the Court awarded her EUR 60,000 for moral harm,[501] although in a case in which three applicants had denounced the death

[499] E.g. J.-F. Flauss, 'La réparation due en cas de violation de la Convention européenne des droits de l'homme', *Journal des Tribunaux* 4, no. 25 (1996), at 14.

[500] For example, the 1993 Vienna Declaration and Programme of Action (adopted 25 June 1993, UN Doc. A/CONF.157/23) stated that '[t]he international community must treat human rights globally in a fair and equal manner, on the same footing, and with the same emphasis': see para. 5 of Part I.

[501] *Ghimp and Others v. Moldova*, no. 32520/09, 30 October 2012.

of their father and husband, they received only EUR 50,000 jointly.[502] Normally, when both substantive and procedural aspects of a violation are at stake, compensation is higher.

When only the procedural limb of Article 2 has been disregarded – in other words, the authorities have failed to conduct an effective investigation into the circumstances of a victim's death – the sums awarded are relatively lower and, exceptionally, the Court may even consider that the finding of a violation is sufficient.[503] It appears from Annex 1 that the reference amount is under EUR 20,000. The judges adapt that standard to the circumstances of each case, although they do not reveal the criteria upon which they have based the increase or decrease of the reference amount. In the absence of a clear set of equitable principles, the use of standards cannot eliminate the wide discretion, and eventually interferes with the consistency of the case law. Thus, when shortcomings have been found in two separate investigations conducted in the same state, it may be difficult to understand why, for example, the parents denouncing the investigation into their son's death received jointly half of the amount awarded to an applicant complaining about the investigation into his brother's death.[504]

4.2.3.2 Torture or inhuman or degrading treatment and deprivation of liberty

Article 3 prohibits torture and inhuman or degrading treatment or punishment. Breach of that article, similarly to Article 2, can also take the form of a substantive and/or procedural violation, but the compensation for moral prejudice is significantly lower than for loss of life. It depends on whether the state has been found in violation of both the substantive and procedural aspects or was only responsible for the absence of an effective investigation. The most serious interference in that category is undoubtedly torture.

Lately, there has been an increase in cases referring to inappropriate conditions of detention, but the compensation for the moral harm is quite low, frequently under EUR 10,000. It may vary greatly, even in

[502] *Dimov and Others v. Bulgaria*, no. 30086/05, 6 November 2012.

[503] See, e.g., *Pleşca v. Romania*, no. 2158/08, 18 June 2013.

[504] Compare *Prynda v. Ukraine*, no. 10904/05, 31 July 2012, where the two applicants received jointly EUR 6,000, with *Yuriy Slyusar v. Ukraine*, no. 39797/05, 17 January 2013, where the applicant received EUR 12,000.

respect of the same country at a certain moment.[505] Slightly higher amounts are given when the plaintiff has suffered ill-treatment by state agents. Here again, it is not possible to discern an objective pattern. The sums vary according to the victim's condition and intensity of the treatment. The Court may also declare that the finding of a violation constitutes in itself sufficient reparation. Such is the case when there are substantial grounds for believing that the applicant, if deported, would be exposed to a real risk of treatment contrary to Article 3.

The Court may allocate in full the claimed amount if it is reasonable as to quantum, even if it is higher than that usually granted in similar cases. It is a matter of discretion which may also reveal a lack of harmonization between the Court's different Sections. As an illustration taken from Annex 2, the Third Section accepted a claim for EUR 20,000 for a procedural violation of Article 3,[506] while the practice for this type of violation is to award an amount below EUR 10,000. By contrast, in the same one-month period, to victims who had sought EUR 10,000 in a case of excessive use of force by the police, the Second Section awarded EUR 7,500,[507] yet only EUR 5,000 to victims who had claimed EUR 10,000 for both a substantive and a procedural violation of Article 3.[508]

Article 5 consecrates the right to liberty and security of person. Deprivations in that respect are common in all countries, and usually take the form of arbitrary detention or deficient procedural guarantees. Given that normally the physical integrity of the victim is not affected, the moral harm is perceived as being less important than under Article 3. Yet, it is difficult to assess the exact sum assigned by the judges to an Article 5 violation because, generally, such cases denote several breaches and the award is made in respect of the whole injury.

The cases selected in Annex 3 disclose the extent to which awards may vary even when made in respect of victims complaining against the same state. A good illustration is provided by the cases against Russia in respect of detention pending extradition, where all efforts to anticipate the awards for unlawful detention or for lack of a speedy review would probably prove futile. It is thus commendable that there are still examples in which the Court has given reasons to justify a different treatment

505 Annex 2 shows that the redress granted by the Court in June–July 2012 in respect of conditions of detention in Romania fluctuated from EUR 3,000 to EUR 20,000.

506 *Otamendi Egiguren v. Spain*, no. 47303/08, 16 October 2012.

507 *İşeri and Others v. Turkey*, no. 29283/07, 9 October 2012.

508 *Réti and Fizli v. Hungary*, no. 31373/11, 25 September 2012.

of comparable cases with respect to redress. In *Stokłosa v. Poland*, even if it found that a national assessor had not been independent of the executive – as it had also established previously in *Mirosław Garlicki v. Poland* – the Court declared that the finding of a violation was sufficient, as opposed to the other case, in which EUR 6,000 had been awarded, because there were no suspicions that the assessor could have been taking an interest in the proceedings against the applicant.[509] Such a practice should definitely be encouraged.

4.2.3.3 Fair trial

By and large, length-of-proceedings and non-enforcement disputes are normally brought under the Article 6 heading of a right to a fair trial. The compensation awarded is fairly comparable for the two categories. It is important to note that cases denouncing non-execution of domestic judgments, in so far as they relate to possessions, have a material component which will certainly increase the total reparation.

As far as delays in domestic proceedings are concerned, cases where the Court has found a violation when the duration was less than four years are fairly rare. There are nonetheless exceptions, which take into account the type of proceedings and the victim's personal situation. The *Apicella* example mentioned above reveals the method of calculation. The judges take an objective reference amount and then adjust it to the specific circumstances. The approach seems reasonable, although it still confers a broad discretion, but at least there is a starting point in further developing the concrete assessment and then expanding it to other violations.

However, the lack of transparency in the application of the *Apicella* formula may give rise to inconsistencies, as is evident in Annex 4, especially when comparing the cases of *Bodnár v. Hungary*[510] and *Çelikalp v. Turkey*.[511] The cases were brought against states with a comparable level of economic development, they both concerned civil proceedings and were both considered at two levels of domestic jurisdiction. But in the absence of any reasoning, it is difficult to understand the logic in giving, for a period of some fourteen and a half years, a slightly higher amount than for one of more than twenty years; all the

[509] *Stokłosa v. Poland*, no. 32602/08, 3 November 2011, para. 38, which referred to *Mirosław Garlicki v. Poland*, no. 36921/07, 14 June 2011, para. 154.

[510] *Bodnár v. Hungary*, no. 46206/07, 15 November 2012.

[511] *Çelikalp v. Turkey*, no. 51259/07, 18 December 2012.

more so because in the latter case the proceedings were also pending for some nine years before ratification of the Convention. The problem is that, besides mentioning the exact length of proceedings, the Court finds a violation on the basis of the all-encompassing formula of 'its case law on the subject', with no further explanation when making an award. It is sometimes difficult to deny that the latest judgments suffer from an argumentative simplicity and seem to encourage a copy/paste drafting policy.

As far as disputes in respect of non-execution are concerned, the Court seemingly applies the same method of calculation, depending on the number of years until the effective execution. The judges should take into account that any execution mechanism needs a grace period to be able to secure enforcement. In addition, one may wonder if what is at stake in non-enforcement cases is not more important than an excessive length of proceedings. In the final analysis, a victim would be more affected by a realization that justice is ineffective.

What is completely striking, though, is that in some cases it takes more time for the Court itself to decide on an application than the period taken by the domestic courts to end a set of proceedings that it finds *in casu* to be unreasonable. As rightly noted by one of the Court's judges, it took the former Commission and the Court almost four years in *Zimmermann and Steiner v. Switzerland* to conclude that a term of nearly three and a half years at national level amounted to a breach of the reasonable time requirement.[512]

4.2.3.4 Private and family rights, and personal freedoms

In the Article 8 area, similarly to the context of the cases where extradition would expose the plaintiff to inhuman or degrading treatment, the Court has also admitted that expulsion may have adverse effects on the applicant's family rights. Even if the state had not yet performed the illegal activity, the judges have aptly considered that the very menace posed by the prospects of taking official action occasioned a moral prejudice. The level of compensation is fairly similar to that applied to redress for a violation already performed.[513] Such an approach may be

[512] Dissenting opinion of Judge Myjer in *Gheorghe and Maria Mihaela Dumitrescu*, note 487.

[513] See, e.g., EUR 9,000 in *Alim v. Russia*, no. 39417/07, 27 September 2011.

accepted, because comparable stress and anxiety in respect of family relations is produced not only by the perpetration, but also by the indubitable likelihood of execution of an order given by authorities in that sense.

The higher awards in this category are made in respect of breaches affecting the relations between family members, in particular when they interfere with the right of access to a child. In that sense, the consequences of the violation are decisive. Thus, on the one hand, the judges awarded EUR 20,000 when the authorities' passivity caused the severance of the relationship between a child and her father, in the context that the former's grandparents had refused to return the child to her father after the death of the applicant's wife.[514] On the other hand, in a case where at the end of a holiday the applicant's wife refused to return to her home country and placed her daughter in a location unknown to her husband, the Court held the authorities responsible for not taking adequate measures aimed at enforcing the complainant's right to the return of his daughter, but awarded only EUR 7,000 for non-pecuniary injury.[515] In the absence of any explanation, one may reasonably question the logic of the Court in those two cases and wonder what had justified such a discrepancy between the two awards. In any event, Annex 5 shows that, except for cases where the authorities may be held responsible for preventing family reunification, awards are often under EUR 10,000. The lowest amounts are usually allocated for interferences with the right to correspondence.

The three personal freedoms listed in the treaty are the freedom of thought, conscience and religion, the freedom of expression, and the freedom of assembly and association. They may sometimes be connected, in the sense that, for example, the freedom of religion may also imply a freedom of assembly. As to the compensation received for the moral harm caused by an interference with personal freedoms, a comparison between Annexes 5 and 6 reveals a slightly lower level. There is no rare occurrence when the Court has declared that the finding of a violation offers sufficient redress. According to the examples provided in Annex 6, the reference amount seems to be EUR 5,000, which is then adjusted so as to reflect the personal aspect of a breach of those freedoms.

[514] *Amanalachioai v. Romania*, no. 4023/04, 26 May 2009.
[515] *Stochlak v. Poland*, no. 38273/02, 22 September 2009.

4.2.3.5 Protection of property

Protection of property is a right where the pecuniary aspect prevails. In contrast to the mainly personal rights guaranteed in the treaty, the right to peaceful enjoyment of property revolves around material interests and has been included in a separate protocol to the Convention. The Court requires relevant evidence for the assessment of the financial damage incurred as a result of an alleged interference. Nevertheless, the prejudice suffered cannot be of an exclusively pecuniary nature. Even if not linked to personal attributes, a violation does cause moral harm, but given its inherent material connotations, the compensation for non-pecuniary damage is generally at the lowest level when compared with other violations.

However, some awards in similar cases may be difficult for an outsider to explain. Annex 7 shows that the cases of *Pascucci*[516] and *Giannitto*[517] were brought against the same contracting party and both concerned a constructive expropriation by the Italian state. They were decided in a two-week interval by the same judges, who based their finding of a violation on the same reasons. Yet, for the moral suffering, the former applicant received twice as much compensation as the latter. No reasoning was provided by the judges that would allow the reader to discern the basis for that different treatment. A decisive influence may have been the fact that, before the Court, the former applicant also secured compensation for pecuniary damage, while the latter had already received appropriate compensation at the internal level.

Now the question may arise: should the moral harm sustained be considered as directly proportional to the value of the material damage? While a victim would certainly suffer greater frustration when deprived of a higher value, it is questionable whether the compensation offered can be at the same level as that afforded for ill-treatment or restriction of personal freedom. And yet, such was the case, for instance, with the *Guiso-Gallisay* case, where the three applicants received jointly a total sum of EUR 45,000 corresponding to the moral harm sustained in relation to deprivation of a property compensated by the Court with EUR 2,100,000.[518] It may be speculated that the Court, given that

[516] *Pascucci v. Italy*, no. 1537/04, 14 January 2014.
[517] *Giannitto v. Italy*, no. 1780/04, 28 January 2014.
[518] *Guiso-Gallisay* (just satisfaction), note 366, paras. 106–10.

plaintiffs usually find it impossible to provide evidence as to the loss of benefit or other profit, includes that loss, to a certain extent, in the moral damage.

4.2.4 Declaratory judgments

In *Golder v. the United Kingdom*, where they found a violation of the applicant's right of access to a court and respect for correspondence, the judges initiated a long and controversial practice of declarations to the effect that the circumstances of a case may not justify any reparation other than that offered by the simple finding of a violation.[519] In one of their early rulings, they defined such a remedy as moral satisfaction.[520] It is not a situation in which the Court considers that no award should be made, but one in which it admits the necessity of redress and assumes that the judicial recognition of the infringement offers sufficient reparation.[521] For that reason, when it is the victims themselves who declare that a finding of a violation would in itself provide sufficient just satisfaction, the Court does not make any award.[522]

The method has been contested from the beginning, even by the Court's judges, on the grounds that it would be 'difficult to accept the proposition that the finding by the Court of a breach of the substantive provisions of the Convention, whilst constituting a condition for the application of Article 50, can at the same time be the consequence in law following from that same provision'.[523] The present section will therefore analyse the application *in concreto* of the principle in order to reach a conclusion on the propriety of such an approach for a human rights system of reparation.

[519] *Golder v. the United Kingdom*, 21 February 1975, Series A no. 18, para. 46 *in fine*.

[520] *Deweer*, note 355, para. 60.

[521] As rightly emphasized, in that respect, the Court's judges and Registry lawyers have sometimes confused matters in so far as the reasoning of a judgment rejects the claim for damage, but then the operative part declares that the finding of a violation represents in itself sufficient reparation for moral damage: see S. Touzé, 'Les limites de l'indemnisation devant la Cour européenne des droits de l'homme: le constat de violation comme satisfaction equitable suffisante', in Flauss and Lambert Abdelgawad, note 104, footnote 16 at 132.

[522] *A.A. v. the United Kingdom*, no. 8000/08, 20 September 2011, para. 75.

[523] Separate opinion of Judges Ganshof van der Meersch and Evrigenis in *Engel and Others v. the Netherlands* (Article 50), 23 November 1976, Series A no. 22.

4.2.4.1 Present practice

The ILC Articles mention acknowledgment of the breach by the wrongdoing state as an example of satisfaction in international law for injury which is not financially assessable. While the second paragraph of Article 37 does not refer to a judicial act of recognition emanating from a court or tribunal, the reason was simply because the Articles are not concerned with the primary rules of responsibility, i.e., which authority has jurisdiction over a dispute.[524] Accordingly, the International Court of Justice accepted in *Corfu Channel* the capacity of a declaration of wrongfulness to provide by itself appropriate satisfaction.[525]

While the Convention system has not included 'satisfaction' as a form of reparation, it has nonetheless admitted that the Court's judgments may procure a declaratory relief per se. In so far as that approach is supported by general international law, it has legal justification. It is used only as a remedy for non-pecuniary prejudice, not for material damage.[526] The Inter-American Court also upheld the compensatory role of a judgment,[527] but certainly not in situations of extreme gravity.[528] So, may that remedy be adapted to all types of violations?

In *Golder*, the victim did not even seek compensation. The Court raised the question on its own motion. Leaving aside the fact that the judges overruled the principle that reparation is given only when expressly claimed, they have certainly perceived a minimum level of prejudice. However, even when the plaintiff sought a symbolic award of one Belgian franc, the judges simply perceived that claim as deserving no more than judicial recognition.[529] Once initiated, the Court started to apply the formula to relatively simple cases, such as when a hearing was not public[530] or when the number of letters stopped or delayed by the authorities, in violation of the applicants' right of respect for correspondence, was very small compared with the number of letters which

[524] Crawford, note 43, at 233. [525] *Corfu Channel*, note 47, at 35.

[526] Normally it is used in cases where the violation was of little significance, where the victim had the possibility of obtaining redress at the internal level, where the national authorities clearly expressed the will to change the legislation or practice that had provoked the violation or where the victim had the possibility of requesting the reopening of the domestic proceedings: see para. 8 of the partly dissenting opinion of Judges Spielmann and Malinverni in *Prežec v. Croatia*, no. 48185/07, 15 October 2009.

[527] See, e.g., *Acosta-Calderón* (merits, reparations and costs), note 58, para. 159.

[528] See, e.g., *El Amparo* (reparations and costs), note 420, para. 35.

[529] *Marckx*, note 111, para. 68.

[530] *Engel* (Article 50), note 523, para. 11 *in fine*, and *Le Compte, Van Leuven and De Meyere v. Belgium* (Article 50), 18 October 1982, Series A no. 54, para. 16.

they were allowed to send.[531] Progressively though, it has extended it to encompass several different situations. The Grand Chamber has recently declared that '[i]n many cases where a law, procedure or practice has been found to fall short of Convention standards this is enough to put matters right'.[532]

Therefore, the Court's judgment constitutes in itself just satisfaction when damage appears to be minimal, as in the case of procedural violations under Articles 5 and 6. Such a remedy would normally not be appropriate for serious violations such as those of the right to life or torture and ill-treatment. Given that the victim does not receive any tangible reparation, those rulings have only a pedagogical role, the respondent state being nonetheless bound to execute them. For instance, following the judgment in *Golder*, the government took administrative action and proposed legal amendments.[533]

But would it be impossible to establish some further criteria for the application of that principle? It may be assumed that the first step has been the introduction of the admissibility condition of a significant disadvantage. The recurrent practice of declaratory awards seems to have provided a pertinent reason for not even examining such complaints. The approach may nonetheless be criticized, because it offers more discretionary power to the Court in deciding what human rights breaches deserve its attention.

The judges should objectively individualize the types of breaches when the moral prejudice may be reasonably assumed to be of minor importance, such as the publicity of the hearings or the public pronouncement of a judgment. An objective identification of those categories has the advantage that it does not discriminate among victims. Certainly, in the specific circumstances of execution, the same kind of violation may generate either more serious or less serious effects, and the reparation should be adjusted accordingly. For example, since its judgment in *Soering*, the Court has developed a practice according to which, when the expulsion of the applicants would place them at risk of torture or inhuman or degrading treatment in the receiving country, it may consider that its endorsement of that possibility constitutes sufficient just satisfaction for the plaintiffs.[534]

[531] *Silver* (Article 50), note 287, para. 10.

[532] *Varnava*, note 157, para. 224 and the cases cited.

[533] Resolution DH(76)35 of 22 June 1976.

[534] See, e.g., *Soering*, note 258, para. 127; *Chahal v. the United Kingdom* [GC], 15 November 1996, *Reports of Judgments and Decisions* 1996-V, para. 158; *Ahmed v. Austria*, 17 December 1996, *Reports of Judgments and Decisions* 1996-VI, para. 51; *Hilal v. the*

From a technical point of view, as already explained, that seems to be the right solution emerging from the interpretation of Article 41, because the Court did not find that a violation had already been committed, and therefore could not afford pecuniary reparation.[535] But from a more humanistic perspective, it may be questionable whether, even in the absence of an effective execution of the expulsion order, those who know and have the official confirmation of what they may endure experience only a minimum and unimportant level of anxiety and distress. In *Ahmed v. Austria* the applicant even committed suicide.[536] Should those claimants have absolute confidence and certitude that the state concerned will indubitably accept the Court's rulings, no matter what their diplomatic relations with third states, and thus they are safe by the simple fact that the judges recognize the situation? Yet, it is precisely on account of the absence of an effective violation that it is difficult to accept that the Court ought to order monetary compensation in those types of cases. Moreover, it should be noticed that in some cases the complainant obtained a residence permit,[537] while in *Soering* he was extradited under certain favourable conditions.[538]

Curiously though, the Court has also stated that the finding of a breach constitutes by itself sufficient just satisfaction for any non-pecuniary damage that the applicant may have suffered, even when it has not established that the claimant had suffered such harm. In a recent case where the applicant company sought compensation for loss of its reputation in international trade, the Court was unable to reach a conclusion on the existence of a causal link between the violation and the non-pecuniary damage alleged, but held that '[n]o award is therefore made under this head and the Court considers that the finding of a violation constitutes in itself sufficient just satisfaction for any non-pecuniary damage that the applicant company might have suffered'.[539] Otherwise stated, the judges have offered a sort of satisfaction for unproved injury.

United Kingdom, no. 45276/99, ECHR 2001-II, para. 83; and *Daoudi v. France*, no. 19576/08, 3 December 2009, para. 82.

535 See above, Subsection 3.2.1 of Chapter 3.

536 Resolution DH(2002)99 of 7 October 2002.

537 Resolution DH(2001)119 of 15 October 2001 in *Chahal*; Resolution DH(2010)138 of 15 September 2010 in *Hilal*; and Resolution DH(2011)102 of 14 September 2011 in *Daoudi*.

538 Resolution DH(90)8 of 12 March 1990.

539 *Forminster Enterprises Limited v. the Czech Republic* (just satisfaction), no. 38238/04, 10 March 2011, paras. 24–6.

That approach seems to be inappropriate, because even if some damage caused by the infringement may be theoretically accepted, the Court should not make any award if its practical existence has not been demonstrated. However, the issues raised by similar situations may rather pertain to legal theory, as long as the practical position of the opponent in a dispute, which is the respondent state, is not impaired by such statements.

A declaratory judgment may nonetheless generate further positive consequences for the victim. A successful applicant in Strasbourg may use that ruling before municipal courts, if internal legislation admits such an effect, in order to seek redress. To that end, the majority of contracting parties have already introduced the possibility to reopen proceedings and re-examine cases when the Court has found a violation of the Convention.

4.2.4.2 Suitability of the approach

Does a declaratory judgment offer effective reparation? In *Corfu Channel* that remedy was provided because the victim state had not sought any other form of satisfaction. In other words, such a declaration may not be mechanically associated with the remedy of satisfaction, because it is inherent to any finding of a violation, as a necessary part of deciding a case, and also precedes any form of reparation.[540] Is that the use of the concept that the Strasbourg judges make?

The Court's case law reveals an unwritten rule that non-pecuniary prejudice may always be transformed into money. It follows that the judges use that formula when the financial equivalent of the moral harm is deemed to be unimportant. What seems to emerge from relevant practice, as in the context of the use of equity, is that the judges know beforehand, on the basis of precedent rulings, that the victim should not be granted any compensation. There would be nothing wrong with considering that a complainant has not sustained prejudice that would deserve an award or that the injury caused is mainly his own fault. One may therefore raise the question: why do the judges not simply state that the circumstances of a violation do not call for an award?

Several of the Court's judges have contested that formula. Some have adopted the view that it is unacceptable not only that a court of justice compensates victims 'with a mere handout of legal idiom', but also that the Court has disregarded its own practice to give full reasoning for all

[540] Crawford, note 43, at 233.

decisions and has 'failed to suggest one single reason why the finding should also double up as the remedy', showing little intention to change that approach.[541] Others have questioned the suitability of the approach from the perspective of the principle that victims should as far as possible be put in the original position. Indeed, one may reasonably question the compatibility of declaratory redress with the standard of *restitutio in integrum*, in so far as the very finding of an infringement denotes existence of moral damage.

As far as inter-state applications are concerned, the issue has not been raised in the recent ruling on reparation delivered in *Cyprus v. Turkey*, which is the first award of damages in this type of dispute. One may only speculate as to the application of that formula in disputes between states. Given the fairly extensive practice on satisfaction in international law, and also in virtue of wide acceptance that declaratory judgments may offer appropriate satisfaction, there is no formal impediment to applying that approach to the Convention parties. The Court has so far delivered declaratory judgments only in respect of individual applicants. From a practical point of view, at a moment when the Court is simply asphyxiated by requests, unmeritorious applications may be thus discouraged from coming to Strasbourg if claimants are aware that they cannot obtain what they consider appropriate reparation, allowing the judges to concentrate on more important cases.

The Strasbourg judges have therefore adapted to the treaty-based regime a notion used in international law to offer remedy to states, by way of satisfaction, for non-pecuniary injury which is not financially assessable. The difference is that they use declaratory judgments as a form of just satisfaction whenever they consider that the monetary equivalent is irrelevant. Some breaches of procedural rules may well be included in such a category, although the judges often embrace that argument also in the context of interference with the substantive aspect of a right. In repetitive cases, however, lack of financial awards may 'encourage' the offender to continue its wrongful activity, because it would go 'unpunished' anyway. To that extent, the protection of human rights offered by the system proves ineffective.

To conclude, the use of declaratory judgments is indeed justified in the specific circumstances of some cases. The question is: why does the

[541] Partly dissenting opinion submitted by Judge Bonello in *Nikolova* and *Aquilina* (note 276), as well as in *T.W. v. Malta* ([GC], no. 25644/94, 29 April 1999).

Court prefer to transform the finding of a violation, which gives entitlement to reparation, into reparation itself, instead of simply declaring that the circumstances of the case do not justify an award? Article 41 empowers the judges to make reparation only 'if necessary'. So, when they decide that the prejudice is too insignificant to be compensated, they may simply declare that financial compensation is not necessary. There are enough cases where the Court did so and there are also judges who have expressly raised this issue in their separate opinions.[542] The finding of a violation is first and foremost linked to state responsibility. As aptly noted by Shelton, '[i]t is the beginning of remedies, not the end'.[543] A reasoned choice between the two solutions used concurrently in the practice would confer more consistency on the case law.

4.2.5 *Symbolic awards and profiles of victims*

A request for a symbolic award is to some extent linked with the profile of the victim. It denotes a person who seeks justice in the first place. Such claims are rather exceptional, because the overwhelming majority of plaintiffs claim substantial and even exaggerated reparation. As for the Court, it does not normally accept them, and it does not even take them into account, presumably because they bear some punitive connotation for the respondent state.

One exception was the case of *Engel and Others v. the Netherlands*, where both the victims and the government sought a 'purely symbolic sum'.[544] The case concerned a deprivation of liberty, but the Court took into account the brevity of detention and the fact that the first applicant had already been compensated for the damage sustained. Therefore, it afforded 'a token indemnity of one hundred Dutch guilders'.[545] Such an award is nonetheless exceptional; it was the fifth judgment of the Court on just satisfaction and it came after the aforementioned judgment in *Golder*, where it introduced the practice of declaratory awards. It is thus reasonable to assume that the judges were experimenting with new methods of redress. But while the approach initiated in *Golder* was very successful, probably because it was in the state's interest, the

[542] See, e.g., the separate opinion of Judge Ziemele in *Barborski v. Bulgaria*, no. 12811/07, 26 March 2013.

[543] D. Shelton, *Remedies in International Human Rights Law* (Oxford University Press, 2005), at 268.

[544] *Engel* (Article 50), note 523, paras. 6 and 8. [545] Ibid., para. 10.

symbolic award in *Engel*, which may bear some punitive intentions, seems to have encountered fierce opposition.

The judges also debated if symbolic compensation was appropriate in *Marckx v. Belgium*, where they considered that the inheritance law discriminated against children born out of wedlock, as was the situation of the complaining mother and daughter, and thus imposed restrictions on the latter's capacity to receive property from her mother and also deprived her of inheritance rights on intestacy over the estates of her near relatives on her mother's side. The applicants sought one Belgian franc as compensation for moral damage, but the Court considered that it was not necessary to afford them any just satisfaction other than that resulting from the finding of several violations of their rights.[546]

The suitability of upholding that symbolic claim was discussed in a separate opinion attached to that judgment, which means that the question was also debated during deliberations. Some of the judges believed that the applicants had a personal interest in being recognized individually as victims of that legal situation, especially as 'neither in the Convention nor in the principles of international law are there to be found any rules preventing the grant, on such facts, of a token satisfaction appropriate to the individual concerned'.[547] Indeed, symbolic awards have already been given at international level, for example in *I'm Alone*, where United States officers sank a Canadian vessel engaged in smuggling liquor into the United States. Although no compensation was due for loss of ship or cargo, the United States was recommended not only to formally acknowledge the illegality and present apologies, but also to pay 25,000 United States dollars (USD) in respect of the wrong.[548]

In another dispute, *Lorsé and Others v. the Netherlands*, the Court found that the first applicant had endured weekly strip-searches for a period of more than six years while in detention, which amounted to inhuman or degrading treatment. The victim claimed only a symbolic amount equivalent to some EUR 454, which the judges granted him, in the absence, as expected, of any comments by the respondent government.[549] However, the Court simply ignored the 'symbolic' characterization, and would certainly have been willing to afford higher

[546] *Marckx*, note 111, para. 68.

[547] Joint dissenting opinion of Judges Balladore Pallieri, Pedersen, Ganshof van der Meersch, Evrigenis, Pinheiro Farinha and García de Enterría.

[548] *I'm Alone (Canada v. United States)* (1935), 3 RIAA 1609, at 1618.

[549] *Lorsé and Others v. the Netherlands*, no. 52750/99, 4 February 2003, paras. 98–100.

compensation if it had not been impeded *in casu* by the principle of *ne ultra petita*. It did the same in *Agga v. Greece*, where the applicant sought one symbolic Greek drachma for non-pecuniary damage, but the Court, 'given his request', considered that the finding of a violation offered adequate reparation.[550] It thus equated 'symbolic award' with 'no award', that is to say, it preferred to 'punish' the victim rather than the offending state.

In general, the Court does not even discuss the possibility of awarding plaintiffs a symbolic sum.[551] Even when a government itself has proposed a symbolic amount to be granted to a victim, the judges have frequently remained silent on the matter and allocated the usual sums,[552] nonetheless making a few exceptions.[553] To some extent, the situation was different when the Committee of Ministers exerted quasi-judicial powers and decided applications. On occasion, the Committee has ordered the respondent state to pay the token sum of one French franc[554] or one escudo[555] for the excessive length of domestic proceedings, or one Belgian franc for non-pecuniary damage caused by a breach of the property right and lack of effective remedies.[556]

In view of the low gravity of the violation, those awards were indeed trying to emphasize that the state conduct had been unlawful, not that the prejudice was minimal. What is striking, however, is that, while through the intermediary of the Committee of Ministers the contracting states themselves have accepted such awards, the Court still hesitates to make them. It may be that it is a method of constraint reserved only to the states parties to the Convention, as a means to manifest disapproval towards the offender for the breach of the treaty.

A claim for a symbolic award is therefore connected to the victim's personal thirst for individual justice; not all of them are motivated by a greedy impulse. It has nothing to do with the particular material loss, but with moral satisfaction. It may also denote a few instances when the

[550] *Agga v. Greece (no. 2)*, nos. 50776/99 and 52912/99, 17 October 2002, paras. 65–6.

[551] See, e.g., *Xenides-Arestis* (just satisfaction), note 164, paras. 44 and 47.

[552] See, e.g., *Avşar*, note 415, paras. 444–5; *Fadeyeva v. Russia*, no. 55723/00, ECHR 2005-IV, paras. 137–8; *Osmanoğlu v. Turkey*, no. 48804/99, 24 January 2008, paras. 126–7; and *Sangariyeva and Others v. Russia*, no. 1839/04, 29 May 2008, para. 128.

[553] See, e.g., *Vaney v. France*, no. 53946/00, 30 November 2004, paras. 55–7.

[554] Resolution DH(91)2 of 13 February 1991 in *Barany v. France*, and Resolution DH(93)48 of 9 November 1993 in *D.T. v. France*.

[555] Resolution DH(91)36 of 13 December 1991 in *Manuel Mendes Godinho e Filhos v. Portugal*.

[556] Resolution DH(95)105 of 11 September 1995 in *Dierckx v. Belgium*.

general interest outweighs the personal interest. While the overwhelming majority of plaintiffs are mainly concerned with their personal interest, some want to see the government's policy, or particular legislation or practice, changed,[557] while others are prepared to invest time and energy in the hope only to see their violation recognized and the state called to account.[558] However, a symbolic award does not seem appropriate as a form of effective reparation, except for the cases in which it is what the victims ask for.

The victims' profiles may thus be different, not only in respect of their underlying interest, but also depending on their personal situation. First of all, applicants may be natural or legal entities, including states. Natural persons, as the beneficiaries of all the rights protected by the Convention, are by far the main victims. Their specific condition may further affect their vulnerability in the Strasbourg proceedings. The Court has found several interferences with prisoners' right of petition, or potential violations of some core personal rights in cases concerning the expulsion of foreigners to a third country. National minorities or ethnic groups may also be confronted with illegitimate conduct by the authorities.

The Court has further admitted the particular vulnerability of young persons and the special psychological factors involved in cases concerning the sexual assault of children.[559] Expectations may also differ when addressing the Court. Relatives of those who have disappeared or been killed by security forces would presumably seek justice in the first place. In general, in situations in which plaintiffs do not claim compensation or reimbursement of costs and expenses, their requests before the Court can reasonably reveal their thirst for justice. This may suggest that they are more interested in the final outcome than in financial gain. By contrast, there are those who have been deprived of their property for a long time and who find in Strasbourg the support for recovering those assets, together with ensuing loss of profit or benefit, even if the impact of dispossession may have been attenuated in the meantime, especially when it is the heirs, not the victims, who lodge the complaint. Therefore, the victims' profiles vary greatly before the Court. It would

[557] See, e.g., M.-B. Dembour, 'What It Takes to Have a Case: The Backstage Story of *Muskhadzhiyeva v. Belgium* (Illegality of Children's Immigration Detention)', in Lambert Abdelgawad, note 208.

[558] See, e.g., *Komarova v. Ukraine*, no. 13371/06, 16 May 2013, para. 86.

[559] See, e.g., *M. and C. v. Romania*, no. 29032/04, 27 September 2011, para. 119.

be simplistic to assume that all of them seek financial redress, but it would also be a fruitless effort to contemplate that the prospects of an official recognition of their sufferings would leave the victims insensitive to the idea of an immediate monetary gain.

4.3 Costs and expenses

Costs and expenses are a matter treated under the heading of just satisfaction, but separately from pecuniary and non-pecuniary damage.[560] On the first occasion that it reimbursed them, in 1974 in *Neumeister v. Austria*, the Court admitted that they did not represent injury arising directly from a violation, but a victim's efforts to prevent and redress the resulting effects.[561] While not mentioned in the text of Article 41 on just satisfaction, it will compensate them in so far as they pertain to a state interference pronounced by the Court. The Inter-American Court has admitted that function of the costs as well, and has also included them in the concept of reparations established by Article 63(1) of the American Convention.[562]

If the entire application or specific complaints have been declared inadmissible or have not led to a pronouncement as to the existence of an infringement, the Court will reject the related claims in respect of costs and expenses, because they must necessarily be linked to the breach.[563] They have their legal basis in Article 41, and so they depend upon the existence of a violation, not of injury. Moreover, since they are an exclusively financial burden, the judges have justly asserted that 'it is difficult to imagine that the finding of a violation could of itself constitute just satisfaction as regards costs'.[564]

[560] See, among others, J. L. Sharpe, 'Awards of Costs and Expenses under Article 50 of the European Convention on Human Rights', *Law Society's Gazette* (1984); N. Sansonetis, 'Costs and Expenses', in Macdonald, Matscher and Petzold, note 32; A. R. Mowbray, 'The European Court of Human Rights' Approach to Just Satisfaction', *Public Law* (1997), at 652–7; L. J. Clements, N. Mole and A. Simmons, *European Human Rights: Taking a Case under the Convention* (London: Sweet & Maxwell, 1999), at 91–7; and Reid, note 206, at 865–9.

[561] *Neumeister* (Article 50), note 90, para. 43.

[562] See, e.g., *Garrido and Baigorria v. Argentina* (reparations and costs), 27 August 1998, Series C no. 39, para. 79.

[563] See, among many other authorities, *Beyeler* (just satisfaction), note 118, para. 27, and *Sahin v. Germany* [GC], no. 30943/96, ECHR 2003-VIII, para. 105.

[564] *The Sunday Times* (Article 50), note 268, para. 16.

As with claims for damage, costs and expenses are not granted automatically; an applicant must submit a specific request. The Court will not compensate them of its own motion, given that no question of public policy is involved,[565] but, as in the case of damages, the judges enjoy wide discretion, because 'the injured party is not entitled to his costs as of right'.[566] The plaintiff should therefore produce evidence, such as itemized bills and invoices, and demonstrate that costs have been actually and necessarily incurred, with a view to preventing or redressing a breach of the Convention, and were also reasonable as to quantum. These are the four criteria established in practice by the Court, with a view to permitting the recovery of costs and expenses incurred in both domestic and Strasbourg proceedings.[567]

4.3.1 Criteria for making an award

Costs and expenses have been actually incurred when applicants have paid them or are legally liable in that respect. Claims are usually dismissed when a lawyer has acted free of charge,[568] when a plaintiff has only estimated the costs in the eventuality of a hearing at the Court,[569] or when the legal costs were paid by an association.[570] On the contrary, fees may be recovered when a counsel has allowed the petitioner effectively to pay the charges only after a ruling from Strasbourg. The situation is different if the complainant and his adviser have fixed a sum on the basis of a contingency agreement, that is, a percentage of the amount, if any, awarded by the Court. The Court has admitted those arrangements only if recognized by the internal law.[571] It will also deduct any sums already received domestically or from the Council of Europe as free legal aid. However, the fact that a claimant has in fact paid those amounts does not automatically lead to their reimbursement, because the other conditions should further be met.

565 See, among others, *Benthem v. the Netherlands*, 23 October 1985, Series A no. 97, para. 45.

566 *The Sunday Times* (Article 50), note 268, para. 15.

567 See, e.g., *Zimmermann and Steiner v. Switzerland*, 13 July 1983, Series A no. 66, para. 36.

568 *McCann*, note 269, para. 221.

569 *De Cubber* (Article 50), note 227, paras. 30 and 33.

570 *Dudgeon* (Article 50), note 236, para. 22.

571 For that reason, such an arrangement was admitted in *Kamasinski v. Austria* (19 December 1989, Series A no. 168, para. 115), but refused in *Dudgeon* (Article 50) (note 236, para. 22).

The inevitability of costs is a highly subjective criterion; the Court, at its own discretion, determines whether expenses were avoidable or not. It all depends on the circumstances of the case, because the Court has not fixed any standard. Costs to attend Strasbourg hearings or translation fees are usually covered, while personal expenses, excessive sets of internal proceedings aiming at the same result, or the cost of several legal advisers may reasonably appear redundant. For instance, in *Sporrong and Lönnroth v. Sweden*, the Court was not persuaded that there were any necessarily incurred fees for preparing documents which had not been taken into account, sums paid to jurists for consultations, research work and for registration for a course on European procedure, or costs for which bills had not yet been received.[572]

The necessity of legal costs is further connected to their purpose. The Court accepts compensation only for the amounts aimed at preventing and redressing a breach of the treaty before domestic courts and the consequent extension of the proceedings before the European judges, in order to have the violation established and to secure reparation. In that context, when challenging procedural failures directly in Strasbourg, as in the case of defiance of the reasonable time requirement, an applicant may be successful in respect of costs incurred in proceedings before the Court, but not for those before the municipal courts.[573] Plaintiffs may recover costs and expenses in the Convention proceedings a lot easier than those occasioned by domestic litigation, because an individual usually invokes the treaty only when unhappy with the outcome of internal proceedings.

Legal costs and expenses should also be reasonable as to quantum. As noted in the past, but still relevant, the Court most often considers that 'what is "reasonable" is synonymous with what is "equitable"'.[574] It would normally refuse to cover them when they are deemed excessively high in view of the lack of complexity of the procedure or of the issues at stake.[575] Claimants also frequently inflate lawyers' fees, but the Court has declined to apply domestic standards or scales in respect of charges without, however, failing to draw inspiration from them.[576] When

[572] *Sporrong and Lönnroth* (Article 50), note 441, para. 39.

[573] See, e.g., *Sobierajska-Nierzwicka v. Poland*, no. 49349/99, 27 May 2003, para. 121, and *Ciută*, note 479, para. 41.

[574] Sansonetis, note 560, at 769.

[575] See, e.g., *King v. the United Kingdom*, no. 13881/02, 16 November 2004, para. 52.

[576] See, e.g., *Venema v. the Netherlands*, no. 35731/97, ECHR 2002-X, para. 116, and *M.S.S. v. Belgium and Greece* [GC], no. 30696/09, 21 January 2011, para. 420.

several petitioners bring a claim to Strasbourg, they are expected to make efficient use of specialist legal advice, such as a Convention expert, so as to minimize costs.[577]

The Court is very strict in assessing those conditions, which means that it conceives of reimbursement of costs and expenses as an assessment of material damage. It seems that the judges are not guided in the field by reasons of equity or logic, but by evidence. In a recent case where the applicant claimed approximately EUR 13 for postal expenses, a Chamber of the Court unanimously dismissed that request on the grounds that there was 'no clear connection to the proceedings at Strasbourg'.[578] How 'clear' should the fact that every applicant must evidently correspond with the Court and that postal services are not free of charge be? Bearing in mind that, not only for damages but also in respect of costs and expenses, the judges themselves have affirmed that 'the matter falls to be determined by the Court at its discretion, having regard to what is equitable',[579] the example amounts to some unlimited discretionary conduct. This is borne out by the fact that in another dispute the Grand Chamber awarded EUR 200 '[f]or the applicant's own out of pocket expenses, which are largely un-itemised'.[580] Given that the judges often put forward the principle of equity, would it have been inequitable to reimburse that plaintiff with EUR 13 for some costs that he evidently had to bear?

4.3.2 *Reimbursement of domestic and Strasbourg costs and expenses*

Domestic costs and expenses must first and foremost be occasioned by unsuccessful attempts to prevent a violation of the Convention or to remedy its adverse effects. They include lawyers' fees and fees for expert reports, stamp duties, mailing charges, or transport and accommodation when the plaintiff lives in another place, as proceedings are not necessarily conducted at home. Costs in Strasbourg may also refer to travel and accommodation in the case of a hearing, legal representation, translations, photocopies and postal services. There is no fee for lodging an

[577] *I.J.L., G.M.R. and A.K.P. v. the United Kingdom* (just satisfaction), nos. 29522/95, 30056/96 and 30574/96, 25 September 2001, para. 21 *in fine*.
[578] *Lavrov v. Russia*, no. 33422/03, 17 January 2012, para. 51.
[579] *The Sunday Times* (Article 50), note 268, para. 15.
[580] *Hirst v. the United Kingdom (no. 2)* [GC], no. 74025/01, ECHR 2005-IX, para. 98.

application. There is, however, a requirement to use one of the two official languages in respect of a hearing or after the communication of an application to the state concerned, but the President of the Chamber may grant leave to a petitioner for the use of the official language of a contracting party, in which case the costs for interpretation and translation are supported by the organization.[581] If the defendant government requests and is granted such leave, it is its responsibility to bear those costs.[582]

A successful claim for costs and expenses incurred in municipal and Convention proceedings must be quantified and supported by relevant evidence,[583] brought within the procedural time limit, and also linked to the violation found. Quantification and a detailed breakdown of how they are computed are not as fundamental as submitting invoices and vouchers to prove and justify their existence. The judges may still offer some compensation on the basis of information in their possession,[584] but if the lack of details does not allow them to distinguish between costs and the legal aid received, they will dismiss the whole claim.[585] When the question of just satisfaction is reserved for a further ruling, the Court may even reimburse them in the judgment on the merits and then cover only the interval between the two decisions.

An award should also be predictable, at least theoretically when the aforementioned criteria are met, if allegations are not contested by the defendant government.[586] In practice, however, the opposing party rationally attempts to establish the inadequacy of compensation, otherwise it risks paying for that. For example, in *Loizidou*, the government did not comment on the applicant's submissions, which may have contributed to an important award of around 185,000 pounds sterling (GBP).[587] In inter-state cases, in virtue of the general principle that states

[581] Rule 34(3) of the Rules of Court. [582] Rule 34(4) of the Rules of Court.

[583] According to Rule 60(2) of the Rules of Court, '[t]he applicant must submit itemised particulars of all claims, together with any relevant supporting documents', failing which the judges may dismiss a claim in whole or in part. See, among many others, *Cumpǎnǎ and Mazǎre v. Romania* [GC], no. 33348/96, ECHR 2004-XI, paras. 133–4.

[584] See, e.g., *Seceleanu*, note 72, paras. 60–2.

[585] See, e.g., *Musiał v. Poland* [GC], no. 24557/94, ECHR 1999-II, para. 61.

[586] See, e.g., *Jersild*, note 385, para. 45, and *De Haes and Gijsels v. Belgium*, no. 19983/92, 24 February 1997, paras. 67–9.

[587] *Loizidou* (Article 50), note 164, the partly dissenting opinion of Judge Mifsud Bonnici.

bear their own costs in disputes before international courts, costs and expenses may not be recovered.[588]

Some commentators have suggested in the past that the Court should introduce a common standard of compensation, a sort of 'European scale', in order to avoid discrepancy between the sums awarded.[589] Those propositions, while not irrelevant, were made in the context of certain homogeneity of economic conditions in the member parties of the Council of Europe, but, following the eastwards enlargement of the organization, contrasts have become evident. Thus, as in the case of moral damage, a uniform scale does not seem to be workable, because different economic standards call for different weight in terms of monetary equivalent. The Court itself admitted in a 1995 judgment that 'given the great differences at present in rates of fees from one Contracting State to another, a uniform approach to the assessment of fees under Article 50 of the Convention does not seem appropriate'.[590]

Consequently, the Court is apparently not bound by any hypothetical thresholds, but rather verifies whether the claimed amounts have been effectively and reasonably spent. Important sums were granted in cases revealing an infringement of the right to protection of property, especially when the related possessions were of high value. For instance, in *Stran Greek Refineries*, where the applicants received the equivalent of several million euros for material damage, the Court awarded GBP 125,000 for costs, in equity and without too much explanation.[591] It also granted large amounts for other types of violation, for instance GBP 100,000 in *Observer and Guardian*, where it found a breach of the freedom of expression.[592] However, such examples should not give the wrong idea that the Court may admit any plausible demand, because the judges do impose some limits based on the above-mentioned criteria. Thus, when it awarded pecuniary damage of more than EUR 13 million in the *Former King of Greece*, the Court had no doubt that the fees of almost GBP 1 million were actually incurred, but declared them excessive and reduced them to EUR 500,000.[593]

[588] Ibid., para. 48. [589] Sharpe, note 560, at 907, and Sansonetis, note 560, at 773.
[590] *Tolstoy Miloslavsky v. the United Kingdom*, 13 July 1995, Series A no. 316-B, para. 77 *in fine*.
[591] *Stran Greek Refineries*, note 55, para. 87.
[592] *Observer and Guardian v. the United Kingdom*, 26 November 1991, Series A no. 216, para. 84.
[593] *Former King of Greece* (just satisfaction), note 114, paras. 106–7.

Most issues arise from an assessment of lawyers' charges for representing or assisting a petitioner, especially in the Convention proceedings. Representation before the Court is mandatory only after notification of an application to the state involved, as well as at any hearing, but in both situations the President of the Chamber may grant leave to plaintiffs to present their own cases.[594] A decision in that sense relies on the complexity of the dispute, not on the claimant's financial condition. There is no need to be represented in repetitive cases, such as those concerning the length of proceedings or non-enforcement of domestic judgments.

It follows that the Court would not fully reimburse a lawyer's fees, even if they were effectively paid by the claimant, when the application is of a repetitive nature and does not raise any complex issue. There are, nonetheless, inconsistencies even in that context, as in two similar and repetitive applications brought by the same person and decided by the same Section of the Court over a two-month interval. In one of them, the petitioner claimed EUR 3,449 for costs and expenses before the Court, and the judges awarded him EUR 3,400, from which EUR 1,740 had to be paid by the government directly to his counsel.[595] In the other case, he sought recovery of EUR 3,569, but received only EUR 1,160, out of which again EUR 1,000 had to be paid directly to the same lawyer.[596] The cases concerned attempts by the plaintiff to recover two different apartments situated in the same building, in comparable sets of internal proceedings. Hence, the work of the adviser to present each of the two applications to the Court would presumably have been almost identical. In both claims for costs and expenses, the applicant sought similar amounts and also declared that he had already paid EUR 1,500 to his lawyer. And yet, in one of the cases, the Court increased that sum, but in the other it reduced it, mentioning, however, that the dispute lacked complexity. It may well be an unfortunate exception or it may reveal a dangerous challenge to the consistency of the case law. For that applicant and lawyer, and also for the general observer, what was the justification of the Court?

Only the victims of a breach may seek recovery of legal costs, given that they are an injured party for the purpose of just satisfaction and because they must prove that they had effectively paid the alleged

594 Rule 36(2) and (3) of the Rules of Court.

595 *Simionescu-Râmniceanu v. Romania*, no. 16272/03, 21 July 2009, paras. 45–7.

596 *Simionescu-Râmniceanu v. Romania (no. 2)*, no. 43953/02, 22 September 2009, paras. 38–40.

amounts. Counsels who have defended applicants free of charge or who have applied legal aid rates have no standing before the Court to request any fee or to seek additional fees.[597] The judges may order that reimbursement of charges be made directly to the lawyer.[598] In doing so, or by mentioning what amount is allocated to representation, they avoid a possible argument between adviser and client as to the worth of legal counsel. At the other end of the spectrum is the practice of granting a lump sum for costs and expenses. In that event, there is no evidence if, or to what extent, a lawyer's fees have been reimbursed. While it may certainly facilitate that problem, the Court is not to be blamed for not solving it. It may be assumed that an applicant has diligently chosen an adviser.

Counsels often exaggerate the number of hours spent on a case or claim excessive hourly rates, but the Court has always moderated such attempts. It has even declared in one of its early cases that 'high costs of litigation may themselves constitute a serious impediment to the effective protection of human rights' and that '[i]t would be wrong for the Court to give encouragement to such a situation'.[599] The judges have refrained from imposing or suggesting a standard, and usually avoid establishing themselves an appropriate amount or number of hours for the service provided by a lawyer, preferring instead to amalgamate the fee with the rest of the costs.[600] In particular, the Court has pertinently refused to make an award in respect of the time spent by applicants themselves working on the case, considering that it did not represent costs actually incurred by them.[601]

Recently, however, the Court has even stopped mentioning in its rulings how many working hours the counsel has invoked or what the hourly fee was. For example, in *Sanoma Uitgevers B.V. v. the Netherlands*, it specified without any further detail the amounts claimed in respect of domestic and Convention proceedings, although it conceded that they were supported by time-sheets, and eventually declared that 'the sums

[597] See, e.g., *Luedicke, Belkacem and Koç v. Germany* (Article 50), 10 March 1980, Series A no. 36, para. 15, and *Delta v. France*, 19 December 1990, Series A no. 191-A, paras. 44–7.

[598] See, e.g., *Nachova and Others v. Bulgaria* [GC], nos. 43577/98 and 43579/98, ECHR 2005-VII, para. 175, and *Imakayeva*, note 414, point 13(a)(iii) of the operative part.

[599] *Young, James and Webster* (Article 50), note 411, para. 15.

[600] See, e.g., *Nikolova*, note 276, paras. 77–9.

[601] See, among others, *Narinen v. Finland*, no. 45027/98, 1 June 2004, para. 50, and *Steel and Morris v. the United Kingdom*, no. 68416/01, ECHR 2005-II, para. 112.

claimed are not reasonable as to quantum either as regards the hourly rates applied or as regards the number of hours charged'.[602] Is that omission so important? How should someone know what would amount to exaggeration? There is no doubt that the parties in that dispute were well aware of the basis for that decision, but the outside observer ventures in uncertainty. While such examples are fairly sparse for the time being, they still raise questions as to the impact of the high number of cases on the quality of the Court's judgments, and ultimately on its credibility.

The Court has frequently upheld claims in respect of fees for a counsel when the issues raised were complex.[603] The applicant must provide evidence, such as contracts for judicial assistance, so as to establish to what set of proceedings the alleged assistance or representation referred.[604] While there are limits as to the number of advisers used for a case before the Court, there is none as to the choice of lawyer. Fees are reimbursed when a plaintiff prefers a counsel from a richer country, and, as a result, it is more expensive than the national offer.[605] The Court normally takes into account whether or not all complaints have been successful and will thus reduce the amount accordingly if some of them were dismissed or declared inadmissible.[606] However, even when a case has been discontinued, and therefore the judges do not make a pronouncement as to the existence of a breach, the Court enjoys discretion to award costs.[607]

If applicants are in financial difficulty as to the presentation of their case, the Court may grant free legal aid, either at their request or of its own motion.[608] The matter lies within the discretion of the President of the Chamber. Although the system is completely original as compared to

[602] *Sanoma Uitgevers B.V. v. the Netherlands* [GC], no. 38224/03, 14 September 2010, paras. 104–12.

[603] See, e.g., *Housing Association of War Disabled and Victims of War of Attica and Others v. Greece* (just satisfaction), no. 35859/02, 27 September 2007, paras. 33–6.

[604] See, e.g., *Dolneanu v. Moldova*, no. 17211/03, 13 November 2007, paras. 59–61.

[605] See, e.g., *Kurt*, note 249, para. 179, and *Aktaş*, note 414, para. 369.

[606] See, e.g., *Benham v. the United Kingdom* [GC], 10 June 1996, *Reports of Judgments and Decisions* 1996-III, paras. 69–71, and *Salomonsson v. Sweden*, no. 38978/97, 12 November 2002, paras. 48–50.

[607] Rule 43(4) of the Rules of Court. As examples see, among many others, *Shevanova v. Latvia* (striking out) [GC], no. 58822/00, 7 December 2007, paras. 52–6, and *Grüne Alternative Wien v. Austria* (striking out), no. 13281/02, 29 November 2011, paras. 30–3.

[608] Rules 100–5 of the Rules of Court. On this topic see, among others, Clements, Mole and Simmons, note 560, at 98–101.

other international courts and tribunals, it has been suggested that it may also be questionable in so far as, on the one hand, it is meant to secure access to the Court for all individuals, irrespective of their financial condition, but on the other hand, legal aid is granted only for deserving applications, that is, those which are communicated for observations to the government concerned.[609] Still, it is precisely on account of the fact that not all the allegations transmitted in Strasbourg are founded or worthy of in-depth consideration that it is difficult to argue that they should be further encouraged. Given the small number of allegations that pass the admissibility test, when compared to the amount of applications received, it would not make sense for the states parties to contribute more for the legal-aid scheme and thus to pay for every aberration. Plaintiffs are therefore financially responsible for the initial stage of the proceedings.

The rates are fixed in accordance with the legal-aid scales in force and paid by the Council of Europe. Their purpose is to cover the fees for representation in particular, but also other necessary expenses, such as travel to a hearing. They are normally payable to the lawyers, not to the applicants.[610] At present, legal aid is fixed at EUR 850 per case, apparently without taking into account the gravity of the violation, the economic situation of the offending state or the number of petitioners.[611] There are, however, exceptions,[612] and the amount is normally higher in Grand Chamber proceedings.[613] Obviously, complainants may also receive legal aid from their own state.

609 E. Lambert Abdelgawad, 'La saisine de la Cour européenne des droits de l'homme', in H. Ruiz Fabri and J. M. Sorel (eds.), *La saisine des juridictions internationales* (Paris: Pedone, 2006), at 218.

610 Rule 103(1) of the Rules of Court.

611 See, e.g., *Dikici v. Turkey*, no. 18308/02, 20 October 2009, para. 35; *Clift v. the United Kingdom*, no. 7205/07, 13 July 2010, para. 92; *Ali v. Romania*, no. 20307/02, 9 November 2010, para. 117; *Meidl v. Austria*, no. 33951/05, 12 April 2011, para. 79; *Schönbrod v. Germany*, no. 48038/06, 24 November 2011, para. 119; and *Biziuk v. Poland (no. 2)*, no. 24580/06, 17 January 2012, para. 80.

612 See, e.g., EUR 1,650 in *Tătar v. Romania* (no. 67021/01, 27 January 2009, para. 136); EUR 1,494 in *Opuz v. Turkey* (no. 33401/02, ECHR 2009, para. 213); EUR 1,450 in *Muñoz Díaz v. Spain* (no. 49151/07, 8 December 2009, para. 88); and EUR 1,150 in *Gillan and Quinton v. the United Kingdom* (no. 4158/05, ECHR 2010 (extracts), para. 97).

613 See, e.g., EUR 1,854.86 in *Micallef v. Malta* ([GC], no. 17056/06, ECHR 2009, para. 115); EUR 1,755.20 in *Taxquet v. Belgium* ([GC], no. 926/05, ECHR 2010, para. 108); and EUR 1,150 in *Al-Khawaja and Tahery v. the United Kingdom* ([GC], nos. 26766/05 and 22228/06, ECHR 2011, para. 174).

What is striking, though, is that even after thousands of judgments delivered by the Court and even when represented by a lawyer, applicants continue to inflate claims for costs and expenses. At least in the presence of a legal adviser, claims should be more realistic, because a counsel is theoretically supposed to be familiar with the Court's case law on the matter, and in particular with the sums accepted by the judges for representation. The relatively low legal-aid provision available through the Council of Europe is a further hint. And yet, even for assistance in repetitive cases, when the practice is already well established, some of the claims are patently excessive. It may be that either those lawyers act in bad faith when claiming high charges for preparing an application, or they are only attempting to seize their chance in Strasbourg.

In any event, there is reason to surmise that the Court will continue to impose some discipline in the field. An alternative may be to introduce a set of standard charges for representation in Strasbourg, on the basis of the type and gravity of the breach, on the number of violations found and on the number of applicants. Inspiration may also be drawn from the existing system of legal aid. Nevertheless, as the Court has already warned in its early cases, low fees may deter qualified lawyers from offering their expertise.[614] Ultimately, whether or not claimants obtain adequate reparation depends almost decisively on specialist counsel.

4.4 Concluding remarks

4.4.1 *Some predictability in respect of awards for pecuniary damage*

Some violations are more suitable than others for an assessment of the adverse financial effects. Certainly, material damage resulting from an interference with the right to peaceful enjoyment of property is much easier to calculate than the pecuniary consequences of a breach of the procedural rights of a fair trial. Indeed, the judges only occasionally launch into speculation as to those damages and offer compensation for loss of opportunity. In fact, when the existence of injury is evident, but its extent is not known, the judges do have absolute discretion for fixing an amount. Such is the case with loss of earnings.

[614] *Luedicke, Belkacem and Koç* (Article 50), note 597, para. 15.

4.4.1.1 Higher predictability for *damnum emergens*

The loss actually sustained is fairly predictable, at least to the extent that it will be granted if the Court has found a violation on the merits and if the victim demonstrates the causal link and submits relevant evidence as to the quantum. An expert report or court decision would evidently multiply the chances for the applicant. The Court will generally use discretion as to the method of calculation, as in the mentioned case of change of jurisprudence in respect of constructive expropriations.

Material injury caused by breaches, other than those affecting the property right, is even easier to demonstrate. It should not be difficult for the judges to respond by ensuring that illegally obtained fines are repaid or that expenses incurred for medical treatment resulting from the consequences of the state's interference in the victim's health are reimbursed by the state.

4.4.1.2 Lower predictability for *lucrum cessans*

Lucrum cessans contains an inherent element of speculation. It is always uncertain what would have happened but for the violation. Even when its existence is uncontested, its extent may only be determined by approximation with comparable situations. The judges enjoy large discretion under the shield of equity, as proved by similar examples with arable land, when they may award it or not. Applicants must adduce strong evidence and prove manifest causation in order to increase the probability of having the lost profits or benefits reimbursed. The situation is slightly more to the victims' advantage when they should receive a sum of money, because in that case they may at least secure the interest.

4.4.2 Large discretion as to awards for non-pecuniary damage

4.4.2.1 The 'most expensive' violations

There is no formal hierarchy of rights and freedoms in the Convention, but the treaty itself accepts that some rights are of a fundamental nature, if one considers the derogations permitted in time of emergency.[615] It is beyond doubt that torture would cause more suffering than unreasonable length of proceedings. The highest awards for moral prejudice should normally be allocated for breaches of the right to life and of prohibition of torture or inhuman or degrading treatment. While they

[615] Article 15(2) of the Convention.

usually are, there are also sufficient examples where the judges have granted comparable amounts, especially for interference with the right to peaceful enjoyment of property.

For example, in *Demades v. Turkey*, the applicant received EUR 785,000 for loss of access to and use of his property, and EUR 45,000 for 'anguish and feelings of helplessness and frustration'.[616] The same amount was awarded to the applicants in *Guiso-Gallisay*, for 'feelings of powerlessness and frustration arising from the unlawful dispossession of their property'.[617] Similarly, in some cases brought by private companies which, in Strasbourg, eventually recovered millions of euros for pecuniary prejudice, the Court also awarded EUR 25,000 to them for non-pecuniary damage.[618] And this in spite of the fact that when plaintiffs from the same country, having sought EUR 20,000 for moral damage sustained as a result of inhuman conditions of detention and failure by the authorities to provide timely medical assistance, or for ill-treatment by the police and lack of investigation, received only EUR 4,000 and EUR 9,000, respectively.[619] Is not that an authentic perversion of human rights?

It is indeed completely striking that awards for so-called 'considerable' moral harm suffered in property cases may correspond to the compensation for moral injury offered to those who had lost family or who had been subjected to torture or ill-treatment. When examining property disputes, the judges mechanically grant moral damage, usually higher when the value of the assets is greater, without even questioning *in concreto* what kind of moral harm precisely that person has suffered. One judge has aptly criticized such a perversion of the course of justice in a case of unlawful killing where the Grand Chamber refused to compensate the loss of earnings, although automatic and hypothetic awards had been previously given in some property and length-of-proceedings disputes, concluding that '[i]n the Strasbourg market it seems that life comes cheap, and killing is a tremendous bargain'.[620]

616 *Demades v. Turkey* (just satisfaction), no. 16219/90, 22 April 2008, para. 29.

617 *Guiso-Gallisay* (just satisfaction), note 366, para. 110.

618 *Oferta Plus S.R.L. v. Moldova* (just satisfaction), no. 14385/04, 12 February 2008, para. 76, and *Dacia S.R.L. v. Moldova* (just satisfaction), no. 3052/04, 24 February 2009, para. 62.

619 *Ciorap v. Moldova (no. 2)*, no. 7481/06, 20 July 2010, paras. 31 and 33, and *Parnov v. Moldova*, no. 35208/06, 13 July 2010, paras. 43 and 45.

620 Partly dissenting opinion of Judge Bonello in *Oğur v. Turkey*, note 168. Judge Myjer also wrote: 'Human rights indeed. The European Court of Human Rights puts less of a price on the right to life or the prohibition of torture than on the peaceful enjoyment of

Moreover, if one takes the example of the cases of nationalization or confiscation of immovable property by the former communist regimes in Central and Eastern Europe, it is normally the heirs, not the victims of the deprivation, who seek redress in Strasbourg. The act of nationalization or confiscation usually took place before those heirs had even been born. To what kind of moral harm have they been subjected? It is somewhat unfortunate that the judges frequently develop the notion of moral damage in cases where it is obvious that it has been produced, for instance, unlawful death or forced disappearance, inhuman or degrading treatment, while in disputes arising from deprivation of property, non-enforcement or delayed execution of domestic judgments, they do not question *in casu* what type of non-pecuniary damage the victim has suffered.

A standardized approach may be a solution, with the condition of diminishing the amounts, although it is still open to discussion whether or not the value of the property should be the only criterion when fixing compensation for moral damage, or whether the wealth of the complainant should not also play a role. Ultimately, those applicants may be held to have rather suffered a loss of opportunity, a chance to enjoy their possessions. However, it seems that the Court avoids speculating on the loss of opportunity, preferring instead to include it in moral damage, which may nonetheless cause further inconsistency. For example, in *Pétur Thór Sigurðsson v. Iceland*, it awarded a fairly excessive amount of EUR 25,000 for the presumed anguish and distress sustained by the applicant, who could have entertained reasonable fears that the Supreme Court lacked the requisite impartiality. As one of the judges has rightly noted, '[t]he award is way beyond the level of awards for non-pecuniary damage offered by this Court to people or relatives of people who have even suffered outrageous human rights violations that fall under the provisions of Articles 2 and 3 of the Convention'.[621] By contrast, in a subsequent case decided the same year by the same Section with only one different judge in composition, the Court considered that 'the finding of a violation in respect of the trial by a tribunal which lacked independence and impartiality constitutes in itself sufficient

mere possessions': see E. Myjer, 'Article 1 Protocol 1 and the Entitlement of Just Satisfaction', in H. Vandenberghe, M. Muylle and T. Viaene (eds.), *Propriété et droits de l'homme = Property and Human Rights* (Bruges: Die Keure/La Charte; Bruylant, 2006), at 101.

[621] See the end of the partly concurring and partly dissenting opinion of Judge Greve in *Pétur Thór Sigurðsson v. Iceland*, no. 39731/98, ECHR 2003-IV.

compensation for any non-pecuniary damage suffered by the applicant'.[622]

4.4.2.2 Different standards for moral damage

The problem with the awards in respect of moral damage is not the Court's discretion per se, because any judge would practically enjoy certain discretion when ruling on an equitable basis for an injury that is hardly assessable in money, but lies in the quantification and the criteria used for selecting to which victims a sum of money should be allocated, or to whom to declare that the very finding of a breach offers adequate reparation. Is that discrimination? Even if the intensity of the harm is obviously higher or lower, they are all victims of an infringement. Bearing in mind that the Practice Direction for just satisfaction claims acknowledges that 'the Court will normally take into account the local economic circumstances',[623] and having regard to the extensive case law, it is beyond doubt that the tables used by the Court distribute money according to the economic level of the respondent state. Victims from more developed countries will obtain higher amounts for similar breaches, considering that claims are in general brought by nationals against their own state.

The essential question is therefore: is that differentiation among victims justified? In other words, would it be preferable to have a sort of worldwide scale for pain and suffering? What are the causes and effects? To start with, there seem to be two different answers, depending on the angle from which the problem is being viewed. On the one hand, if one looks from the theoretical angle, the human rights philosophy ought to be uniform, treat all individuals in the same manner and therefore not make discriminations, but advocate against them. As has been suggested, '[t]here is state responsibility for this violation and as regards the measures of damages, the Court, the guardian of pan-European values, naturally could not, and should not, say that a life in, e.g., Turkey is worth less than a life in, e.g., Sweden'.[624]

But on the other hand, viewed from the practical angle and as asserted by Grotius – and cited in *Lusitania* – 'money is the common measure

[622] *Alfatlı and Others v. Turkey (as regards the applicant Mahmut Memduh Uyan)*, no. 32984/96, 30 October 2003, para. 50.
[623] Para. 2 of the Practice Direction, note 143.
[624] I. Cameron, 'Damages for Violations of ECHR Rights: The Swedish Example', *Swedish Studies in European Law* 1 (2006), at 121.

of valuable things'. And given that the level of economic development differs greatly among the member parties of the Council of Europe, it is both logical and judicious to adapt an award to the economic situation of the place where the applicant effectively lives. Otherwise, the judges would create further injustice. But what happens if at some point after suffering a violation an applicant has permanently moved to a more developed country? What matters, the economic level in the respondent state or the victim's permanent place of living?

In *Apicella*, the judges clearly referred to the standard of living in the country concerned. That approach seems to be inappropriate, because the victim will not spend the money in that place. Inasmuch as the Court's awards are not intended to be punitive, what should matter is the victim's situation, not that of the respondent state. If the breaching state is poor and the applicant, who was a former citizen, now lives permanently in a richer country, the pecuniary compensation should also be higher. The same amount of money cannot have the same value, and thus offer the same benefit, in countries with different levels of economic development. The purchasing power will be more or less than anticipated by the judges at the moment of their ruling. For that reason, the Court should rethink its approach.

Ultimately, the moral harm per se is the same for all individuals, only the concrete redress differs, that is, the sum of money assigned, not the form of reparation. However, no pattern can be discerned within the Court's case law which allows the conclusion that financial awards are predominantly made in respect of rich countries, and that most declarations in which the finding of a violation is enough are made in the case of poor countries. The level of compensation depends on the nature of the infringement. There may nonetheless be a certain type of wrongful conduct prevailing in some countries, according to their democratic level of development.

While it is commendable that the Court employs various solutions to assure consistency of its impressive case law, it is highly questionable why it prefers to do so to the detriment of transparency. The Grand Chamber, confronted with a disappearance case, denied the existence of 'specific scales of damages that should be awarded',[625] and put forward the ambiguous principle of equity. Why are those standards not revealed to the public? Are there any arguments for the confidentiality of the

[625] *Varnava*, note 157, para. 225.

tables on Article 41 claims? At this point it might be worth wondering what the practical effects may be.

First and foremost, if those tables were made public, they would certainly represent a valuable tool for both applicants and domestic courts. To express it in a pragmatic, lawyer's language, plaintiffs would be aware that the monetary value of their personal suffering does not weigh more. They would be prevented from bringing patently excessive claims. The municipal courts would also benefit from guidance in making awards for moral harm, which would reinforce the meaning of the principle of subsidiarity and thus simplify the work of the Court. Furthermore, the Court may expand those tables so as to include much larger and more diverse groups of violations. In that respect, it may take guidance, for example, from the UN Compensation Commission, which has already established ceilings for compensation for mental pain and anguish which are dependent upon the category of claimant and types of violation and injury.[626]

In revealing and further developing those tables, the Court may also avoid a degree of subjectivity on the part of its judges, who come from different legal and cultural backgrounds. Even if it leads to the objectification of the moral suffering, an objective approach based on legal reasoning is to be preferred to the present subjective discretion hidden behind the shield of an allegedly inspiring equity. Therefore, what would be the negative consequences?

The most undesirable effect appears to be that states would know the price for their wrongful conduct and would thus be 'encouraged' to persist in their activity instead of changing internal legislation and practice, which would probably cost more. But are not states already aware how much the Court awards for a violation, especially if it is a repetitive one? The case law is fairly abundant and it would be difficult to argue that governments do not keep the evidence. The proof lies in their observations on the merits of a case and particularly on just satisfaction, where they mention jurisprudence in their favour.

Another effect might be that governments would probably disagree with the amounts allocated for specific violations, and also with

[626] Decision 8: Determination of Ceilings for Compensation for Mental Pain and Anguish (UN Doc. S/AC.26/1992/8, 27 January 1992), taken by the Governing Council of the United Nations Compensation Commission during its Fourth Session, at the 22nd meeting, held on 24 January 1992. For a study, see V. Heiskanen, 'The United Nations Compensation Commission', *Collected Courses of the Hague Academy of International Law* 296 (2002).

the distribution according to the economic development of the state concerned. Scholars and practitioners would also comment on the matter. However, standards are in any case applied, and the Court's practice stands for that. The judges would be bound by some more objective criteria and, even if not more transparent, at least they would be more consistent.

Other predictable consequences would reverberate on the Court's activity. It is highly arguable that the existence of standardized tables would increase the number of applications, on the grounds that plaintiffs would have nothing to lose if they send their claims to Strasbourg. This is because in any event the statistics show that more than 90 per cent of applications are declared inadmissible, a figure which demonstrates that complainants have always submitted, and will always submit, unfounded allegations. Nonetheless, the tables may offer victims a sort of incentive to wait and hope for the highest sum, instead of being interested in reaching a friendly settlement with the government, and thus relieving the judges of further pronouncement on the merits. While it is true that the Court's statistics for 1959–2013 show that friendly settlements/strike-out judgments accounted for some 6 per cent,[627] one should also take into account that friendly settlements are normally concluded by those plaintiffs who do not want to wait several years for the Convention proceedings, but prefer instead to get some money more easily.

The figures may also deter governments from launching into friendly-settlement discussions, preferring instead to wait for the Court's judgment in view of the fact that the corresponding award is likely to be low. Such a scenario is also doubtful, because that strategy would ultimately cost states more than the individual payments. The Court may at any moment consider that an accumulation of similar cases denotes a structural failure which demands general measures from the state. The effect will be that the state concerned must allocate internal resources to change the legal framework. Rational states therefore have an interest in avoiding by all means a finding of a violation, not only because of negative publicity, but also for financial reasons.

To conclude, can it be assumed that some human rights violations are less important than others, in so far as standards of compensation are different? Is there hierarchization among different rights or among victims of a violation of the same right? In fact, the system of protection

[627] See the statistics on violations by article and by state (1959–2013), available on the Court's website (www.echr.coe.int/Pages/home.aspx?p=reports&c=).

admits entitlement to moral damage for all breaches, without distinction. Differentiation comes only in the context of a concrete assessment of reparation, which reasonably and normally depends on the type and gravity of a violation, according to the circumstances of each case. It should be conceded that some infringements are less serious than others, not necessarily because they concern different rights, but because of the specific conditions of perpetration. This is not to say that the corresponding rights guaranteed by the Convention are less important, but only that an interference may produce effects which are more severe. A different assessment is accepted as long as it is not arbitrary.

4.4.3 *The middle way for awards in respect of costs and expenses*

While conceptually less important than moral damage, the Court used in the past to give more reasons for a reimbursement of costs and expenses than for an award in respect of non-pecuniary harm. This has led the former to be slightly easier to anticipate. However, the continuous increase of the caseload reverberates negatively on the quality of the Court's judgments, and thus on predictability. In some cases, without even mentioning if a plaintiff has submitted any evidence in support of his allegations, the Court first considers the conditions for making an award, and then admits or rejects a claim with the following laconic copy/paste formula: '[i]n the present case, regard being had to the documents in its possession and the above criteria . . . '.[628] Does this interfere with the predictability of compensation for legal costs?

The Court's discretion is not as great as in the context of moral injury, although in many cases reimbursement is allowed on a reasonable basis. It still exercises discretion, although, by the definition that the Court itself has given, costs must have been actually incurred, and therefore they should be calculated, not estimated. As a drafting strategy, the judges usually declare that they have examined all the documents in their possession. From the perspective of the predictability of an award, such a decision must be read between the lines; for example, when the Court does not mention that allegations have been supported by evidence, it means that they have not, hence the reason why they have been rejected. In consequence, if plaintiffs submit relevant documentation

[628] Compare two judgments delivered on the same day by two different Court Sections: *Szerdahelyi v. Hungary*, no. 30385/07, 17 January 2012, paras. 40–2, and *A.A. v. Russia*, no. 49097/08, 17 January 2012, paras. 109–11.

and if their claims meet the well-established criteria for making an award, the prospects for reimbursement of costs and expenses are reasonably good.

4.4.4 *Awards that denote some punitive character*

The general and uncontested rule in international law is that punitive damages are not accepted.[629] At the moment of codification of the rules of state responsibility, during the controversies raised by the concept of international crimes of states, the ILC was confronted with proposals to introduce a possibility for 'payment of damages reflecting the gravity of the breach'.[630] Although there was agreement that this sort of 'aggravated' damages was not equivalent to punitive damages, in order to avoid any provision with punitive connotations in the field of state responsibility it was decided to remove the concept altogether.[631] Some punitive element may nonetheless be perceived in the remedy of satisfaction, because it is not precisely focused on reparation, but rather on the victim's personal satisfaction of seeing the perpetrator regret the unlawful conduct.[632]

Both the European and Inter-American systems of human rights protection resort to the general theory. The Inter-American Court has clearly declared that the system of reparation is compensatory, not punitive, and that the practice of some domestic courts to award exemplary awards in order to deter repetition is not applicable in international law.[633] On the contrary, the Strasbourg Court's position is not so firm. While it is true that it has not accepted such requests, neither has it absolutely excluded such a possibility. The Practice Direction for just satisfaction claims reads as follows:

[629] On punitive damages, see C. Gray, *Judicial Remedies in International Law* (Oxford: Clarendon Press, 1990), at 26–8; N. Jorgensen, 'A Reappraisal of Punitive Damages in International Law', *British Yearbook of International Law* 68 (1997); S. Wittich, 'Awe of the Gods and Fear of the Priests: Punitive Damages in the Law of State Responsibility', *Austrian Review of International and European Law* 3 (1998), and, by the same author, 'Punitive Damages', in Crawford, Pellet and Olleson, note 46; and Shelton, note 543, at 354–67. For an analysis of punitive and aggravated damages in domestic systems, see the contributions in H. Koziol and V. Wilcox (eds.), *Punitive Damages: Common Law and Civil Law Perspectives* (Vienna: Springer, 2009).

[630] Crawford, note 43, at 36. [631] Ibid.

[632] Barthe-Gay, note 447, at 124, and Gray, note 629, at 43.

[633] *Velásquez-Rodríguez* (reparations and costs), note 152, para. 38.

> The purpose of the Court's award in respect of damage is to compensate the applicant for the actual harmful consequences of a violation. It is not intended to punish the Contracting State responsible. The Court has therefore, until now, considered it inappropriate to accept claims for damages with labels such as 'punitive', 'aggravated' or 'exemplary'.[634]

The text holds that 'until now' the Court has not admitted such requests. Indeed, the Court has either simply rejected claims for punitive and exemplary damages,[635] or declared that it does not accept them or they are not appropriate in the circumstances of the case,[636] without any further comment or reference to the international law standards on the matter. It therefore leaves the door open for any new development in the field, particularly as the European Convention is *lex specialis* in relation to general international law. Practice reveals examples of reparation for material or moral prejudice where punitive intentions may be inferred, not only with respect to the breaching state, but also relative to applicants.

4.4.4.1 With respect to the breaching state

The Court has a broad discretion under Article 41 as to when and how to make reparation, and also in respect of the concrete amount. It usually follows its previous jurisprudence, in an attempt to secure consistency of the case law. On occasion, the awards are inexplicably higher, particularly as the Court does not give further details as to calculation. Such awards may raise questions as to the intention behind them, especially when corroborated by separate opinions from some judges. They are a fairly reliable element, in so far as their point of view will have already been made known to the other judges at the moment of deliberations, but nonetheless the majority, having preferred to maintain its position on the matter, will have done so without even giving some further arguments to assure the outsider that an exceptional award had been occasioned by the specific circumstances of the case, and not by any intention

634 Para. 9 of the Practice Direction, note 143.

635 See, e.g., *Selçuk and Asker*, note 167, para. 119; *Orhan v. Turkey*, no. 25656/94, 18 June 2002, paras. 447–9; *Tepe v. Turkey*, no. 27244/95, 9 May 2003, paras. 216–19; *İkincisoy v. Turkey*, no. 26144/95, 27 July 2004, paras. 147–50; and *Stefanou v. Greece*, no. 2954/07, 22 April 2010, para. 82.

636 See, e.g., *Cable and Others v. the United Kingdom* [GC], nos. 24436/94 et seq., 18 February 1999, para. 30; *Hood v. the United Kingdom* [GC], no. 27267/95, ECHR 1999-I, paras. 88–9; *Lustig-Prean and Beckett* (just satisfaction), note 399, para. 12; and *Greens and M.T. v. the United Kingdom*, nos. 60041/08 and 60054/08, 23 November 2010, para. 97.

to inflict a punishment or to act as a deterring example to the breaching state.

Such was the case with *Gaygusuz v. Austria*, where the Court found violations of the prohibition of discrimination and of the right to protection of property on the grounds that the plaintiff, because of his nationality, was not entitled to emergency assistance under the legislation in force. It compensated the victim with 200,000 Austrian schillings (ATS). One of the Chamber judges has nonetheless perceived a punitive intention on the part of the Court, in so far as 'however the sums are calculated, and accepting the hypotheses most favourable to the applicant (unrealistic though they are), the maximum amount he could have received in emergency assistance was about ATS 80,000'.[637]

Then, in the aforementioned *Aktaş* case, the Court awarded EUR 226,065 for future loss of earnings. The national judge expressed a dissenting opinion giving examples of previous awards.[638] Indeed, the calculation was wholly speculative and it may be reasonably perceived as a message to the respondent state, a usual 'client' of the Court as far as disappearances and unlawful killings are concerned. Moreover, the fact that the judges also found a violation of the state's treaty obligation to furnish all necessary facilities to the Commission and Court in their task of establishing the facts should not be disregarded.[639]

A further illustration, this time in respect of non-pecuniary injury, is *Ouranio Toxo and Others v. Greece*,[640] where a political party defending the Macedonian minority living in Greece and two of the members of its political secretariat alleged interference with their freedom of association on account of acts directed against them with the participation of the clergy and municipal authorities, and also in respect of the inactivity of the police when a group of demonstrators broke into and ransacked the party headquarters. The Court eventually accepted that the local population, at the instigation of the authorities, attacked and destroyed the party headquarters. The police refused to intervene, and the public prosecutor did not consider it necessary to investigate the incidents. The Court found a violation of the freedom of association and of the reasonable length of proceedings, and granted the plaintiffs a total sum of

[637] Partly dissenting opinion of Judge Matscher in *Gaygusuz v. Austria*, 16 September 1996, *Reports of Judgments and Decisions* 1996-IV.

[638] Partly dissenting opinion of Judge Gölcüklü.

[639] *Aktaş*, note 414, paras. 343–6.

[640] *Ouranio Toxo and Others v. Greece*, no. 74989/01, ECHR 2005-X (extracts).

EUR 30,000 for non-pecuniary damage. According to the two dissenting judges, that amount was excessive, in so far as it was comparable with that allocated for violations of the right to life or for torture or inhuman or degrading treatment. Hence, it would have been justified only if the Court had been allowed to establish punitive damages.[641]

In order to avoid criticism, the Court officially continues to assure states that its awards have no punitive intentions. Such was the case in *Scordino v. Italy*, where it revealed that it had used a standardized approach in respect of violations of the reasonable time requirement, making awards that were higher than those usually made before 1999. The judges have nonetheless comforted the state involved by declaring that the increase was not a punitive measure, but an encouragement for states in general to find viable solutions and also a way to compensate applicants for lack of domestic remedies.[642]

The same seems to have happened in *Pontes v. Portugal*, which concerned the removal of a child from his parents and his ultimate adoption. The Court awarded EUR 32,500 jointly to the parents, but declared that its sole intention had been to compensate their moral suffering.[643] The dissenting judges pointed to the disproportionate character of that amount not only when compared with similar breaches of the right to visit, but also when considering more serious violations in which families of persons who had disappeared received in compensation only a third of that amount.[644]

The judges have wisely transformed a punishment, which operates for a past activity, into incentives for future conduct, but the effect beyond philosophy is still the same: the wrongdoing state should avoid non-repetition. Ultimately, as aptly observed by a judge in a separate opinion, the Court also performs a pedagogical function and thus, '[t]he award of just satisfaction, besides reinstating the victim in his fundamental right, serves as a concrete warning to erring governments'.[645]

641 Partly dissenting opinion of Judges Lorenzen and Vajić.

642 *Scordino*, note 372, para. 176.

643 *Pontes v. Portugal*, no. 19554/09, 10 April 2012, para. 114.

644 Para. 22 of the separate opinion of Judges Sajó and Pinto de Albuquerque.

645 Partly dissenting opinion of Judge Bonello joined by Judge Maruste in *Nikolova*, note 276. For a view that punitive damages are necessary in the European system of human rights protection, see paras. 12–19 of the concurring opinion of Judge Pinto de Albuquerque, joined by Judge Vučinić, in *Cyprus v. Turkey* (just satisfaction), note 325.

4.4.4.2 With respect to the applicant

Some punitive intentions may also be perceived in the context of awards for moral damage to the benefit of those whose behaviour was anything but moral, for example those convicted in domestic proceedings or even presumed guilty. Such may be the case of *Minelli*, a journalist investigated for a defamatory publication, but in whose respect the prosecution had been terminated on account of limitation. The domestic courts still ordered him to pay a part of the costs of the proceedings, on the presumption that he should probably have been convicted of defamation. The Court found a breach of the presumption of innocence, but considered that the finding of a violation offers sufficient redress for non-pecuniary injury. What leaves the impression that the judges condemned his conduct is that they deemed it necessary, as a sort of justification, to raise, under the heading of non-pecuniary damage, the fact that the applicant had, in the press, accused third parties of improper commercial dealings and that the prosecution had nonetheless started the investigation at the request of those persons.[646]

In another case, which concerned an order to return to the United States a child whose mother had taken her to Belgium without her father's consent or that of the American courts, the Court compensated only the child.[647] Although it found a violation in respect of both the child and her mother, it established a causal link between breach and harm only with respect to the child. In their separate opinion, the dissenting judges denounced the majority for the punitive approach they had taken, stating that such an approach was tantamount to condemning the actions of the mother.[648]

Similarly, the Court has been little impressed by the moral prejudice alleged by criminals in respect of the regime and conditions of detention. Even if they have indeed found a violation of the prohibition of inhuman and degrading treatment, the judges have awarded relatively low amounts. Such was the case with an applicant who had killed three children, who received EUR 1,500,[649] or with a plaintiff who had killed both his first and second wives, who received EUR 2,000.[650] Although the Court may only assess an individual's rights

646 *Minelli v. Switzerland*, 25 March 1983, Series A no. 62, para. 44.
647 *B. v. Belgium*, no. 4320/11, 10 July 2012, para. 87.
648 Partly dissenting opinion of Judges Tulkens, Jočienė and Keller.
649 *Iorgov v. Bulgaria*, no. 40653/98, 11 March 2004, para. 97.
650 *G.B. v. Bulgaria*, no. 42346/98, 11 March 2004, para. 97.

under the Convention, and do so without being subjective, it would not be unreasonable to speculate that it disapproves of such behaviour, especially in view of the fact that it has included in those judgments the government's statement that a claim by that person would have been immoral and would have constituted an insult to the memory of the victims.

However, as the title of this section suggests, the likely punitive manifestations concern the applicant in the general sense, not necessarily the direct victim of a violation. A good illustration is provided by the well-known case of *McCann and Others v. the United Kingdom*, where, although they found a violation of the right to life, the judges 'punished' the plaintiffs for the victims' objectionable conduct and refused to make reparation for pecuniary and non-pecuniary damage. The Grand Chamber unanimously declared that 'having regard to the fact that the three terrorist suspects who were killed had been intending to plant a bomb in Gibraltar, the Court does not consider it appropriate to make an award under this head'.[651]

The Grand Chamber reiterated the *McCann* approach in a subsequent case which involved persons suspected of committing the terrorist attacks of 11 September 2001. It has thus distinguished the case of *A. and Others v. the United Kingdom*, on the grounds that 'it has not been established that any of the applicants has engaged, or attempted to engage, in any act of terrorist violence'.[652] Yet, although it acknowledged the large sums allocated in the past for unlawful detention, the Court underlined the emergency situation created by those attacks and decided 'that the circumstances justify the making of an award substantially lower than that which it has had occasion to make in other cases of unlawful detention'.[653]

However reprehensible the victims' actions were, the very existential logic of the Court is to apply the Convention and to decide on state responsibility, as well as to afford redress when the circumstances so justify. The general rule in international law is that the obligation of reparation arises in connection with 'the injury caused by the internationally wrongful act',[654] and is therefore an objective notion. From a

[651] *McCann*, note 269, para. 219.
[652] *A. and Others v. the United Kingdom* [GC], no. 3455/05, ECHR 2009, para. 251.
[653] Ibid., para. 253. [654] Article 31 of the ILC Articles.

legal perspective, the Strasbourg judges have erroneously linked the necessity of redress with a subjective element, that is, the victim's personality. The victim's condition may play a role, but simply for individualizing the level of compensation, not for deciding entitlement to reparation. As aptly noted by Tomuschat, the absence of compensation in such a case where the right to life was disregarded 'can easily be misinterpreted as a sign of tacit approval of the police action, notwithstanding its formal condemnation'.[655]

Apparently, on occasion, the judges use their broad discretion not merely to apply the treaty, but also to effect some justice and penalize the victims for their criminal intentions. Even when it awards *ultra petita*, such as in the above-mentioned cases, besides exceptional human intentions, the Court may also send a message to the state concerned that it is not allowed to go unpunished after committing serious breaches of human rights, such as those affecting the right to life.

Impulses to condemn the petitioners' inappropriate behaviour are also evident at the level of the Council of Europe. In a 2001 report on the future effectiveness of the Court, an Evaluation Group considered that the Court should play a more proactive role in the friendly-settlement discussions between the parties. It was also suggested that when applicants unreasonably refuse an offer, the judges could dispense with their consent in discontinuing their case.[656] The Court has been very receptive to that proposition and has implemented, even in that year, the practice of unilateral declarations examined in the next chapter. Such a practice of deciding a case only to the advantage of one party is arguably in conflict with the individual right of petition, and thus a sanction against the victim's unwillingness to accept the terms of an agreement with the offender.

4.4.5 *Award of a lump sum – useful practice?*

The Court often awards a lump sum in respect of both pecuniary and non-pecuniary damage or in respect of costs and expenses. To award a lump sum means to allocate an amount for the entire damage or for the entire costs claimed by the victim, without differentiating between the

[655] Tomuschat, note 266, at 1428.

[656] Para. 62 of the Report of the Evaluation Group to the Committee of Ministers on the European Court of Human Rights, EG Court(2001)1, 27 September 2001 (available at https://wcd.coe.int/ViewDoc.jsp?id=226195&Lang=fr).

two types of damage or between the different costs involved in the internal proceedings and the Strasbourg proceedings. The question is, who benefits from that practice?

First and foremost, the lump-sum practice is a useful tool in the hands of the judges. They do not have to categorize the prejudice or to assess its limits. They only allocate a sum that appears to be equitable in the circumstances of the case. In reality, however, it seems that they choose the lump-sum award when they find it difficult to assess the moral damage. When the plaintiff has demonstrated the material loss, it is a convenient practical solution to round that sum up so as to reflect, more or less, the additional moral harm. It is also an alternative to appease a divergent practice of the Court. If there are discrepancies in previous awards made for similar types of damage, by awarding a lump sum the judges avoid taking a clear stance on the matter.

Another aspect is that the practice reflects the large discretion normally enjoyed by the judges in the field of reparation. A lump sum does not allow differentiation between the heads of damage. It may thus create a certain frustration for the applicants, in so far as they see their claim amalgamated and treated as if their individualization has little significance for the judges. In fact, a lump-sum award deprives a judgment of its pedagogical function. Neither the plaintiff nor the defendant government are given any indication as to the manner in which the Court has weighed the effects of a violation. When that sum is given in respect of costs and expenses, a claimant who is represented by a lawyer cannot assess the concrete amount allocated for representation before the Court. It may thus generate some arguments between lawyer and client as to the amount awarded for legal services, and indirectly as to the necessity and quality of that assistance.

Also, when the Court has found several violations, a lump sum does not permit an observer or prospective complainants to understand what the judges deemed as being appropriate compensation. In the absence of clarification, such an award may very well conceal an intention on their part to 'punish' the breaching state or even to apply different standards for a plurality of infringements. In any event, when the value of the material prejudice at stake is significant, a lump sum may denote an intention by the judges to bypass the moral damage, especially in property disputes where the pecuniary loss may largely outweigh the non-pecuniary harm. However, the part of the sum corresponding to the non-pecuniary prejudice may be easily estimated by reference to previous awards for moral damage in similar cases.

A lump-sum award seems to be a very convenient and practical solution for the Court, inasmuch as it allows the judges to easily appreciate the whole damage suffered by the victim and to give no further explanation for their choice. This is plainly illustrated by the recent award in *Cyprus v. Turkey*, where the Court has allocated considerable amounts without revealing any basis for calculation. The practice thus stands in conflict with a desire for a transparent and consistent system of reparation. In other words, it should not be overused, because it may give the impression that the Court deals with reparation superficially. If the Court were to adopt, as advocated at the end of the present study, a standardized approach to reparation based on a set of equitable principles, the lump-sum practice would lack justification.

5

Procedure and execution

Claims for just satisfaction are generally considered at the same time as the finding of a violation. When the question is not ready for decision, the Court may adjourn it. The state may express its willingness to make reparation before the Court's ruling on the applicant's demands. It may do so domestically, by reopening the case and providing compensation, or in Strasbourg, by proposals for a friendly settlement or through a unilateral declaration. In any event, the reparation offered to the applicant comes under the Court's scrutiny.

Owing to the fact that in the drafting of the Convention, express proposals to give the Court a power to annul legislation and other domestic acts, or to direct the responsible state to take particular action, were rejected, the judges have always declined to interpret the former Article 50 and the present Article 41 in that sense. They dismissed requests to annul or repeal legal provisions,[657] to annul disciplinary sanctions or sentences,[658] and to order a state either to make a specific declaration[659] or to take measures for preventing future violations.[660] However, the Court has recently started, in the context of systemic violations, to suggest the need for general measures. Apparently, the broad language of Article 41 does not prevent the Court from indicating specific measures, be they individual or general.

5.1 Compensation following the finding of a violation

Obtaining redress is not an automatic consequence of the finding of a violation. If an applicant has not claimed any compensation, the Court

[657] For example, in *Marckx*, note 111, para. 58.

[658] See, e.g., *Albert and Le Compte v. Belgium* (Article 50), 24 October 1983, Series A no. 68, para. 9.

[659] See, e.g., *Dudgeon* (Article 50), note 236, para. 15, and *Campbell and Cosans* (Article 50), note 418, paras. 15–16.

[660] *McGoff v. Sweden*, 26 October 1984, Series A no. 83, paras. 30–1.

will not consider the matter of its own motion.[661] Yet, there have been some perhaps unfortunate exceptions when an applicant sought redress only for non-pecuniary damage, but the judges held that 'he undoubtedly suffered some pecuniary and non-pecuniary damage' and allocated an amount for both heads of damage.[662] If the judges need further elements to decide on the matter, then the application of Article 41 will be included in a separate judgment.[663] Normally, applicants must observe certain requirements when seeking compensation because, if not raised in the proper form, they risk their claims being rejected.

5.1.1 Procedural requirements when lodging a claim for compensation

Plaintiffs must lodge a specific claim within the mandatory time limit, which is usually the same as that for submitting observations on the merits of the dispute. In this respect, at the time of communication, notice is given to the applicants as to the text of Rule 60 of the Rules of Court, which deals with claims for just satisfaction. According to that provision, a plaintiff must submit itemized particulars of all claims, together with any relevant supporting documents. The Court is generally very strict as to these conditions and often rejects, in whole or in part, all demands which are not made in due time, or are not supported by evidence.[664] The applicant's claims for just satisfaction are then submitted to the government concerned for comments. Before the old Court, the Commission was also invited to submit comments.

The Practice Direction for just satisfaction claims provides that the Court will reject claims raised in the application form but not resubmitted at the appropriate stage of the proceedings, which means normally in the plaintiff's response to the government's observations on the merits.[665] There are, nonetheless, examples when the Court did award compensation for claims raised only in the application form, especially

[661] See, e.g., *Francesco Lombardo v. Italy*, 26 November 1992, Series A no. 249-B, para. 25.

[662] *Burczy v. Poland*, no. 43129/04, 11 February 2014, paras. 46 and 48, and point 3 of the operative part.

[663] Rule 75(1) of the Rules of Court.

[664] See, among many others, *Sýkora v. Slovakia*, no. 26077/03, 18 January 2011, paras. 30–3.

[665] Para. 5 *in fine* of the Practice Direction, note 143. For an example, see *Fadıl Yılmaz v. Turkey*, no. 28171/02, 21 July 2005, para. 26.

in repetitive cases, and even when the plaintiff was represented by a lawyer in the Strasbourg proceedings and thus was presumed to have known the procedure.[666] However humane this attitude may be, it overcame the judges' awareness of the need for consistency of the case law.

A petitioner may also waive the right to claim reparation. Most of the waivers in the Court's jurisprudence pertain to procedural rights, but there may also be cases raising the issue of waivers of substantive rights, such as the right to just satisfaction.[667] Certainly, the question appears to be mainly theoretical, because the whole logic of the protection system is to establish responsibility and provide redress. But the issue did come up in the Court's early practice, in *Neumeister*. The government argued that the victim had benefited from the pardoning of his prison sentence and thus renounced his right to claim compensation before the Court, whereas the applicant contended that he would have withdrawn his claim only if the state had waived all possible claims against him arising out of the facts leading to his conviction. Confronted with such an ambiguous situation, the judges dismissed the government's submissions on the grounds that the alleged waiver had not resulted from unequivocal statements or documents.[668] However, given the specificity of entitlement to reparation, it cannot be said that a waiver would run counter to any important public interest that would justify the continuation of the examination.[669]

A claim for redress may also be nullified by a Court decision to strike out the application. According to Article 37 of the Convention, the judges may discontinue a case on either subjective or objective grounds. They may thus consider that a plaintiff's behaviour denotes no intention to pursue the application, that the matter under dispute has been resolved or that some other reasons justify termination of the proceedings. In that case, the petitioner loses the prospect of obtaining redress in Strasbourg, unless the general interest of respect for human rights requires continuation of the examination or, exceptionally, the judges subsequently decide to restore the application.

[666] See, e.g., *Chiorean v. Romania*, no. 20535/03, 21 October 2008, paras. 31–4, where the Court dismissed the claims for costs and expenses as being unsubstantiated, not because they were not submitted at the appropriate stage of the proceedings.

[667] See L. Caflisch, 'Waivers in International and European Human Rights Law', in M. H. Arsanjani et al. (eds.), *Looking to the Future: Essays on International Law in Honor of W. Michael Reisman* (Leiden: Martinus Nijhoff Publishers, 2011), at 421–31.

[668] *Neumeister* (Article 50), note 90, para. 36.

[669] *Håkansson and Sturesson v. Sweden*, 21 February 1990, Series A no. 171-A, para. 66.

5.1.2 *Is the question of just satisfaction ready for decision?*

The Court has adopted a practical and objective approach, based on the circumstances and evidence in each particular case, but also having due regard for the interest of the good administration of justice. In the great majority of cases, it rules on just satisfaction on the basis of all the relevant documentary evidence already submitted by the parties in support of their allegations as to the existence and amount or value of damage. In the event of an award, it mentions in the operative part of its judgment the amounts of money, the type of damage covered and the currency in which those sums are to be paid.

When in doubt about the application of Article 41, the Court invites the parties to submit written observations on the matter and, in particular, to notify it of any agreement that they may reach. Depending on the complexity of the case, the deadline for observations is either three or six months from the date on which the judgment on the merits becomes final,[670] as before that date the parties also have the possibility to request referral to the Grand Chamber within the three-month period from the date of delivery of the judgment. Even if the issue of reparation is adjourned, the Court may still suggest to the respondent state that some individual measures would be appropriate.[671] The question of just satisfaction shall be decided, as far as possible, by the same judges who considered the merits of the case.

The Court reserved for the first time the question of just satisfaction in the *Belgian linguistic* case in 1968.[672] The case was brought by French-speaking parents of Belgian nationality, who wanted their children to be educated in French. The majority of the Plenary Court considered that a domestic legal provision prevented certain children, solely on the basis of the residence of their parents, from having access to the existing French-language schools, and further reserved for the applicants concerned the

670 There may also be exceptions: for example, the Court reduced that time limit to one month in *Gatt v. Malta* (no. 28221/08, ECHR 2010, point 4(b) of the operative part). By contrast, in *Cyprus v. Turkey* the judges have not imposed any time limit for the parties to submit their just satisfaction claims, hence a delay of almost nine years was not considered as being problematic: see *Cyprus v. Turkey* (just satisfaction), note 325, paras. 23–30.

671 For example, in the above-mentioned *Gatt* case, the judges considered that '[b]earing in mind the urgent need to put an end to the violation of Article 5 § 1 . . . the respondent State should in any event give consideration to securing the applicant's immediate release from detention' (para. 59 *in fine*).

672 *Belgian linguistic*, note 13.

right to claim just satisfaction. Given that no subsequent claim was lodged, the case was closed by the Committee of Ministers, while noting the legislative measures taken by the state.

The question of just satisfaction is normally reserved when the dispute is very complex, or when the judges do not dispose of all elements for taking a decision. As is well known, the ruling on reparation in *Cyprus v. Turkey* has been delayed for thirteen years. Mostly, such may be the case when the plaintiff has not formulated a detailed claim,[673] when expert reports are needed for the evaluation of property,[674] or when there is great discrepancy between the expert reports already submitted by the parties.[675] If only one of the parties submits evidence, and if it is pertinent, the Court usually considers the pecuniary loss on the basis of those submissions, without asking for justifications from the other party as well. The judges are not proactive in this respect because it is the parties' obligation to produce pertinent evidence in support of their allegations. In general, claims for compensation for taking of property or payment of large amounts are normally, albeit not necessarily, attested by an expert report.

In addition, the matter may be adjourned when, according to the parties, the internal law may afford *restitutio in integrum*. For example, in *Schuler-Zgraggen v. Switzerland*, the government informed the Court about the introduction of a new law allowing the reopening of the proceedings following a finding of a violation in Strasbourg. The Court reserved the issue of pecuniary damage, but eventually found that, although the government had made a retroactive payment of an invalidity pension, it had failed to pay interest on the sums returned to the applicant.[676] In situations of this type, when the question of just satisfaction is reserved on the grounds that a victim may obtain redress at home, the Court gives such opportunity to the respondent government, but also verifies whether the reparation made is in agreement with the Convention standards. In other words, it may lead to a duplication of work, with the Court having the final word.

The Court may also reserve the question of just satisfaction when in doubt about the existence of one of the conditions for making an award.

[673] *Gatt*, note 670, para. 58. [674] *Papamichalopoulos* (Article 50), note 91, para. 48.

[675] *Petroiu v. Romania*, no. 33055/09, 24 November 2009, paras. 29 and 31, where the value of the property at issue amounted to EUR 1,464,000 according to the expert report submitted by the applicant, and to EUR 259,603 according to the government's expert report.

[676] *Schuler-Zgraggen* (Article 50), note 400, para. 15.

In *Kostovski v. the Netherlands*, where the constraints affecting the rights of the defence were contrary to the right to a fair trial, the Court adjourned its ruling on compensation in the absence of any information as to whether and, if so, to what extent the internal law allowed redress for the consequences of the violation found.[677] Eventually, following a friendly settlement between the parties, the Court discontinued the application.

In some cases, only a part of the claims for reparation need further consideration. In general, the Court does not reserve exclusively the question of moral damage, because non-pecuniary damage, by its very nature, does not lend itself to precise calculation, so there is usually no need for other evidence. It can be assessed on the basis of the violation found. Yet, the judges may reserve assessment of both pecuniary and non-pecuniary damage. As for costs and expenses, when not adjourned with the other types of prejudice, they may be supplemented in the later judgment.

Most often when the just satisfaction is reserved in part, it is only the question of pecuniary damage which may not be ready for decision at the moment of the examination on the merits. The reasons may be the same as those mentioned above, namely the complexity of the case and the lack of pertinent evidence necessary in order to assess the loss of or divergence between data submitted by the parties. When adjourning the question of pecuniary damage, the Court may also take into account the possibility of further individual or general measures to be taken by the respondent government.[678]

What seems to emerge from the relevant practice before establishment of the full-time Court is that the old Court used to give preference to separate judgments on just satisfaction. To be sure, the judges were not dealing with the same number of cases as they were in the post-1990 era, when almost all of the Central and Eastern European countries, including Russia, joined the Council of Europe.

The two methods both have pros and cons. A separate judgment on just satisfaction, in those situations in which the Court had reserved the question only in part, allows a victim to complain that the state has not executed its obligation. The applicant may thus claim interest for the sums awarded in the principal judgment but not paid, or not paid in due time.[679] Another advantage would be that a separate judgment

[677] *Kostovski v. the Netherlands*, 20 November 1989, Series A no. 166, para. 48.
[678] See, e.g., *Hutten-Czapska v. Poland* [GC], no. 35014/97, ECHR 2006-VIII, para. 247.
[679] See, e.g., *Hentrich* (Article 50), note 166, para. 14.

theoretically allows the state to make reparation at home, although in practice this rarely happens. What is more likely to happen though is that, following a violation on the merits, the parties may be more disposed towards a friendly settlement, as was the case in *Broniowski v. Poland*, where the violation of the applicant's property right originated in a widespread, systemic problem affecting a whole class of persons.[680] This may absolve the Court's judges from abstract calculations, still without exempting them from assessing the domestic compensation. Furthermore, if the state provides redress at national level, there is a considerable prospect of the victim being malcontent or distrustful, and thus complaining again to the Court about the type or amount of reparation.

However, lately the ever-increasing backlog leaves the Court no other practical choice than to dispose of cases, whenever possible, in a single judgment. This method has the uncontested advantage of celerity. The applicant is thus not left in uncertainty for some extra time, and the Court quickly disposes of the case, concentrating its resources on the other petitions. Indeed, the Registry lawyers do not have to look at the circumstances of a case on two separate occasions and draft two judgments. Moreover, the judges refrain from speculation as to the possible conduct of the state once it has been found in violation.

The Inter-American Court has adopted a similar approach. Its Rules of Procedure have been modified several times, but maintain the possibility of making a specific ruling on reparations in the judgment on the merits. The latest rules approved in 2009 have also introduced the possibility for the Court of San José to decide upon the preliminary objections, the merits, and the reparations and costs of the case in a single judgment.[681] Certainly, when circumstances so justify, the judges will leave the question of reparation for subsequent consideration.

5.2 Compensation when the state is willing to settle the dispute

The Convention system gives an applicant the possibility to receive compensation even if the proceedings are not concluded by a Court

680 *Broniowski v. Poland* (friendly settlement) [GC], no. 31443/96, ECHR 2005-IX. Also see Myjer, note 620, at 110.

681 Article 42(6). Article 37(6) of the 2003 Rules provided only for the possibility of deciding the preliminary objections and the merits of the case in a single judgment. The Rules of the Inter-American Court are available on its website (www.corteidh.or.cr/index.php/en/about-us/reglamento/reglamento-vigente).

judgment. It means that plaintiffs may obtain redress even in the absence of an official finding of a violation, because states may be interested in settling a dispute and making reparation before a pronouncement by the judges, in order to avoid some bad publicity. States are reasonably more inclined to do so when a complaint follows the well-established case law of the Court – regardless of the type of violation alleged – and thus the outcome would be rather predictable.

When the state is inclined to settle a dispute in anticipation of the Court's ruling, the applicant's reaction would normally direct the conflict in one of two directions. On the one hand, when the petitioner is ready to negotiate the terms of an agreement with the government, and if eventually both parties consent, they conclude a friendly settlement. The reparation is fixed jointly by the conflicting parties. On the other hand, when the applicant unreasonably refuses or abandons discussions with the adverse party, or when the parties fail to agree on a compromise, the government may still submit an offer for compensation by way of a unilateral declaration. The reparation is established in this case by a unilateral decision by the government.

In both situations, the Court is called upon to endorse the course of action. If the Court agrees, it may strike the entire application, or part of it, out of its list of cases. It may do so only if it considers that it is no longer justified to continue the examination of the application, and if it is also satisfied with respect for human rights as defined in the treaty.[682] As aptly noted some decades ago, that scrutiny performed by the Court confirms the principle of public order attached to the protection of human rights under the Convention.[683]

It may be arguable whether applicants should be compelled to end a dispute only because the government wants to. Yet, an Evaluation Group created to make proposals aimed at securing the effectiveness of the Court considered that 'the conclusion of a friendly settlement can involve substantial budgetary savings for the Court', and therefore suggested reinforcement of so-called 'incentives to settle'.[684] In the opinion of that Group, the Court should deprive petitioners of part of their costs in cases where they had declined a settlement offer deemed by the Court

682 Article 37(1) *in fine* of the Convention.

683 P. Vegleris, 'Modes de redressement des violations de la Convention européenne des droits de l'homme: esquisse d'une classification', in *Mélanges offerts à Polys Modinos: problèmes des droits de l'homme et de l'unification européenne* (Paris: Pédone, 1968), at 373.

684 Para. 62 of the Report of the Evaluation Group, note 656.

to be reasonable, or even dispense with their consent in striking out their case if their refusal to accept a settlement offer was unreasonable.[685] However exaggerated these proposals would have appeared back in 2001 when they were made, they have nonetheless been implemented by the judges. While it is almost impossible to prove the infliction of a pecuniary punishment on recalcitrant plaintiffs, albeit that it is not unreasonable to apply one, the second approach of ignoring the claimant's approval of terms of settlement has been openly endorsed by the Court in the form of recognition of unilateral declarations submitted by the government concerned.

A detailed analysis of friendly settlements and unilateral declarations is therefore in order. Both are procedural incidents that put an end to a dispute in Strasbourg without the need for examination of the merits of a case. Therefore, do they offer effective reparation to the applicant? In fact, what do the judges consider before reaching a decision? Is the desideratum of human rights protection maintained by dispensing with the Court's scrutiny of an alleged violation? At first glance, the policy of friendly settlements and unilateral declarations seems to be fairly problematic.

5.2.1 *Friendly settlement*

5.2.1.1 Notion

A friendly settlement may be defined as a compromise between the conflicting parties to terminate the proceedings. The parties thus avoid a win–lose epilogue to their dispute and generate gain on both sides. The procedure draws upon the international law rules on peaceful settlement of disputes. Within the Strasbourg system, it is also an expression of the underlying principle of subsidiarity, according to which it is the role of the states to protect human rights in the first place and thus to offer remedies. Article 39 of the Convention allows the Court to place itself, at any stage of the proceedings, at the disposal of the parties concerned with a view to securing a friendly settlement. Whether the applicant, the defendant government or the Court itself takes the initiative or makes a proposal is less important. What matters is that the parties agree on a common position.

Prior to the latest amendments effectively brought about by Protocol No. 14 in 2010, the treaty provided that the Court was to be involved in

685 Ibid.

friendly-settlement discussions only if it had declared an application admissible. The new procedure is therefore more permissive, with a view to reducing the workload, and plaintiffs are encouraged to negotiate an agreement from the very beginning of their request. As rightly observed, it simply represents codification of the existing practice, given that even before that amendment the judges used to apply that principle in virtue of the Rules of Court.[686] However, the Court has the power, not an obligation, to place itself at the parties' disposal.

Negotiations for agreement are confidential and cannot be used or referred to in the contentious proceedings.[687] They usually take the form of letters between the parties, passing through the Registry. In fact, all documents deposited within the framework of friendly-settlement negotiations are not accessible to the public.[688] A breach of the confidentiality principle may lead to an application being declared inadmissible on grounds of abuse of the right of petition. The parties are thus given confidence to launch discussions and to make concessions in an attempt to put an end to their dispute as quickly as possible, at the same time being assured that, in case negotiations fail, their submissions or their attitude towards settlement will be treated without prejudice to their arguments on the merits or in respect of any claims for just satisfaction. Indeed, neither the parties nor the Court make any pronouncement as to the merits of the case.

Friendly settlements are frequently concluded in repetitive cases, but petitioners should not be subjected to any form of pressure from the authorities.[689] Statistics demonstrate that agreements became popular among applicants especially after the entry into force of Protocol No. 11 in 1998. For example, 2001 statistics show that friendly settlements amounted to 20 per cent of the applications declared admissible.[690] It is difficult, however, to draw accurate graphics based on the Court's official statistics, because disputes ending in a friendly settlement are struck out by decisions, and statistics usually count only the total number of decisions, without mentioning their specific type. There are also decisions which terminate the proceedings on the basis of a friendly settlement concluded before or even after the communication of a case,

[686] F. Ang and E. Berghmans, 'Friendly Settlements and Striking Out of Applications', in Lemmens and Vandenhole, note 201, at 91.

[687] Article 39(2) of the Convention and Rule 62(2) of the Rules of Court.

[688] Rule 33(1) of the Rules of Court.

[689] *Kurt*, note 249, paras. 159–60.

[690] Van Dijk et al., note 241, at 228.

but generally before a pronouncement on admissibility. Those decisions are not taken into account in the Court's statistics.

Friendly settlement of international litigation is not an exclusive feature of the Strasbourg system. The American Convention also offers that possibility, building upon the European model.[691] The question is whether the prospect of an agreement between the parties, which would prevent the Inter-American Court from exercising scrutiny over the level of protection, is appropriate for that particular regime. One cannot but agree that, even if the number of judgments delivered by the two courts is completely incomparable, unlike the average type of dispute coming to Strasbourg,[692] the American system of control is predominantly confronted with gross violations of human rights.

5.2.1.2 Evolution

In its original wording, the Convention expressly reserved for the Commission the principal role in friendly-settlement proceedings. By contrast with the present version of the treaty, according to which 'the Court *may* place itself at the disposal of the parties',[693] the former text provided that the Commission '*shall* place itself at the disposal of the parties'.[694] What for the Court is an option, for the Commission was an obligation.

Agreements were possible not only before adoption of the Commission's report on the merits of a case, but also when the dispute was further referred to the Court or to the Committee of Ministers.[695] The Commission, through its Secretariat, used to make pecuniary

691 Article 48(1)(f) of the American Convention.

692 According to the Court's statistics for the whole period 1959–2013, in respect of the subject matter of the Court's violation judgments, 43.13% concerned the right to a fair trial, 12.64% concerned the protection of property, and only 12.00% concerned the right to liberty and security, 8.98% concerned the prohibition of torture and inhuman or degrading treatment, and 4.34% concerned the right to life. See the Court's statistics, note 627.

693 Article 39(1) of the Convention, emphasis added.

694 Former Article 28(b) of the Convention, emphasis added.

695 Friendly settlement is an option at the parties' disposal only as from 1 January 1983 before the Court and as from June 1987 before the Committee of Ministers: see C. A. Nørgaard and H. C. Krüger, 'Article 28-1-b et Article 28-2', in Pettiti, Decaux and Imbert, note 17, footnotes 2 and 3 at 662. For a survey of friendly-settlement proceedings before the Convention organs prior to Protocol No. 11, see V. Berger, 'Le règlement amiable devant la Cour', in Pettiti, Decaux and Imbert, note 17; I. Cabral Barreto, 'Le règlement amiable devant la Cour européenne des droits de l'homme', *Bulletin des droits de l'homme* 10 (2002); and Keller, Forowicz and Engi, note 460, at 18–31.

proposals, and hardly ever made suggestions for legislative or administrative reform.[696] There were no cases when a friendly settlement was refused and, during its existence, about 12 per cent of cases were settled in this way.[697] The first friendly settlement before the Commission was reached in 1965,[698] and up to the end of 1998, when it ceased to exist, the Commission had drafted 412 such reports.[699]

The role played by the Commission in bringing parties to a compromise was of certain importance, at least in theory. Former Article 47 of the Convention mentioned that an application declared admissible was to be referred to the Court only after the Commission had certified the failure of friendly-settlement discussions.[700] The Commission also had the power to issue a provisional opinion on the merits of a case. That information was a key element in shaping the parties' motivation for a compromise. It was communicated exclusively to them, without the authorization to be used outside the friendly-settlement framework.[701] In general, the effectiveness of those agreements was open to doubt, because the Convention was not providing for an express supervision of the execution of the obligations undertaken by the parties as a part of their agreement. The Commission's report was transmitted to the Committee of Ministers only for information.

The Commission played an active role in negotiations for settlement in some inter-state applications. Thus, in the proceedings established by the first two cases lodged by Cyprus against Turkey, it aborted the attempts to compromise owing to Turkey's refusal to co-operate. Also, in the dispute brought by France, Norway, Denmark, Sweden and the Netherlands against Turkey, following the involvement of the Commission, the breaching state agreed to communicate the measures taken at the internal level, then, after each report, to engage in a dialogue with the delegates of the Commission, and finally to submit a final report on the effective implementation of the friendly settlement.[702]

[696] Cabral Barreto, note 695, at 32. [697] Costa, note 324, at 11.

[698] *Boeckmans v. Belgium*, no. 1727/62, Commission's report of 17 February 1965.

[699] Cabral Barreto, note 695, at 46.

[700] The Commission acknowledged that in a standard paragraph, but it did not imply that effective negotiations must have taken place in each case: see Nørgaard and Krüger, note 695, at 663.

[701] For an example where the Commission struck out a case because its provisional opinion on the merits was made public, see *Familiapress Zeitungs-GmbH v. Austria*, no. 20915/92, Commission's report of 3 March 1995.

[702] Commission's report of 7 December 1985, note 342.

The old Court did not participate in negotiations, nor had it any initiative in this respect, but was entitled to discontinue an application in the case of an agreement.[703] If necessary, it had the possibility to request observations from the parties, and also from the delegate of the Commission, the latter arguing mainly whether the arrangement secured respect for human rights. In practice, the old Court, like the former Commission, never refused a friendly settlement.[704] It used to strike out cases by way of judgments, which, unlike the Commission's reports, were transmitted to the Committee of Ministers for supervision of execution.

When a dispute was not referred to the Court, but was to be decided by the Committee of Ministers under former Article 32, the parties were still free to find a common denominator. Like the Court, the Committee was not involved in negotiations, but had the power to terminate the proceedings if an agreement was consistent with human rights protection. The Committee did not actually have too many occasions when, as a result of friendly settlements, it was able to discontinue applications. Only five such cases have been identified.[705]

The major transformation introduced for friendly-settlement proceedings by the entry into force of Protocol No. 11 is that the new Court took over the powers held previously not only by the old Court, but also by the former Commission and by the Committee of Ministers. Apparent confusion was produced by the drafters as to the form of the Court's decision. The amended text of the treaty provided that, in a case of agreement, the Court was to strike out applications by means of a decision.[706] On the contrary, the Rules of Court mentioned the form of a judgment.[707] Court decisions, unlike judgments, do not come under the express power of the Committee to supervise execution. The Court used to approve settlements through judgments. The latest Protocol No. 14 clarified that theoretical contradiction and established the form of a decision, with the particularity that its execution comes under the supervision of the Committee.[708] The Explanatory Report justified the choice of a decision instead of a judgment by referring to

[703] The parties had the possibility of reaching a friendly settlement before the Court's judgment on the merits or, if the question of reparation had been reserved, before the judgment on just satisfaction.

[704] Cabral Barreto, note 695, at 37. [705] Ibid., at 38.

[706] Former Article 39 of the Convention.

[707] Former Rule 44(2) of the Rules of Court.

[708] Article 39(3) and (4) of the Convention and Rule 43(3) of the Rules of Court.

some negative connotations which the latter may have for the state, and therefore the difficulty it may create for reaching a friendly settlement.[709] What is important is that this provision secures performance of the obligations resulting from the parties' agreement.

The Court places itself at the disposal of the parties for negotiations through the Registrar, not through the judges. The Registrar, acting on the instructions of the Chamber or its President, may enter into contact with the parties once an application has been declared admissible, but most of the time it intervenes when the case is communicated to the government involved. Given that, as a general rule since the exponential increase in the Court's backlog, the judges examine whenever possible the admissibility and the merits of a case in the same judgment, the parties are usually invited at the time of communication to include in their observations any proposals for a friendly settlement.

The Commission's power to deliver a provisional opinion on the merits of a case has not been preserved by the new system. But the Registrar may take the initiative and make concrete proposals for an agreement. In this respect, a few remarks may be apt. The number of communicated cases which end in the finding of at least one violation is considerably higher than those in which no violation is found. The Court's statistics for 2013 mention 797 judgments finding at least one violation, as opposed to 96 judgments finding no violation. For the entire period 1959–2013 the figures are 14,121 and 1,156, respectively. Statistics also show that fewer than 10 per cent of the applications are communicated for observations, the rest of them being disposed of at the admissibility stage.

It is not therefore unreasonable to speculate that, when a case is communicated, or has already been declared admissible, the chances for an applicant to see his or her allegations – or part of them – endorsed by the Court are fairly high. The government may also be aware of the implications of a judgment. It follows that the parties ought to proceed with extreme caution when presented with a proposal by the Registrar. That proposal is based on some scrutiny of the application materials, and is therefore the result of a general estimation of the final outcome. Moreover, the Court's Registry has the possibility to make specific proposals based on previous agreements in similar cases.[710]

[709] Para. 94 of the Explanatory Report, note 202. [710] Harris et al., note 30, at 831.

5.2.1.3 Terms of settlement

A settlement involves concessions from both sides. The parties trade their chance to win the Strasbourg proceedings. On the one hand, the government may be aware that the case is not the first raising a particular question, therefore the probability of being found in breach of the complainant's rights is rather high. Hence, it has the possibility to weigh its offer against the compensation granted in similar cases. By entering into a friendly settlement, the state avoids a judgment of a violation with inherent negative reactions, as well as its costs in the Convention proceedings. Friendly settlements do not imply recognition of a breach, either by the state or by the Court. Therefore, settlements in repetitive cases are particularly attractive for states.

On the other hand, plaintiffs may be motivated by the certitude of an immediate gain, without having to wait several more years to see their case resolved, and without having to keep asking themselves whether they will, in any case, get something or how much. Other reasons include changes in personal life, fear of publicity or repercussion following the pronouncement of a violation, pressure by the government, or a lawyer's insistence.[711] Undoubtedly, some petitioners entering into a friendly settlement may live under the impression that they would have obtained more compensation in a Court judgment, but pragmatic applicants should inquire into the Court's case law and compare their claims with awards in similar cases which – very importantly – have been brought against the same contracting party. Practice shows, for instance in the context of violations for unreasonable length of proceedings, that the amount awarded by the Court for the same delay is generally slightly higher when the breach comes out of criminal or commercial proceedings, and is also higher in cases brought against richer member countries.

However, especially in cases in which several violations have been alleged, plaintiffs are very reluctant to accept proposals coming from the government, or even from the Registry. The balance between what is expected and what is offered is offset by the applicants' lack of knowledge of the Court's jurisprudence. On the one hand, applicants usually live under the impression that all their allegations are well founded, notwithstanding statistics for the cases declared inadmissible, which show by far that in fact it is the contrary. On the other hand, while not necessarily the

[711] Berger, note 695, at 789–90.

case for the government, the Registry certainly takes into account in their proposals only the complaints which appear admissible prima facie.

But is there any difference between the financial awards in terms of quantity? Are the financial awards in friendly settlements defined according to standards other than those in Article 41? The question seems to arise only when the sum is proposed by the Court, because the opposing parties in a dispute may agree on whatever amount they choose. It may be logical that the Registry would first look to the compensation allocated in similar disputes and propose a sum that would be equitable for both parties. It may even suggest a slightly higher figure, as an incentive for the applicant to accept an agreement.[712] In fact, it seems that the Registry has already developed some 'standards of good practice',[713] which means that, when fixing an amount, it is not necessarily guided by the text of Article 41 but by precedent.

The compensation covers both pecuniary and non-pecuniary damage, as well as costs and expenses. There are cases in which reparation was granted in the form of compensation by cancellation of debt owed by the applicant.[714] In other cases, only the costs and expenses were reimbursed.[715] The sum is free of any taxes that might be applicable, and will be payable within three months from the date of notification of the decision taken by the Court to strike the case out of its list of cases. In the event of failure to pay this sum within that period, the government will also pay simple interest on it, from expiry of that period until settlement. The payment constitutes the final resolution of the case.

As in the case of a Court pronouncement on just satisfaction, friendly settlements may include, in addition to money, other individual measures. For example, in immigration cases, foreign applicants may receive a residence permit, and even a work permit, as well as assurances that they will not be expelled.[716] In criminal proceedings, agreement may be

[712] Keller, Forowicz and Engi, note 460, at 65 and 78. According to the authors, when the Registry is making a proposal, the practice is to suggest an amount that is about 10 per cent higher than that usually allocated to similar cases, in order to create an incentive for the applicant to agree with the settlement. That amount is usually reduced if the applicant disagrees and the government submits a unilateral declaration.

[713] Ibid., at 141.

[714] *Wilhelm Peyer v. Switzerland*, no. 7397/76, Commission's report of 8 March 1979.

[715] *Van Hal International Piershil B.V. v. the Netherlands*, no. 11073/84, Commission's report of 9 March 1987.

[716] *Bulus v. Sweden*, no. 9330/81, Commission's report of 8 December 1984, and *Ahmed v. Sweden*, no. 9886/05, 22 February 2007, para. 20.

reached in respect of a reopening of internal proceedings,[717] a quashing or pardoning of a prison sentence,[718] or a mention in the applicant's criminal record.[719] In civil proceedings, the terms of settlement depend on whether the adverse party is a private person or the state. Given that the state cannot intervene to the detriment of a third person's rights, a plaintiff may conclude an agreement with the government only when the civil proceedings are brought against the authorities. In that case, an applicant may, for instance, secure payment of a debt,[720] or assume an obligation in the interests of a child.[721] The government may also express regret for the events leading to the application, although not necessarily acknowledging a violation of the Convention.[722]

In addition to individual measures ordered for the applicants' sole benefit, governments may engage in general measures when the violation at issue is likely to touch upon a larger category of persons. This occurs in the context of shortcomings in internal law or practice which call for new amendments. While measures coming under the government's executive power should not pose any problem, difficulties may arise when the initiative belongs to another state branch. The principle of separation of powers prevents governments from engaging in obligations of result, instead of mere obligations of means. What a government may do is propose legislative amendments,[723] or draw the attention of the national judicial authorities to the Court's case law.[724]

In *Broniowski*, one of the most famous friendly settlements, the government assumed responsibility for legislative changes in the domestic legal order as a way to afford redress to a large number of individuals in the same situation as the applicant. Following the terms of the agreement, the Grand Chamber did not content itself with merely taking note

[717] *Jager v. Switzerland*, no. 13467/87, Commission's report of 11 December 1989.

[718] *Nagel v. Austria*, no. 7614/76, Commission's report of 2 May 1978, and *Zimmerman v. Austria*, no. 8490/79, Commission's report of 6 July 1982.

[719] *Widmaier v. the Netherlands*, no. 9573/81, Commission's report of 7 October 1986, *Decisions and Reports* (DR) 48.

[720] *Leemans-Ceurremans v. Belgium*, no. 11698/85, Commission's report of 13 November 1987.

[721] *Dunkel v. the Federal Republic of Germany*, no. 10812/84, Commission's report of 14 May 1987.

[722] *Köksal v. the Netherlands*, no. 31725/96, 20 March 2001, para. 14.

[723] *B.H. v. the United Kingdom*, no. 30307/96, Commission's report of 30 June 1998, para. 12.

[724] *Samkova v. the Slovak Republic*, no. 26384/95, Commission's report of 15 January 1997, para. 21.

of those engagements, but also analysed at length their scope. As a matter of principle, general measures are not established by the Court, because its judgments are essentially declaratory in nature. States are free to choose the appropriate measures, but the judges still apply some scrutiny, at least in theory, because such measures have to be based on respect for human rights as defined in the treaty.[725]

States may also change domestic legislation or practice before entering into friendly-settlement discussions, and then invoke those modifications in order to reach agreement.[726] A compromise is facilitated when those changes have already been implemented, it being unlikely that a complainant would abandon his application on the basis of a promise of future amendments.[727] Given that the Court generally endorses friendly settlements, it is difficult to assess whether it exercises any scrutiny over those modifications at the internal level.

Personal interest usually prevails for applicants entering into a settlement with the government. There are nevertheless examples when general measures outweighed the compensation received by the victim.[728] Plaintiffs may also accept some extra commitments, besides the classical obligation to waive any further claims based on the same facts, like renouncing internal remedies or performing certain formalities.[729]

The monetary compensation that a petitioner receives in a friendly settlement, especially when the allegations concern only one or a few violations, is usually comparable with that awarded by the Court in similar cases. It is particularly the government, rather than the applicant, which is familiar with the case law on just satisfaction, and thus may propose an amount which is more or less realistic. Leaving aside a claimant's moral expectations with regard to the outcome of a dispute, one cannot but agree that friendly settlements can save a great amount of time and stress on both sides. Inflation is not necessarily a factor, as the monetary award is normally made in euros and will be converted into the national currency of the state at the rate applicable at the date of settlement.

725 *Broniowski* (friendly settlement), note 680, para. 42.

726 *Millan i Tornes v. Andorra*, 6 July 1999, *Reports of Judgments and Decisions* 1999-IV, para. 21.

727 Nørgaard and Krüger, note 695, at 671 and examples cited at footnote 4.

728 Ibid., footnote 1 at 669.

729 Ibid., footnotes 1–5 at 668, and Cabral Barreto, note 695, footnote 23 at 33.

5.2.1.4 Effects

An agreement between the parties does not officially announce that the state was in breach of the treaty. States may admit their fault,[730] but given that they are not obliged to do so, they often include in the terms of a declaration the provision that they are making an *ex gratia* payment, which means that reparation is made without any acknowledgment of a violation. Governments usually offer petitioners a sum of money against their undertaking to waive any further claims in respect of the facts giving rise to their application. These two factors have a very important legal consequence for the applicant. In the context of a large number of member parties having accepted reopening of domestic proceedings as a result of a Court judgment, and given that the state has not accepted responsibility, a plaintiff entering into agreement can no longer challenge those facts at the internal level. But even if not offering any moral satisfaction to the plaintiff, the terms of a declaration may still amount to *restitutio in integrum* if the applicant so conceives. After all, re-establishment of the original condition bears more significance when decided by the alleged victim.

Friendly-settlement negotiations do not suspend the proceedings on the merits. In this way, if the former fail, the latter are not delayed. When informed of an agreement, the Court verifies that it has been achieved on the basis of respect for human rights,[731] and will decide whether the matter has been resolved such that the case can be closed. The aim of that control is to make sure that the compromise is fair, as well as to balance the inequality of bargaining power between states and individuals.[732] The judges weigh both the personal and the general interest. The former translates into the reparation effectively secured by the applicant, whereas the latter seeks to defend the human rights philosophy underlying the control system.

In general, the judges endorse any arrangement between the parties, as a proficient tool to dispose of the caseload, but while consistency of the case law must certainly be preserved, they should be more proactive by going beyond the terms of settlement and assessing the wider effects that an agreement may have for other persons in a similar situation to the petitioner. In fact, the judges should decline a compromise when the state concerned, although aware of the measures that it should take in

[730] See, e.g., the cases cited in Nørgaard and Krüger, note 695, footnotes 1 and 2 at 667.
[731] Rule 62(3) of the Rules of Court. [732] Costa, note 324, at 11.

order to prevent future violations, remains passive.[733] What the Court has done in practice, however, is that it has mentioned, in some judgments delivered as a result of an accord between the parties, previous similar disputes where it had already indicated to the respondent state the need for general measures.[734]

Examples of when the Court has dismissed a friendly settlement and continued to examine the case are fairly rare, and depend on the manner in which a compromise has been reached or on the evident discrepancy between the terms of settlement and the gravity of the alleged violation.[735] Such was the case, for instance, with *Ukrainian Media Group v. Ukraine*, where the Court dismissed the friendly settlement reached by the parties and continued the examination of the case on the basis of the serious nature of the complaints raised in respect of the alleged violation of the applicant's freedom of expression.[736] In a later case, *Paladi v. Moldova*, the Court also found that the equivalent of almost EUR 600 agreed in the friendly settlement bore no reasonable relationship to the plaintiff's allegations of insufficient medical treatment and unlawful detention, and concluded that he should have benefited from legal advice on the matter before renouncing his complaints.[737]

Applicants have the alternative option of withdrawing their request on the grounds that the matter has been resolved, instead of informing the Court of a friendly settlement. This is likely to occur especially when a compromise has already been executed by the government, when the issue at stake has in the meantime been considered by the Court, or when the applicant's main purpose was not reparation, but prevention of similar violations.[738] Such a decision may be taken for whatever reason, on the complainant's own motion or at the request of the government,[739] but it is not automatically accepted by the Court. Proceedings are terminated on the grounds that the plaintiff has lost interest in pursuing the case only if considerations of public interest do not oppose doing so.

[733] O. De Schutter, 'Le règlement amiable dans la Convention européenne des droits de l'homme: entre théorie de la fonction de juger et théorie de la négociation', in *Les droits de l'homme au seuil du troisième millénaire: mélanges en hommage à Pierre Lambert* (Brussels: Bruylant, 2000), at 230.

[734] Ibid. [735] Harris et al., note 30, at 831.

[736] *Ukrainian Media Group v. Ukraine*, no. 72713/01, 29 March 2005, para. 36.

[737] *Paladi v. Moldova*, no. 39806/05, 10 July 2007, paras. 60–6.

[738] For instance, when the applicant militates for general protection of human rights or performs a repetitive activity: see De Schutter, note 733, at 230 and the cases cited.

[739] See, e.g., *Janab v. the United Kingdom*, no. 10579/83, Commission's decision of 9 December 1987, and *Kastrati v. Bulgaria* (dec.), no. 41348/98, 30 November 2000.

However, the Court has also struck out cases even if the applicant opposed that decision, when it is in possession of a fact which would provide a solution to the matter.[740] Given that, in all these cases, the matter is considered as being resolved, the Court does not order any reparation, except for costs, which are at its own discretion.[741]

Friendly settlements have no judicial character, and therefore cannot be invoked as precedent in subsequent proceedings.[742] But they have incontestable benefits for both parties, although, generally speaking, human rights protection suffers because the supreme authority in the field is prevented from pronouncing on the matter. In other words, justice may not be done,[743] and certainly the Court suffers a limitation of both its role and judicial function.[744] Negotiations for a compromise usually take place after the communication of a case, which means that the Court has already got an idea as to the problems raised. It may therefore be assumed that the chances of a finding of a violation are rather high. Yet, it is the applicants' choice to put an end to their requests, as it was their choice to institute proceedings. Given that quite a large number of cases have been amicably settled so far, it might be worth pondering what it is that prevails in the applicants' expectations: recognition and protection of their rights or an award of compensation. Certainly, the two are closely related, the latter being the consequence of the former, but one may wonder whether the quest for reparation has not gained primacy over the need for justice.[745]

5.2.2 *Unilateral declaration*

Only in September 2012 were rules on unilateral declarations introduced in the Rules of Court,[746] as a codification of the Court's

[740] See, among many others, *B.B. v. France*, 7 September 1998, *Reports of Judgements and Decisions* 1998-VI, and *Haziri v. Sweden* (dec.), no. 37468/04, 5 September 2006.

[741] Rule 43(4) of the Rules of Court. Unlike striking out applications because of friendly settlements, Article 37 of the Convention provides that when an application is discontinued because the matter has been resolved, the Court may subsequently decide to restore it to its list of cases if it considers that the circumstances justify such a course.

[742] A. Kiss, 'Conciliation', in Macdonald, Matscher and Petzold, note 32, at 703.

[743] For a criticism of friendly settlements in general, see O. Fiss, 'Against Settlement', *Yale Law Journal* 93, no. 6 (1984).

[744] Berger, note 695, at 788–9.

[745] On this point, also see J.-F. Flauss, 'Convention européenne des droits de l'homme: une nouvelle interlocutrice pour le juriste d'affaires', *Revue de jurisprudence de droit des affaires* 6 (1995).

[746] Rule 62A of the Rules of Court.

practice.[747] Accordingly, when a friendly-settlement procedure fails, the government has the possibility of making a declaration by which it clearly acknowledges a violation of the Convention and undertakes to provide the plaintiff with adequate redress. The novelty of this provision is that it has specifically linked such a declaration with an express statement on the part of the defendant state that it has violated the Convention. If the declaration complies with the objective of respect for human rights as defined in the treaty, the Court may decide to discontinue the case. Nonetheless, it may later decide to restore the application to its list of cases if it considers that the circumstances justify such a course.

The first unilateral declaration was accepted by the Court in 2001, in *Akman v. Turkey*, which concerned unlawful killing of the applicant's son by the security forces. The case was declared admissible, but then both parties filed proposals for an agreement. In the absence of a compromise, the government sought termination of the case by a unilateral declaration. It expressed regret for the occurrence of individual cases of death resulting from the use of excessive force, as in the circumstances of the applicant's son, and offered to pay the applicant GBP 85,000. It must be emphasized that the government has merely expressed its regrets, but has not acknowledged existence of a breach. Although the claimant opposed this, the Court drew attention to the fact that the parties were unable to agree on the terms of a friendly settlement and held that, in view of that declaration and of the already existing case law on the matter, it was no longer justified to continue the examination of the application.[748]

The Grand Chamber later established the principles for a unilateral declaration in *Tahsin Acar v. Turkey*. The case concerned the enforced disappearance of the applicant's brother. The Court refused the government's unilateral declaration, and presumably felt bound to develop the reasons for doing so, although it has not produced an exhaustive list. Pertinent elements include the nature of the allegations, the evidence which supports them, whether they follow well-established

[747] For a short presentation, see C. Rozakis, 'Unilateral Declarations as Means of Settling Human Rights Disputes: A New Tool for the Resolution of Disputes in the ECHR's Procedure', in Kohen, note 245.

[748] *Akman v. Turkey* (striking out), no. 37453/97, ECHR 2001-VI. Also see P. Sardaro, '*Jus Non Dicere* for Allegations of Serious Violations of Human Rights: Questionable Trends in the Recent Case Law of the Strasbourg Court', *European Human Rights Law Review*, no. 6 (2003), at 620–30.

case law, the measures taken by the government in the context of the execution of judgments delivered in previous similar disputes and their impact on the case at issue, as well as any admission of the breach and intention to provide redress.[749]

Even in the absence of a firm requirement in that sense, the Court was very receptive to any official acknowledgment in relation to the violations alleged and to any offer of reparation. While full admission of liability was not an express condition for submission of unilateral declarations, it was still a significant element in the government's advantage. There was, however, one exception, which referred to cases brought in respect of persons who had disappeared or had been killed by unknown perpetrators, and where the complainant denounced a defective investigation. If the Court happened to find that evidence in the file supported the applicant's allegations, it would not allow a unilateral declaration unless the government at least acknowledged the faulty investigation and undertook to conduct a new investigation in full compliance with the requirements of the Convention.[750] It was in the absence of such admission and corresponding obligation that the Grand Chamber dismissed the unilateral declaration made in *Tahsin Acar*.

On occasion, however, the defendant government has admitted the existence of a breach, but then offered to pay compensation *ex gratia*. There is an obvious contradiction in terms and the Court has properly called attention to that inconsistency. Not surprisingly, it refrained from defining it as an unfortunate mistake or even as bad faith. It preferred instead to dismiss those declarations on the grounds that the compensation proposed was substantially less than that awarded in similar cases and thus did not justify discontinuance of the application.[751]

As far as the proceedings stage is concerned, the government usually submits a unilateral declaration after the friendly-settlement negotiations have proved unsuccessful. The new rule of the Rules of Court provides that such a declaration may, in exceptional circumstances, be submitted even in the absence of previous attempts to reach a friendly settlement.[752] However, while the filing of a declaration must be made in public and adversarial proceedings,[753] the statements made by the

[749] *Tahsin Acar v. Turkey* (preliminary issue) [GC], no. 26307/95, ECHR 2003-VI, para. 76.

[750] Ibid., para. 84.

[751] See, e.g., *Dmitrijevs v. Latvia* (dec.), no. 37467/04, 7 September 2010, para. 65, and *Bazjaks v. Latvia*, no. 71572/01, 19 October 2010, para. 52.

[752] Rule 62A(2) of the Rules of Court.

[753] Rule 62A(1)(c) of the Rules of Court.

parties during discussions for an agreement remain confidential and are not taken into account by the Court. It seems nonetheless logical to have a clear connection between the financial awards granted in the form of a friendly settlement and the amount proposed by the government in a unilateral declaration.[754] As expected, the plaintiff will normally oppose the termination of the proceedings, but the Court, besides the applicant's subjective perception of the facts, will also take into account the objective factors.

The Court ought to take extreme care when examining and accepting such declarations, because the applicant's consent will not have been given. At least in theory, they come under attentive scrutiny by the Convention organs, in an attempt to avoid further abuse by the state. In practice, however, the overwhelming majority of unilateral declarations are accepted. Given that such declarations typically come after the communication of a case, it cannot be asserted that all these complaints were considered prima facie as being manifestly ill-founded. What can be inferred, though, is that these declarations are predominantly accepted in repetitive cases, when there is sufficient practice as to the outcome of similar disputes and also as to the reparation granted. In that context, the Court seems to have abandoned the victim-oriented approach and adopted instead a case-oriented response. Nevertheless, as has been noted in a concurring opinion in *Tahsin Acar*, unilateral declarations should not become a sort of sanction for the petitioners who opposed a friendly settlement.[755]

In some cases, the government may propose a unilateral declaration only for some of the complaints, most probably for those which are not manifestly ill-founded. In this way, it avoids unnecessary admissions in respect of the remaining allegations, which would probably be graver if proved true. That was the case, for instance, with a declaration made only in respect of the length of domestic proceedings, although the plaintiff further alleged violations of the right to a fair trial and of the right to protection of property. The Court accepted the unilateral declaration and struck out that part of the application, then concluded that the other

[754] Keller, Forowicz and Engi, note 460, at 114, who reveal the practice of the German government to offer in a unilateral declaration 90 per cent of the amount proposed by the Registry in view of a friendly settlement; the rationale of the fact that the government proposed a slightly lower amount is that it has also admitted responsibility for the violation, so the applicant was entitled to less money.

[755] Joint concurring opinion of Judges Bratza, Tulkens and Vajić.

complaints were inadmissible.[756] Had the government admitted an interference with the other rights, especially with the property right, it would have been expected to have offered a higher amount in compensation.

5.2.3 *Concluding remarks*

Friendly settlements and unilateral declarations are two procedural tools that allow the Court to discontinue a complaint and to afford redress without a need to examine the merits of a dispute. The Court does not pronounce on the responsibility of the defendant state and until recently the state was also not obliged to admit the existence of a breach. However, the modifications brought to the Rules of Court in 2012 expressly require the state to do so in the event of a unilateral declaration. Overall, the practice does not reflect the underlying desire for human rights protection, but rather a necessity to facilitate the good functioning of the Court. The practical effects cannot be ignored.

Thus, in cases of petitions with several applicants, it may be that only some of them are willing to reach a compromise with the government. The Court will inquire into the terms of settlement and, if agreed, will strike the case out in respect of those plaintiffs. For the others, it will continue with the examination of their complaints.[757] Similarly, when two or more applications concerning the same matter have been joined in order to be treated more expeditiously, if only one of the claimants agrees with the government on a friendly settlement, the Court may disjoin his or her application from the others and strike it out of its list of cases.

The same occurs in respect of unilateral declarations in cases with several applicants. Moreover, the government has the possibility to limit the terms of declaration only to a part of the petition. In that case, the Court will confine the assessment of the declaration to the complaints to which it refers, and then will continue to examine the remaining complaints.[758] Generally, this is unlikely to happen in cases of friendly settlement, because both parties aim at ending the entire dispute as quickly as possible. At least the plaintiff would seem to have little interest

[756] *Fedorova and Shakhov v. Russia* (dec.), no. 50537/06, 17 February 2011.

[757] See, e.g., *Luedicke, Belkacem and Koç* (Article 50), note 597, and *Foti and Others v. Italy* (Article 50), 21 November 1983, Series A no. 69.

[758] See, e.g., *Grabinski v. Poland* (dec.), no. 1237/07, 30 November 2010, and *Fedorova and Shakhov*, note 756.

in reaching a compromise only for some complaints, and to let the Court decide the others, because applicants usually believe that they may reach a higher compensation figure with the Court than with the defendant government. But even partial settlements would help petitioners to see at least some of their claims materialize and, furthermore, the Court would process that application more easily.

Friendly settlements may also be reached, and unilateral declarations may also be made, exclusively in respect of just satisfaction. This is the case when the Court finds a violation, but reserves the question of compensation. The Court, when adjourning the matter, usually invites the parties to notify it of any possible agreement. It is beyond doubt that, at this moment of the proceedings, when the applicant's allegations or at least a part of them are officially confirmed, an agreement certainly does secure some benefit for the work of the Court, which may save some time instead of performing any complex calculations. Predictably, the applicant may be less inclined towards a compromise when so close to the final outcome, which definitely appears to be in his advantage.

Nonetheless, there are important distinctions in terms of quality between friendly settlements and unilateral declarations. In friendly settlements, both parties agree to put an end to their dispute, whereas in the context of unilateral declarations, the plaintiff normally opposes discontinuance of the proceedings. Then, there is the issue of the acknowledgment by the state of its responsibility as to the violations alleged. On the one hand, in a compromise, the absence of such an admission or even a statement to the contrary may be outweighed by the applicant's readiness to settle the case. On the other, in a unilateral declaration, even before the latest changes introducing the condition of an express acknowledgment of a violation, the Court was more demanding with the government's submissions, because the applicant's opposition was rather ignored. As rightly emphasized, such a clear acknowledgment compensates, to a certain extent, the absence of the claimant's agreement,[759] although whether that payment is made *ex gratia* or not generates different legal consequences, that is, it shapes the applicant's ability to reopen a case at domestic level.

At this point, doubts may reasonably arise as to the utility and also justification of bilateral agreements and unilateral declarations. While the former are beneficial for both parties, the latter profit only the

[759] Keller, Forowicz and Engi, note 460, at 105.

government involved. As for the Court, both are advantageous, because the Registry lawyers save a great deal of time with the drafting, as well as with calculations for compensation. A strike-out decision is usually shorter and contains fewer facts than a judgment on the merits. The procedure is thus accelerated and it should come as no surprise that the Court itself encourages such a practice. The number of applications disposed of in this way has recently increased substantially, to the extent that there has been a 94 per cent rise in these decisions in 2010 and a further 25 per cent in 2011.[760] However, as already mentioned, the general protection of human rights may suffer in the absence of a ruling by the Court on alleged infringements by the contracting states. The Court's main role is to adjudicate, not to facilitate compromise.

On the other hand, the Court functions in a treaty framework, not under the public law, and those two alternatives of terminating the proceedings are now expressly provided for in the Convention and in the Rules of Court. Extreme care should be taken by the judges in order to avoid situations in which a state would seek to buy off violations instead of running the risk of being found in violation of its international commitments. It is not mere theory that friendly settlements or unilateral declarations may conceal grave or even systemic violations. For instance, some allegations brought in respect of ill-treatment may reveal certain police practice on the edge of the law, but a friendly settlement would prevent the Court from carefully assessing compatibility with the treaty standards. As far as systemic violations are concerned, the case law also shows that, for example in the context of the reasonable length-of-proceedings requirement for a fair trial, certain countries prefer to reach financial agreement with a victim of a violation rather than devote significant costs and efforts to changing the domestic system.

There are still exceptions when those instruments may provide benefit to human rights protection. Thus, the state may undertake to propose administrative, legal or judicial changes. In this case, the effects of the state's conduct go beyond the applicant's interests, and spread out to other persons in a similar situation. However, according to some authors, there are disputes in which the Court itself is believed to have

[760] Para. 11 of the Preliminary opinion of the Court in preparation for the Brighton Conference (adopted by the Plenary Court on 20 February 2012, available at www.echr.coe.int/Pages/home.aspx?p=court/reform&c=).

allowed termination of the proceedings although new questions of principle were at issue.[761]

Another issue concerns the justification to endorse friendly settlements or unilateral declarations. Their excessive use, although to the Court's benefit in view of its growing workload, should not be encouraged, because the Convention system would become a system akin to money laundering in so far as violations would be transformed into money in the absence of a severe scrutiny of the state activity. Without doubt, this is an exaggerated scenario, but steps in that direction should be carefully avoided. The role of the Court is to decide on state responsibility for breaches of international obligations to respect human rights.

Obviously, the Court's role is limited by the fact that the Convention is a regional treaty. The member states have agreed that the Court will deal with certain issues, and the power to endorse friendly settlements and unilateral declarations is one of them. Contested or not for their influence on the Court's adjudication role, the Strasbourg organs will continue to encourage compromise between the conflicting parties. Even recently, following a high-level conference on the future of the Court, the contracting states have been expressly invited to give priority to resolution of repetitive disputes by way of friendly settlements or unilateral declarations, with the Court getting actively involved in the process.[762] In consequence, as already explained, the practice of unilateral declarations has been codified in the Rules of Court, along with the already existing conditions for a friendly settlement. It seems that the urgent necessity to dispose of a huge backlog has gained impetus at all costs. What is to be hoped is that the judges will carefully balance the conflicting interests at stake.

5.3 Court recommendations with respect to execution

5.3.1 Notion

States found in violation of the Convention have the consequent obligation to make reparation. The scope of that commitment is neither defined nor delimited by the Court, but governed by the core principle of *restitutio in integrum*, applied by the judges when deciding on just

[761] F. Sudre, 'Existe-t-il un ordre public européen?', in P. Tavernier (ed.), *Quelle Europe pour les droits de l'homme? La Cour de Strasbourg et la réalisation d'une 'Union plus étroite' (35 années de jurisprudence: 1959–1994)* (Brussels: Bruylant, 1996), at 69.

[762] The 2011 Izmir Declaration, note 463.

satisfaction. In fact, the whole process of fixing and enforcing awards of reparation in Strasbourg has become an interplay between judicial and political organs. A wrongdoing state is not absolved of responsibility by the simple fact that it pays the amount decided by the judges. As is well known, the Court is entitled by Article 41 of the Convention to grant just satisfaction, while Article 46 empowers the Committee of Ministers to supervise the execution of a judgment, including assessment of necessary individual and/or general measures to be taken by the state as a component of the general obligation to make *restitutio in integrum*.[763] Only after their adoption will the Committee close the examination of a case by a final resolution. For that reason, those measures are activities performed by the state in addition to an award, but in the accomplishment of the duty to make full reparation. They may also be taken on the state's own initiative when the question of just satisfaction has been reserved for a subsequent judgment,[764] or as part of a friendly settlement.

Individual and general measures have a distinct scope and justification. The former are connected with individual breaches and aim to protect a personal interest by reinstating the *status quo ante*, whereas the latter are intended to redress the situation not of the very person who has lodged a complaint with the Court and whose claim is decided by the judges, but of those who are in the same position. General measures therefore apply to domestic systemic problems which have caused or are likely to produce widespread violations, and may either have a preventive character, a sort of guarantee of non-repetition, or bring a continuous infringement to an end.[765] But even general measures emerge from and are associated with personal interferences, because the Court does not admit *actio popularis*. There are even some atypical cases where they have essentially been ordered with a view to remedying the applicant's condition, for example adoption of subsidiary legislation on gender reassignment of transsexuals[766] or modification of an educational system with regard to religious instruction.[767]

While such measures required for the enforcement of a Court judgment come by definition under the authority of the Committee of

[763] *Scozzari and Giunta*, note 296, para. 249.

[764] See, e.g., *Bönisch* (Article 50), note 436, para. 9.

[765] See, among others, V. Colandrea, 'On the Power of the European Court of Human Rights to Order Specific Non-Monetary Measures: Some Remarks in Light of the *Assanidze*, *Broniowski* and *Sejdovic* Cases', *Human Rights Law Review* 7, no. 2 (2007).

[766] *L. v. Lithuania*, no. 27527/03, ECHR 2007-X, para. 74 and point 5 of the operative part, and also the partly dissenting opinion of Judge Fura-Sandström.

[767] *Hasan and Eylem Zengin v. Turkey*, no. 1448/04, ECHR 2007-XI, para. 84.

Ministers, the judges have stepped gradually into the process. What has legitimized such interference? As may easily be appreciated, they have done so with the permission of the contracting states, as it would have been difficult for a treaty organ to assume more powers than those expressly conferred by the parties. The Committee, in its capacity as the voice of the member states, has issued a number of recommendations which have opened the way, either in a more implicit or in a fairly explicit manner, for progressive involvement of the Court. Depending on the circumstances of a case, and on its own conviction, the Court has started to indicate general and individual measures.

On the one hand, the participation of the judges was easily and overtly accepted in the context of a call for general measures whenever needed, as an expression – and example at the same time – of enthusiastic association of the contracting parties to prevent large-scale human rights violations in Europe. In that sense, by a resolution of May 2004, the Committee has invited the Court to identify in its rulings the structural or general deficiencies in national law or practice, in order to facilitate execution of judgments, but also to preserve the effectiveness of the system.[768]

On the other hand, indication of individual measures has been made as a matter of inference. Thus, in reference to the subsidiarity of the mechanism of supervision, the Committee has made particular calls to states for implementation of effective domestic remedies, while accepting that the obligation to abide by a judgment may entail adoption of individual and/or general measures so as to ensure *restitutio in integrum*.[769] Given that the ability to utilize the control machinery was not challenged, the Court has not been expressly invited to give indications when examining a case, but the judges have nonetheless deemed it useful and even necessary to suggest means for securing effective redress. It matters little if they do so also to help respondent states to conform to Convention standards. By and large, the direct recipient is the individual applicant, who thus benefits from what is considered at the European level to be an effective form of redress. Admittedly, such actions are particularly constructive, inasmuch as the philosophy of human rights and the efficiency of the system of reparation are further promoted and preserved.

768 Resolution Res(2004)3 of 12 May 2004 on judgments revealing an underlying systemic problem, available on the Council of Europe's website (https://wcd.coe.int/ViewDoc.jsp?id=743257).

769 Recommendation R(2000)2, note 142.

Overall, at least at a theoretical level and leaving aside the frictions likely to arise from a potential defiance of the principle of separation of powers within the system, one cannot but agree that it is more pertinent to have a judicial organ, rather than a political one, to individualize and adapt those actions. The Court is more equipped than the Committee in that sense, having not only the advantage of judicial expertise, but also knowledge of the circumstances of a case. It is therefore the most competent entity to examine and determine the compatibility of those measures with the treaty standards. By using this approach, one may avoid a duplication of efforts and redundancy, in so far as dissatisfied applicants or the Committee would not have to come again before the judges in order to contest those measures. In any case, it should be conceded that it is rather extraordinary for the Court to indicate individual or general measures, as it usually limits itself to pecuniary awards.

In conclusion, while the main Strasbourg organ in charge of the imposition of individual and/or general measures in the execution of a judgment and accomplishment of *restitutio in integrum* is the Committee of Ministers, the judges may still give some guidance. Practice shows that the position of the Court in that respect has evolved from a firm non-participation to a rather active involvement. What has prompted such a development?

5.3.2 Evolution

The Court has traditionally refrained from prescribing specific measures that wrongdoing states should take in order to redress the adverse effects of a breach on the applicant or to prevent further violations. It used to say that it was not empowered under the Convention to provide for the quashing of a judgment or to give any directions. It did so, for instance, in *Hauschildt v. Denmark*, where the applicant submitted that, in the event of a violation of the right to a fair trial, his conviction should have been quashed and any disqualifications or restrictions placed on him removed.[770] This is also the case for legislative amendments aimed at a wider category of persons. In fact, since a 1979 decision in *Marckx*, the Court has insisted that its judgments are essentially declaratory and

[770] *Hauschildt*, note 227, para. 54. Also see, e.g., *Le Compte, Van Leuven and De Meyere* (Article 50), note 530, para. 13; *Dudgeon* (Article 50), note 236, paras. 13–14; *Campbell and Cosans* (Article 50), note 418, para. 16; *Gillow* (Article 50), note 389, para. 9; and *Belilos v. Switzerland*, 29 April 1988, Series A no. 132, para. 76.

allow the state to choose the means to be utilized in its domestic legal system in order to abide by the Court's rulings.[771]

The complexity of the issues brought to Strasbourg has gradually evolved since that judgment, and the Court has been confronted with grave violations and systemic failures. In that context, as a promoter of a human rights philosophy, it could not have remained passive. It has progressively adjusted the traditional approach and affirmed that, exceptionally and with a view to helping a respondent state to fulfil its duty of execution, it may indicate various options for putting an end to a systemic deficiency, leaving however the choice to the state's discretion, except for disputes where the nature of the violation gives no real alternative, when it may specify a particular measure.[772] Such is the case with physical liberty, where the Court has radically changed perspective. For example, in *Saïdi v. France* the applicant sought a retrial in the first place, but the judges reflected that the Convention had not given them jurisdiction to direct the French state to open a new trial.[773] And yet, while it has previously declined requests to order reopening of domestic proceedings, the Court has eventually started to recommend a retrial. Often, suggestions for individual redress are still connected with physical liberty, but they are not excluded from other areas such as restitution of property, execution of domestic judgments or fair-trial guarantees.

Only in 2000, in *Scozzari and Giunta v. Italy*, which was a case about interference with family rights, did the Court for the first time make explicit reference to a need for individual and general measures. The judges disapproved of the placement of the first applicant's children into the care of a questionable community, and to the delayed and limited contact visits, and thus compensated the damages. Given that the infringement by the Italian authorities was evidently of a continuous nature – a factor coupled with the sensitive matter under examination – the Court deemed it necessary, in the context of reparation, to remind all the contracting states about their responsibility to abide by final judgments. In that respect, the judges interpreted the scope of Article 41 as

771 *Marckx*, note 111, para. 58. Also see, among many others, *M.S.S.*, note 576, para. 399.

772 See, e.g., *Öcalan v. Turkey* [GC], no. 46221/99, ECHR 2005-IV, para. 210, and *Scoppola v. Italy (no. 2)* [GC], no. 10249/03, 17 September 2009, para. 148.

773 *Saïdi v. France*, 20 September 1993, Series A no. 261-C, para. 47. Also see *Pelladoah v. the Netherlands*, 22 September 1994, Series A no. 297-B, para. 44.

extending beyond a mere duty of payment, thus giving rise to a legal obligation to adopt appropriate individual and/or general measures that would put an end to the violation and redress its effects.[774]

It is therefore laudable for the European system that states cannot achieve execution by a simple remuneration for their wrongful behaviour, but are required to restore as far as possible the situation existing before the breach and to avoid future violations. Even if states are free to choose the means by which they will discharge those two obligations of personal reparation and general prevention, the Committee of Ministers may suggest a particular action. However, in *Scozzari and Giunta*, it took nearly eight years for the state to execute the judgment,[775] a fairly long period in which to implement the requisite measures. While it is true that the Committee's pressure is mainly political and that only the latest changes to the Convention have introduced the possibility to institute infringement proceedings against a state which does not execute a ruling by the Court, it is too soon to tell whether they will form a stronger deterrent.

Now the question may arise: what made the new permanent Court, established in 1998, suddenly change the previous rigid approach of non-involvement in domestic affairs? It seems to be an act of judicial activism induced by a structural exigency to implement new methods for a more efficient functioning of the Court in the context of an ever-increasing caseload. No matter how much some of the Strasbourg judges are determined to defend the Court's prestige by declaring that its legal principles are estranged from any pragmatic reason,[776] and while accepting that such indeed should be the case, it would nonetheless be simplistic to suppose that conceptual transformations in the system are permitted without the consent of the member states. The Court is a treaty organ and does what it is entitled and allowed to do. Only the contracting parties may adjust its tasks. Given that the states' representatives have agreed within the Committee of Ministers to provide for legal means in their domestic systems so as to be able to achieve *restitutio in integrum* and to further invite the Court to identify systemic failures, the judges have used that framework to develop a practice of active involvement as to what are *in casu* the proper measures.

[774] *Scozzari and Giunta*, note 296, para. 249.

[775] Resolution DH(2008)53 of 25 June 2008.

[776] Concurring opinion of Judge Zupančič in *Broniowski v. Poland* [GC], no. 31443/96, ECHR 2004-V.

5.3.3 *Individual measures*

Individual measures are relevant only to an applicant. Their aim is to remedy the effects of a violation beyond a simple payment of compensation, that is, to bring a continuous breach to an end and to reinstate the *status quo ante*, because the concept of just satisfaction is meaningless if the wrongful conduct of a state is further tolerated. Individual measures need to adapt to the situation created by the infringement and to the applicant's condition. They include actions such as the release from detention, reopening of proceedings, reinstatement in the previous post or in an equivalent job, modifications to a criminal record, recognition of legal capacity or personality, or granting access to a child. In spite of their evident utility, the judges resort to them in only a few cases, and not necessarily in all the cases that are similar. They usually decline specific requests by the applicants. Therefore, on what grounds, if any, does the Court order an individual measure? Does it depend on the circumstances of a dispute, including the claimant's demeanour, or is it a matter of discretion and policy?

Although the judges have not mentioned any particular measure, the *Scozzari and Giunta* case has nonetheless set the stage for the subsequent evolution in the Court's attitude towards the measures that states are expected to take in order to acquit themselves of the obligation to make full reparation. Since then, respondents have progressively received explicit indications as to the anticipated conduct, besides having to pay a fixed amount. And yet, was that case the first time in which such an occasion arose?

The judges certainly dealt with comparable applications even before that judgment, and occasionally made rather indirect, albeit unequivocal, suggestions as to the proper course of action. For instance, in the well-known case of *Soering v. the United Kingdom*, where the plaintiff was detained in prison in England pending extradition to the United States to face charges of murder, the Court declared that his extradition would expose him to inhuman or degrading treatment caused by the 'death row phenomenon'.[777] The Court did not call for a specific measure, being evidently unable in that special context to interfere in a member state's relations with a third party,[778] but nonetheless made it

[777] *Soering*, note 258, para. 111 and point 1 of the operative part.

[778] The Court affirmed in a later case that 'the Convention does not require the Contracting Parties to impose its standards on third States or territories': see *Drozd and Janousek v. France and Spain*, 26 June 1992, Series A no. 240, para. 110.

clear that not taking that particular measure would amount to a breach of the Convention. Logically, the state was eager to avoid condemnation in Strasbourg and, although it had not revoked the extradition, at least obtained assurances from the United States that the applicant would not be prosecuted for capital murder.[779] That successful formula applied by the Court has been repeatedly used in other cases and further extended to other violations, to the benefit of claimants facing the probability of deportation in precarious conditions.[780] Evidently, in the absence of serious grounds, the judges have not opposed extradition.[781]

The Court continued to foster that proactive approach, but sometimes in a more contestable way. Thus, in *Papamichalopoulos*, the judges found a violation on the basis of an irregular *de facto* expropriation which had lasted for more than twenty-five years. They aptly considered that the return of the land in issue would restore the situation before the breach, but additionally held that otherwise the state had to pay a considerable amount of money.[782] As already mentioned, there is nothing conceptually wrong in establishing an alternative obligation for the offender in property cases, given that adequate grounds may justify compensation instead of restitution. It is precisely on account of the fact that the Court has not requested persuasive justification based on evidence for any alleged impossibility of restitution that it is difficult to accept that the principle of *restitutio in integrum* was correctly applied. For that reason, such alternative obligations are not genuine individual measures as defined in the introductory part, because their central purpose is not to restore the situation existing before the breach, but to assist the state in execution. They are not primarily directed towards the individual's situation, in order to assure effective reparation, but rather towards the need to secure implementation of the Court's judgments.

Moreover, when confronted again with a simple dispossession, but this time with heavy political implications, the approach was inadequate from a legal point of view, albeit suitable from a political one. That was the case with *Loizidou*, which concerned the applicant's continuous dispossession owing to the presence of the Turkish army in northern

[779] See the resolution of the Committee of Ministers, note 538.

[780] See, e.g., *Chahal*, note 534, para. 107 and point 1 of the operative part; *Saadi v. Italy* [GC], no. 37201/06, ECHR 2008, para. 149 and point 2 of the operative part; and *Nunez v. Norway*, no. 55597/09, 28 June 2011, para. 85 and point 2 of the operative part.

[781] See, e.g., *N. v. the United Kingdom* [GC], no. 26565/05, ECHR 2008, para. 51 and point 2 of the operative part.

[782] *Papamichalopoulos* (Article 50), note 91, paras. 38–9.

Cyprus, a long-lasting international problem. Although the Court concluded that there was, and continued to be, a breach of the applicant's property rights,[783] it only compensated her for the damage sustained,[784] instead of requesting Turkey to return the property, or even better, imposing some further general measures for the benefit of those in a similar position. That solution indeed offered some compensation to the plaintiff, but was that reparation effective for her case in so far as the Court had left intact the wrongdoing conduct of the breaching state? By all means, in Strasbourg, victims seek justice from the Court, not from the offending state.

If the judicial mechanism intended to preserve its efficiency, a desire for a bold standpoint in respect of measures that would secure full redress would thus become evident. It seems that the Grand Chamber considered the case of *Scozzari and Giunta* as being a good opportunity to assume a more active role in execution, inasmuch as the dispute was not very complex, notwithstanding what was at stake for the applicants, and also had no implications for the international politics of individual states, as was the case in *Soering* and *Loizidou*. However, it had not indicated any measure in *Scozzari and Giunta*.

The next step forward was thus to specify clearly, in addition to compensation for material and moral damage, the particular remedies that would assure full reparation. The Court's judges have expressed dissenting opinions in which they have called for an effective means of redress in domestic law, such as retrial, when a criminal procedure had become vitiated.[785] The first occasion arose out of a series of cases directed against Turkey and calling into question the independence and impartiality of national security courts, which used to try civilians for acts allegedly interfering with state security. Inasmuch as those courts included a military judge, the Court concluded that the presence of a member of the armed forces raised legitimate doubts about their independence and impartiality.[786] The respondent has been very receptive to

[783] *Loizidou v. Turkey* (merits), 18 December 1996, *Reports of Judgments and Decisions* 1996-VI, para. 64 *in fine*.

[784] *Loizidou* (Article 50), note 164, paras. 34 and 40.

[785] Partly dissenting opinion of Judge Zupančič in *Cable*, note 636.

[786] See, among many others, *Incal v. Turkey*, 9 June 1998, *Reports of Judgments and Decisions* 1998-IV, para. 72, and *Karataş v. Turkey* [GC], no. 23168/94, ECHR 1999-IV, para. 62.

those findings and, by a legislative reform, removed the military judges from their composition.[787]

In such cases, the Court used to consider that the finding of a violation represented sufficient reparation, but after dealing for more than five years with a number of similar applications lodged before those amendments, and also having regard to the length of prison sentences imposed by those courts,[788] it eventually decided in 2003 to indicate in *Gençel v. Turkey* – and in other cases examined the same day – that the most appropriate remedy for individuals convicted by such tribunals would be to reopen the proceedings with the required fair-trial guarantees.[789] It is hard to discern why it has taken so long for the judges to stipulate explicitly an individual measure, when they already had not only the *Scozzari and Giunta* precedent, but also the general consensus among the member states to introduce in their domestic legal order the possibility of reopening proceedings and re-examining cases.[790]

Once this process had started, individual measures were quickly extended to other guarantees of the right to a fair trial,[791] and also to other groups of violations.[792] For instance, when confronted with complaints in respect of properties unlawfully taken by the former communist regimes in Eastern Europe, the judges held that the return of property would be the most appropriate form of *restitutio in integrum*.[793] The problem is that the provision for alternative payment without requiring the state to prove the impossibility of restitution tends to

[787] The state security courts were abolished in June 2004: see *Halis v. Turkey*, no. 30007/96, 11 January 2005, para. 21.

[788] L. Caflisch, 'La mise en oeuvre des arrêts de la Cour: nouvelles tendances', in Salerno, note 206, at 160.

[789] There were thirteen cases decided on 23 October 2003 where the Court established that measure: see, e.g., *Gençel v. Turkey*, no. 53431/99, para. 27; *Peker v. Turkey*, no. 53014/99, para. 32; and *Eren v. Turkey*, no. 46106/98, para. 29.

[790] Recommendation R(2000)2, note 142.

[791] For instance, the applicant's right to participate in his trial (*Somogyi v. Italy*, no. 67972/01, ECHR 2004-IV, para. 86); for lack of legal assistance (*Shulepov v. Russia*, no. 15435/03, 26 June 2008, para. 46, and *Salduz*, note 132, para. 62); or for lack of prior notice of the hearing of a cassation appeal (*Maksimov v. Azerbaijan*, no. 38228/05, 8 October 2009, para. 46).

[792] For example, measures to redress the effects of any past or future damage to the applicant's career as a result of the disciplinary sanction imposed on him, which was considered as unlawful interference with the freedom of association, in the case of *Maestri* (note 31, para. 47), or the victim's reinstatement in her previous post or in an equivalent job or, if this was not possible, reasonable compensation or a combination of these and other measures in *Ursan v. Romania* (no. 35852/04, 6 April 2010, para. 46).

[793] See, in particular, *Străin*, note 136, para. 80.

make solutions look good exclusively on paper, because an offender may prefer to pay the monetary alternative. However, the practice does offer examples of the state returning the property in question, mostly when it had not been transferred into the possession of third persons or when its monetary equivalent did not justify allocations from public expenditure.[794]

Questionable rulings may still surface in this field. In *Ştefanescu v. Romania*, the Court found a violation on account of non-enforcement of a domestic judgment by which a national ministry had been ordered to reinstate the applicant in his previous post and to pay his salary. In the meantime, the plaintiff had already found another job, but under the heading of just satisfaction, although he had not sought reinstatement, the judges directed the government to reinstate him in an equivalent job.[795] They have nonetheless provided for an alternative pecuniary obligation, but the example proves the occasionally negative impact that the Court's objective to produce impressive numbers of judgments may have on the quality of its rulings.[796]

The Court's final development in respect of individual measures, which is indeed evidence of an effective mechanism of reparation, was to include an injunction in the operative part of its judgments and thus make them binding. It follows that the call made by judges to that end has eventually been fruitful.[797] The first time that it did so was in *Assanidze v. Georgia*, which concerned the applicant's arbitrary detention. The Grand Chamber, in addition to a generous amount in respect of all the damage sustained, ordered the state to release him as soon as possible.[798] The claimant was liberated the day after the Court's judgment,[799] which incontestably made a real success out of that strategy.

[794] See, e.g., the Resolution adopted in the case of *Brumărescu and 30 other cases against Romania*, note 135.

[795] *Ştefanescu v. Romania*, no. 9555/03, 11 October 2007, paras. 33–7.

[796] Equally striking in that pronouncement is that the judges awarded compensation for pecuniary damage even though only a violation of the right of access to court has been found (para. 38). As already explained in the context of the need for a causal link, claims for material damage are normally connected to the right to protection of property, not the right to a fair trial.

[797] See, e.g., the joint concurring opinion of Judges Spielmann and Malinverni in *Vladimir Romanov v. Russia*, no. 41461/02, 24 July 2008; the concurring opinion of Judge Spielmann in *Polufakin and Chernyshev v. Russia*, no. 30997/02, 25 September 2008; and the joint concurring opinion of Judges Rozakis, Spielmann, Ziemele and Lazarova Trajkovska in *Salduz*, note 132.

[798] Point 14(a) of the operative part in *Assanidze*, note 140.

[799] Resolution DH(2006)53 of 2 November 2006.

Yet, the achievement seems to have been of limited value. Three months later, the Grand Chamber delivered a ruling in the case of *Ilaşcu and Others v. Moldova and Russia*, where the claims of the Moldovan plaintiffs were mainly linked to their unlawful detention in Transdniestria, a territory under *de facto* Russian control. The judges placed responsibility on both states for ill-treatment and arbitrary detention, and requested them to secure the immediate release of those applicants still imprisoned.[800] But unlike the good example given by Georgia, the Russian authorities in particular were little impressed by the Committee of Ministers' repeated actions of 'deeply deploring' and 'regretting profoundly' the non-enforcement.[801] In the face of a strong international actor such as Russia, the Convention mechanism proved limited.[802] It is not unreasonable to speculate that Russia may have perceived, and therefore opposed, the judges' attitude as intervention in internal business. It was only three years after the judgment that the Committee finally noted 'with relief' that the two detained applicants had been released.[803] Ultimately, political pressure appears to have been more effective than legal reasoning, which is why the assignment of the responsibility of execution to a political organ confers efficiency on the Convention system.

Plausible questions were raised by former practitioners at the Court in respect of the criteria used by the judges when deciding individual measures in a particular case,[804] but no answers were given. In the absence of any directions in the legal framework or in the case law, it is only the margin of discretion that the Court enjoys in the field of reparations that may offer a reasonable explanation. The judges have specified individual measures not only in the context of serious violations of human rights such as inhuman and degrading treatment[805] or

[800] *Ilaşcu*, note 210, para. 490 and point 22 of the operative part.

[801] Interim Resolutions DH(2005)42 of 22 April 2005, DH(2005)84 of 13 July 2005, DH(2006)11 of 1 March 2006 and DH(2006)26 of 10 May 2006.

[802] Another illustration is given by the fact that Russia was the only state out of the forty-seven members of the Council of Europe that refused for some four years to ratify Protocol No. 14, thereby delaying implementation of the latest reform of the Convention mechanism.

[803] Interim Resolution DH(2007)106 of 12 July 2007.

[804] De Salvia, note 105, at 52–3.

[805] See, e.g., *Aleksanyan v. Russia*, no. 46468/06, 22 December 2008, para. 240 and point 9 of the operative part, and *Sławomir Musiał v. Poland*, no. 28300/06, 20 January 2009, point 4(a) of the operative part.

retrospective application of criminal law,[806] but also for less grave infringements such as exceeding a reasonable length of proceedings[807] or unlawful dispossession;[808] hence, not only for cases with some distinctive features,[809] but also for those that are repetitive. While a pattern cannot be discerned, it is commendable that the Court primarily takes into account the applicant's situation and interest, and not a state's capability to execute.

Such a victim-oriented approach builds confidence in the system. Certainly, there is a reasonable limit conferred by a member state's relations with a third state. When confronted with deportation orders issued despite the risk of inhumane treatment in the country of destination or disregarding the plaintiff's right to respect for family life, the Court prefers a more cautious attitude. To this end, instead of pronouncing the revocation of those orders, it declares that the Convention would be violated if the expulsion were carried out.[810] It is a legal artifice that may nonetheless act as a deterrent for the state concerned.

5.3.4 General measures

General measures account for the preventive role of human rights protection. They surpass the situation of the individual petitioner and anticipate the propagation of the violation to persons in a similar position. Thus, they reveal a systemic deficiency which has already caused and is further likely to produce a large number of identical complaints. In virtue of their scope and effects, they pertain to repetitive cases. Therefore, in opposition to individual measures assigned to redress a defective application of legal provisions, the necessity to adopt general measures emerges from the very existence of structural

[806] See, e.g., *Scoppola*, note 772, para. 154 and point 6(a) of the operative part.

[807] See, e.g., *Naime Doğan and Others v. Turkey*, no. 76091/01, 17 July 2007, para. 34.

[808] See, e.g., *Brumărescu v. Romania* (just satisfaction) [GC], no. 28342/95, ECHR 2001-I, para. 22 and point 1 of the operative part.

[809] See, e.g., stipulation to confirm an acquittal and erase a conviction in *Bujniţa v. Moldova* (no. 36492/02, 16 January 2007, para. 29), or to examine an appeal by the applicant against a judgment in *Malahov v. Moldova* (no. 32268/02, 7 June 2007, para. 47), or an order to transfer the applicant's pension rights to a specific pension fund in *Karanović v. Bosnia and Herzegovina* (no. 39462/03, 20 November 2007, para. 30 and point 3(a)(i) of the operative part).

[810] See, among others, *Sufi and Elmi v. the United Kingdom*, nos. 8319/07 and 11449/07, 28 June 2011, paras. 304 and 312, and point 3 of the operative part, and *Alim*, note 513, para. 100 and point 3 of the operative part.

shortcomings in internal law or practice. It matters little whether the failure has affected the whole legislation in a field or simply a legal provision.

The role of general measures is twofold, and their effects go beyond the particular case. On the one hand, they seek to avoid large-scale violations, but on the other hand they aim to alleviate the Court's work by directing states to solve their structural problems themselves, so as to deter applicants from coming to Strasbourg. Indeed, when domestic remedies prove to be defective, states are recommended to adapt their legislation to the Convention standards or to provide in practice for new facilities. Inasmuch as the execution of the Court's judgments is supervised by the Committee of Ministers, states have thus agreed to submit the propriety of the changes in their legal order to the scrutiny of the other contracting parties.

The Court imposed general measures for the first time in 2004, in *Broniowski*, following the express invitation by the Committee to identify in its judgments what may denote structural deficiencies in national law or practice. Given that the same year it also ordered individual measures in the operative part of the aforementioned *Assanidze* judgment, it seems to have been a concerted implementation of general and individual measures, but only with prior authorization by the Committee of Ministers. In this area, the judges have previously avoided proposing solutions, but have nonetheless not refrained from reporting widespread problems in domestic affairs. For example, in *Bottazzi*, the Grand Chamber still declared that the numerous breaches of the reasonable-time requirement in cases brought against Italy reflected an internal practice which was incompatible with the Convention.[811] While the judges have not specified the need for general measures, the message was evident. The state has subsequently introduced an internal remedy called the Pinto law.

In *Broniowski*, the applicant claimed compensation for property abandoned in the so-called 'territories beyond the Bug River'. Those were regions lost by Poland following a westwards shift of its borders at the end of the Second World War. The issue of compensation of the population repatriated to Poland who had left behind their property was intended to be regulated by domestic law. The Court examined and disapproved of the malfunctioning of the internal legislation, declaring

[811] *Bottazzi v. Italy* [GC], no. 34884/97, ECHR 1999-V, para. 22.

that not only was the applicant's entitlement to compensation illusory, but so was that of other potential claimants.[812] It meant that a systemic violation represented shortcomings in the legal order affecting a whole class of individuals and was likely to generate numerous subsequent well-founded applications.[813]

The negative impact on the plaintiff's rights was not the result of the authorities' subjective conduct, but the consequence of objective legal regulations. The failure to implement an appropriate mechanism of compensation, which had affected a large number of persons, was deemed to represent not only an aggravating factor for state responsibility, but also a threat for the efficiency of the Strasbourg mechanism.[814] The Grand Chamber followed the *Assanidze* precedent and, in the operative part of its judgment, included the necessity for legal measures and administrative practices to secure the implementation of the property right.[815] This time, however, it did so not because of some pressing need to ameliorate the plaintiff's condition, but owing to the wide scope of those measures. The judges were very attentive not to assume more powers than those conferred by the Convention. They examined the need to remedy the systemic nature of the violation in the context of the state's obligation under Article 46 to abide by the Court's judgments, and not as a matter of reparation for a potential breach under Article 41, which expressly covers past, not future, infringements.

In the circumstances of the *Broniowski* case, where general measures were expected from the state, the Court reserved the question of pecuniary and non-pecuniary damage. More importantly, and for the first time, it adjourned consideration of similar claims pending the implementation of the relevant general measures.[816] That was in agreement with the latest policies seeking to release the Court from the overburden of unceasing applications, and also in line with the subsidiarity principle promoted by the Convention, according to which redress should be secured at home in the first place. The judges were aware that a firm deadline for the state to adopt general measures would have been unrealistic, so they only mentioned a vague condition of a reasonable time. It was for the Committee of Ministers to exert pressure for execution.[817]

[812] *Broniowski*, note 776, paras. 185–7. [813] Ibid., para. 189. [814] Ibid., para. 193.
[815] Ibid., point 4 of the operative part. [816] Ibid., para. 198.
[817] Interim Resolution DH(2005)58 of 5 July 2005.

The merits being decided, the controversy over reparation was then conveniently resolved by a friendly settlement.[818] On the one hand, the applicant received compensation, and on the other hand, the state had already amended and further undertaken to improve the relevant legislation. The personal interest was fully satisfied, while the general interest received no more than a promise. It was, however, the only plausible solution, for the Court had no other choice than to be confident in the government's commitment to take the necessary measures. Hence, it discontinued the case. The agreement had *res judicata* authority only for the parties to the dispute, not also for the many other individuals in the same situation. The Polish authorities eventually adopted new legislation, which was subsequently examined by the Court and declared to correspond to an effective compensation scheme.[819] The first pilot judgment was therefore a success.

The way being opened by *Broniowski*, the Court has continued to order general measures whenever it considered that several applications disclosed a systemic problem. The question is: how many similar cases are necessary before the Strasbourg judges accept the existence of an internal malfunction and prescribe general measures? In *Broniowski*, the Court identified 167 cases on its docket and a potential total of some 80,000 complainants.[820] In *Lukenda v. Slovenia*, 500 length-of-proceedings applications were pending before the Court, and in addition several statistics confirmed that delays in judicial proceedings were a major problem in that country.[821] In *Hutten-Czapska v. Poland*, where the underlying systemic problem originated in the malfunctioning of the housing legislation, the Grand Chamber identified some 600,000 persons potentially affected.[822] In *Yuriy Nikolayevich Ivanov v. Ukraine*, where the failure consisted in non-enforcement or delayed enforcement of domestic decisions, the judges pointed to more than 300 judgments already delivered and some 1,400 applications pending, but further highlighted that any national who had obtained a final domestic decision ran the risk of being deprived of proper enforcement.[823]

818 See the judgment of 28 September 2005.

819 *Wolkenberg and Others v. Poland* (dec.), no. 50003/99, 4 December 2007, para. 74, and *Witkowska-Toboła v. Poland* (dec.), no. 11208/02, 4 December 2007, para. 76.

820 *Broniowski*, note 776, para. 193.

821 *Lukenda v. Slovenia*, no. 23032/02, ECHR 2005-X, paras. 91–2.

822 *Hutten-Czapska*, note 678, para. 236.

823 *Yuriy Nikolayevich Ivanov v. Ukraine*, no. 40450/04, 15 October 2009, paras. 83 and 86.

However, the Court bases its orders not only on existent statistics, but also on its inner conviction. For instance, in *Scordino v. Italy*, where it ordered the government to adopt general measures for two types of structural failures, i.e., unjustified hindrance in obtaining reasonable compensation for expropriation and excessive length of proceedings, the Grand Chamber employed expressions such as 'large number of people' and 'dozens of applications before the Court',[824] respectively, '[h]undreds of cases are currently pending before the Court'.[825] In other length-of-proceedings cases against Italy decided on the same day, the Grand Chamber also had regard to the hundreds of cases brought in Strasbourg.[826] In *Dybeku v. Albania*, the Court simply urged the government to take general measures in order to secure appropriate conditions of detention and adequate medical treatment for those prisoners who, like the applicant, need special care owing to their state of health.[827] While such indications do not generally give particular suggestions as to any required number of persons in a similar position, the main assumption is that there should be many. It would be difficult to agree on a threshold in that respect, particularly as the judges take into account not only the applications pending on the Court's docket, but also the potential inflow of future cases.[828] Flexibility may be accepted in this area in so far as it permits judges to exert certain leverage on states as to due conduct.

The problem with the general measures is that they are not precise. Unlike individual measures, the Court does not indicate a course of action, but leaves the choice to the breaching state. In fact, the 2004 resolution of the Committee of Ministers, which is the legal basis for the Court's recommendations, has invited the judges to identify only the existence and the source of a systemic problem, 'so as to assist states in finding the appropriate solution' and the Committee to supervise the execution.[829] The Court was denied permission to meddle in internal affairs. Indeed, it would even have been inappropriate to give it such

[824] *Scordino*, note 372, para. 235. [825] Ibid., para. 238.

[826] *Cocchiarella v. Italy* [GC], no. 64886/01, ECHR 2006-V, para. 127; *Musci v. Italy* [GC], no. 64699/01, ECHR 2006-V (extracts), para. 127; *Riccardi Pizzati v. Italy* [GC], no. 62361/00, 29 March 2006, para. 124; *Giuseppe Mostacciuolo v. Italy (no. 1)* [GC], no. 64705/01, 29 March 2006, para. 125; *Giuseppina and Orestina Procaccini v. Italy* [GC], no. 65075/01, 29 March 2006, para. 125; *Ernestina Zullo*, note 465, para. 129; *Apicella v. Italy* [GC], no. 64890/01, 29 March 2006, para. 124; and *Giuseppe Mostacciuolo v. Italy (no. 2)* [GC], no. 65102/01, 29 March 2006, para. 124.

[827] *Dybeku v. Albania*, no. 41153/06, 18 December 2007, para. 64.

[828] See, e.g., *Hutten-Czapska*, note 678, para. 236. [829] Resolution Res(2004)3, note 768.

power, given that governments are better equipped than an international institution to redress domestic legal shortcomings. Still, the Court may give some more precise indications to the state: for example, in the context of the length of municipal proceedings, that domestic decisions should be executed within a six-month period.[830]

5.3.5 *Role and justification*

Practice reveals that individual and general measures are frequently used in cases where the breach is continuous, and those measures require an active intervention from the Strasbourg mechanism in order to provide effective reparation. Hence, the scope of those measures is rather limited. The Court does not prescribe individual measures when both the violation and all its effects have already occurred, or general measures if the internal systemic problem has been properly remedied in the meantime. Moreover, while the role of individual measures is to secure personal relief, and thus provide benefit exclusively to the victim, the general measures, besides their main preventive function, are also an important tool for the Court in facilitating its work by anticipating and easily disposing of a great number of repetitive cases.

States have taken and implemented individual and general measures even before the Court has started to make specific suggestions or to include injunctions in the operative part of its judgments. It has been an important element of the proceedings for the enforcement of the Strasbourg rulings because the Committee of Ministers has regularly inquired into the measures taken by offending states as a consequence of a Court judgment.[831] Therefore, why did the judges consider it necessary to refer themselves to such measures and to what extent has that approach conferred more efficiency on reparation? Was it justified? In other words, what were the purpose and implications of that so-called assistance? Should that practice be further encouraged?

First of all, the Court's approach is very cautious in the absence of a treaty provision to allow it to indicate a course of action, and also given that member states are extremely sensitive to any unjustified intervention in their own affairs. The Court has endeavoured to evade any

[830] See, e.g., *Scordino*, note 372, para. 240 *in fine*.

[831] See, e.g., Resolution DH(85)12 of 31 May 1985 in *Piersack v. Belgium*; Resolution DH(89)2 of 18 January 1989 in *Unterpertinger v. Austria*; and Resolution DH(89)18 of 15 June 1989 in *Weeks v. the United Kingdom*.

possible accusation that it assumes more powers than it has under the Convention, or that it becomes involved in the tasks of another treaty organ. In so far as it needed a justification in that respect, the Court associated its new ability to give directions with a form of co-operation with the Committee for a better and easier execution of its judgments, not with a power per se. Thus, whatever the case, the judges attach their entitlement to suggest general measures to the state's obligation to abide by the Court's decisions, not to their own power to afford just satisfaction. Otherwise stated, those measures are not linked directly to a treaty violation, but are mentioned in order to assist the execution. In the absence of an agreement by states, the judges had the only solution of accentuating the contracting parties' existing obligations instead of developing proactive theories of human rights protection. Is that condemnable?

The answer seems to be in the negative, if one looks beyond that official position. Given that the Court had no authority to claim additional powers, it sought justification in the treaty and other documents adopted by the Committee of Ministers. In practice, its recommendations are accepted, being regarded as legal advice on how to achieve *restitutio in integrum*. For the victims, they assure effective reparation. Nonetheless, it may be reasonable to encourage the judges to associate those measures only with serious violations, so as to prevent reticence on the part of the states or of the Committee. As rightly pointed out, even if the member states are in favour of closer co-operation between the Court and the Committee, turning the judges' assistance into a systematic practice would interfere with the principle of the separation of powers.[832]

The Court has officially dismissed any association with an intrusion into the role of the Committee of Ministers. Such was the case, for example, in *Sejdovic v. Italy*, where the government considered that only the Committee, during the execution, was entitled to affirm that a general measure was necessary.[833] The Grand Chamber insisted that the Court's approach to systemic problems in the national legal order is primarily designed to assist the member states in fulfilling their treaty obligations.[834] However, the Court had no difficulty in prescribing measures that were in conflict with the domestic law of a state. Thus, in *Laska and Lika v. Albania*, although reopening of proceedings was not

[832] Caflisch, note 788, at 165.
[833] *Sejdovic v. Italy* [GC], no. 56581/00, ECHR 2006-II, paras. 115–18.
[834] Ibid., para. 120.

available under internal law, the Court suggested that the state introduce such a possibility, which would be in line not only with the recommendations of the Committee of Ministers, but also with the general principles of international law.[835] The judges have not included that injunction in the operative part of the judgment. Given that it is well known that only the operative provisions are binding, such an equivocal position seems to have been rather calculated.

Yet, is there any difference if individual and general measures are situated in the reasoning or in the operative part of a judgment? Or, is that the case if they are indicated under Article 41 on just satisfaction or under Article 46 on binding force and execution of judgments? The importance is both pedagogical and practical. On the one hand, the Court has to give consistency to its case law, but on the other hand the victim must receive from the state the reparation ordered in Strasbourg.

The Court's case law offers examples of all of these situations. At the beginning, the need for additional measures was mentioned exclusively in the reasoning part. Even at present that practice has been maintained in some cases.[836] Can it be assumed that, if not inserted in the operative part, the principle of *restitutio in integrum* has no effective application? It may be hard to believe that in this way the need for additional measures would remain undetected at the moment of execution. But in order to avoid some doctrinal discussions whenever a measure is crucial for an applicant – especially when the applicant is to be released from unlawful detention[837] or when the state ought to return property[838] or to execute a domestic decision[839] – the judges have included an injunction in the operative part. General measures are introduced in the operative part mainly when there is pertinent evidence as to the widespread negative effects of the state conduct,[840] or when, although the Court has already indicated the need for legislative reform, the state has not taken any effective measure.[841] Given that the operative provisions are

[835] *Laska and Lika v. Albania*, nos. 12315/04 and 17605/04, 20 April 2010, paras. 74–7.
[836] See, e.g., *Gatt*, note 670, para. 59 *in fine*.
[837] See, e.g., point 6 of the operative part in *Fatullayev v. Azerbaijan*, no. 40984/07, 22 April 2010.
[838] See, e.g., point 7(a) of the operative part in *Borzhonov v. Russia*, no. 18274/04, 22 January 2009.
[839] See, e.g., point 3(a) of the operative part in *EVT Company v. Serbia*, no. 3102/05, 21 June 2007, and point 3(a) of the operative part in *Nicolescu v. Romania*, no. 31153/03, 20 January 2009.
[840] See, e.g., point 4 of the operative part in *Broniowski*, note 776.
[841] See, e.g., points 3 and 4 of the operative part in *Hutten-Czapska*, note 678.

binding, the state may not contest them. In addition, the Committee has a clear indication as to the matter under supervision. On the whole, the reparation and its effective execution benefit from maximum efficiency. Hence, that practice should be further encouraged. Several of the Court's judges have advocated such a practice.[842]

As to the second question in respect of where to ground the individual and general measures, in Article 41 or in Article 46, it bears less significance for the system of effective reparation, but is more significant from an academic perspective. While the case law is not coherent in that sense, the Court generally develops the general measures under Article 46. They are an obligation of the states as a part of their commitment to abide by the Court's judgments, and the judges only indicate them because the Committee of Ministers has invited them to do so. As for individual measures, in so far as they are viewed as an element of the state's obligation to provide full reparation, they are normally ordered under Article 41, as a component of the effective application of the principle of *restitutio in integrum*.

Are the individual and general measures interdependent or autonomous? Prima facie, one may be tempted to assume that when a systemic violation calls for general measures, the applicant's situation, provoked by the same deficiency, must also be redressed by some individual remedy. While it may be true having regard to the case law,[843] that is not necessarily the case, because the plaintiff may receive pecuniary compensation for material and moral damage, without it being necessary to carry out some further particular measures. Such is usually the case with violations of the right to protection of property when restitution is not possible. Moreover, even if general measures are indicated as a consequence of individual breaches, the category of violation to which they are assigned is quite different. Individual measures are intended to remedy the personal effects of an application of the law *in concreto*, whereas general measures are directed towards an objective deficiency in the internal legislation, irrespective of any particular application.

[842] See, e.g., the joint concurring opinion of Judges Rozakis, Spielmann, Ziemele and Lazarova Trajkovska in *Salduz* (note 132); the concurring opinion of Judge Malinverni, joined by Judges Casadevall, Cabral Barreto, Zagrebelsky and Popović in *Cudak* (note 88); and the concurring opinion of Judges Malinverni and Sajó in *Lalas v. Lithuania* (no. 13109/04, 1 March 2011).

[843] See, e.g., *Driza v. Albania*, no. 33771/02, ECHR 2007-XII (extracts), paras. 126 and 135, and *Dybeku*, note 827, para. 64.

In conclusion, the Court has developed a steady practice of imposing, to a lesser or greater extent, individual and general measures. Their place and role has gained acceptance within the system, although discussions may persist as to their justification. From a pragmatic victim-oriented point of view, the beneficial effects of those indications are undisputed. The very purpose of individual and general measures is to restore the *status quo ante* and to prevent future violations. It is not unreasonable to speculate that they will be further developed, as long as their use is not exaggerated.

5.4 The execution stage

5.4.1 Supervision by the Committee of Ministers

It is common knowledge that there is no such notion as forced execution in international law. The majority of the states parties to the Convention comply with the Court's judgments and execute them without any constraint. The system needs, however, powers to cope with instances of late or non-execution, especially with the ones from those few states which not only supply the greatest number of applications, but also pose the main problems in respect of execution.

The Statute of the Council of Europe, as well as the Convention, is based on separation of powers within the organization. The fact that the Committee of Ministers supervises the execution gives a rather political connotation to the binding effect of the Court's judgments. Execution is an integral part of the system, although the judgments are not directly enforceable at domestic level. This is a matter to be regulated by the internal law. The Court's authority and the system's credibility both depend to a large extent on the effectiveness of this process of execution.[844] It is a general legal principle that a judgment which is not enforced renders the judicial process ineffective.

Execution implies not only payment of just satisfaction, but also individual or more general measures, including change of practice or legislative amendments.[845] Such suggestions are made either when

[844] Para. 16 of the Explanatory Report to Protocol No. 14, note 202.

[845] See, e.g., H.-C. Krüger, 'Reflections on Some Aspects of Just Satisfaction under the European Convention on Human Rights', in G. Cohen-Jonathan, J.-F. Flauss and P. Lambert (eds.), *Liber Amicorum Marc-André Eissen* (Brussels: Bruylant, 1995), at 256.

examining the merits of the violations alleged,[846] or when considering the claims on just satisfaction.[847] As for the applicant, the only requirement is to provide the government with a bank account for payment. States have a large margin of appreciation in respect of the means required to fulfil the obligation to abide by the final judgment. It is essentially an obligation of result, based on the principle of subsidiarity, and the Court has generally refused to give indications in this respect.[848]

The Committee performs an important role by monitoring the execution. It meets in four three-day sessions each year and examines whether the state has paid the reparation ordered by the Court,[849] and whether it has taken any other individual or general measures to redress the violation found and to prevent further breaches. It may thus assist the states in finding remedies, in order to avoid further violations. According to the Rules adopted by the Committee for that purpose, states are invited to inform it of the measures already implemented or intended to be taken as a consequence of a judgment.[850] If satisfied that the state has acquitted itself of all obligations, the Committee will adopt a resolution in that respect, otherwise it will keep the matter on the agenda. Theoretically, the Secretary-General of the Council of Europe may also request explanations from the member states as to the manner in which their internal law ensures the effective implementation of the Convention,[851] but this procedure is hardly used in practice.

A complainant has also the possibility to come back to the Court if the respondent state disregards its obligations. That was the case, for instance, with *Verein gegen Tierfabriken Schweiz*, where the Court

[846] See, among others, *Vallée*, note 480, para. 49, and *Karakaya v. France*, 26 August 1994, Series A no. 289-B, para. 43.

[847] See, e.g., *X v. the United Kingdom* (Article 50), note 287, para. 15, and *Dudgeon* (Article 50), note 236, paras. 11–12.

[848] See, among many others, *Scordino*, note 372, para. 233.

[849] For possible issues related to payment, see Monitoring of the payment of sums awarded by way of just satisfaction: an overview of the Committee of Ministers' present practice, CM/Inf/DH(2008)7 final, 15 January 2009 (available at https://wcd.coe.int/ViewDoc.jsp?id=1393941&Site=CM).

[850] Rule 3 of the Rules adopted on 10 January 2001 by the Committee of Ministers for the application of Article 46, paragraph 2, of the European Convention on Human Rights (available at https://wcd.coe.int/ViewDoc.jsp?id=744279&BackColorInternet=9999CC&BackColorIntranet=FFBB55&BackColorLogged=FFAC75), confirmed by Rule 6 of the Rules of the Committee of Ministers for the supervision of the execution of judgments and of the terms of friendly settlements, adopted on 10 May 2006 (available at https://wcd.coe.int/ViewDoc.jsp?id=999329).

[851] Article 52 of the Convention.

found a violation of the applicant association's freedom of expression. The petitioner sought a review of the initial judgment delivered by the domestic courts, but its application was dismissed and the Committee of Ministers concluded the supervision of the execution of the Court's judgment. The continuous infringements of its rights prompted the applicant to invoke a fresh violation before the Court.

In the proceedings before the Grand Chamber, the Swiss government submitted, *inter alia*, that it was only the Committee which had jurisdiction at the execution stage, and that body terminated the monitoring proceedings. The Court held in its turn that it had jurisdiction over all issues raised by the interpretation and application of the Convention, also being the sole authority which may decide whether it has such jurisdiction. It therefore dismissed the government's objection and found that the Committee had ended the supervision of the execution without being informed by the government that a domestic judgment had declined the plaintiff's request to reopen the internal proceedings following the Court's pronouncement. The judges eventually established a new violation of the applicant's freedom of expression.[852]

What is somewhat disappointing is that, although they underlined the importance of executing the Court's judgments, the judges have not considered that case also from the standpoint of a violation of the state's obligation to execute those rulings. Even if that was not expressly raised by the parties, the Court had the possibility, as on many other occasions, to requalify the complaints or to raise of its own motion the question of execution. It has thus declined to take a firm position on the question of state responsibility under an international treaty and, instead of delivering a judicial opinion, left the matter in the hands of the Committee, a political body which has already been criticized by some of the Court's judges for 'a certain tolerance and an ineffective monitoring'.[853]

The Committee's supervision is mainly in the form of political and diplomatic pressure. Positive reaction by the member states was achieved following specific recommendations in respect of some wide-ranging breaches or problems encountered during the execution. An increasing number of states have already introduced in their legal order the possibility to reopen proceedings. Further impact on the Court's case law is

[852] *Verein gegen Tierfabriken Schweiz (VgT) v. Switzerland (no. 2)* [GC], no. 32772/02, ECHR 2009.

[853] Dissenting opinion of Judge Loucaides in *Toğcu v. Turkey* (striking out), no. 27601/95, 9 April 2002.

expected from recommendations in respect of the verification of the compatibility of internal draft laws, existing laws and administrative practice with the Convention standards, and on the improvement of domestic remedies.[854] To this may be added more specific actions: for example, the numerous resolutions in respect of the applications brought against Italy for length of internal proceedings, which were subsequently considered by the Court as a practice incompatible with the treaty, with aggravating effects.[855]

The long expected entry into force of Protocol No. 14 is deemed to increase the effectiveness of the mechanism, although the achievements have proved of limited impact. As regards the execution phase, the Protocol bestows upon the Committee a new prerogative to bring infringement proceedings in the Court against a state which refuses to abide by a final judgment.[856] The Explanatory Report admits the extreme and rather counter-productive character of this measure, and calls for its use only in exceptional circumstances. The drafters envisaged that the procedure's mere existence, with the resulting political pressure, would translate into an effective incentive for executing the Court's judgments.[857] However, as rightly noted, it is doubtful that referral of a political issue back to the Court would solve matters, except for some extra time for political bargaining.[858]

The infringement proceedings are dependent on two procedural constraints. The state is first served a formal notice, and then the Committee may decide to refer the question to the Court, but only by a majority vote of two-thirds of the representatives entitled to sit on the Committee. In the absence of any example so far, it is difficult to argue about the value of this new procedure. Doubts may further arise as to the usefulness for the execution stage of a new judgment ruling that a state has failed to fulfil its obligations, and the question may be raised as to what legal 'sanction', if any, the Court should apply.

854 Recommendation Rec(2004)5 of the Committee of Ministers to member states on the verification of the compatibility of draft laws, existing laws and administrative practice with the standards laid down in the European Convention on Human Rights, 12 May 2004, available on the Council of Europe's website (https://wcd.coe.int/ViewDoc.jsp?id=743297), and Recommendation Rec(2004)6 of the Committee of Ministers to member states on the improvement of domestic remedies, 12 May 2004, available on the Council of Europe's website (https://wcd.coe.int/ViewDoc.jsp?id=743317).

855 Costa, note 324, at 14, and the cases cited.

856 Article 46(4) of the Convention.

857 Para. 100 of the Explanatory Report, note 202.

858 Harris et al., note 30, footnote 313 at 866.

In theory, the Committee may also use the available measures of suspension of voting rights or expulsion from the organization, but in practice this is hardly conceivable. Can Russia be expelled from the Council of Europe? Better results would certainly produce clear directives from the Court, in the operative part of its judgments, as to the manner in which the state would be discharged of its obligations emerging from its breaching conduct. In that case, the Committee would simply need to assess whether the state has fully complied with those indications. It would improve matters if the system were more transparent, thus inspiring – and thus conveying to the states – more confidence.

If the supervision of the execution is hindered by a problem of interpretation, the Committee has been empowered by Protocol No. 14 to ask the Court for a ruling on the matter.[859] The referral decision also requires a majority vote of two-thirds in order to avoid an excessive burden on an already overloaded Court. The aim of this new procedure is to enable the Court to deliver an interpretation of its rulings, not to assess the propriety of the measures taken by states at the execution stage.[860] Here again, in the absence of any practice, it is difficult to assign it an effective role. Theoretically, interpretation of a decision by the very body which delivered it is certainly highly beneficial, but realistically it seems fairly doubtful that the judges, when confronted with a heavy caseload, would have any time to spare for interpretation in addition to adjudication.

5.4.2 *Time limit for execution and interest for belated payment*

At the end of 1990 the Committee of Ministers, faced with reluctance from the Italian government to pay several applicants, set a time limit of three months, but only with respect to that country. The following year, both the old Court and the Committee introduced a deadline by which a government ought to have performed the obligations ordered by the Strasbourg organs.[861] Initially, it was calculated from the date of the

[859] Article 46(3) of the Convention. [860] Para. 97 of the Explanatory Report, note 202.

[861] See, in this sense, J.-F. Flauss, 'La "satisfaction équitable" devant les organes de la Convention européenne des droits de l'homme: développements récents', *Juris-Classeur Europe* 2, no. 6 (1992). The Inter-American Court had established such a deadline as long ago as its first judgment on reparations in July 1989: see *Velásquez-Rodríguez* (reparations and costs), note 152, para. 26.

delivery of the judgment,[862] but later that time limit took into account the possibility for the parties to request referral to the Grand Chamber and therefore started when the judgment became final in accordance with Article 44(2) of the Convention.

As a general rule, the time limit is set at three months, but the Court may consider that a longer period would be appropriate. This was the case, for instance, with *Papamichalopoulos*, where the Court gave the state six months to return to the applicants a plot of land measuring 104,018 sq. m, including the buildings on it, or else to pay them compensation. It seems that the Court makes provision for a longer period only when it orders the state to do something, not when the state just has to pay a sum of money, even if the amount is fairly large.[863] Thus, in another two cases against Greece, the Court followed the three-month rule, although it had ordered impressive amounts of several millions of euros.[864] In one of them, the government even submitted that it was not able to make immediate full payment because of the size of just satisfaction and of the internal economic problems. For the Committee, that implicit request for a postponement appeared contrary to the obligations following on from the Court's judgment, and it ordered payment without delay.[865]

A case in which there was a serious delay in payment was *Loizidou*.[866] The government proposed that payment should be made following a global settlement of all similar cases concerning Cyprus. Although the Committee repeatedly held that the Turkish position was in breach of its international obligations,[867] Turkey did not pay until 2003, namely five years after the judgment on just satisfaction. It will be interesting to see how long it will take Turkey to pay the sum of EUR 90 million awarded in the case of *Cyprus v. Turkey*, for which the Court established a time limit of three months. Another case with a very long delay in execution

[862] Point 1 of the operative part in *Moreira de Azevedo v. Portugal* (Article 50), 28 August 1991, Series A no. 208-C, which is the first case where the Court mentioned a delay for payment.

[863] See, e.g., point 4(a) of the operative part in *Niţescu v. Romania*, no. 26004/03, 24 March 2009.

[864] *Stran Greek Refineries*, note 55, point 6 of the operative part, and *Former King of Greece* (just satisfaction), note 114, point 1 of the operative part. Greece paid the sums ordered on 17 January 1997 and on 5 December 2002, respectively.

[865] Interim Resolution DH(96)251 of 15 May 1996 in *Stran Greek Refineries*.

[866] *Loizidou* (Article 50), note 164. See Harris et al., note 30, at 874.

[867] Interim Resolutions DH(99)680 of 6 October 1999, DH(2000)105 of 24 July 2000, DH(2001)80 of 26 June 2001 and DH(2003)174 of 12 November 2003.

was that of *Dorigo v. Italy*, where the Commission and then the Committee found a violation of the right to a fair trial because the victim had been unable to examine witnesses against him when sentenced to over thirteen years' imprisonment.[868] It took more than eight years for the Committee to close that case, and the plaintiff has thus been obliged to serve nearly all the prison sentence passed on him in the unfair trial.[869] Delays in enforcement are also inevitable in cases where the Court has ordered or found necessary general measures. The Committee's powers to secure enforcement of the Court's judgments in due time are therefore subject to reasonable doubt.

Delays in execution may generally be caused by the parties or by the procedural steps to be taken. They include domestic bureaucracy, internal economic problems, requests by one party or both parties to refer the case to the Grand Chamber, the applicant's refusal to receive payment or a wrong address. When the Strasbourg organs introduced that time limit, no sanction was provided for the cases in which the state deferred payment, except maybe for political pressure by the Committee, which used to restate consideration of a case at each of its following meetings, until effective payment.[870]

In order to enhance the effectiveness of supervision, the Committee also decided to establish execution timetables, as well as a grace period of around one year from the date on which the judgment became final. After that period, it should be clear whether or not the execution process will be finished in the short term. If the general measures required by the Court are likely to be taken in the near future, the case will continue to be examined according to the normal time limits, but if they take some more time, then the Committee will adopt an execution framework with longer-term planning.[871]

[868] *Dorigo v. Italy*, no. 33286/96, Commission's report of 9 September 1998, and Committee of Ministers Resolution DH(99)258 of 15 April 1999; also see Harris et al., note 30, at 876.

[869] Final Resolution DH(2007)83 of 20 June 2007.

[870] That was the case, for instance, with *Azzi v. Italy* (no. 11250/84, Commission's decision of 13 October 1988) and *Lo Giacco v. Italy* (no. 10659/83, Commission's decision of 5 December 1988), where the Committee of Ministers reconsidered the cases three times until effective payment.

[871] Human rights working methods – Improved effectiveness of the Committee of Ministers' supervision of execution of judgments, Information document, CM/Inf (2004)8 final, 7 April 2004 (available at https://wcd.coe.int/ViewDoc.jsp?Ref=CM/Inf (2004)8&Language=lanEnglish&Ver=final).

One particular problem that may arise during the execution phase is when an applicant has been deported to a country which is not a member of the Council of Europe, and thus the Court, or his representatives, have lost contact with the victim. The issue arose in two Russian cases where the petitioners had been expelled to Uzbekistan. The Court reiterated the principle that 'the Convention must be interpreted and applied in such a way as to guarantee rights that are practical and effective' and ordered the breaching state to secure the execution of the just satisfaction award by facilitating contact between the victims and the Committee of Ministers or the applicants' representatives.[872] In order to make that order effective, the judges inserted the injunction in the operative part of their rulings.

Given that the Court in its early years was dealing with fewer cases and with lower awards, as opposed to the sums allocated in the present property cases, the system did not generally encounter any particular problem as to the enforcement of judgments.[873] For example, when the applicants sought interest until payment in the case of *The Sunday Times*, the Court replied that 'it may be assumed that the United Kingdom will comply promptly with the obligation incumbent on it', and dismissed the claim.[874]

That sort of bond of trust could not have survived the progressively increasing number of applications. Therefore, in cases where the question of reparation had been reserved for a separate judgment, but the government had not paid the amounts already fixed in the judgment on the merits, the Court upheld the applicant's request for interest.[875] At the beginning of 1996, the Court revised its position on the matter and thus started to order payment of interest until effective settlement, equal to the statutory rate of interest applicable in the respondent state at the date of adoption of its judgment.[876] Besides coercion, interest was further intended to counter a possible devaluation of an amount, inasmuch as the old Court used to make awards directly in the national currency.

[872] *Muminov* (just satisfaction) (para. 19) and *Kamaliyevy* (just satisfaction) (para. 14), cited at note 430.

[873] Nonetheless, the Committee of Ministers was confronted with overdue payments by some of the member parties: see the examples given by Flauss, note 499, footnote 26 at 10.

[874] *The Sunday Times* (Article 50), note 268, para. 44.

[875] *Hentrich* (Article 50), note 166, paras. 12–14.

[876] *John Murray v. the United Kingdom* [GC], 8 February 1996, *Reports of Judgments and Decisions* 1996-I, para. 80.

The statutory rate of interest varied greatly among the contracting parties.[877] For that reason, in 2002 the Court fixed sole interest for all countries, based on the marginal lending rate of the European Central Bank, to which it adds three percentage points.[878] The possibility to award interest for delay in execution has also been introduced in the Rules of Court,[879] but as a power that judges have, not an obligation or a right of the applicants. However, the current practice is automatically to make provision for such an award, apparently as an 'encouragement' for governments to execute the Court's judgments in due time. Hence, the relevance of the issue at present is more theoretical than practical.

5.4.3 *Currency of the award*

Traditionally, the Court has awarded reparation in the plaintiff's national currency. It has been pointed out that such an approach was likely to produce a financial loss for the petitioner, resulting from the conversion of currencies. The problem arose particularly in the context of legal aid obtained from the Council of Europe by the victim. That amount was paid in French francs and deducted from the costs reimbursed by the Court. An issue would have arisen when the judgment was executed months or even years later, because the judges made compensation at the rate available at the date of their ruling, whereas the victim may have received that amount at a different rate at the moment of actual payment.[880]

Things have changed with the adoption of the euro. In 2002, after making awards in euros even though the plaintiff claimed redress in another currency,[881] the Grand Chamber decided to change the previous practice of making reparation in the applicant's currency and established, in principle, the euro as the reference currency.[882] *In concreto*, when the euro is not the victim's national currency, the Court awards just satisfaction in euros, but orders that amount to be converted into the

[877] For example, the annual rate at the same month level was 4 per cent in *Josef Fischer v. Austria* (no. 33382/96, 17 January 2002, para. 30), and 30 per cent in *Mączyński v. Poland* (no. 43779/98, 15 January 2002, para. 45).

[878] *Öneryıldız v. Turkey*, no. 48939/99, 18 June 2002, para. 168.

[879] Rule 75(3) of the Rules of Court.

[880] Sansonetis, note 560, at 762.

[881] See, e.g., *Öneryıldız v. Turkey* [GC], no. 48939/99, ECHR 2004-XII, paras. 156–67.

[882] *Christine Goodwin v. the United Kingdom* [GC], no. 28957/95, ECHR 2002-VI, para. 123.

respondent state's national currency at the rate applicable on the date of settlement. The logic of making awards in euros is to overcome the effect of the instability of the national currency. Still, if the exchange rate is fluctuating, it may cause some prejudice.

Some have adopted the view that 'it would be more convenient for the Court' to award just satisfaction in the currency specified in the applicant's submissions, in order to prevent the negative impact of fluctuating exchange rates.[883] In reality, such a solution seems to offer little benefit in so far as the Registry lawyers would have to convert that sum into euros, in order to allow all the judges deliberating on a case to appreciate the equivalent of the claimed amount. Moreover, the value attached to a national currency depends on its strength vis-à-vis the euro.

An award in euros is only the general rule, therefore the Court does not exclude the possibility of making awards in the currency proposed by the plaintiff. Normally, it does so in respect of the pecuniary damage claimed by the victim and also for costs and expenses.[884] As for redress for moral prejudice, the judges continue to make awards in euros. In the absence of any explanation, one may only speculate on the practicality of such an approach. First, the judges order compensation directly in the national currency only when the applicants so claim. In any event, especially when assessing the value of a property at the time of deliberations, the Court has to convert a plaintiff's claims in the local currency in order to have an indication of the price on the local market. Second, it is easier for the judges to value the non-pecuniary harm directly in euros, as they already have the example of previous awards in similar cases. Finally, moral damage is the area where the Court needs acutely to give a sense of consistency to its practice. After all, pecuniary damage sustained by victims and the costs involved are inherently different from case to case, but compensation for moral suffering may and should be established along some objective lines. However, when the petitioner has claimed compensation in the national currency, whether reparation is ordered directly in the local currency or in euros, and then converted at the time of settlement, does not make any important difference. In addition, interest for delay in execution is paid for all the amounts granted by the Court.

[883] Becue et al., note 208, at 145.

[884] See, e.g., *Parolov v. Russia*, no. 44543/04, 14 June 2007, paras. 43–8, and *Dementyev v. Russia*, no. 3244/04, 6 November 2008, paras. 37–44.

5.4.4 Rights of creditors against an applicant who is a debtor

There have been cases where creditors of a plaintiff sought to seize the sums awarded by the Court in respect of just satisfaction. There is no difficulty when the creditors claim their right after payment by the respondent government, because the applicant has the possibility to make a claim in internal law. Questions arise when such a claim is made before payment.[885] The applicants have sometimes come back to Strasbourg with a request for interpretation of the Court's judgment.

That issue first appeared in *Ringeisen*. The parties argued whether the sum granted should be paid to the petitioner directly or could be claimed by his creditors. The judges left the matter to the discretion of the national authorities, but suggested that the government exempt that compensation from seizure.[886] The government made the sum available to the applicant's creditors, so he requested interpretation of the judgment, persuaded that the compensation should have been paid to him personally and free of all seizure or attachment. The Court allowed his request and ruled that the compensation for non-pecuniary damage was to be paid to the applicant personally and free from attachment.[887] A practice was thus initiated, based on the principle that a personal indemnity for moral damage may not be seized by an applicant's creditors.

In a subsequent case, *Allenet de Ribemont v. France*, the Court awarded just satisfaction for both pecuniary and non-pecuniary damage, without distinguishing between the two. Moreover, upon a request by the applicant, it declined jurisdiction to pronounce in advance on the seizable character of that award.[888] The amount was eventually seized by the applicant's creditors. The applicant sought interpretation of the judgment and, taking into account that pecuniary awards in respect of moral damage were already held to be free from attachment, requested the Court to distinguish between the attachable and non-attachable parts of that compensation. The Court declined to identify the proportions corresponding to pecuniary and non-pecuniary damage, as it was often difficult to make such a distinction, and concluded that its judgment was clear enough.[889]

885 Flauss, note 499, at 11–12. 886 *Ringeisen* (Article 50), note 90, para. 27.

887 *Ringeisen v. Austria* (interpretation), 23 June 1973, Series A no. 16, para. 15. Also see the separate opinions of Judges Verdross and Zekia.

888 *Allenet de Ribemont v. France*, 10 February 1995, Series A no. 308, paras. 63 and 65.

889 *Allenet de Ribemont v. France* (interpretation), 7 August 1996, *Reports of Judgments and Decisions* 1996-III, paras. 22–3.

The Committee of Ministers, under its former judicial powers, also ruled in favour of payment of the sums for non-pecuniary damage personally and free from seizure,[890] although it had allowed an attachment by domestic courts in respect of maintenance payments owed by the applicant to his son.[891] As for awards for costs and expenses, the Committee seems to have admitted, on the contrary, that they were not free from attachment. It has therefore allowed the state to set up those amounts against the sums owed by the victim for previous internal proceedings.[892]

Certainly, an applicant may agree to pay his creditors, but is not obliged to do so. The Court, although it had clearly recognized that at least compensation paid for moral damage should be free from attachment, usually refrains from inserting specific injunctions in that respect, on the same grounds as in the context of individual and general measures, namely that it does not have jurisdiction to make such an order. But even though the Court declined to issue a statement that the sums awarded should be exempt from attachment,[893] it nevertheless gave an opinion on the issue. In *Selmouni v. France* and *Velikova v. Bulgaria*, the judges considered that the whole compensation should be exempt from attachment, including costs and expenses, but left the point to the discretion of the national authorities. They held that 'the purpose of compensation for non-pecuniary damage would inevitably be frustrated and the Article 41 system perverted' if the state were to allow the attachment of that amount.[894]

Therefore, the nature of the awards was no longer a decisive factor. In the absence of a binding ruling by the Court, it would be the national authorities which would decide whether the awards from Strasbourg may be seized by creditors, before their payment to the applicant. It is expected, though, that they will follow the indications given by the Court. At least France gave assurances to the Committee of Ministers, at the time of execution of the obligations deriving from the *Selmouni* case, that the sums would not be attached.

[890] See, e.g., Resolution DH(94)66 of 19 October 1994 in *F.W. Kremzow II v. Austria.*

[891] The resolution in *Unterpertinger*, note 831.

[892] See, e.g., Resolution DH(84)5 of 7 December 1984 in *Eckle v. Germany*, and Resolution DH(91)9 of 13 February 1991 in *Hauschildt v. Denmark.*

[893] *Philis v. Greece (no. 1)*, 27 August 1991, Series A no. 209, para. 79.

[894] *Selmouni*, note 454, para. 133, and *Velikova v. Bulgaria*, no. 41488/98, ECHR 2000-VI, para. 99.

5.4.5 *Concluding remarks*

The supervision of execution of the Court's judgments comes out of the legal sphere and is entitled to a political organ. The question is whether the system thus designed is efficient and also sufficient, given that the few states that contribute the majority of cases are also those which pose problems. More difficulties arise in the context of pilot judgments, where general measures require legislative reform. Apart from political pressure, the Committee of Ministers has no efficient powers to apply any sanction on a state delaying or refusing to execute a judgment. This reveals the limits of the monitoring system. Exclusion from the organization is too extreme to be easily used, and the new infringement proceedings still have to prove their value. As to the latter solution, one may even ask how efficient such a power may be, when the very organ in charge of execution, and also the only one which may initiate such infringement proceedings, may itself be responsible or even unaware of a defective execution.[895]

The members of the Council of Europe still have to work on a more efficient mechanism for supervision, as well as on more authority and appropriate means, be they political or judicial, to force reluctant states to perform their commitments in due time. Instead of an effective system of implementation, there are envisaged only palliative measures aimed at political co-operation.[896] Would some political measures alleviate the judicial problems that undermine the Court's efficacy? The answer cannot be entirely positive, and the same is true with all instruments negotiated in the political arena.[897] The whole Convention system is a result of political co-operation and negotiation between sovereign states, so there should be no surprise that politics often outweighs the judiciary. The problematic question is this: to what extent can a political organ successfully replace a judicial one?

The alternatives offered by the Council of Europe are mainly recommendations and resolutions adopted by the Committee of Ministers.

[895] See the execution issues raised in *Verein gegen Tierfabriken Schweiz*, note 852, as well as the examples of tolerance in non-execution cited in a dissenting opinion to the *Toğcu* case, note 853.

[896] S. Greer, 'Reforming the European Convention on Human Rights: Towards Protocol 14', *Public Law* (2003), at 670–3.

[897] L. Caflisch, 'L'efficacité du système européen de protection des droits de l'homme', in L. Caflisch et al. (eds.), *El derecho internacional: normas, hechos y valores: Liber Amicorum José Antonio Pastor Ridruejo* (Madrid: Universidad Complutense, 2005), at 58.

Those documents are not binding on the member states, but certainly they have some effect when taken in the Convention framework. The Strasbourg institutions are therefore in pursuit of new solutions to adapt a system that risks being the victim of its own success. Political action is deemed more suited to the regional interference of powerful states. The compromise may be accepted if it secures effective protection of human rights. However, where remedies for the breaches found are not to the victim's benefit, or where states are not able to take appropriate measures in order to prevent repetition of similar violations, the Court's efficiency and credibility is in doubt.

6

What future for just satisfaction?

6.1 Need for explanation of the Court's quantification

The present study has largely demonstrated the inconsistency of the Court's rulings on just satisfaction. In particular, the practice in respect of compensation for moral prejudice is rather unpredictable, even if the judges use a confidential standardized approach. One may reasonably discern that the Court has an attraction for methods and concepts which give it discretion, such as the sometimes misused concept of 'equity'.

It is somewhat unfortunate that in Strasbourg, beside some often empty words merely stating that the Court has ruled in equity, there is no concrete reference as to what connotations equity has taken in the specific circumstances of a case. Further action seems indispensable. Such action should require a transparent enactment and an additional development of the standardized approach already used to calculate compensation. A model is proposed in the final section of this chapter. Based on objective standardization, the judges may further elaborate a theory of equity that would allow adjustments in accordance with the particular and often subjective circumstances of each case. In doing so, the Court would offer some grounds for its decisions.

What is equally striking is that the Court, when analysing the characteristics of internal law, held in *The Sunday Times* that:

> Firstly, the law must be adequately accessible: the citizen must be able to have an indication that is adequate in the circumstances of the legal rules applicable to a given case. Secondly, a norm cannot be regarded as a 'law' unless it is formulated with sufficient precision to enable the citizen to regulate his conduct: he must be able – if need be with appropriate advice – to foresee, to a degree that is reasonable in the circumstances, the consequences which a given action may entail.[898]

[898] *The Sunday Times v. the United Kingdom (no. 1)*, 26 April 1979, Series A no. 30, para. 49.

Now the question is: does the Court itself respect the conditions it demands from the member states? The answer should be obvious. There is neither predictability, nor consistency in its rulings on just satisfaction. Tomuschat has rightly observed that '[w]hat since Sunday Times the Court itself has viewed as an essential requirement of a legal rule, namely that the consequences of its application should be foreseeable, is lacking in its own jurisprudence'.[899]

For Jennings, '[t]he judicial function is an art not a science', in so far as 'the application of the law is [not] a mere technical process excluding discretions'.[900] The present analysis does not argue for the transformation of the Strasbourg system of reparation into a *fully* objective mechanism. That is not even possible, in so far as it cannot ever be conceived that two victims would suffer exactly the same type and degree of damage. Especially the moral harm depends on the personal characteristics of each victim. What this study aims to do is to reveal the inconsistencies in the Court's practice on reparation and to promote a higher degree of objectivization. On closer scrutiny, it appears that the field of reparations can be transformed into a more technical mechanism, which would exclude the judges' discretion to the greatest possible extent. The judges have already embarked upon an objective approach, but, inasmuch as they refuse to assume legal responsibility for its effective application, it is only a tool for exercising greater discretion and a reason not to be preoccupied with what equitable principles would imply.

In fact, practice shows that the Court does not offer grounds for different treatment of fairly similar cases. Is it not rather arbitrary to allow the judges to grant or refuse reparation without having to give any reason or explanation? Even a former President of the Court has admitted that, despite the fact that it has a large practical importance for applicants, 'the way in which just satisfaction is calculated – in spite of the efforts made by the case law – does not offer full legal certainty'.[901] Thus, after being confronted with an interference with their own rights, most of the victims must face again a discretionary ruling for reparation. In so far as awards are not predictable, a plaintiff who was not able to assess his chances of success before a decision in his case will still be no wiser, even if there eventually is the finding of a violation.

[899] Tomuschat, note 266, at 1427.

[900] R. Y. Jennings, 'The Judicial Function and the Rule of Law in International Relations', in *International Law at the Time of Its Codification*, note 170, Vol. III, at 148.

[901] Costa, note 324, at 16.

Some awards for moral damage are quite illustrative in this sense. In *Rukas v. Ukraine* the applicant claimed EUR 2,000 and received EUR 1,800;[902] in *Nozhkov v. Russia* the applicant claimed EUR 3,000 and received EUR 2,600;[903] and in *Suso Musa v. Malta* the applicant claimed EUR 25,000 and received EUR 24,000.[904] Given the fairly small difference between what was sought by the victims in terms of reparation and what was awarded by the Court, why did the judges not deem it equitable to allocate the full amount? Do such awards conceal a punitive attitude towards victims? Or is it just a mechanical calculation and application of some undisclosed formulae?

Usually, when the Court's lack of consistency is challenged, not only by individuals, but also by governments, the judges, even sitting in a Grand Chamber formation, avoid giving an explanation. Such was the case in two disputes decided the same day, *Arvanitaki-Roboti* and *Kakamoukas*, where the government asserted that 'when examining other cases concerning Greece in which it had found more serious violations than that of the right to a hearing within a reasonable time, the Court had awarded smaller sums'.[905] The Grand Chamber has not dealt expressly with those allegations, though in the presence of explicit requests by the states parties, the Court, which is a treaty organ created to interpret and apply the Convention, should take the opportunity to clarify the manner in which it applies that instrument.

To the frequent absence of explanations in respect of the criteria used to assess the reparation, one may add the lack of reasoning for the high percentage of applications declared inadmissible by the single judges or by the Committees of three judges. As rightly emphasized, there is a real danger that the category of manifestly ill-founded requests is used as a tool to control the caseload, a practice which eventually interferes with the Court's legitimacy.[906] Given that the decision-making process in Strasbourg is based on drafts prepared by the Registry lawyers, which necessarily rely on legal arguments, and in view of the extensive caseload

902 *Rukas v. Ukraine*, no. 15879/06, 15 October 2009, paras. 23 and 25.

903 *Nozhkov v. Russia*, no. 9619/05, 19 February 2013, paras. 51 and 53.

904 *Suso Musa v. Malta*, no. 42337/12, 23 July 2013, paras. 125 and 127.

905 See the cases of *Arvanitaki-Roboti* (para. 25) and *Kakamoukas* (para. 37), cited at note 478.

906 H. Keller, A. Fischer and D. Kühne, 'Debating the Future of the European Court of Human Rights after the Interlaken Conference: Two Innovative Proposals', *European Journal of International Law* 21, no. 4 (2010), at 1046.

and for the sake of transparency and guidance to national courts, one may even wonder if it would not be worthwhile to ask the judges to include a short reasoning for their decision.[907]

Therefore, the principal negative effect of the Court's lack of transparency is that it undermines its authority. The 2012 High Level Conference in Brighton on the future of the Court acknowledged that judgments need to be clear and consistent because this promotes legal certainty.[908] If the Court is not able to give consistency to its practice, it will lose credibility. It should not be disregarded that, while it is not always just about monetary compensation, the Strasbourg proceedings are used to a large extent for the very purpose of obtaining relief for a victim of a state violation. An incoherent approach has no beneficial effects on the confidence that the Court has already gained.

Moreover, inconsistent practice does not offer efficient guidelines, neither to the domestic courts in respect of the Convention standards of protection and reparation, nor for potential applicants as to the prospects of their complaints being upheld. Thus, the most sensitive issue remains the judges' unwillingness to give legal reasoning for their awards of reparation and their preference to resort to the absolute discretion that they enjoy under the treaty in the field of just satisfaction. But is that important, as long as the plaintiff secures reparation? The answer is entirely in the affirmative, because arbitrariness reflects negatively on the Court's legitimacy.

The solution proposed is to adopt a transparent, mainly objective system of redress, and to limit the judges' discretion to the minimum possible extent. That would assure more consistency to the case law. To explain the method of calculation and to establish the highest and lowest limits of pecuniary compensation for each type of violation would even prevent a number of disputes from coming to Strasbourg in the first place, because victims would be made aware that there would be no reasonable prospects for higher reparation. In the end, it would benefit the Court, unless the intention behind the Court's approach is to curb the influx by switching from an individual approach to a constitutional review of the law when faced by allegations of human rights violations.

907 A. Lester, 'The European Court of Human Rights after 50 Years', in Christoffersen and Madsen, note 188, at 108.

908 Para. 23 of the Brighton Declaration, note 179.

6.2 Should the Court act more like an international or more like a constitutional court?

6.2.1 The basis of inquiry

A factor of great influence over the capacity of individual victims to secure reparation in Strasbourg is the possibility for the Court to assume a constitutional mission at the expense of the right of individual petition. It has been noted that '[t]he original purpose of the Convention was not primarily to offer a remedy for particular individuals who had suffered violations of the Convention but to provide a collective, inter-state guarantee that would benefit individuals generally by requiring the national law of the contracting parties to be kept within certain bounds'.[909] The system appears to have been designed as a mechanism for revealing breaches of states' obligations, not for compensating the individual victim, and thus, from the beginning, it did not even provide a right of individual petition before the Court.[910] As is well known, the system has evolved, and the right of individual application lies at the heart of the protection mechanism. Therefore, what is the role of the Court, to apply the treaty on a case-by-case basis, so as to establish the responsibility of contracting states, or to impose norms and standards?

In 1995, in *Loizidou*, the Grand Chamber defined for the first time the Convention as 'a constitutional instrument of European public order'.[911] It took that expression from the previous Commission report of 1991 on the admissibility of that case.[912] But while no other open reference to constitutional powers had been made before by the Convention organs, the idea is far from being new in Strasbourg. As early as 1958, in a speech delivered at the ceremony marking the fifth anniversary of the entry into force of the Convention, the first President of the former Commission referred to the treaty as 'a constitutional instrument – as a European Bill of Rights for the individual'.[913] At the same time, he acknowledged that 'the very word "Convention" serves as a warning that our Bill of Rights

[909] Harris et al., note 30, at 33. [910] Ibid.

[911] *Loizidou v. Turkey* (preliminary objections), 23 March 1995, Series A no. 310, para. 75.

[912] *Chrysostomos, Papachrysostomou and Loizidou v. Turkey*, Commission's report of 4 March 1991, *Decisions and Reports* (DR) 68.

[913] C. H. M. Waldock, 'The European Convention for the Protection of Human Rights and Fundamental Freedoms', *British Yearbook of International Law* 34 (1958), at 359.

may have the features more of European international than of European constitutional law'.[914]

Recent Presidents of the Court have revived the debate over the transformation of the Convention into a constitutional instrument.[915] Along that same line of reasoning, in a report prepared in 2006 by a Group of Wise Persons set up by the states parties of the Council of Europe with the purpose of evaluating the long-term effectiveness of the control mechanism, the members of that group considered that:

> This protection mechanism confers on the Court at one and the same time a role of individual supervision and a 'constitutional' mission. The former consists in verifying the conformity with the Convention of any interference by a state with individual rights and freedoms and making findings as to any violation by the respondent state. Its other function leads it to lay down common principles and standards relating to human rights and to determine the minimum level of protection which states must observe.[916]

In view of the ongoing debate over the Court's constitutional role, it might be worth wondering what the difference is between a constitutional court and an international court, in order to determine what is, or what should be, the practical position of the Strasbourg Court. The present section argues that the Convention, as it stands, has not provided the Court with constitutional powers. It is only by an extensive interpretation of the treaty that the judges have embarked on a constitutional mission, most probably as an alternative to the continuing increase in the caseload. The question is whether they should continue in that direction.

There are some analogies that may be drawn between an international and a constitutional court, especially in the case of a human rights court, but of more relevance for the present inquiry are their distinctive features. International courts and tribunals are usually created by a treaty

[914] Ibid., at 356.

[915] See, by L. Wildhaber, 'A Constitutional Future for the European Court of Human Rights?', *Human Rights Law Journal* 23, nos. 5–7 (2002); '"Constitutionnalisation" et "juridiction constitutionnelle": le point de vue de Strasbourg', in Hennette-Vauchez and Sorel, note 181; and 'Rethinking the European Court of Human Rights', in Christoffersen and Madsen, note 188. Also see Costa, note 324, at 15.

[916] Para. 24 of the Report of the Group of Wise Persons to the Committee of Ministers, CM (2006)203, 15 November 2006 (available at http://https://www.wcd.coe.int/ViewDoc.jsp?id=1063779%26Site=CM). Also see para. 81.

with the very purpose of interpreting and applying that instrument. Their composition and area of jurisdiction are also defined in the treaty. They have limited powers. Thus, the international human rights courts, i.e., the European, Inter-American and African Courts, have been created to decide whether the contracting states are responsible for the alleged breaches of the corresponding treaties.

A further characteristic of international courts is that they are composed of judges with different legal and cultural backgrounds, but an essential distinction between international and constitutional courts may be found in the effects of their judicial review. Whereas a decision of a constitutional court invalidates a law with effects *erga omnes* in national legislation, or at least denies its application to a concrete litigation, a judgment by an international court may only declare that a law or its applications are incompatible with the specific treaty, without directly affecting the validity of that law in the internal order.[917] That is what the Strasbourg Court does, given that it has traditionally refrained from annulling legislation.

The features of a constitutional court, in so far as there is no international constitutional court, may only be extracted from national jurisdictions. They too function under the law and include members of high professional authority; they too have exclusivity in the field, their rulings being final and not challengeable before other institutions, but their role and tasks are completely different from that of an international court. Their principal authority is to establish *in abstracto* whether particular laws are in conflict with the constitution. As a result, they have a power to annul laws.

The European Court has features of both of these types of courts, which has occasioned a long debate as to what attributes should prevail. The pilot-judgment procedure has decisively altered the traditional approach of refusing to review domestic laws. It seems that the judges have adopted a new mentality. In fact, it is not the procedure per se, but the interpretation given by the Court, which has entitled it to pronounce on an incompatibility with the Convention. While the Court itself cannot declare legislation null and void, in practice it may achieve the same result. Ultimately, though, such an active involvement may hardly be condemned, as long as it reinforces protection of human rights for large-scale violations.

[917] Bernhardt, note 14, at 297.

6.2.2 *The pilot-judgment procedure: identification of systemic or structural problems*

The pilot-judgment procedure goes a step further towards what many like to call 'the Court's constitutional mission'. It is uncontested that this new development no longer aims at individual justice, but at collective protection of human rights. Will that lead to a decline in the Court's interest for personal redress and, eventually, of the right of individual petition?

First and foremost, the initiative belongs to the states, not to the judges. In its 2004 resolution, the Committee of Ministers invited the Court

> as far as possible, to identify, in its judgments finding a violation of the Convention, what it considers to be an underlying systemic problem and the source of this problem, in particular when it is likely to give rise to numerous applications, so as to assist states in finding the appropriate solution and the Committee of Ministers in supervising the execution of judgments.[918]

In a further recommendation adopted the same day, the Committee encouraged the member states to

> review, following Court judgments which point to structural or general deficiencies in national law or practice, the effectiveness of the existing domestic remedies and, where necessary, set up effective remedies, in order to avoid repetitive cases being brought before the Court.[919]

Some particular features of the pilot-judgment procedure emerge from those statements, and have been further developed in the Court's judgments. In 2011, a specific rule was inserted into the Rules of Court.[920] The procedure can be initiated either by the Court of its own motion or at the request of the parties in a dispute. The judges will first find a violation which affects a larger group of individuals who have either already lodged applications or are prospective complainants. In other words, they identify a systemic problem. Automatically, the Court pronounces the need for general measures and gives some guidance to the state. For more authority, it normally reinforces that obligation in the operative part of its ruling. It may also decide to adjourn examination of all similar cases, and it usually specifies a time limit for adopting

[918] Resolution Res(2004)3, note 768. [919] Recommendation Rec(2004)6, note 854.
[920] Rule 61.

measures, normally six months or one year. Given that a pilot-judgment procedure is always attached to a particular dispute, an applicant in such a case would receive the usual reparation.

According to the official texts cited above, the procedure involves equally the Court and the member states. The judges should identify the systemic failures, as well as the type of remedial measures, and the states would take effective action.[921] But this is hardly applied in practice; the judges have taken over the state's attributes, and started to decide themselves what the proper conduct should be.[922] Would that amount to intrusion into internal affairs?

Since the early cases, some of the judges have clearly opposed such an attitude on account of the weakness of the legal basis of the pilot-judgment procedure. For them, the Court has no justification to indicate in the operative provisions that the state should amend its legislation, either in virtue of the aforementioned two documents issued by the Committee of Ministers, or on the grounds of Article 46 of the Convention, which only provides for the duty to abide by the Strasbourg rulings.[923] Others have moderated those fears by arguing that the Court would not 'usurp' a constitutional role, but would simply refer to minimum standards, exerting though some functions which are somewhat similar to those of constitutional courts.[924] After all, the member parties have agreed that the Court will deal with these issues which might otherwise be considered internal affairs.

The pilot-judgment procedure should not be confused with a simple order for general measures.[925] Whereas both situations denote a widespread problem, the Court identifies a systemic failure in the internal order only in a pilot judgment, and may decide on the procedure to be followed in cases stemming from the same systemic problem. Moreover, the Court is more willing to give explicit guidance to the state. However, in addition to offering a remedy for past violations, both situations correspond implicitly to the general requirement in international law

921 Rule 61(3) of the Rules of Court.

922 See, e.g., point 4 of the operative part in *Suljagić v. Bosnia and Herzegovina*, no. 27912/02, 3 November 2009.

923 Partly dissenting opinion of Judge Zagrebelsky in *Hutten-Czapska*, note 678. Also see V. Zagrebelsky, 'Violations structurelles et jurisprudence de la Cour européenne des droits de l'homme', in Salerno, note 206, at 154–5.

924 Partly concurring and partly dissenting opinion of Judge Zupančič in *Hutten-Czapska*, note 678.

925 E.g., *Xenides-Arestis v. Turkey*, no. 46347/99, 22 December 2005, para. 40.

for guarantees of non-repetition, whose pertinence to the Convention system will be examined in the next section.

An inherent effect of a pilot judgment is that it goes beyond the normal *inter partes* authority of the Court's rulings.[926] That is indeed a constitutional feature. The procedure has been very much welcomed by the judges, who conceive it as a tool for disposing of a great number of present and future repetitive applications. The Court has initiated the procedure with the *Broniowski* and *Hutten-Czapska* judgments, and then continued to apply it to several types of violations, such as non-enforcement or delayed enforcement of domestic judgments,[927] restitution or compensation for nationalized property,[928] amendments to the electoral law,[929] compensatory remedies for the unreasonable length of civil,[930] criminal[931] or administrative[932] proceedings, and inhuman or degrading conditions of detention.[933]

Except for the cases in which the fundamental nature of the right at stake renders inappropriate the adjournment of the examination of similar complaints,[934] the pilot-judgment system would inevitably delay the prospects for other victims who want to see their disputes examined. Whether they have already brought proceedings in Strasbourg or not, they have to wait until the state implements general measures. Other complainants will receive compensation at international level only if the Court deems those measures inappropriate. Otherwise, they will be directed to address their petitions to the internal authorities. Similarly, those potential victims who do not have their case

[926] G. Nicolaou, 'The New Perspective of the European Court of Human Rights on the Effectiveness of Its Judgments', in C. Hohmann-Dennhardt, P. Masuch and M. Villiger (eds.), *Grundrechte und Solidarität: Durchsetzung und Verfahren: Festschrift für Renate Jaeger* (Kehl: N. P. Engel, 2011), at 172.

[927] See, e.g., *Burdov v. Russia (no. 2)*, no. 33509/04, ECHR 2009; *Olaru and Others v. Moldova*, nos. 476/07, 22539/05, 17911/08 and 13136/07, 28 July 2009; and *Yuriy Nikolayevich Ivanov*, note 823.

[928] See, e.g., *Maria Atanasiu*, note 380. [929] See, e.g., *Greens and M.T.*, note 636.

[930] *Finger v. Bulgaria*, no. 37346/05, 10 May 2011.

[931] *Dimitrov and Hamanov v. Bulgaria*, nos. 48059/06 and 2708/09, 10 May 2011, and *Michelioudakis v. Greece*, no. 54447/10, 3 April 2012.

[932] *Rumpf v. Germany*, no. 46344/06, 2 September 2010, and *Vassilios Athanasiou and Others v. Greece*, no. 50973/08, 21 December 2010.

[933] *Ananyev and Others v. Russia*, nos. 42525/07 and 60800/08, 10 January 2012, and *Torreggiani and Others v. Italy*, nos. 43517/09, 46882/09, 55400/09, 57875/09, 61535/09, 35315/10 and 37818/10, 8 January 2013.

[934] For example, complaints about inhuman or degrading treatment: see *Ananyev*, note 933, para. 236.

on the Court's docket may be requested to exhaust the new domestic remedy before coming to Strasbourg,[935] which will create further uncertainty.[936]

Some of the Court's judges have pointed to other undesirable effects. Thus, the measures taken by the state may subsequently be deemed inappropriate by the Court, which means that the judges will have to examine those cases, a situation that they sought to prevent by adjourning the consideration of those applications pending the pilot-judgment procedure.[937] Yet, the procedure has been introduced in order to prevent large-scale violations.

It may still be premature to pronounce on the effectiveness of such an approach, but recent signs are not encouraging. In a press release of February 2012,[938] the Court decided to resume examination of applications concerning the non-enforcement of domestic decisions in Ukraine, given that the state had not adopted the required measures following a pilot judgment. The judges further noted the existence of some 2,500 similar cases on the docket. In other words, those petitioners have waited for nothing. The Court should reflect on that situation in its future rulings.

In conclusion, the system needs solutions for securing effective enforcement of pilot judgments. It seems that the states need more impetus to put things in order. In that sense, building on the pilot-judgment procedure, the Brighton Declaration invited the Committee of Ministers to design a procedure by which the Court would choose only a small number of repetitive cases, which are representative for a certain group of violations, and then determine if they constitute a breach of the treaty. That determination will then be applicable to the whole group of cases.[939] Thus, states parties will be more 'pressed' to adapt legislation to the Convention standards, not only in the context of systemic failures generating widespread effects, but also when in the presence of a

[935] See, e.g., *Nagovitsyn and Nalgiyev* (dec.), nos. 27451/09 and 60650/09, 23 September 2010, and *Balan v. Moldova* (dec.), no. 44746/08, 24 January 2012.

[936] B. Nascimbene, 'Violation "structurelle", violation "grave" et exigences interprétatives de la Convention européenne des droits de l'homme', in Salerno, note 206, at 147.

[937] D. Popovic, 'Pilot Judgments of the European Court of Human Rights', in Steering Committee for Human Rights (ed.), *Reforming the European Convention on Human Rights: A Work in Progress* (Strasbourg: Council of Europe, 2009), at 360.

[938] Procedure following pilot judgment in *Yuriy Nikolayevich Ivanov v. Ukraine*, published on 29 February 2012, and available on the Court's website, through the Hudoc search engine.

[939] Para. 20(d) of the Brighton Declaration, note 179.

problem that simply has the prospect of repetition. While in theory the proposal can be welcomed, in so far as it strengthens the level of human rights protection, there still remains the practical test of effective implementation.

6.2.3 *Which way for the Court?*

The Convention is not a European human rights constitution, even if it contains a list of rights and guarantees that must be included in the national systems of the contracting states. It is an international treaty and, unlike a domestic constitutional instrument, the parties may formulate reservations or even denounce it. An important difference between treaty-based and constitution-based regimes is that 'whereas treaty-based regimes impose legal obligations on states that are both fixed at the outset and consensual, constitutional entities have the ability to impose obligations on states that are neither'.[940] This is an argument that weighs heavily against the contention that the Convention is akin to a constitution. It would be difficult to argue that the states parties would accept obligations against their sovereign power of decision. Even the pilot-judgment procedure has been initiated with their express consent.

Some perceive the Convention mechanism as a 'transnational system of constitutional justice' which influences national legal orders so as to obtain adjustments to their system of human rights protection.[941] But as far as the Court's constitutional status is concerned, authors are generally divided. Some argue against constitutional tasks,[942] while others have adopted the view that, in order to provide authoritative pan-European standards, the Court, rather than delivering a personal remedy to each deserving applicant, should be encouraged further in the constitutional tasks direction.[943] What should be the most suitable orientation for the system is still under debate, though it should be admitted that 'the claim has never been that the Convention system is

[940] S. Gardbaum, 'Human Rights and International Constitutionalism', in J. L. Dunoff and J. P. Trachtman (eds.), *Ruling the World? Constitutionalism, International Law, and Global Governance* (Cambridge University Press, 2009), at 245.

[941] A. Stone Sweet, 'On the Constitutionalisation of the Convention: The European Court of Human Rights as a Constitutional Court', *Faculty Scholarship Series* 71 (2009), at 10.

[942] See, e.g., E. A. Alkema, 'The European Convention as a Constitution and Its Court as a Constitutional Court', in Mahoney et al., note 266.

[943] Wildhaber, 'A Constitutional Future', note 915, at 161 and 163.

fully "constitutional"'.[944] In fact, all these statements put the accent on the inherent constitutional feature of human rights, omitting the very important institutional aspect. After all, it is the member states that decide what powers the Court should have.

In cases brought by private persons, in contrast to those lodged by states, the judges have traditionally refused to examine domestic law in the absence of individual measures of implementation, albeit some rulings may have led to a similar result.[945] Admittedly, they declared in *Marckx* that, although they were not required to undertake an examination *in abstracto* of the impugned legal provisions, 'it is inevitable that the Court's decision will have effects extending beyond the confines of this particular case, especially since the violations found stem directly from the contested provisions and not from individual measures of implementation, but the decision cannot of itself annul or repeal these provisions'.[946] In that case, they did indeed assess the compatibility of Belgian law on maternal affiliation and the Convention standards.

Thus, even if the Court's judgments had officially been deemed to be 'essentially declaratory' and the choice of the means of domestic assimilation had been left to the wrongdoing state,[947] in some of its early cases, there was nonetheless perceived 'a real temptation . . . to act in a way it has no jurisdiction to do, namely to declare certain legislative acts to be incompatible with the Convention, instead of strictly limiting its pronouncements to the individual measure which was the subject of the original application'.[948] While such an active stance towards annihilation of standards conflicting with the Convention is hardly condemnable from the point of view of effective protection of human rights, it evidently runs against the original intention of the drafters, who promptly opposed a power by which the Court could annul legislation. In fact, it runs against the intention of the contracting states to abide by the terms of the treaty as it stood at the moment of ratification.

[944] Bates, note 6, at 153.

[945] In cases where the applicant was not able to demonstrate concrete interference (*Klass*, note 246, paras. 33–4), when the law imposed modification of conduct (*Dudgeon* (Article 50), note 236, para. 41), or when the applicant belonged to a class of persons at risk of being affected by certain legislation (*Johnston*, note 257, para. 42, and *Open Door and Dublin Well Woman*, note 393, para. 44).

[946] *Marckx*, note 111, para. 58. [947] Ibid.

[948] H. Golsong, 'The European Court of Human Rights and the National Law-Maker: Some General Reflections', in Matscher and Petzold, note 37, at 242.

Turning to more recent developments, one should agree that the pilot-judgment procedure does allow the judges to examine specific legal provisions in a larger context than that of the particular circumstances of the case. The Court does not confine its analysis to a simple remedy *in casu*, but further recommends or even orders the breaching state to change its legislation so as to reach the level of treaty standards. The difference is that, through the intermediary of the above-mentioned recommendations by the Committee of Ministers, the judges now have the express approval of the member states to do in practice what in theory they have usually declined authority to do, namely to review internal legislation. Is that a voluntary submission by the states parties to a sort of constitutional order? Would that further empower the Court with some constitutional power? Is that an attempt to distract the Court's attention away from the individual victim of a breach and to focus instead on theoretical debate as to how the internal law should be? Definitely, the judges should not assume constitutional tasks at the expense of the right of individual petition. If the latter is abolished, the entire protection of human rights will become an illusion.

States, when becoming parties to the Convention, agree to comply with the legal standards established by that instrument, standards that are not imposed by a supranational entity, but accepted by them through the simple act of ratification. The Court has nonetheless performed an extensive interpretation of the states' obligation to abide by its final rulings, and thus has started to firmly impose general measures. While the Convention clearly provides for reparation for the past consequences of a violation, the judges have also been concerned with the future effects of the states' unlawful conduct. That development can only be welcomed, in so far as it assures a more effective protection and also aims at prevention. At the same time, it must be conceded that only exceptionally does the Court impose general measures. Review of legislation *in abstracto* is not its main task, as in the case of constitutional courts. By contrast, the Inter-American Court has not hesitated to declare the general incompatibility of legislation with the American Convention, for instance in the case of amnesty laws.[949]

The Strasbourg judges may also use Article 13 of the Convention, which confers on victims a right to an effective remedy before a national authority. The provision is vague enough to permit the Court to inquire into the scope and efficiency of domestic means to provide redress. The

[949] *Barrios Altos v. Peru* (merits), 14 March 2001, Series C no. 75, paras. 41–4.

judges also use that article as a ground for the principle of subsidiarity, according to which the states are better equipped to cope with human rights violations at home. In so far as the Court insists on its subsidiary role – a principle inserted in the Convention's preamble by Protocol No. 15 – it is not prepared to assume a full constitutional mission. Moreover, the judges permit the member states to enjoy a certain margin of appreciation in respect of legislation at internal level. The two principles are incompatible with the functioning of a constitutional court.

Nevertheless, additional constitutional prerogatives may prove beneficial for the promotion of human rights, although it is rather doubtful that the Court may discharge an extra function without affecting its present role, at a moment when it is confronted with an increasing number of cases. But if the judges were entrusted with constitutional powers, would that exclude a high level of discretion on their part when defining human rights principles and theories? The present record on reparation proves the contrary. There would be discussions and contradictions as to what would be the proper norm. One should also take into account that the Convention itself imposes a certain standard. The national constitutional courts may deal better with those questions of incompatibility between laws. A further aspect is that the Strasbourg judges cannot have complete knowledge of all internal legal orders.

In conclusion, the European Convention is an international treaty and the Court is a treaty organ that has been created and operates within the framework of that instrument. The member states have not committed themselves to any formal constitutional supervision on the part of the Strasbourg judges. The drafters clearly refused a power for them to strike down legislation. As long as the states do not agree to the contrary, the Court cannot perform tasks akin to those conferred on constitutional courts, for it cannot extend its authority of its own motion. Otherwise, it risks being accused of abuse of power.

Still, it would be simplistic to deny completely any constitutional dimension to the system. The Court interprets the Convention and imposes standards as to the level of protection: for example, as to the guarantees for a fair trial or for an effective investigation, or as to the conditions of detention in the member countries. Such a development has been perceived by some of the judges as denoting that 'the character of the Convention as a "Human Rights Constitution" has become more important than the treaty character'.[950] At the same time, it cannot be

[950] Bernhardt, note 14, at 304.

ignored that the system of control was originally conceived as a mechanism of inter-state applications. In those cases, a member state is indeed allowed to challenge *in abstracto* a legal provision or practice from another state party, without necessarily claiming to have suffered prejudice. Yet, the practice is highly disappointing from that point of view, given the extremely few inter-state disputes. That was presumably the reason why the states have decided to grant the individual a direct right of application, in order to balance their hesitation to launch into politically unfriendly activities. The result was far beyond expectations, the Court presently struggling with the enormous influx of requests.

Therefore, individual justice has proved successful and it also stands as evidence of how many states respect the Convention. When considering the number of violations, the result is fairly alarming. Directing the Court from individual redress towards constitutional standardization would ultimately lead to progressive degradation of the system of protection, even if in theory the right of individual petition is further maintained. The so-called constitutional mission would be of benefit to the system, but only in addition to individual justice, not through replacement. In that sense, it has been suggested that a constitutional role may be reinforced, for instance by increasing the *erga omnes* effects of judgments, by granting the Court more constitutional 'tools', or even by creating an additional tribunal and then dividing the two roles between the two institutions, but with the condition that the right of individual petition should remain unaffected, especially as the two functions are not diametrically opposed to each other.[951]

Whatever solution is adopted, the debate over the future of the Court should be oriented towards a harmonious coexistence of the two roles, not towards their mutual exclusion. It seems that the legitimate ambition to eliminate a tremendous backlog tends to prioritize a constitutional mission *over* individual justice. The lack of financial resources has a deterrent effect on the Court's enthusiasm for human rights protection. But until there is official recognition of some constitutional powers, the Court should continue to identify shortcomings in domestic legislation and firmly direct the states to adopt general measures to remedy the existing problems. In that mission, the support of the Committee of Ministers is crucial, inasmuch as non-enforcement of general measures annihilates their utility. Moreover, the role and effect of those measures is closely linked to another principle that the Strasbourg mechanism

[951] Vanneste, note 201, at 83–6.

should further develop, which is that of firmly requesting from the offending states guarantees for the non-repetition of the breaching conduct.

6.3 Guarantees of non-repetition

Conceptually, reparation is made for the injury that a violation has already caused. It is mainly concerned with the past. But the period of time which follows a Court's pronouncement may be equally important for assessing the extent of the damage generated by a violation, such as in the context of estimating the loss of earnings or when the state is ordered to offer free and full medical cover during the victim's lifetime.[952] On the contrary, the general obligation to offer assurances and guarantees of non-repetition, while occasioned by past conduct, is always provided for the future.[953] So, are they a form of reparation?

The UN Basic Principles and Guidelines on the Right to a Remedy and Reparation clearly say so.[954] However, the Commentary to Article 30(b) of the ILC Articles insists on their future-looking characteristic, with the consequence that '[t]hey focus on prevention rather than reparation'.[955] They may be claimed as satisfaction, such as in the case of the repeal of legislation or preventive measures to avoid repetition, but their main purpose is 'the reinforcement of a continuing legal relationship'.[956] They have been claimed in the *Gabčíkovo–Nagymaros Project* case, but the International Court of Justice has not made any reference to them.[957] It nonetheless examined their suitability for the first time in *LaGrand* and appreciated that the commitment undertaken by the offender to implement specific measures represented a general assurance of non-repetition.[958] While a simple verbal promise may

952 *Oyal v. Turkey*, no. 4864/05, 23 March 2010, para. 102.

953 See, in particular, S. Barbier, 'Assurances and Guarantees of Non-Repetition', in Crawford, Pellet and Olleson, note 46.

954 Principle 18 of the Basic Principles and Guidelines on the Right to a Remedy and Reparation for Victims of Gross Violations of International Human Rights Law and Serious Violations of International Humanitarian Law, 19 April 2005, UN Doc. E/CN.4/2005/L.10/Add.11.

955 Crawford, note 43, at 198. 956 Ibid., at 199.

957 *Gabčíkovo–Nagymaros Project (Hungary/Slovakia)*, Judgment, ICJ Reports 1997, p. 7, paras. 14(5) and 127 *in fine*.

958 *LaGrand (Germany v. United States of America)*, Judgment, ICJ Reports 2001, p. 466, paras. 124, 125 and 127, and also points 6 and 7 in the operative part. For a discussion, see G. Palmisano, 'La garantie de non-répétition entre codification et réalisation

suffice as assurance, guarantees imply more than that, and thus are better suited for a system of human rights protection. In fact, the states parties to the European Convention have given an assurance that they will respect those rights by the very act of ratification. Looking to the amplitude of the Court's case law, there is no need to point to the value of those assurances. Therefore, only the pertinence of guarantees will be examined.

In the Strasbourg system, guarantees of non-repetition may only be seen as a complementary element for realization of *restitutio in integrum* for the very act of violating the treaty, not in the sense of individual redress offered to a victim. To that extent, they perform the function assigned by general international law; that is, assuring the other contracting states that the wrongful conduct will not be replicated. In any event, guarantees of non-repetition, even in the context of the particular regime created by the Convention, would be given to the other states in relation to a specific official activity, not with reference to the effects on the individual victim. It would be an exaggeration to request a state to assure each victim that it will not interfere again with his or her rights. Those guarantees should aim at the act per se, not at its distinctive consequences, being thus attached to the legal obligation.

There is no treaty provision in respect of guarantees of non-repetition. When clearly sought by applicants, the judges have refused to make an order on the grounds that they have not been empowered to direct the state to take such action, the respondent having the choice of the means by which it would discharge its obligation to abide by the Court's ruling.[959] During supervision of the execution, the practice of the Committee of Ministers has been to request information from the respondent state as to the measures taken as a result of the finding of a violation. States have usually submitted information as to the measures effectively adopted, which may have included actions such as changes in administrative practice and dissemination of the Strasbourg ruling,[960] or elimination of the administrative discretion as to construction and operation of places of worship.[961] Therefore, states have an obligation

juridictionnelle du droit: à propos de l'affaire *LaGrand*', *Revue generale de droit international public* 106 (2002).

959 *McGoff*, note 660, para. 31. Moreover, in a recent case where the applicant clearly requested guarantees of non-repetition, the Court did not even examine such a claim, at least not expressly: *Stojanović v. Serbia*, no. 34425/04, 19 May 2009, paras. 83 and 85.

960 Resolution DH(2003)177 of 6 January 2004 in *D.N. v. Switzerland*.

961 Resolution DH(2005)87 of 26 October 2005 in *Manoussakis and Others v. Greece*.

to prevent future interferences, albeit not to offer formal guarantees for that. But looking beyond denomination, may they be considered as guarantees of non-repetition? It may be hard to contest that such changes, in so far as they do not amount to new violations, have the effect of preventing recurrence.

Moreover, not only the Committee, but also the Court itself has directed on occasion the wrongdoing state to prevent recurrence, normally on the grounds of the same obligation of abiding by its rulings. The most common example is that of legislation in disagreement with the Convention, where the simple existence of that law, not particular acts of implementation, constituted an infringement. For instance, in *Norris v. Ireland*, where legislation prohibiting male homosexual activity interfered with the applicant's private life, the Court instructed the state to take the necessary measures in order to discharge its obligation of execution.[962] The judges were restricted from ordering the state to amend or annul legislation by the legal norm, but the message was fairly evident and the state acted in consequence and has modified the criminal legislation regarding homosexual acts.[963]

Recently though, the Court has identified weaknesses in domestic legislation and recommended states to take action for the very purpose of putting an end to the existing situation and to prevent future violations of the right to a trial within a reasonable time,[964] or of overcrowding in prisons.[965] It was nonetheless a simple suggestion, without any formal binding effect, because the Court had not identified 'a structural problem consisting of "a practice that is incompatible with the Convention" nationwide',[966] which would have entitled it to apply the pilot-judgment procedure.

In essence, it is laudable that the Strasbourg mechanism has not tolerated mere assurances, but has endeavoured to provide effective guarantees of non-repetition, even if not labelled as such and even if not clearly demanded. In the context of the pilot-judgment procedure, the Court gives an express order to the respondent state to adopt and implement general measures. It is not simply an implied element of the

[962] *Norris*, note 257, para. 50. [963] Resolution DH(93)62 of 14 December 1993.
[964] *Lukenda*, note 821, para. 98.
[965] See, e.g., *Štrucl and Others v. Slovenia*, nos. 5903/10, 6003/10 and 6544/10, 20 October 2011, para. 140, and *Mandić and Jović v. Slovenia*, nos. 5774/10 and 5985/10, 20 October 2011, para. 127.
[966] Ibid.

execution phase, confined to political supervision. In the presence of a still incipient practice, it is too soon to tell whether or not it is effective. It is expected that states will take it seriously.

One may here again ask whether these general measures, either suggested in particular cases or imposed in pilot-judgment proceedings, may represent guarantees of non-repetition. In order to answer this, one should return to the above-mentioned Commentary to Article 30(b) of the ILC Articles, which puts the accent on the future-looking element and on the preventive character of those guarantees; the same is true with regard to the Basic Principles and Guidelines.[967] By contrast, the principal aim of the pilot-judgment procedure is to redress the situation of a large number of persons who, like the victims in the particular case, are affected by the situation found to be incompatible with the Convention.[968] While it is true that such judgments also denote a preventive character, that is not their main purpose. Hence, they may not be properly called guarantees of non-repetition.

In so far as the Court derives the legal basis of general measures from Article 46 instead of Article 41, they cannot be considered as a form of reparation, but as an element of the states' obligation to abide by final judgments, which includes the responsibility to adopt, when appropriate, general and/or individual measures in order to put an end to the violation and to redress so far as possible its effects. The ILC Articles have also treated them separately from reparation, but together with the obligation of cessation of the wrongful act, if it is continuing.[969] The Convention system has therefore fallen back on the general rule. Those general measures, except for those implied by the pilot-judgment procedure, may reasonably be equated with guarantees of non-repetition. Until such an obligation is distinctly provided in the treaty, the Court will continue to aptly make recourse to a legal artifice and incorporate them into the more general obligation of execution.

In international law, guarantees of non-repetition are claimed by the states, in so far as they are the principal actors. In the Strasbourg system, it is the Court that must exert that authority, the individual applicant having no influence and the other states, regrettably, having no apparent interest. It may be that in the absence of a generally accepted theory of

[967] See Principle 23. [968] See, e.g., *Maria Atanasiu*, note 380, para. 231.
[969] Article 30 of the ILC Articles.

legal prejudice,[970] the contracting states lack enthusiasm for couching their disagreement for a breach of the treaty in official action against the wrongdoer. It should be deplored that law is overshadowed by politics.

A better solution would therefore be for the member parties to agree to introduce them directly in the treaty and thus make them binding. In this way, guarantees of non-repetition would be placed under judicial, not political, control. The Convention, as the Court itself has declared on several occasions, is a living instrument which must be adapted to present-day conditions.[971] The current practice, in addition to a fairly impressive rate of interference, reveals some systemic deficiencies which have already given rise, or may give rise, to large-scale violations. Theoretically, there should be no impediment to requiring guarantees in those situations. And yet, it ultimately depends on member states' willingness to make further commitments so as to reinforce the rights and freedoms accepted by them in the treaty. Certainly, it is not in their best interest to engage in such a process, but it is absolutely a precondition for a truly efficient system of protection.

The necessity for guarantees of non-repetition may thus emerge from the circumstances of a case, without any limitation to the classic repetitive cases, but nonetheless when the judges consider that the unlawful activity may be repeated. Article 30(b) of the ILC Articles also mentions the obligation to provide them when the circumstances so require. Their role is to prevent recurrence, not to repair what has already been done. That would indeed represent full protection of human rights, which should aim not only at redressing illegality, but also at preventing replication.

The Court puts great emphasis on states' duty to guarantee the rights and freedoms provided by the Convention. In doing so, it uses not only its role of establishing responsibility, but also its prerogative of awarding reparation. Thus, it may grant reparation even with the more far-reaching aim of deterring repetition, or at least such was declared in *Scordino*, where it allocated higher awards than in the past in order to encourage states to find themselves reasonable solutions for their structural deficiencies.[972] However, the ever-increasing case law demonstrates that the objective of

[970] It has been argued that cessation and non-repetition may be justifiable consequences of legal injury: see B. Stern, 'The Elements of an Internationally Wrongful Act', in Crawford, Pellet and Olleson, note 46, at 194–200.

[971] *Tyrer v. the United Kingdom*, 25 April 1978, Series A no. 26, para. 31.

[972] *Scordino*, note 372, para. 176.

non-repetition is far from being reached. The latest pilot-judgment procedure is confined to exceptional cases denoting a 'recurrent and persistent nature of the problem, [a] large number of people it has affected or is capable of affecting, and [an] urgent need to grant them speedy and appropriate redress at the domestic level'.[973]

By contrast, the Inter-American system does provide for guarantees of non-repetition. They aim at non-recurrence of human rights violations and, similarly to the pilot-judgment procedure under the European system, are mainly concerned with structural problems. According to their nature and purpose, those guarantees have been classified as follows: measures to adapt domestic law to the parameters of the American Convention; human rights training for public officials; and adoption of other measures to guarantee the non-repetition of violations.[974]

It would therefore be a positive development for the Convention mechanism to draw inspiration from general international law and from the example provided by the Inter-American system, and to further expand the scope of the pilot-judgment procedure in order to include larger types of violations. The Court should not wait until the structural problem generates a high number of applications, but should assess the impact of doubtful legislation from the first signs of repetition, as suggested even by the member states in the Brighton Declaration.[975] A further possibility, with better prospects, is to introduce directly into the treaty an express requirement for guarantees of non-repetition. Protection of human rights, by its very definition, should not be limited to the victim's personal interest, but should also defend the general interest. In the very first article of the Convention, the states parties undertook the obligation to respect human rights, which necessarily implies a commitment to avoid reiteration of wrongful conduct. An effective system of protection should go beyond simple reparation for the harm sustained, and should prevent recurrence. To that end, when the particular circumstances of a breach so justify, states should be directed to give effective guarantees of non-repetition.

6.4 Just satisfaction division

The Court's organization reveals the existence of a just satisfaction division within the Registry, but its role and tasks remain undisclosed

[973] *Ananyev*, note 933, para. 190. [974] 2012 Annual Report, note 48, at 18.
[975] Para. 20(d) of the Brighton Declaration, note 179.

to the public. Given that it is placed under the authority of the Jurisconsult in charge of research and case-law information,[976] it presumably has an advisory role, which is to provide guidance on the Court's awards, so as to ensure consistency to the practice. It may also be involved in defining the scope of the latest criterion of inadmissibility, i.e., the significant disadvantage. Would it not be appropriate to give that division an active role in the decisional process?

First and foremost, the judges are the ultimate decision makers. While it should be accepted that such a unit may indeed give some positive input, the just satisfaction division cannot by itself secure consistency, but only strive for greater jurisprudential coherence among the Court's Sections and in respect of different countries. It may also supervise the proposals for a friendly settlement made by the Registry. But it would be excessive to involve that division in the process of establishing specific awards in each case. The lawyers have better knowledge of all the particularities of a dispute and can make a better proposal as to the appropriate reparation. They may resort to advice from that division whenever necessary. There should therefore be a concerted effort from both lawyers who work on cases and judges who decide them and, when needed, a harmonization by the just satisfaction division.

Another probable task of that division appears to be the creation and modification of those tables of compensation which the Court still declines to reveal. The implementation and adjustment of that standardized approach should indeed be that division's main task. After gaining approval from the judges, the Registry lawyers should be encouraged to use those tables as a valuable tool for their daily work. Not only the judges, but also the lawyers should become aware that an international court needs consistency in its decisions.

It is therefore commendable that the Court, as an institution, strives for coherence in its practice. If adjusted accordingly, a standardized approach may offer greater harmony. The just satisfaction division has therefore an important role in carrying out research and coming up with effective proposals. Yet, it is not a solution in itself inasmuch as, in the last resort, it is the judges who decide compensation in each case.

[976] See the Organization Chart, available on the Court's website (www.echr.coe.int/Pages/home.aspx?p=court/howitworks&c=).

6.5 Rethinking the Convention system of reparation?

6.5.1 The cause for concern

The present study has largely demonstrated the existence of several failures in the Strasbourg system of reparation. Things do go wrong and something should be done. In essence, the Court's practice lacks consistency and predictability. This is owing to reluctance on the part of the judges to engage in a systematic interpretation of Article 41 on just satisfaction and to elaborate a clear theory of reparation. It is precisely on account of that unwillingness that it is difficult to discern any logic in the current practice of the Court. The most evident example is the use of the principle of equity which, along with the principle of necessity, represents the source of the Court's discretionary power in deciding awards of just satisfaction. It is doubtful that the drafters of the Convention anticipated the extraordinary development of the system of protection, with the resulting influence on the question of reparation. They feared that the Court would not have enough cases to resolve and, in any event, believed that the mechanism of control would be based on inter-state complaints. As is well known, this has not been the case. On the contrary, there have been only a few inter-state disputes, and the system is quite asphyxiated by requests from private persons. It thus necessitates a readjustment to the existing conditions.

The alternative proposed by this study is the implementation of a method of calculation based on predefined figures, supported by the elaboration of a theory of equity and of a test of necessity in order to apply those standards. To have amounts allocated for each type of violation but not to dispose of a set of equitable principles that would permit their adjustment to each particular case would not alter significantly the present state of affairs. It is therefore of utmost importance to establish criteria of application of the standards of reparation. This would ensure transparency in the decision-making process and build confidence in the system, and also facilitate the work of the judges. To be a judge should not be the equivalent of having discretion, but of doing justice. If that aim is attained, the Strasbourg regime would serve as an example not only for the consecration of the right of individual petition and of an enforcement mechanism, but also in respect of a reliable and effective system of reparation.

Even if the system may draw some inspiration from the regime of reparation under general international law or under other special regimes, the judges have rather occasionally resorted to fields outside the realm of the Convention. Apparently, they did so when trying to secure a larger authority for their own interpretation of the treaty. In any event, there is no formal obligation for them to fall back on general international law. The Court may nonetheless resort more often to general international law in a quest for consistency for its rulings and to strive to place them in the wider framework of the international legal order. One should not forget that the Convention is an international treaty and that the Court does not operate in a vacuum, but within the framework of international law, its work being widely used in international practice.

A true challenge to the Court's evolution towards a system of effective reparation is posed by the increasing number of complaints. The latest developments reveal that the decision makers seem to be more inclined to stop that influx of applications by limiting the right of individual petition rather than by expanding the organizational structure. The reform introduced by Protocol No. 14 has already proved to be insufficient in providing the Court with the necessary tools to dispose of the existing caseload. In addition, there is a long debate as to whether or not the Court should be transformed into a constitutional court, in order to abandon the present individual assessment of human rights violations and to focus on imposing general standards. But if the member states are really willing to guarantee efficient protection, they should maintain the actual system of individual justice. The record stands for the extent to which states are capable of securing internal protection. The Court itself has recently admitted that '[i]t is the individual complaint which triggers the Convention review and enables the Court to identify shortcomings at national level'.[977]

The system of protection should therefore be improved so as to confer effective redress on the victims and to assure predictability and, above all, consistency. From that perspective, one should rethink the theory of reparation and define the principles of equity and necessity, not only on purely theoretical grounds, but also taking into account a practical feasibility of the approach that is proposed. The most suitable alternative would be to introduce transparent standardization, which would subsequently allow the judges to develop a theory of equitable criteria based on some fixed values. The result would be an improvement of the

[977] Para. 3 of the Preliminary opinion of the Court in preparation for the Brighton Conference, note 760.

process of effective assessment of compensation and a higher degree of consistency for the awards in respect of non-pecuniary injury.

At present, the practice of the Court is to declare that it awards in equity a certain amount, without any further reasoning. Except for the obvious cases, there is no explanation as to why the Court considers compensation necessary and as to how it establishes the amount. Equally striking is the fact that it may have recourse to some tables of compensation that are only for internal use, which is in conflict with the very idea of a court of law. Predefined standards of reparation, especially with respect to moral damage, would confer both a transparent and a predictable basis for the reparation claimed by victims, whereas a set of equitable principles would allow a proper adjustment of objective figures to the subjective elements of a dispute. It may be difficult to anticipate *in abstracto* all the conditions of perpetration for each type of violation, therefore a certain degree of generalization should be accepted. Evidently, a good starting point is the extensive case law, and then the list may be periodically updated.

6.5.2 Standardization

First and foremost, it is important to clarify what would imply a standardized approach for non-pecuniary damage. In essence, the intention is to create an objective basis for the process of calculation, which should use a set of equitable criteria in order to individualize that basis. In other words, the aim is to fix general minimum and maximum limits for awards, in respect of each right and type of violation, and then to establish the particular compensation in accordance with a set of circumstantial factors, such as the importance of the right and the gravity of the violation or the victim's fault in causing damage. It is what the UN Compensation Commission has already done by fixing ceilings for compensation for mental pain and anguish. For example, for Category A in that classification, which refers to cases where a spouse, child or parent of an individual suffered death, a threshold of USD 15,000 per claimant and USD 30,000 per family unit has been agreed.

It is also what some national jurisdictions use when compensating personal injury.[978] For instance, all the British judges involved in hearing personal injury cases will receive a copy of updated guidelines for the

[978] See examples in W. V. Horton Rogers (ed.), *Damages for Non-Pecuniary Loss in a Comparative Perspective* (Vienna: Springer, 2001). Also see E. Dwertmann, *The*

assessment of general damages in personal injury cases. These guidelines provide in great detail the amounts to be allocated for several types of injury.[979] The Strasbourg case law is already largely repetitive, and there are relatively few distinct cases as compared to the amplitude of the precedent. There is sufficient practice to extract a pattern and create models. In the absence of the Court's willingness to reveal the method of calculation that it already uses, one must presume that it is based on previously fixed figures.

A good start is the above-mentioned case of *Apicella*, which concerned the unreasonable length of internal proceedings. The Court applied a variable limit of between EUR 1,000 and EUR 1,500 per year's duration of the internal proceedings, which was to be increased by EUR 2,000 if what was at stake for the victim was particularly important. What is 'particularly important' remains an unavoidable matter within the judges' discretion, which is very likely to disperse if they elaborate a clear theory of equity, as will be discussed in the next section. However, their discretion is greatly restricted by the fact that they are supposed to follow effective provisions in respect of the sum to be allocated. In that particular case, the judges have nonetheless omitted to reveal the extent to which the sum may have been decreased if the plaintiff had contributed to the protraction of the litigation or if the dispute had not been complex. Logically, it seems that the amount may be decreased towards zero when the victim's fault does not justify an award. On the contrary, the maximum of the increase is EUR 2,000. Between these limits, the judges enjoy a power of subjective appreciation.

Another example is that of an arrested person who has not benefited from a prompt appearance before a judge or judicial officer. In such a case, some judges have inferred from the practice that the Court uses values between EUR 450 and EUR 500 to compensate each day of delay.[980] The Court itself may sometimes offer an indication as to how it arrived at a certain figure. In a case where the three applicants' detention became arbitrary after the expiry of their tariffs, when making redress, the judges specified the exact period of unlawful detention.[981]

Reparation System of the International Criminal Court (Leiden: Martinus Nijhoff Publishers, 2010), at 172–8.

979 J. Burnett et al. (eds.), *Guidelines for the Assessment of General Damages in Personal Injury Cases* (Oxford University Press, 2012).

980 Concurring opinion of Judge Türmen in *Çelik and Yıldız v. Turkey*, no. 51479/99, 10 November 2005.

981 *James, Wells and Lee v. the United Kingdom*, nos. 25119/09, 57715/09 and 57877/09, 18 September 2012, para. 244.

When weighting the difference between awards against the difference between the periods of detention, it is possible to see that it results in an amount of EUR 200 for each month.

The main advantage of those approaches is that the limits are clearly established. The victim is well aware in advance of the prospects of success. Based on the precedent, a would-be applicant may even predict the likely amount that he or she may secure in Strasbourg. The other side of the coin is that states may also be inclined to buy off violations, when aware of the price they have to pay. The method may easily be implemented for the majority of treaty violations. The most difficult thing would be to agree on the thresholds, but, given the extensive case law, they can easily be extracted from the prevailing awards.

Those effective limits can be further developed in the context of a theory of equity. They must reflect not only the nature of the right guaranteed, but also the gravity of the breach. In this way, those cases where the judges allocate comparable amounts to those who have been tortured and those who were deprived of the use of their property may be removed from the Court's practice. Then, it is only an exercise of adjusting those amounts to the individual situation of the victim, based on equitable criteria.

The basic idea is to perform a subjective assessment, rooted in equity, but on a transparent basis. It would be unacceptable for a human rights court to award compensation mechanically on the sole objective ground of the type of violation. One cannot establish a fixed amount for what amounts to ill-treatment because, depending on the method of execution of the unlawful acts, the result may be limited to mental suffering or be accompanied by physical harm. The reparation should therefore be adapted to each particular victim and to the circumstances of perpetration of the illegal activity, in order to provide effective redress, but, at the same time, it should follow objective standards. It is an interplay between standardization and equity, which aims at consistency in the Court's practice. The judges' discretion should be limited as far as possible, because absolute power may lead to abuse.

The awards thus agreed should be further adjusted according to the economic level of development in each member country. In fact, they should depend on the economic level of the country where the victim lives on a permanent basis. A good reference point in adjusting those amounts is offered by the figures published annually by the World Bank in respect of the gross national income per capita. In order to facilitate calculation, the Court may classify the contracting states into several groups. It would thus create a greater harmony among states with comparable economic levels.

In essence, standardization may be carried out in two ways: in the treaty or in the practice. The strongest effects would certainly be secured by an amendment of the Convention, in all probability in the form of a subsequent protocol. As a result, codification of the existent practice would gain more authority and the judges would be bound by it. At the same time, as argued earlier in this chapter, it would be useful to introduce into the treaty the possibility of claiming guarantees of non-repetition. However, all these changes require agreement between the member states, which may prove to be a difficult process. Until then, the judges should direct the practice towards an objective approach. In that sense, the Court may adopt a practice direction.

The great advantage of a standardized approach is transparency. In so far as the Court promotes its subsidiary role in the field of reparation, it may give valuable guidance to domestic courts as to the Strasbourg standard of compensation. In this way, plaintiffs may get redress locally and will be dissuaded from coming before the Court when aware that they may not obtain higher compensation. This would facilitate the Court's work and relieve it of the burden of repetitive claims. For example, when confronted with applications exclusively in respect of the length of internal proceedings, it may simply dismiss them on the basis of the municipal award. It would be a replication on a larger scale of what the system has already done by introducing the admissibility requirement of a significant disadvantage, where the judges look first at the amount at stake.

The disadvantage of standardization may be that plaintiffs would perceive an opportunity for financial gain, irrespective of the soundness of their claims. They may apply to the Court only because they have nothing to lose, and thus suffocate the system with requests. But one should not confuse the provision of compensation standards with a right to obtain those amounts. By no means is a victim entitled as a matter of right to secure those sums. Even if a violation is found, the Court may still decide that the circumstances of the case do not justify an award. Yet, it would certainly be more difficult for the judges to change those standards. Their margin of appreciation would lessen and they might feel constrained in their ruling capacity and decisional autonomy.

Standardization should not be limited to establishing specific amounts in respect of non-pecuniary injury. The Court must also adopt an objective approach for some heads of material damage, in particular for compensation of loss of profit caused by expropriations. In that context, it should clearly decide when to make such awards and also the method of calculation, including whether an award should take into account the value of the buildings erected by the state or whether it should be confined to interest on the principal sum. The judges must engage in interpretive exercises as to the test of necessity and fairness. In that sense, they may inquire into the profit obtained by a similar property. Moreover, as far as costs and expenses are concerned, the Court may also establish tables for lawyers' fees in Strasbourg proceedings. Those fees should also be adapted to the economic situation of the country where the lawyer is based.

6.5.3 *A theory of equity*

Standardization must be supported by a theory of equity. The two are interrelated. In order to secure efficiency in the decision-making process, the judge needs the proper tools and the criteria of application. The predefined tables are the tools and the equitable criteria are the principles for a coherent application of those figures. In other words, it is equitable to apply some standards and the standards should be applied equitably. As rightly emphasized, '[i]n each case the judge has to decide what the various criteria are and their relative weight in the special circumstances'.[982] *In concreto*, 'those principles must be capable of being applied in a consistent and coherent manner, so that the amount awarded can be regarded as just, not merely by reference to the facts of this case, but by comparison with other cases'.[983] Therefore, when engaging in that exercise, the judge must define equity and must establish standards and limits, because otherwise the concept becomes extra-judicial.

The Court has extracted the equity from the text of Article 41; they use equity *infra legem*, which means that it is derived from the interpretation of the legal norm. That provision on reparation makes a double reference to fairness: on the one hand, it lays down the principle that the standard of reparation under the treaty is that of fair, just compensation, and on the other, it entitles the judges to grant redress only 'if necessary'. That necessity can very well be treated as an element of equity – when the judges deem it necessary to make an award, it means that they consider

[982] Lapidoth, note 171, at 145.
[983] Para. 7 *in fine* of the declaration of Judge Greenwood in *Diallo*, note 145.

that it is equitable to make such an award. The drafters of the Convention have not provided for a right to reparation, but simply for a possibility. They empowered the judges to decide when it is equitable, hence necessary, to make redress. The judges may very well decide that the finding of a violation constitutes in itself sufficient just satisfaction. The problem is that the lack of a theory of equity and of a test of necessity reverberates negatively on the Court's practice.

For Koskenniemi, 'the construction of equity means simply the giving of effect, not to somebody's theory of justice but to the *intrinsically equitable (or just) character of the criteria used*'.[984] The Strasbourg judges do not use any criteria when deciding reparation in equity, but only discretion. That goes against a uniform application of equity. The Court is divided into five Sections and each judge comes from a different cultural and legal background. In the absence of criteria, it must be conceded that each judge construes equity in his or her personal system of values. And yet, the Court should strive for a harmonious use of equity at an institutional level. That can be realized by establishing a clear theory of equity and a test of necessity that would limit the personal and discretionary interpretation. As aptly noted, '[t]he great qualities of law are its generality, clarity, certainty and predictability. None of these virtues would exist in an individualized system of equity.'[985] The individual interpretation given to equity should therefore be replaced with a generally accepted theory at the level of the system of reparation. That would secure consistency and uniformity in application. If willingness exists, it should not be difficult to elaborate such a theory. A good starting point would be to establish the concrete criteria of application for the above-mentioned model of compensation. Then the judges only have to adjust the standard to the particular circumstances of a case.

In concreto, the Court should first establish the factors that may justify a variation towards the lower or the higher limit of the sums allocated for each type of violation. The judges should have a clear representation of the circumstances which are to be taken into account and of those which are irrelevant. Certainly, the reference amount will be decreased when the victim is at fault for the prejudice. It may also be decreased when there are several applicants in a dispute, in particular when they are close

[984] M. Koskenniemi, *From Apology to Utopia: The Structure of International Legal Argument* (Cambridge University Press, 2005), at 468 (emphasis in original).

[985] Lapidoth, note 171, at 146.

relatives. For example, when deprivation of property affects husband and wife, it would be exaggerated to treat them as distinct entities and to allocate separately to each of them the same compensation for moral prejudice that would have been given to a singular victim in a similar situation. The same applies to a plurality of plaintiffs who continue the Convention proceedings in the name of a victim who has died during the litigation. It is therefore logical to allocate them jointly the amount that would have been awarded to the victim. In fact, in this specific case, the plaintiffs are not the direct victims of a violation. There may also be situations in which the victim is no longer alive because of the violation. In that case, it would be equitable to compensate the relatives in function of the family link to the victim.

Then, the judges should agree under which circumstances an increase of the reference amount would be justified. Obviously, the most serious violations, such as deprivation of life and torture, require higher amounts of compensation. Equally relevant is the number of violations. The judges may take as a reference the compensation allocated for the most serious of them, and then add on a certain percentage corresponding to each extra violation. Given that it is a singular person who suffers a plurality of interferences, it seems exaggerated to make the final sum equal to the total of the individual parts of the compensation provided for each violation.

As already mentioned, the Court has adopted in practice a set of rules for the examination of the length of domestic proceedings. The judges will first determine the period at stake and the levels of jurisdiction, and then they will inquire into the specific circumstances of the case. Relevant factors are: the complexity and nature of the internal dispute; the conduct of the applicant and of the relevant authorities; what was at stake for the victim; and the number of victims. That example may be reasonably replicated and adjusted to violations of other rights. In addition, an increase may be justified by the sex, age and physical or mental condition of the victim, as well as by the specific circumstances in which the wrongful act was committed. The economic development of the country where the victim lives should also be taken into account, otherwise the Court itself generates inequitable treatment between the victims when the practical value of compensation does not serve its very purpose.

As an illustration, the Court may agree on a predefined standard of compensation between EUR 50,000 and EUR 100,000 for torture. That is the objective standard. When the judges have before them a case of torture, they need to adapt that standard to the circumstances of the case. To do that, they need a set of equitable criteria. Thus, if the victim is particularly vulnerable or has lost a limb, the award will go towards the maximum limit. If the authorities failed to provide an effective investigation into the allegations of torture, the sum may further increase. However, if the victim lives in a developing country, the amount should be decreased so as to reflect the economic level. Another illustration can be offered by a case of ill-treatment. The standard of compensation may be fixed between EUR 20,000 and EUR 40,000, and then the award may be adjusted towards the maximum if the victim has suffered a permanent disability or has been hospitalized.

All these standards, while normally used in assessing the compensation for moral harm, may also be relevant to reparation for pecuniary damage. While material harm is by definition a prejudice that has to be proved and thus allows accurate evaluation, there are nonetheless factors that may only be established in equity. The most evident example is the loss of earnings, where the judges must decide the financial input which would have been generated by – and therefore for the use of – the victim or, in a case of death, for the use of the relatives of the victim, and then speculate on the period of time over which the victim, but for the violation, would have been securing that income. The loss of opportunity and even the reimbursement of costs and expenses may also be based on equitable grounds.

Overall, the use of equity should be further encouraged in Strasbourg, but only on the basis that its application derives from well-established criteria. The concept cannot be removed altogether because there can be no conceivable system of reparation which relies entirely on objective standards of compensation. The circumstances of perpetration of the wrongful act, the victim's personal condition and the concrete negative effects obviously differ in every case. Equity thus allows the law to be adapted to the facts. As Lapidoth aptly put it:

> The advantages of the application of equity are obvious: in adjudication, it enhances the chances of bringing the law nearer to justice, which is one of the main objects of every legal system. It makes it possible to adapt the rule to individual cases and to prevent injustice resulting from the generality of law and from the impossibility of the legislature to predict in advance all the possible situations that might arise.[986]

[986] Ibid.

6.5.4 Further developments

In addition to standardization and definition of a set of equitable criteria for compensation, there are some other elements that merit reconsideration. The judges should reinforce the principle of *restitutio in integrum* not only by giving specific indications as to the necessary measures that would reinstate the *status quo ante*, but also by initiating a practice of requiring breaching states to prove an impossibility of restitution in property disputes. As the practice stands, they order restitution alternatively with monetary compensation, which gives the state a choice in its own interest. It should be feasible to require evidence regarding the physical and legal situation of a property.

Moreover, the Court may give more consistency to its practice by making a reasoned choice between declaring, on the one hand, that the finding of a violation offers sufficient reparation and, on the other hand, that the circumstances of a case do not call for an award. However, one cannot argue for the total elimination of that practice, given that the moral harm is often of a level of intensity that does not justify financial compensation.

The Court should also confine itself to the role of an international court, which is to apply the Convention on a case-by-case basis. The treaty has not empowered it with constitutional prerogatives. While it is true that the states themselves have initiated the latest pilot-judgment procedure, the judges have used that provision for assessing the compatibility of the internal legislation with the Convention and for requiring modifications in accordance with particular guidance. The approach is not conceptually wrong, inasmuch as it reinforces the human rights standards, but the judges seem to give it priority at the expense of individual justice, a path that the Court should not follow.

In fact, giving constitutional attributes to the Strasbourg judges would presumably engender some extra discretion. Arguably, the right of individual petition, which makes the European system of human rights protection so successful, would be progressively reduced until its final annihilation. In the presence of a so-called constitutionalist mission being mainly promoted from inside the Court, it is not unreasonable to assume that it does not necessarily come from a conviction, but rather from an effort to reduce the caseload significantly. Any constitutional court decides fewer cases than an ordinary court.

In that sense, the Court has declared in *Salah v. the Netherlands* that 'the awarding of sums of money to applicants by way of just satisfaction is not one of the Court's main duties but is incidental to its task of ensuring the observance by States of their obligations under the Convention'.[987] It is true that the Court's *raison d'être* is '[t]o ensure the observance of the engagements undertaken by the High Contracting Parties in the Convention and the Protocols thereto',[988] but the same parties have committed themselves in the first article of the Convention to respect the human rights and freedoms defined in the treaty. If that is not the case, a state's responsibility is established. In general international law, from which the Court occasionally draws inspiration, the ensuing obligation is to make reparation. The Permanent Court of Justice held in *Factory at Chorzów* that '[r]eparation ... is the indispensable complement of a failure to apply a convention and there is no necessity for this to be stated in the convention itself'.[989] Therefore, while it may be accepted that, under the Convention, reparation is an 'incidental task' to that of deciding responsibility, the judges should not ignore or minimize its role and place in the process of human rights protection.

The Court has successfully implemented a practice of ordering the respondent state to take some individual measures in addition to a specific award of compensation. Situations such as unlawful detention, denial of parental rights or non-enforcement of domestic judgments require prompt intervention on the part of the state. In order to make that state react as quickly as possible, the judges should include the order in the operative part of their ruling. In doing so, the binding effect cannot be contested. Moreover, the Committee of Ministers may effectively check whether the operative provisions in a judgment have been executed.

Finally, at least in theory, the system of execution of the Court's judgments is proving to be fairly effective. The function of supervision entrusted to a political organ is a unique feature within the international field and has provided efficiency to the process. The negative aspect is that enforcement is sometimes delayed by the respondent state, even if the Court has adopted a practice of granting interest for late execution. The recent experience with non-execution of pilot judgments also raises the question of a new means of enforcing that type of judgment. In essence, the Committee should impose clear time limits for execution, in

[987] *Salah v. the Netherlands*, no. 8196/02, ECHR 2006-IX (extracts), para. 70.
[988] Article 19 of the Convention.
[989] *Factory at Chorzów (Jurisdiction)*, 1927, PCIJ, Series A, No. 9, at 21.

accordance with the circumstances of each particular case. It already has the possibility to bring infringement proceedings before the Court. That distribution of roles within the Council of Europe should therefore be further maintained, as long as it has a positive impact.

In conclusion, if proper adjustments are made, the Strasbourg system of reparation may indeed prove effective. The judges cannot fully discharge their judicial function in the presence of unlimited discretion and in the absence of legal reasoning. Consistent practice is a precondition for legitimacy. After all, the prestige of the institution is at stake, not only their professional authority.

7

Conclusions

The present study has performed an in-depth scrutiny of the reparation regime under the European Convention on Human Rights. The thesis advanced, supported by the Court's practice, is that the Strasbourg system of reparation lacks consistency and predictability. In particular, that situation can easily be observed with regard to the awards for non-pecuniary damage. What has caused that state of affairs? First of all, it is the treaty provision on just satisfaction that entitles the judges to make redress only 'if necessary'. Then, the Court has further derived from the text of Article 41 an authorization to make redress in equity. Finally, the judges have made no efforts to engage in interpretive exercises as to the test of necessity and to elaborate a theory of equity. The problem is that broad discretion and lack of reasoning reverberate negatively on the coherence of the system. The result is a practice that may sometimes be characterized as being arbitrary.

In order to understand the phenomenon and be able to propose feasible solutions, the analysis sought to carry out a thorough and systematic consideration of the theory and practice of reparation under the Convention. On occasion, the study placed the treaty into the larger framework of international law, with a special emphasis on the rules of state responsibility and reparation. While the Convention is *lex specialis* and functions on its own rules, it was not conceived in order to exist independently from international law, although the specificity of that regime has made the judges give priority to an interpretation primarily based on rules and precedent within that system. The practice reveals interactions with general international law and with other specialized regimes, in particular those establishing a mechanism for human rights protection, but such references are not made in a systematic way. They occur when the judges seek to ensure consistency in their rulings and to give wider authority to their interpretation of specific subject matters regulated by the Convention. For example, they have expressly made reference to the general regime of reparations and derived the correspondent obligation for the member states, when found in violation of the treaty, to make *restitutio in integrum* for the prejudice occasioned by their unlawful conduct.

Yet, the judges have lacked the same enthusiasm in developing a theory of equity and a test of necessity. While they have interpreted several aspects of Article 41 on just satisfaction, they have not clarified how they transpose effectively into practice the words 'if necessary'. They simply content themselves to invoke the discretion that they enjoy under Article 41 for making an award, a discretion based on the expression 'if necessary' and on the principle of equity, also extracted from the provision on just satisfaction. The problem is that such discretion has sometimes transformed into arbitrariness, in so far as the judges do not consider it necessary to give a legal reasoning for their awards of compensation. That occurs especially in the area of reparation for non-pecuniary damage, where the prejudice is inherently difficult to assess. However, solutions do exist if the Court is really willing to give consistency to its case law.

The alternative proposed at the end of the study is a high degree of standardization in respect of compensation for non-pecuniary damage, based on predefined amounts for each type of violation, and the establishment of a set of equitable principles that would make possible the adjustment of those figures to the specific circumstances of a case. While it is a fact that the judges already use some tables when making awards for non-pecuniary damage, those figures are confidential and do not allow real scrutiny of their effectiveness. In any event, it is difficult to argue that their use has made the practice more predictable. It may ease the work of the judges and of the Registry lawyers, but it does not make the system more transparent. The Court strives to secure its margin of manoeuvrability.

The present study is not confined to a certain type of injury or to a specific mode of redress; it covers the whole regime of reparation under the European Convention. It has therefore been appropriate to put under thorough scrutiny the entire system of reparation. In doing so, the analysis has revealed the weaknesses in the remedial mechanism not only in the specific case of compensation for moral prejudice, but also at the more general level of the underlying philosophy of human rights promoted in Strasbourg. More precisely, while it is laudable that the system officially relies on and further promotes the right of individual petition which allows private persons to bring their claims directly before an international court, the recent developments occasioned by an ever-increasing number of applications have generated a strong debate on the reform of the Court which ultimately impedes, to a limited extent though, the essence of that right. Thus, the Convention was amended in 2010 in the sense that an additional criterion of admissibility, among others, has been introduced. Thereafter, plaintiffs must prove the existence of a significant disadvantage, otherwise their request is declared inadmissible. While accepting that in practice there are indeed complaints which have produced rather insignificant prejudice and being aware of the nature of the Convention as an international treaty where the parties decide its specific conditions of application, it is somewhat unfortunate that a philosophy which has gained a unique status in international protection of human rights is now corrupted by reasons of structural efficiency. It seems that the drafters of the system seek to curtail the influx of petitions rather than to increase the Court's capacity to deal with the backlog that has accumulated over the years.

In theory, the original drafters envisaged a mechanism of protection that would rely on denouncements by the contracting states. Gradually though, that perspective has proved to be unrealistic, given that the states parties aspire to friendly co-operation among themselves and would rather be unenthusiastic about launching into activities that may impede their political relations. Therefore, the system has evolved towards a direct entitlement for individuals to denounce breaches of the treaty. And yet, the Convention has not bestowed a right to compensation upon the victims, but only a right to complain before the Court. When a violation is found, it is the judges who decide whether just satisfaction is necessary.

After setting the theoretical stage of the system of reparation, the study has analysed *in concreto* the forms of redress that a victim can obtain in Strasbourg. The aim of the exercise was to understand the logic used by the judges when they decide the necessity of reparation and when they determine the appropriate type of redress. That is the field where their margin of discretion is at a maximum. The main problem, as already mentioned, is that they have not developed a clear theory of reparations by which they can define, first and foremost, the principles of equity and the test of necessity. The result is an inconsistent practice. That discretion is narrower as far as reparation for pecuniary damage is concerned, but at the highest level as regards compensation for moral prejudice. To the extent that the Convention system does not accept a form of satisfaction within the meaning of the general theory of reparations in international law, the redress secured in Strasbourg is often pecuniary. Conversely, the Court may deliver a declaratory judgment by which it accepts that the very finding of a violation constitutes in itself just satisfaction or may simply state that the circumstances of the case do not justify an award.

The applicants are therefore dwelling in uncertainty until the final pronouncement by the Court. Their 'agony' is accentuated by the lack of consistency and predictability in the case law. They cannot anticipate the redress they would receive in the event of their allegations of infringement being upheld by the Court. They may, however, curtail that 'agony' by reaching a compromise with the defendant government, before the judges give a ruling on the dispute. In doing so, they rapidly secure some form of reparation, without the need to wait for a final decision. In that case, the state is not officially declared responsible for any interference with the claimant's rights. At the same time, the Strasbourg procedure allows the government concerned to submit a unilateral declaration by which it acknowledges the existence of a violation and offers redress to the plaintiff. From a victim-oriented approach, that possibility offered to the defendant is fairly debatable, in so far as it entitles the presumed offender to put an end to the litigation in spite of the manifest opposition of the applicant. Nevertheless, procedural guarantees are in place to ensure that respect for human rights does not call for the continuation of the proceedings. The judges are therefore expected to stay alert as to any temptation by the state to conceal serious violations of human rights.

When a violation is found and reparation is deemed necessary, the Court can make a monetary award or, depending on the special circumstances of the case, can order the state to take individual or general measures. The practice has significantly evolved in that respect. While the judges have traditionally refrained from making recommendations with respect to executions – a task reserved for the Committee of Ministers – they have recently adopted a more proactive and commendable stance. Certainly, they did so with the agreement of the member parties, which have voiced through the intermediary of the Committee of Ministers their commitment to the system of protection. Thus, the Court has ordered the release of detainees, effective contact between family members or return of property.

Moreover, the Court has adopted and implemented a practice of pilot judgments, by which it reveals systemic deficiencies in the internal legal order of the contracting states and indicates the need for general measures to correct and further prevent the adverse effects generated by those shortcomings. The procedure is still in its initial stage and has even denoted the limits of the system in securing the execution of those judgments. There is a need for further improvements, because otherwise the persons affected simply have their prospect for redress delayed.

Having analysed the theory and practice of reparations under the law of the Convention, the time is ripe to introduce proposals for improvement. The scrutiny demonstrates that the large margin of discretion allowed to the Court in the field of reparations has generated arbitrary case law. Therefore, the thesis advocated throughout this study is that the system of just satisfaction under the European Convention should evolve towards effective reparation. Given that the Convention regime functions within a wider international legal system, inspiration can be drawn from international law, to the extent imposed by its *lex specialis* status. At a moment when international law undergoes continuous fragmentation, it is important for the special regimes operating with the same subject matter to adopt a coherent approach. Specialization of field branches is a fact, it cannot be contested or reversed; one should accept it and learn to deal with it. One possible approach is to strive for coherence among the special regimes in the same field. That would reinforce the authority and credibility of the field.

The most recurrent problem revealed by the study is the absence of reasoning for the specific awards of reparation. The judges lack enthusiasm for engaging in interpretive exercises and for establishing a set of clear principles. The ensuing consequence is a divergent practice. The long-term negative effect is that the Court's authority and legitimacy is depreciated. The extraordinary increase in the number of those who claim to be victims of human rights violations cannot be ignored, but trying to prevent them from coming to Strasbourg is not a solution. The philosophy of human rights protection should not be corrupted. An alternative would be to reinforce at the internal level the protection of the Convention rights and to adopt a transparent approach in Strasbourg, thus permitting the victims themselves to realize that national and international levels offer the same standard of protection. Another solution is to introduce into the system, by analogy with general international law, an obligation to provide guarantees of non-repetition. The Court may also promote its constitutional mission, but only in addition to, not in replacement of, individual justice. The system has sufficiently demonstrated that it is the private persons, not the states, who make violations of the Convention known.

The main proposal that this study submits is the introduction of a high level of standardization and the elaboration of a theory of equity that would allow a proper adjustment of objective figures to the subjective elements of each particular case. As expected, standardization is in the first place pertinent to the compensation for moral harm, because the material damage should generally be possible to prove with factual evidence. Implementation of a standard approach would significantly curtail the excessive discretion that the Strasbourg judges enjoy at present in respect of making awards of reparation. The principal benefit is that it would confer consistency and predictability on the system and would further build confidence in its authority. It would also offer a pedagogical role to the control mechanism, in so far as it would give a feasible example of a consistent application of the legal norm.

No system of reparation can be entirely objective, for the simple reason that it is speculative to put value on moral suffering. Moreover, two individuals cannot suffer the same prejudice. But when there are no rules to follow, they should be established, because discretion often leads to arbitrariness. That is the aim of the present study: to raise awareness of the negative implications generated by giving complete discretion to the Strasbourg judges and to propose a realistic alternative based on agreed limits of compensation. However, when all is said and done, the Strasbourg system has a true capacity to offer effective reparation. The fame that the Court has gained makes the effort worthwhile.

ANNEXES: EXPLICATIVE NOTE ON ANNEXES

The following annexes represent a selection of judgments delivered by the Court in respect of different types of violations. The tables contain only the awards made in respect of non-pecuniary damage, when the Court has allocated smaller amounts than those claimed by plaintiffs. They have been arranged in a reverse chronological order, starting with the most recent, except for Annex 6, where the cases also follow the order of the three Convention articles that represent the personal freedoms. The cases that have been chosen are exclusively those where the Court has found one or several violations of a single article of the treaty. In the latter situation, each particular aspect is specified. The purpose of these annexes is to illustrate the variation of the Court's awards for moral damage, not only between different types of violations, but also between countries, in accordance with their level of economic development. Thus, a victim from a richer country will be given higher compensation than one from a poorer country. The logic is that the value of money differs as a function of economic development.

The annexes are provided in particular to support the debate on reparations in Chapter 4. In general, there are more cases in which the Court finds two or more breaches of the Convention than those where only one violation is found. For the purpose of this exercise, only the latter are pertinent. They allow a precise assessment of the sum allocated for each violation in exclusivity. Certainly, a victim will receive higher compensation in respect of moral prejudice when more than one violation is found. Equally important is the number of applicants. The annexes make express reference to their number and to the method of allocation among them.

A further mention should be made in respect of articles which support a violation not only in their substantive limb, but also as regards their procedural element. For example, a finding of a violation of Article 2 on the right to life frequently triggers a procedural violation amounting to a lack of effective investigation. Here again, it is reasonable to speculate that the judges afford a higher amount than when either of the two aspects is individually breached. Examples are therefore provided in order to assess that aspect.

Annex 1 Selected cases

Compensation for non-pecuniary damage for violations of Article 2

Case	Principal issue(s)	Violation(s) found	Award (EUR)
Pozhyvotko v. Ukraine no. 42752/08 17 October 2013	Victim's widow and mother complained about investigation of circumstances of his death.	No thorough investigation.	10,000 to each
Przemyk v. Poland no. 22426/11 17 September 2013	No effective determination of criminal liability arising in connection with circumstances in which applicant's son was killed.	Conduct of criminal proceedings did not afford applicant appropriate redress.	20,000
Cadıroğlu v. Turkey no. 15762/10 3 September 2013	Five applicants – parents and brothers of victim who died when he was sixteen years old – alleged state responsibility for death and ineffective investigation.	Failure to conduct investigation with due expedition.	20,000 jointly
Saidova v. Russia no. 51432/09 1 August 2013	Plaintiff alleged that her son had been unlawfully detained and disappeared.	No effective investigation into circumstance of disappearance.	10,000

Dambean v. Romania no. 42009/04 23 July 2013	No effective and timely investigation into road traffic accident that caused the death of applicant's husband.	No due diligence in investigation.	15,000
Collette and Michael Hemsworth v. the United Kingdom no. 58559/09 16 July 2013	Victim's wife and father complained of unlawful use of lethal force against deceased and also of defective investigation.	Excessive investigative delay.	20,000 jointly
Abik v. Turkey no. 34783/07 16 July 2013	Applicants considered that the death of their son was due to excessive use of force, and alleged ineffective investigation.	No due diligence in investigation.	5,000 to each
Gülbahar Özer and Others v. Turkey no. 44125/06 2 July 2013	Five applicants denounced killing of their five children by a number of soldiers, and lack of effective investigation.	Use of fatal force not absolutely necessary and proportionate. No meaningful investigation.	65,000 to each
Gheorghe Cobzaru v. Romania no. 6978/08 25 June 2013	Killing of applicant's son by a police officer, and ineffective investigation.	Use of lethal force not absolutely necessary and proportionate. No effective investigation.	30,000

Case	Principal issue(s)	Violation(s) found	Award (EUR)
Süleyman Ege v. Turkey no. 45721/09 25 June 2013	Applicant denounced circumstances in which his brother died in hospital.	No due diligence in investigation of circumstances of death.	20,000
Banel v. Lithuania no. 14326/11 18 June 2013	Applicant alleged that the state had failed to protect her son's life and that investigation of his death had not been effective.	No due diligence in protecting right to life of applicant's son.	20,000
Pleşca v. Romania no. 2158/08 18 June 2013	No effective investigation into death of applicant's daughter.	No effective investigation.	Finding of a violation was sufficient.
Nencheva and Others v. Bulgaria no. 48609/06 18 June 2013	Nine applicants – parents of seven children who had died in a facility for children with severe mental illnesses – alleged state's failure to protect their children's lives and defective investigation.	The state failed in its obligation to protect life of vulnerable children placed under its responsibility. No effective investigation.	10,000 to two of them. Finding of a violation was sufficient for the others.
Mehmet Şentürk and Bekir Şentürk v. Turkey no. 13423/09 9 April 2013	Victim's widower and son complained about her death and that of the child she	Owing to a flagrant malfunctioning of hospital departments, the state failed to	65,000 jointly

	had been carrying, as well as about ineffective investigation.	protect victim's physical integrity. No effective investigation.	
Yuriy Slyusar v. Ukraine no. 39797/05 17 January 2013	Applicant denounced investigation of his brother's death.	No effective investigation.	12,000
Kudra v. Croatia no. 13904/07 18 December 2012	Four applicants – victim's parents and brothers – denounced proceedings for failing to establish who was responsible for victim's death.	The domestic system, faced with a case of unintentional deprivation of life, failed to provide effective and prompt response.	20,000 jointly
Gina Ionescu v. Romania no. 15318/09 11 December 2012	Applicant denounced investigation into her husband's death.	No due diligence in investigation.	15,000
Bajić v. Croatia no. 41108/10 13 November 2012	Applicant denounced unreasonably long proceedings related to the death of his sister – while she was receiving health care – which was allegedly caused by medical negligence.	The domestic system as a whole, faced with a case of allegation of medical negligence resulting in a death, failed to provide adequate and timely response.	10,000

Case	Principal issue(s)	Violation(s) found	Award (EUR)
Dimov and Others v. Bulgaria no. 30086/05 6 November 2012	Three applicants alleged death of their father and husband during police operation leading to his arrest, and also defective investigation.	The government failed to prove that force used was no more than absolutely necessary. No effective investigation.	50,000 jointly
Ghimp and Others v. Moldova no. 32520/09 30 October 2012	Four applicants alleged that their husband and relative had been killed by state agents and also alleged ineffective investigation.	The state was responsible for victim's death. No effective investigation.	60,000 to the wife
Çoşelav v. Turkey no. 1413/07 9 October 2012	Death of applicants' son while he was being detained in prison.	The authorities failed to protect victim's right to life. No effective investigation.	45,000 jointly
Prynda v. Ukraine no. 10904/05 31 July 2012	Applicants alleged defective investigation into road traffic accident that caused their son's death.	No effective investigation into suspicious death.	6,000 jointly
Şat v. Turkey no. 14547/04 10 July 2012	Applicant complained about bullet wound he had sustained during operation by security forces in the prison where he was being detained.	Force employed against applicant not absolutely necessary.	15,000

Ülüfer v. Turkey no. 23038/07 5 June 2012	Use of lethal force against the applicant's son, who died after having been shot by police as he was trying to escape, while handcuffed, from a court following hearing in trial against him. Applicant also complained about investigation.	The state failed to provide appropriate framework for use of force and weapons by police, and lethal force in that case was not absolutely necessary. No effective investigation.	40,000
Damayev v. Russia no. 36150/04 29 May 2012	Applicant complained that his wife and five children had been killed by state agents and that the authorities had failed to carry out effective investigation into their deaths.	Applicant's family members died because of disproportionate use of lethal force by state agents. No effective investigation.	600,000
Putintseva v. Russia no. 33498/04 10 May 2012	Plaintiff alleged that her son had been killed during his military service and that the authorities' response to incident had been inadequate.	Legal framework on use of force fundamentally deficient and use of firearms to prevent victim's escape incompatible with the Convention.	45,000
Shafiyeva v. Russia no. 49379/09 3 May 2012	Applicant complained that her husband had disappeared after having been detained by state agents.	No effective investigation.	30,000

Case	Principal issue(s)	Violation(s) found	Award (EUR)
Kleyn and Aleksandrovich v. Russia no. 40657/04 3 May 2012	Applicants are widower and son of victim, who allegedly died as a result of intentional mistreatment in police custody.	No effective investigation.	20,000 jointly
Metin v. Turkey no. 26773/05 5 July 2011	Applicant's son committed suicide during compulsory military service.	The authorities failed to properly assess victim's capacity to serve in the army and thus to prevent risk of loss of life.	18,000
Ciechońska v. Poland no. 19776/04 14 June 2011	Applicant alleged that the state failed in its positive obligation to protect her husband's life and to carry out effective and thorough investigation into his death.	The legal system as a whole, faced with arguable case of negligent act causing death, failed to provide adequate and timely response.	20,000
Peker v. Turkey (no. 2) no. 42136/06 12 April 2011	Applicant alleged that he had been shot in the leg and then beaten up by a number of gendarmes who had been carrying out an operation in the prison where he was being detained.	No plausible explanation as to how applicant suffered his injury while he was in prison. No effective investigation.	18,000

Wasilewska and Kalucka v. Poland nos. 28975/04 and 33406/04 23 February 2010	Applicants are relatives of victim who was killed during special police operation.	Disproportionate use of force and failure to properly prepare for the situation. No effective investigation.	20,000 to each
Eugenia Lazăr v. Romania no. 32146/05 16 February 2010	Applicant complained about inadequate medical treatment of her son who eventually died.	Investigation into death undermined by poor regulatory framework governing forensic investigations.	20,000
Mikayil Mammadov v. Azerbaijan no. 4762/05 17 December 2009	Applicant's wife poured petrol over herself and set herself on fire when police presented her with an expulsion order.	Inadequate investigation marked by a number of omissions.	20,000
Golubeva v. Russia no. 1062/03 17 December 2009	Death of applicant's partner during his arrest at their home.	Arrest was not organized so as to avoid risk of recourse to lethal force by police.	35,000
Maiorano and Others v. Italy no. 28634/06 15 December 2009	Eight applicants – relatives of two girls murdered by dangerous reoffender while he was on day-release from prison.	Failure to show diligence needed to protect right to life.	10,000 to one of them 5,000 to each of the others

Case	Principal issue(s)	Violation(s) found	Award (EUR)
Abdulhadi Yildirim v. Turkey no. 13694/04 15 December 2009	Despite suffering from schizophrenia, applicant's son was conscripted into the armed forces, where, having started serving sentence for desertion, he committed suicide in prison.	The military and prison authorities failed to take minimum precautions to protect victim's life.	12,000
Trufin v. Romania no. 3990/04 20 October 2009	Applicant's brother was found unconscious in the street. Initial medical report mentioned head injury and lesions caused by repeated blows.	Action taken to clarify circumstances of death and identify culprits did not meet requirements of prompt and effective investigation.	8,000
Abdullah Yılmaz v. Turkey no. 21899/02 17 June 2008	Plaintiff's son, aged twenty, committed suicide during his compulsory military service.	Failure by the authorities to do everything in their power to protect victim from improper conduct of his superiors.	12,000
Juozaitienė and Bikulčius v. Lithuania nos. 70659/01 and 74371/01 24 April 2008	Applicants are mother and father respectively of two victims shot dead in a car by police, as police tried to chase that car driven by a third person.	Use of force more than absolutely necessary in order to effect lawful arrest. No effective investigation.	30,000 to each

Budayeva and Others v. Russia nos. 15339/02, 21166/02, 20058/02, 11673/02 and 15343/02 20 March 2008	Series of mudslides destroyed six applicants' homes. They also killed and injured several people.	State's failure to discharge its positive obligation to protect right to life. Lack of adequate judicial response.	30,000 to one of them 15,000 to one of them 10,000 to four of them
Reavey v. the United Kingdom no. 34640/04 27 November 2007	Three gunmen entered applicant's house and shot and killed her three sons.	Lack of independence of Royal Ulster Constabulary during initial stages of investigation.	5,000
Celniku v. Greece no. 21449/04 5 July 2007	Brother of two petitioners killed with firearm when police tried to arrest him.	Deficient organization of police operation. No effective investigation.	20,000 jointly
Karagiannopoulos v. Greece no. 27850/03 21 June 2007	Although he eventually survived, applicant was shot in the head by a police officer while he was being arrested.	The state failed to protect applicant's life, and he became disabled. No effective investigation.	20,000

Case	Principal issue(s)	Violation(s) found	Award (EUR)
Kontrová v. Slovakia no. 7510/04 31 May 2007	Applicant's husband killed their two children and then killed himself. Applicant had already alerted police when, on previous occasion, husband had threatened to kill their children.	The state failed to take measures to protect lives of applicant's children.	25,000
Ramsahai and Others v. the Netherlands no. 52391/99 15 May 2007	Applicants are grandparents and father of victim, who was shot dead by a police officer who was trying to arrest him for stealing a scooter.	No effective and independent investigation.	20,000 jointly
Kamil Uzun v. Turkey no. 37410/97 10 May 2007	Applicant's mother was killed by a mortar shell which landed on her neighbour's house.	No effective investigation.	20,000

Annex 2 Selected cases

Compensation for non-pecuniary damage for violations of Article 3

Case	Principal issue(s)	Violation(s) found	Award
Lapshov v. Russia no. 5288/08 24 October 2013	Appalling conditions in temporary detention centre pending investigation and trial.	Degrading conditions of detention.	EUR 5,000
Aslanis v. Greece no. 36401/10 17 October 2013	Conditions of detention.	The police station was in itself inappropriate for a three-month detention.	EUR 8,000
Douet v. France no. 16705/10 3 October 2013	Ill-treatment by police during applicant's arrest.	The government failed to prove that use of force was proportionate and necessary.	EUR 15,000
Cotleţ v. Romania (no. 2) no. 49549/11 1 October 2013	Conditions of detention during a four-month imprisonment, especially overcrowding and poor conditions of hygiene.	Conditions of detention.	EUR 600

Case	Principal issue(s)	Violation(s) found	Award
Ţicu v. Romania no. 24575/10 1 October 2013	Applicant, diagnosed with mental disorder, complained about conditions of detention and aggression used by other inmates.	Conditions of detention. No effective investigation.	EUR 24,000
Epistatu v. Romania no. 29343/10 24 September 2013	Conditions of detention, especially overcrowding.	Conditions of detention.	EUR 3,000
NA v. Moldova no. 13424/06 24 September 2013	Applicant accused the authorities of having not identified and punished those who had raped her.	No effective investigation.	EUR 10,000
Amine Güzel v. Turkey no. 41844/09 17 September 2013	Ill-treatment during both arrest and time in police custody, and no effective investigation.	No effective investigation.	EUR 12,500
Athan v. Turkey no. 36144/09 3 September 2013	Ill-treatment while in police custody and no effective investigation.	No effective investigation.	EUR 5,000

Rzakhanov v. Azerbaijan no. 4242/07 4 July 2013	Harsh conditions of detention.	Conditions of detention.	EUR 7,500
Mustafa Aldemir v. Turkey no. 53087/07 2 July 2013	Wounded by security forces, applicant alleged excessive and disproportionate use of force and defective investigation.	Both substantive and procedural limbs.	EUR 19,500
Fehér v. Hungary no. 69095/10 2 July 2013	Detention in overcrowded cells.	Overcrowding.	EUR 12,000
Holodenko v. Latvia no. 17215/07 2 July 2013	Ill-treatment by police and defective investigation.	Both substantive and procedural limbs.	EUR 5,000
A.F. v. Greece no. 53709/11 13 June 2013	Conditions of detention, especially overcrowding.	Conditions of detention.	EUR 8,000
Davitidze v. Russia no. 8810/05 30 May 2013	Excessive use of force during arrest and no effective investigation.	Both substantive and procedural limbs.	EUR 7,500

Case	Principal issue(s)	Violation(s) found	Award
E.A. v. Russia no. 44187/04 23 May 2013	Applicant, diagnosed with HIV and hepatitis C, alleged deficiencies in his medical care while in detention.	Inhuman and degrading treatment.	EUR 7,500
Canali v. France no. 40119/09 25 April 2013	Conditions during six months in detention, especially poor conditions of hygiene.	Conditions of detention.	EUR 10,000
Dimitar Shopov v. Bulgaria no. 17253/07 16 April 2013	No effective investigation into an assault against applicant by private individuals.	No effective investigation.	EUR 3,000
Ochelkov v. Russia no. 17828/05 11 April 2013	Torture by police officers on two occasions after applicant's arrest and no effective investigation.	Inhuman and degrading treatment on both occasions. No effective investigation.	EUR 20,000
Böber v. Turkey no. 62590/09 9 April 2013	Ill-treatment by police and no effective investigation.	Both substantive and procedural limbs.	EUR 19,500
Ivakhnenko v. Russia no. 12622/04 4 April 2013	Conditions of detention in remand prison.	Overcrowding.	EUR 6,250

Markaryan v. Russia no. 12102/05 4 April 2013	Ill-treatment in police custody and no effective investigation.	Both substantive and procedural limbs.	EUR 10,000
Valiulienė v. Lithuania no. 33234/07 26 March 2013	The state failed to protect applicant from acts of domestic violence.	No adequate protection given to applicant against acts of violence.	EUR 5,000
Mimtaş v. Turkey no. 23698/07 19 March 2013	Ill-treatment by prison guards and no effective investigation.	Both substantive and procedural limbs.	EUR 9,750
Stana v. Romania no. 44120/10 5 March 2013	Conditions during some ten years in detention.	Overcrowding.	EUR 10,000
Kemal Baş v. Turkey no. 38291/07 19 February 2013	Excessive and disproportionate use of force during arrest and no effective investigation.	Both substantive and procedural limbs.	EUR 9,500
Ciolan v. Romania no. 24378/04 19 February 2013	Conditions during two years and four months in detention.	Overcrowding.	EUR 5,400

Case	Principal issue(s)	Violation(s) found	Award
Gülaydın v. Turkey no. 37157/09 12 February 2013	Ill-treatment by police and no effective investigation.	Both substantive and procedural limbs.	EUR 15,000
Gurenko v. Russia no. 41828/10 5 February 2013	No adequate medical care in detention, despite suffering from a serious heart condition.	No adequate medical treatment during more than six years in detention.	EUR 15,000
Cirillo v. Italy no. 36276/10 29 January 2013	No treatment suited to applicant's medical condition, while in detention.	No adequate medical treatment.	EUR 10,000
Suleymanov v. Russia no. 32501/11 22 January 2013	The authorities' failure to effectively investigate ill-treatment of applicant's son by state agents.	No effective investigation.	EUR 12,500
Jashi v. Georgia no. 10799/06 8 January 2013	Inadequate medical care in prison.	Failure to provide timely and adequate care for applicant's mental health problems in prison.	EUR 3,000
Dvalishvili v. Georgia no. 19634/07 18 December 2012	Ill-treatment by police and no effective investigation.	Both substantive and procedural limbs.	EUR 12,000

Jeladze v. Georgia no. 1871/08 18 December 2012	Inadequate medical treatment in prison.	Applicant was left without appropriate diagnostic treatment for more than fifteen months.	EUR 5,000
Timofejevi v. Latvia no. 45393/04 11 December 2012	Effectiveness of investigation into allegations of excessive use of force during arrest.	No effective investigation.	EUR 4,000
Banu v. Romania no. 60732/09 11 December 2012	Conditions during one year and five months in detention.	Overcrowding.	EUR 3,750
Nieciecki v. Greece no. 11677/11 4 December 2012	Conditions during more than two years and three months in detention.	Overcrowding.	EUR 5,600
Mityaginy v. Russia no. 20325/06 4 December 2012	Ill-treatment by police and no effective investigation.	No effective investigation.	EUR 5,000
Kasperovičius v. Lithuania no. 54872/08 20 November 2012	Conditions during a seven-day detention in a remand facility.	Degrading treatment.	EUR 3,000

Case	Principal issue(s)	Violation(s) found	Award
Longin v. Croatia no. 49268/10 6 November 2012	Conditions during about one year in detention.	Degrading treatment.	EUR 5,000
Ablyazov v. Russia no. 22867/05 30 October 2012	Ill-treatment in police custody and no effective investigation.	Both substantive and procedural limbs.	EUR 15,000
E.M. v. Romania no. 43994/05 30 October 2012	Ineffective investigation into domestic violence.	No effective investigation.	EUR 7,500
Paweł Pawlak v. Poland no. 13421/03 30 October 2012	Imposition of so-called 'dangerous detainee' regime on applicant for about one year and ten months.	Severity of measures taken exceeded legitimate requirements of security in prison.	EUR 12,000
Bureš v. the Czech Republic no. 37679/08 18 October 2012	Ill-treatment in a sobering-up centre and no effective investigation.	Both substantive and procedural limbs.	EUR 20,000

Otamendi Egiguren v. Spain no. 47303/08 16 October 2012	Defective investigation into allegations of ill-treatment while being kept in incommunicado detention.	No effective investigation.	EUR 20,000
Eylem Baş v. Turkey no. 11435/07 16 October 2012	Ill-treatment while in police custody and no effective investigation.	Both substantive and procedural limbs.	EUR 10,000
İşeri and Others v. Turkey no. 29283/07 9 October 2012	Force used by police against four applicants, during their participation in a press conference, was disproportionate.	Excessive use of force.	EUR 7,500 to each
Asyanov v. Russia no. 25462/09 9 October 2012	Conditions during one and a half years in remand prison.	Overcrowding.	EUR 6,500
Bygylashvili v. Greece no. 58164/10 25 September 2012	Conditions during six months in detention, especially overcrowding.	Degrading treatment.	EUR 8,000
Ferhat Kaya v. Turkey no. 12673/05 25 September 2012	Ill-treatment while in police custody and defective investigation.	Both substantive and procedural limbs.	EUR 9,750

Case	Principal issue(s)	Violation(s) found	Award
Muta v. Ukraine no. 37246/06 31 July 2012	Defective investigation into allegations of ill-treatment by a private individual.	No effective investigation.	EUR 7,500
Yerme v. Turkey no. 3434/05 24 July 2012	Excessive use of force by police while arresting applicant. Defective investigation.	Both substantive and procedural limbs.	EUR 19,500
Fűlöp v. Romania no. 18999/04 24 July 2012	Applicant contracted tuberculosis in prison because sick detainees had not been segregated from the others.	Degrading treatment.	EUR 7,500
Iacov Stanciu v. Romania no. 35972/05 24 July 2012	Conditions of detention in various prisons.	Conditions in prison, in particular overcrowding, lack of access to hygiene, and inappropriate medical treatment.	EUR 20,000
Wenerski v. Poland (no. 2) no. 38719/09 24 July 2012	Inadequate conditions of detention.	Cumulative effects of inappropriate living conditions and victim's vulnerable medical condition.	EUR 5,000

Aleksakhin v. Ukraine no. 31939/06 19 July 2012	Ill-treatment by police and lengthy proceedings in a case against a police officer.	Torture. No effective investigation.	EUR 20,000
Budaca v. Romania no. 57260/10 17 July 2012	Conditions during one and a half years in detention.	Conditions of detention.	EUR 4,900
Iorgoiu v. Romania no. 1831/02 17 July 2012	Conditions during more than two years and two months in detention and absence of medical treatment.	Conditions of detention.	EUR 5,100
Radu Pop v. Romania no. 14337/04 17 July 2012	Conditions of detention in different prisons.	Conditions of detention.	EUR 8,400
Vartic v. Romania no. 12152/05 10 July 2012	Conditions during more than eleven years in detention.	Conditions of detention.	EUR 12,000
Taylan v. Turkey no. 32051/09 3 July 2012	Torture while in police custody and length of criminal proceedings against police officers.	Torture. The judges used discretion to minimize consequences of an extremely serious unlawful act.	EUR 45,500

Case	Principal issue(s)	Violation(s) found	Award
Rustamov v. Russia no. 11209/10 3 July 2012	Extradition to Uzbekistan.	If extradited, applicant would face a real risk of treatment proscribed by Article 3.	Finding of a violation was sufficient.
Razvyazkin v. Russia no. 13579/09 3 July 2012	Conditions of solitary confinement in correctional colony's punishment cells; inadequate medical assistance.	Repeated solitary confinement amounted to inhuman and degrading treatment.	EUR 15,000
Kulish v. Ukraine no. 35093/07 21 June 2012	Ill-treatment by police and no proper investigation.	Very serious and cruel suffering that amounted to torture. No effective investigation.	EUR 30,000
Mazâlu v. Romania no. 24009/03 12 June 2012	Conditions of detention in police station cells and at a high-security prison.	Conditions of detention.	EUR 7,500
Răducanu v. Romania no. 17187/05 12 June 2012	Conditions of detention and lack of adequate medical care for venous thromboses in applicant's legs.	Conditions of detention in prison.	EUR 9,000

Buntov v. Russia no. 27026/10 5 June 2012	Torture by officials in penal colony where applicant was being detained. No effective remedy.	Torture. No effective investigation.	EUR 45,000
Ciucă v. Romania no. 34485/09 5 June 2012	Conditions of detention, in particular overcrowding and hygiene.	Conditions of detention.	EUR 3,000
Eski v. Turkey no. 8354/04 5 June 2012	Ill-treatment while in police custody. Length of criminal proceedings against accused police officers.	Inhuman treatment. The judges used discretion to minimize consequences of an extremely serious unlawful act.	EUR 19,500
Şercău v. Romania no. 41775/06 5 June 2012	Ill-treatment by a police officer and no effective investigation.	No proper investigation.	EUR 6,000
Culev v. Moldova no. 60179/09 17 April 2012	Inhuman conditions of detention.	Poor conditions of detention went beyond unavoidable level of hardship inherent in detention.	EUR 4,500
Rizvanov v. Azerbaijan no. 31805/06 17 April 2012	Applicant was victim of police brutality during a demonstration and had no effective investigation.	Both substantive and procedural limbs.	EUR 4,500

Case	Principal issue(s)	Violation(s) found	Award
Kazantsev v. Russia no. 14880/05 3 April 2012	Ill-treatment while in police custody and no effective investigation.	Both substantive and procedural limbs.	EUR 7,500
Dimitar Dimitrov v. Bulgaria no. 18059/05 3 April 2012	Inappropriate use of force by police and no effective investigation.	Both substantive and procedural limbs.	EUR 3,000
Melnītis v. Latvia no. 30779/05 3 April 2012	Conditions of pre-trial detention.	Conditions of detention.	EUR 7,000
Zontul v. Greece no. 12294/07 17 January 2012	Applicant, an illegal migrant, complained that he had been raped with a truncheon by a coastguard officer supervising him and that the authorities had refused to allow him to be examined by a doctor who was on the premises.	Treatment to which victim had been subjected, in view of its cruelty and its intentional nature, had amounted to an act of torture. The authorities failed to allow victim to be involved in proceedings as a civil party.	EUR 50,000
Archip v. Romania no. 49608/08 27 September 2011	Ill-treatment by the authorities and no effective investigation.	No effective investigation.	EUR 10,000

Demian v. Romania no. 5614/05 27 September 2011	No adequate medical treatment for diabetes while in detention and poor conditions in detention.	No adequate medical treatment while in detention.	EUR 10,000
Đurđević v. Croatia no. 52442/09 19 July 2011	Three applicants alleged ill-treatment by police and defective investigation.	No proper investigation.	EUR 6,000 jointly
Hellig v. Germany no. 20999/05 7 July 2011	Applicant complained about being placed naked in a security cell in prison for seven days.	No sufficient reasons which could justify such harsh treatment as to deprive applicant of his clothes during his entire stay.	EUR 10,000
Saçılık and Others v. Turkey nos. 43044/05 and 45001/05 5 July 2011	Twenty-four applicants alleged that, in the course of a security operation conducted in their prison, they had been subjected to ill-treatment. No adequate investigation.	Injuries consistent with excessive use of force. No effective investigation.	EUR 20,000 to each
Păduret v. Moldova no. 33134/03 5 January 2010	Ill-treatment while in detention. No effective investigation within a reasonable time, allowing perpetrators to escape responsibility.	Legislation adopted to prevent and punish acts of ill-treatment by law-enforcement agencies was not given full preventive effect.	EUR 20,000

Case	Principal issue(s)	Violation(s) found	Award
Daoudi v. France no. 19576/08 3 December 2009	Extradition to Algeria.	A serious risk that applicant would be subjected to ill-treatment if decision were enforced.	Finding of a violation was sufficient.
Samoylov v. Russia no. 64398/01 2 October 2008	Ill-treatment by police officers and no effective investigation into the matter.	Ill-treatment inflicted on applicant by policemen. No effective investigation.	EUR 10,000
Kemal Kahraman v. Turkey no. 39857/03 22 July 2008	Applicant was arrested on suspicion of being involved in three bombings: ill-treatment while in police custody.	Torture: no plausible explanation for injuries intentionally inflicted for purpose of extracting confessions.	EUR 15,000

Annex 3 Selected cases

Compensation for non-pecuniary damage for violations of Article 5

Case	Principal issue(s)	Violation(s) found	Award
Öner Aktaş v. Turkey no. 59860/10 29 October 2013	Five-year pre-trial detention.	No sufficient reasons for length of detention.	EUR 5,000
Housein v. Greece no. 71825/11 24 October 2013	Applicant's arrest and detention ignored his status as an unaccompanied minor.	Unlawful detention. Lack of examination by a court.	EUR 12,000
Shyti v. Greece no. 65911/09 17 October 2013	The court's refusal to hear applicant when his detention was decided and no speedy review.	No adversarial and speedy proceedings.	EUR 4,000
Vosgien v. France no. 12430/11 3 October 2013	Length of detention on remand.	No sufficient reasons to justify applicant's detention on remand for four years and three months.	EUR 8,000

Case	Principal issue(s)	Violation(s) found	Award
Gonța v. Romania no. 38494/04 1 October 2013	Length of pre-trial detention.	No sufficient reasons to justify applicant's pre-trial detention for two years and four months.	EUR 3,000
Kvashko v. Ukraine no. 40939/05 26 September 2013	Unlawful administrative detention and arrest, lack of prompt judicial review and no compensation.	Arbitrary detention. No prompt judicial review. Lack of compensation.	EUR 4,500
Danalachi v. Moldova no. 25664/09 17 September 2013	Applicant alleged that she had been unlawfully detained because she could not pay a fine.	The court's decision lacked any justification for detention.	EUR 5,000
Suso Musa v. Malta no. 42337/12 23 July 2013	Unlawful detention and no effective means to challenge its lawfulness.	Arbitrary detention. No effective and speedy remedy to challenge lawfulness.	EUR 24,000

Dinç and Çakır v. Turkey no. 66066/09 9 July 2013	Lengthy detention on remand.	No relevant and sufficient reasons to justify applicants' detention for one year and two months.	EUR 1,200 to each
Abashev v. Russia no. 9096/09 27 June 2013	No effective domestic remedy for a complaint about unlawful arrest.	No enforceable right to compensation.	EUR 5,000
Vassis and Others v. France no. 62736/09 27 June 2013	Applicants were not brought promptly before a judge.	No justification for a forty-eight hour detention.	EUR 5,000 to each
Pletmentsev v. Russia no. 4157/04 27 June 2013	Unlawful detention.	Arbitrary detention.	EUR 7,000
Baran v. Poland no. 53315/09 28 May 2013	Unlawful detention and courts' refusal to compensate applicant.	Unlawful detention. Lack of compensation.	EUR 6,000

Case	Principal issue(s)	Violation(s) found	Award
K. v. Russia no. 69235/11 23 May 2013	No speedy examination of appeals against detention orders.	No speedy review of lawfulness of detention.	EUR 2,000
Zagidulina v. Russia no. 11737/06 2 May 2013	Involuntary placement in a psychiatric hospital.	Unlawful detention.	EUR 7,500
Barjamaj v. Greece no. 36657/11 2 May 2013	Detention of a minor with a view to deportation.	Unlawful detention.	EUR 2,000
Petukhova v. Russia no. 28796/07 2 May 2013	Deprivation of liberty for purposes of conducting an involuntary psychiatric examination.	Unlawful four-hour detention in a police station before hospitalization.	EUR 3,000
Baksza v. Hungary no. 59196/08 23 April 2013	Excessive length of pre-trial detention and no access to relevant material relating to investigation.	Stereotyped reasoning. Principle of equality of arms was ignored.	EUR 6,500

Firoz Muneer v. Belgium no. 56005/10 11 April 2013	Unlawful detention and no effective means to challenge its lawfulness.	Applicant had not been released speedily before any judicial control of his detention took place.	EUR 5,000
Shikuta v. Russia no. 45373/05 11 April 2013	Unlawful and lengthy detention and no speedy review of reasons for detention.	No legal grounds for a five-month detention. No speedy review.	EUR 7,500
Djalti v. Bulgaria no. 31206/05 12 March 2013	Unlawful detention and no effective means to challenge its lawfulness.	Unlawful detention. No speedy review.	EUR 3,500
Salih Salman Kılıç v. Turkey no. 22077/10 5 March 2013	Unlawful and lengthy detention.	Unlawful detention. Applicant was not brought promptly before a judge.	EUR 9,750
Kowrygo v. Poland no. 6200/07 26 February 2013	Excessive length of pre-trial detention.	No relevant and sufficient reasons to extend detention to one year and nine months.	EUR 2,200
Yefimova v. Russia no. 39786/09 19 February 2013	Detention pending extradition.	One period of detention was unlawful. No effective and speedy review.	EUR 20,000

Case	Principal issue(s)	Violation(s) found	Award
Bakoyev v. Russia no. 30225/11 5 February 2013	Detention pending extradition.	Unlawfulness of two periods of detention.	EUR 5,000
Betteridge v. the United Kingdom no. 1497/10 29 January 2013	No speedy review of lawfulness of detention.	No speedy review.	EUR 750
Mihailovs v. Latvia no. 35939/10 22 January 2013	Plaintiff held against his will in a state-run social care institution for more than ten years.	Unlawful detention. No review of the lawfulness of detention.	EUR 15,000
Swennen v. Belgium no. 53448/10 10 January 2013	Detention of a person of unsound mind.	Applicant's confinement in a prison for thirteen years was inappropriate.	EUR 15,000
Baisuev and Anzorov v. Georgia no. 39804/04 18 December 2012	Three-hour detention at police station.	Unlawful and arbitrary detention. Applicants were not informed of the reasons.	EUR 500 to each

Athary v. Turkey no. 50372/09 11 December 2012	Detention with a view to deportation.	Unlawful detention. No notification of reasons. No speedy review.	EUR 9,000
Janiashvili v. Georgia no. 35887/05 27 November 2012	Applicant was remanded in custody for a total period of almost one year.	Unreasonable period of detention.	EUR 600
Khachatryan and Others v. Armenia no. 23978/06 27 November 2012	Detention for an act which did not constitute an offence at the material time and no compensation.	No 'offence' within the meaning of Article 5(1)(c). No enforceable right to compensation.	EUR 6,000 to each
Bilal Doğan v. Turkey no. 28053/10 27 November 2012	Length of pre-trial detention.	Almost ten months of pre-trial detention for a minor was excessive.	EUR 1,000
Horváth v. Slovakia no. 5515/09 27 November 2012	No speedy review of lawfulness of detention.	No speedy determination of lawfulness of applicant's detention.	EUR 4,200

Case	Principal issue(s)	Violation(s) found	Award
Pyatkov v. Russia no. 61767/08 13 November 2012	Unlawful and unreasonably long pre-trial detention and shortcomings in the review of lawfulness of detention.	Periods of unlawful detention. No relevant and sufficient reasons for a pre-trial detention of three years and five months. Appeals decided *in absentia*.	EUR 10,000
Osmanović v. Croatia no. 67604/10 6 November 2012	A complaint against lawfulness of detention was declared inadmissible simply because applicant was no longer detained.	Court's failure to decide complaint on the merits.	EUR 2,500
Buishvili v. the Czech Republic no. 30241/11 25 October 2012	The courts in review proceedings had no power to order applicant's release.	No access to judicial proceedings in which release could be ordered.	EUR 3,000
Rakhmonov v. Russia no. 50031/11 16 October 2012	Detention pending extradition.	Unlawful detention. Lack of a speedy review.	EUR 1,000

Sergey Solovyev v. Russia no. 22152/05 25 September 2012	Unlawful detention.	Unlawful detention until issuing of a new detention order the next day.	EUR 500
Stepanov v. Russia no. 33872/05 25 September 2012	Unlawful detention.	No time limit or grounds for applicant's detention.	EUR 5,000
Dervishi v. Croatia no. 67341/10 25 September 2012	Pre-trial detention of three years and six months.	Lack of reasoning and excessive length of pre-trial detention.	EUR 3,600
Kırlangıç v. Turkey no. 30689/05 25 September 2012	Pre-trial detention of five years and four months.	Stereotyped reasoning.	EUR 5,400
Alikhonov v. Russia no. 35692/11 31 July 2012	Detention pending extradition.	No speedy review.	EUR 3,000

Case	Principal issue(s)	Violation(s) found	Award
Van der Velden v. the Netherlands no. 21203/10 31 July 2012	Confinement in a custodial clinic was extended contrary to domestic law.	Applicant's continued detention beyond a certain date was unlawful.	EUR 43,800
Ceviz v. Turkey no. 8140/08 17 July 2012	Lengthy detention and no effective remedy or compensation.	No communication of prosecutor's written submissions. Lack of compensation.	Finding of a violation was sufficient.
S. v. Germany no. 3300/10 28 June 2012	Retrospective preventive detention.	Unlawful detention.	EUR 12,000
Malkhasyan v. Armenia no. 6729/07 26 June 2012	Unlawful detention.	Unlawful detention. Stereotyped reasoning.	EUR 4,500
Cristian Teodorescu v. Romania no. 22883/05 19 June 2012	Detention of a person of unsound mind.	Unlawful detention for twenty-four hours in a psychiatric hospital.	EUR 4,500

Kislitsa v. Russia no. 29985/05 19 June 2012	Detention on remand was not based on relevant and sufficient grounds.	No sufficient grounds for extending applicant's detention.	EUR 1,000
Kortesis v. Greece no. 60593/10 12 June 2012	Unlawful detention and no information about the reasons.	Unlawful detention. Applicant had to wait twenty-nine hours before being informed of the reasons for his detention.	EUR 2,200
Abidov v. Russia no. 52805/10 12 June 2012	Detention pending extradition.	No speedy review.	EUR 2,000
Muradkhanyan v. Armenia no. 12895/06 5 June 2012	Lengthy detention, not based on a court decision.	Unlawful detention. Lengthy detention.	EUR 6,000
Kozhayev v. Russia no. 60045/10 5 June 2012	Unlawful arrest and detention.	Unlawfulness of detention from time of detention until time that detention order was issued the same day.	Finding of a violation was sufficient.
Shakurov v. Russia no. 55822/10 5 June 2012	Lawfulness of detention was not decided speedily.	Delays in examining appeals against two detention orders.	EUR 2,000

Case	Principal issue(s)	Violation(s) found	Award
Suslov v. Russia no. 2366/07 29 May 2012	Pre-trial detention exceeding maximum allowed by domestic law, and no relevant and sufficient grounds.	No legal basis for repeated extensions of detention period. Lengthy pre-trial detention.	EUR 15,000
Yevgeniy Kuzmin v. Russia no. 6479/05 3 May 2012	Absence of sufficient and relevant grounds for a lengthy detention on remand.	No sufficient reasons to justify continued deprivation of liberty for more than one year and two months.	EUR 1,000
Creangă v. Romania no. 29226/03 23 February 2012	Thirteen-hour deprivation of liberty and subsequent placement in pre-trial detention.	No sufficient legal basis in domestic law for both deprivations of liberty.	EUR 8,000
Valeriy Samoylov v. Russia no. 57541/09 24 January 2012	Unreasonable length of detention pending investigation and trial.	No relevant and sufficient reasons to justify extending applicant's detention to more than two years and one month.	EUR 2,500

Zandbergs v. Latvia no. 71092/01 20 December 2011	Detention on remand unreasonably long and deficient judicial review.	No sufficient reasons for a detention period of three years and three months. Deficient system of appeals.	EUR 3,000
Stoica v. Turkey no. 19985/04 29 November 2011	Detention on remand unreasonably long.	No relevant and sufficient reasons to justify extending detention to some three years and six months.	EUR 4,300
Stokłosa v. Poland no. 32602/08 3 November 2011	Applicant alleged that assessor, who had remanded him in custody, had lacked independence.	Assessor was not independent of the executive.	Finding of a violation was sufficient.
Bruncko v. Slovakia no. 33937/06 3 November 2011	Unlawful detention in custody.	Unlawful detention after the expiry of detention order given at pre-trial stage.	EUR 15,000
Miminoshvili v. Russia no. 20197/03 28 June 2011	Unlawful and unjustified pre-trial detention and unnecessarily long detention proceedings.	Unlawful detention. No relevant and sufficient reasons for continuous detention. No speedy review.	EUR 12,000

Case	Principal issue(s)	Violation(s) found	Award
Mirosław Garlicki v. Poland no. 36921/07 14 June 2011	Detention on remand not imposed by an independent judicial officer.	Assessor was not independent of the executive.	EUR 6,000
Ruprecht v. Poland no. 39912/06 21 February 2011	Pre-trial detention of almost eight years.	Grounds given by authorities could not justify overall period of detention.	EUR 6,000
Michalko v. Slovakia no. 35377/05 21 December 2010	Unlawful pre-trial detention and corresponding procedure.	No relevant and sufficient reasons for denying release. No effective and speedy review. Lack of compensation.	EUR 7,000
Osypenko v. Ukraine no. 4634/04 9 November 2010	Unlawful deprivation of liberty and excessive length of pre-trial detention.	Unlawful detention during a certain period. Unreasonable length of detention.	EUR 2,500

Annex 4 Selected cases

Compensation for non-pecuniary damage for violations of Article 6

Case	Length and type of proceedings	Award
Sereny v. Romania no. 13071/06 18 June 2013	- seven years, four months at two levels of jurisdiction - criminal proceedings	EUR 1,800
Szepes v. Hungary no. 77669/12 11 June 2013	- fourteen years, ten months at two levels of jurisdiction - civil proceedings	EUR 9,000
Akmansoy v. Turkey no. 14787/07 28 May 2013	- more than eleven years, three months at two levels of jurisdiction - civil proceedings	EUR 6,000
Pospekh v. Russia no. 31948/05 2 May 2013	- five years, seven months at two levels of jurisdiction - civil proceedings	EUR 2,000
Goudoumas v. Greece no. 62459/09 2 May 2013	- twelve years, eleven months at three levels of jurisdiction - administrative proceedings	EUR 11,200

Case	Length and type of proceedings	Award
Danilo Kovačič v. Slovenia no. 24376/08 18 April 2013	- fourteen years, two months at four levels of jurisdiction - criminal proceedings	EUR 8,000
Vershinin v. Russia no. 9311/05 11 April 2013	- seven years at three levels of jurisdiction - civil proceedings	EUR 2,100
Aborina v. Russia no. 28222/06 11 April 2013	- nine years, four months at two levels of jurisdiction - civil proceedings	EUR 4,000
Alhan v. Turkey no. 8163/07 2 April 2013	- almost six years at two levels of jurisdiction - civil proceedings	EUR 2,500
Kıranel v. Turkey no. 26964/09 2 April 2013	- seven years, eleven months at one level of jurisdiction - civil proceedings	EUR 5,000
Şercaru v. Romania no. 13088/09 2 April 2013	- six years, one month at two levels of jurisdiction - civil proceedings	EUR 1,500

Sándor v. Hungary no. 31069/11 12 March 2013	- nine years, eleven months at three levels of jurisdiction - civil proceedings	EUR 6,400
Mészáros v. Hungary no. 23559/09 12 March 2013	- eight years at three levels of jurisdiction - civil proceedings	EUR 2,900
Laufik v. Slovakia no. 5718/10 5 March 2013	- more than eleven years, nine months at three levels of jurisdiction - civil proceedings	EUR 7,800
Müller-Hartburg v. Austria no. 47195/06 19 February 2013	- nine years, eleven months at three levels of jurisdiction - disciplinary proceedings	EUR 8,000
A.H. v. Slovakia no. 23386/09 19 February 2013	- five years, four months at two levels of jurisdiction - civil status	EUR 2,400
Tereshkin v. Russia no. 13601/05 19 February 2013	- seven years, ten months at two levels of jurisdiction - disability allowance	EUR 4,500

Case	Length and type of proceedings	Award
Hauser v. Slovakia no. 12583/09 5 February 2013	- more than eight years, eight months at two levels of jurisdiction - civil proceedings	EUR 5,200
Borobar and Others v. Romania no. 5663/04 29 January 2013	- almost eight years at three levels of jurisdiction - criminal proceedings	EUR 2,400 to each
Erkızan v. Turkey no. 17074/09 22 January 2013	- thirteen years, eight months at two levels of jurisdiction - civil proceedings	EUR 9,600
Ferencsik v. Hungary no. 33275/08 22 January 2013	- ten years, six months at one level of jurisdiction - criminal proceedings	EUR 11,500
Lengyel v. Hungary no. 34567/08 18 December 2012	- nine years, three months at two levels of jurisdiction - civil proceedings	EUR 5,800
Çelikalp v. Turkey no. 51259/07 18 December 2012	- twenty years, four months at two levels of jurisdiction - civil proceedings	EUR 13,000

Tumlukolçu v. Turkey no. 33621/09 18 December 2012	- twelve years at two levels of jurisdiction - civil proceedings	EUR 7,000
Gürceğiz v. Turkey no. 11045/07 15 November 2012	- more than seven years at two levels of jurisdiction - criminal proceedings	EUR 3,000
Bodnár v. Hungary no. 46206/07 15 November 2012	- fourteen years, five months at two levels of jurisdiction - civil proceedings	EUR 14,400
Gutman v. Hungary no. 53943/07 8 November 2012	- six years, ten months at two levels of jurisdiction - civil proceedings	EUR 4,300
Karpetas v. Greece no. 6086/10 30 October 2012	- ten years, five months at three levels of jurisdiction - criminal proceedings	EUR 5,000
Barišič v. Slovenia no. 32600/05 18 October 2012	- five years, ten months at two levels of jurisdiction - labour proceedings	EUR 4,000

Case	Length and type of proceedings	Award
Sizov v. Russia (no. 2) no. 58104/08 24 July 2012	- four years, ten months at two levels of jurisdiction - criminal proceedings	EUR 2,000
Chyżyński v. Poland no. 32287/09 24 July 2012	- eleven years, eight months at two levels of jurisdiction - criminal proceedings	EUR 8,000
Szentesi v. Hungary no. 19558/08 12 June 2012	- nine years, four months at two levels of jurisdiction - civil proceedings	EUR 8,000
Sitosilo Volou A.E. v. Greece no. 64846/09 12 June 2012	- ten years at five levels of jurisdiction - civil proceedings	EUR 2,000
Laduna v. Slovakia no. 11686/10 31 May 2012	- more than eight years, ten months at two levels of jurisdiction - civil proceedings	EUR 6,800
TNS s.r.o. v. Slovakia no. 15702/10 31 May 2012	- six years at two levels of jurisdiction - civil proceedings	EUR 3,000

Franc v. Slovakia no. 20986/10 31 May 2012	- more than twelve years in respect of the proceedings at first instance - civil proceedings	EUR 2,500
Masár v. Slovakia no. 66882/09 3 May 2012	- more than four years, five months of pre-trial proceedings - criminal proceedings	EUR 2,500
Cangelaris v. Greece no. 28073/09 3 May 2012	- six years, four months at one level of jurisdiction - civil proceedings	EUR 3,000
Mezzapesa and Plati v. Italy no. 37197/03 24 April 2012	- more than fourteen years at one level of jurisdiction - civil proceedings	EUR 5,500 jointly
Solomakhin v. Ukraine no. 24429/03 15 March 2012	- almost nine years, four months at three levels of jurisdiction - civil proceedings	EUR 2,400

Annex 5 Selected cases

Compensation for non-pecuniary damage for violations of Article 8

Case	Principal issue(s)	Violation(s) found	Award
Someşan and Butiuc v. Romania no. 45543/04 19 November 2013	Right to reputation.	No careful balance between journalist's and applicants' rights.	EUR 4,500 to each
Söderman v. Sweden no. 5786/08 12 November 2013	No remedies against applicant's stepfather's attempt to film her secretly while she was naked in bathroom.	No remedy existed that could enable applicant to obtain effective protection against said violation of her personal integrity.	EUR 10,000
Zelenevy v. Russia no. 59913/11 3 October 2013	Applicants – mother and her son – complained about non-enforcement of judgments fixing the latter's residence.	No adequate measures aimed at reuniting toddler with his mother.	EUR 10,000 jointly
Antoneta Tudor v. Romania no. 23445/04 24 September 2013	Plaintiff was denied access to documents relating to her father, held by the secret service of former communist regime.	The state failed in its positive obligation to secure effective access to information.	EUR 4,500

Bălteanu v. Romania no. 142/04 16 July 2013	Applicant complained that recording of his communications with third parties had been unlawful.	The courts did not examine lawfulness of recordings, thus annihilating legal safeguards.	EUR 4,500
R.M.S. v. Spain no. 28775/12 18 June 2013	Applicant complained about total lack of access to her daughter.	The authorities prevented family reunification solely on financial grounds.	EUR 30,000
Tur v. Turkey no. 13692/03 11 June 2013	Refusal by prison authorities to send an applicant's letter.	Interference not in accordance with the law.	EUR 300
Prizzia v. Hungary no. 20255/12 11 June 2013	Non-enforcement of decisions granting applicant visiting rights in respect of his minor son.	The authorities did not take all steps required to enforce access rights.	EUR 12,500
Avilkina and Others v. Russia no. 1585/09 6 June 2013	Disclosure of medical files to prosecutor's office without applicants' consent and in the absence of any criminal investigation.	Collection by prosecutor's office of confidential medical information was not accompanied by sufficient safeguards.	EUR 5,000 to each
Garnaga v. Ukraine no. 20390/07 16 May 2013	The authorities refused to change applicant's patronymic.	The authorities did not balance relevant interests at stake.	Finding of a violation was sufficient.

Case	Principal issue(s)	Violation(s) found	Award
Udeh v. Switzerland no. 12020/09 16 April 2013	Refusal to grant first applicant, convicted for a drugs offence, leave to remain with the rest of his family.	There would be a violation if expulsion of first applicant were enforced.	Finding of a violation was sufficient.
Zorica Jovanović v. Serbia no. 21794/08 26 March 2013	No information about the real fate of applicant's son, who had allegedly died while still in a state-run hospital.	The state's continuing failure to provide applicant with credible information as to the fate of her son.	EUR 10,000
B.B. and F.B. v. Germany nos. 18734/09 and 9424/11 14 March 2013	Withdrawal of parental authority.	The courts did not provide sufficient reasons for withdrawing applicants' parental rights.	EUR 25,000 to each
Lombardo v. Italy no. 25704/11 29 January 2013	Right to visit.	No adequate measures for an effective implementation of applicant's right to visit.	EUR 15,000
Röman v. Finland no. 13072/05 29 January 2013	Impossibility to have paternity established owing to a legal time limit.	Application of a rigid time limit for the exercise of paternity proceedings.	EUR 6,000

Chabrowski v. Ukraine no. 61680/10 17 January 2013	Authorities' failure to enforce a judgment intended to reunite applicant with his daughter.	Lack of effectiveness of enforcement led to a serious rupture of family ties between applicant and his daughter.	EUR 7,500
Csoma v. Romania no. 8759/05 15 January 2013	Failures in medical treatment leaving applicant permanently unable to bear children.	Applicant was not involved in the choice of treatment and not informed properly of the risks.	EUR 6,000
A.K. and L. v. Croatia no. 37956/11 8 January 2013	Applicant's son was put up for adoption without her knowledge, consent or participation in adoption proceedings.	No adequate safeguards at any stage of process of severing the ties between applicants.	EUR 12,500 to the first applicant
G.B. and R.B. v. Moldova no. 16761/09 18 December 2012	Applicants – husband and wife – complained about the latter's sterilization and nominal amount of compensation awarded to them.	EUR 607 is considerably below minimum level of compensation generally awarded by the Court for Article 8 violations.	EUR 12,000 jointly
Vuldzhev v. Bulgaria no. 6113/08 18 December 2012	Prisoner's correspondence with his lawyer.	Unjustified monitoring of correspondence.	EUR 1,200

Case	Principal issue(s)	Violation(s) found	Award
Meirelles v. Bulgaria no. 66203/10 18 December 2012	Failure to take interim custody measures without delay.	No sufficient measures to ensure effective contact between applicant and her child.	EUR 1,500
Remetin v. Croatia no. 29525/10 11 December 2012	Applicant, having been attacked and beaten by an unknown man, alleged inadequate protection.	Defective proceedings which eventually led to prosecution becoming time-barred.	EUR 7,500
Butt v. Norway no. 47017/09 4 December 2012	Deportation.	There would be a violation if deportation order were ever to be enforced.	EUR 3,000
Hamidovic v. Italy no. 31956/05 4 December 2012	Applicant was expelled and thus forced to leave her husband and children.	Measure was not proportionate.	EUR 15,000
Joanna Szulc v. Poland no. 43932/08 13 November 2012	Unsuccessful attempts to obtain access to all documents collected on applicant by communist-era secret services.	No effective and accessible procedure to contest applicant's classification by security services as their secret informant.	EUR 5,000
Alkaya v. Turkey no. 42811/06 9 October 2012	Applicant, a notorious comedienne in Turkey, denounced the press for publishing her address.	No fair balance between competing interests at stake.	EUR 7,500

Godelli v. Italy no. 33783/09 25 September 2012	Applicant complained that she had been unable to obtain non-identifying information about her birth family.	Absence in the law of any balance between competing rights and interests at stake.	EUR 5,000
Buckland v. the United Kingdom no. 40060/08 18 September 2012	Applicant is a gypsy and had a licence agreement terminated.	Applicant was dispossessed of her home without any possibility to have proportionality of her eviction assessed.	EUR 4,000
Costa and Pavan v. Italy no. 54270/10 28 August 2012	Applicants, a couple who are healthy carriers of cystic fibrosis, wanted, with the help of medically assisted procreation and genetic screening, to avoid transmitting disease to their offspring.	Disproportionate interference with their right to respect for their private and family life on account of inconsistent domestic legislation.	EUR 15,000 jointly
Robathin v. Austria no. 30457/06 3 July 2012	Search and seizure of electronic data.	Seizure and examination went beyond what was necessary to achieve a legitimate aim.	EUR 3,000
Bjedov v. Croatia no. 42150/09 29 May 2012	Order to vacate a flat in violation of right to respect for home.	Lack of analysis of proportionality of measure by an independent court.	EUR 2,000

Case	Principal issue(s)	Violation(s) found	Award
Santos Nunes v. Portugal no. 61173/08 22 May 2012	Lack of diligence in enforcing a custody order.	No adequate efforts to enforce custody order.	EUR 15,000
İlker Ensar Uyanık v. Turkey no. 60328/09 3 May 2012	At the end of a holiday in Turkey, applicant's wife refused to return to the United States with their daughter.	The courts did not perform a thorough analysis of familial situation.	EUR 12,500
Yordanova and Others v. Bulgaria no. 25446/06 24 April 2012	Twenty-three applicants of Roma origin complained that authorities decided to remove them from their homes.	There would be a violation if order were enforced.	Finding of a violation was sufficient.
Pontes v. Portugal no. 19554/09 10 April 2012	Decisions that led to one of the applicants' children being removed from them and eventually adopted.	Decision to place child for adoption not based on relevant and sufficient reasons.	EUR 32,500 jointly

Strömblad v. Sweden no. 3684/07 5 April 2012	Protracted custody proceedings.	The courts did not deal diligently with applicant's request to grant him custody of his daughter.	EUR 7,000
Romet v. the Netherlands no. 7094/06 14 February 2012	Applicant complained that unknown persons had been able to abuse his driving licence after he had reported it lost or stolen.	Swift administrative action to deprive a driving licence of its usefulness as an identity document was possible and practicable.	EUR 9,000
A.M.M. v. Romania no. 2151/10 14 February 2012	Long and ineffective paternity proceedings.	In paternity proceedings, the courts must take into account the child's interests.	EUR 7,000
Kopf and Liberda v. Austria no. 1598/06 17 January 2012	Two applicants denounced the courts for their decisions to refuse them access to their former foster child.	The courts did not deal diligently with applicants' request for visiting rights.	EUR 5,000 jointly
Prodělalová v. the Czech Republic no. 40094/08 20 December 2011	Visiting rights and custody proceedings.	No sufficient measures to protect applicant's parental rights.	EUR 5,000

Case	Principal issue(s)	Violation(s) found	Award
Bergmann v. the Czech Republic no. 8857/08 27 October 2011	Visiting rights.	No sufficient measures to ensure effective contact.	EUR 10,000
Khelili v. Switzerland no. 16188/07 18 October 2011	Applicant was classified as 'prostitute' in police database.	Retention of the word 'prostitute' for years was neither justified nor necessary.	EUR 15,000
S.I. v. Slovenia no. 45082/05 13 October 2011	Length of custody proceedings and judge's refusal to enforce provisional contact arrangements.	The authorities failed to meet their obligations in proceedings for child custody and contact rights.	EUR 4,000
Schneider v. Germany no. 17080/07 15 September 2011	Applicant claimed to be F.'s biological father and denounced the courts for their refusal to allow any contact or information about his development.	No fair balance between interests at stake.	EUR 5,000
Shaw v. Hungary no. 6457/09 26 July 2011	Access and custody rights following child's abduction by applicant's ex-wife.	No adequate measures to facilitate reunification of applicant with his daughter.	EUR 20,000

Larisa Zolotareva v. Russia no. 15003/04 26 July 2011	Applicant complained that bailiff had failed to respect her private life and home when carrying out her eviction.	While the domestic authorities declared bailiff's actions unlawful, they did not offer any compensation to applicant.	EUR 5,000
Liu v. Russia (no. 2) no. 29157/09 26 July 2011	Refusal of a residence permit to first applicant and his administrative removal to China.	No adequate procedural safeguards and no fair balance between the interests at stake.	EUR 1,800 jointly
Grimkovskaya v. Ukraine no. 38182/03 21 July 2011	Nuisances caused by routeing a motorway via applicant's street, which had been ill-equipped for such a purpose.	Applicant had no meaningful opportunity to adduce her viewpoints before an independent authority.	EUR 10,000
Jarnea v. Romania no. 41838/05 19 July 2011	Access to personal files held by former secret services under communist regime.	No effective access to relevant information concerning applicant.	EUR 5,000
K. v. Slovenia no. 41293/05 7 July 2011	Child custody and contact arrangements.	Applicant's contact with his daughter was severely restricted for three years.	EUR 6,000

Case	Principal issue(s)	Violation(s) found	Award
Akar v. Turkey no. 28505/04 21 June 2011	Refusal by the prison authorities to send an applicant's letter.	Interference not in accordance with the law.	EUR 300
Orlić v. Croatia no. 48833/07 21 June 2011	Eviction.	No adequate procedural safeguards.	EUR 2,000
Krušković v. Croatia no. 46185/08 21 June 2011	Recognition of applicant's paternity.	The claim by applicant was ignored for no apparent reason.	EUR 1,800
Pascaud v. France no. 19535/08 16 June 2011	Applicant's inability to secure judicial recognition of his true relationship with his biological father.	No fair balance between competing interests.	EUR 10,000
Zoltán Németh v. Hungary no. 29436/05 14 June 2011	Non-enforcement of access rights.	The authorities did not make reasonable efforts to facilitate reunion, but tolerated mother's unlawful actions.	EUR 20,000

Saleck Bardi v. Spain no. 66167/09 24 May 2011	Applicant was deprived of custody of her daughter, who had been placed in a host family.	The authorities did not make reasonable efforts to facilitate reunion.	EUR 30,000
Abou Amer v. Romania no. 14521/03 24 May 2011	Prosecutor's order to deport the first of two applicants and to ban him from Romania for ten years.	The applicants did not enjoy minimum degree of protection against arbitrariness.	EUR 8,000 jointly
Gluhaković v. Croatia no. 21188/09 12 April 2011	No effective right to contact between applicant and his daughter, given that the courts had ignored his work schedule.	The authorities failed to adequately secure applicant's right to effective contact with his daughter.	EUR 15,000
Di Cecco v. Italy no. 28169/06 15 February 2011	Monitoring of applicant's correspondence with the Court while he was in prison.	Interference not in accordance with the law.	EUR 1,000
Lesiak v. Poland no. 19218/07 1 February 2011	Monitoring of applicant's correspondence with the Court while she was in prison.	Interference not in accordance with the law.	EUR 800

Case	Principal issue(s)	Violation(s) found	Award
Mikolajová v. Slovakia no. 4479/03 18 January 2011	Conclusion in a police decision that applicant had committed a criminal offence, despite complaint against her having been dropped.	Insufficient safeguards to avoid arbitrariness and to secure rights of individual against abuse.	EUR 1,500
Bordeianu v. Moldova no. 49868/08 11 January 2011	Non-enforcement of a judgment granting applicant custody of her daughter.	The authorities' passivity was responsible for severance of relationship between child and her mother.	EUR 10,000
Nurzyński v. Poland no. 46859/06 21 December 2010	During his detention, applicant was deprived of personal contact with his wife and mother.	Refusal to allow applicant to receive family visits was not in accordance with the law.	EUR 1,500
Anayo v. Germany no. 20578/07 21 December 2010	Applicant complained about refusal to grant him access to his children.	No consideration of question as to whether contact would be in children's best interest.	EUR 5,000

Annex 6 Selected cases

Compensation for non-pecuniary damage for violations of Articles 9, 10, 11

Case	Principal issue(s)	Violation(s) found	Award
Eweida and Others v. the United Kingdom nos. 48420/10, 59842/10, 51671/10 and 36516/10 15 January 2013	Restrictions placed by employer on wearing of a cross worn visibly by four applicants.	As to first applicant, no evidence of any real encroachment on interests of others.	EUR 2,000 to first applicant
Fusu Arcadie and Others v. Moldova no. 22218/06 17 July 2012	Eight applicants complained that they were unable to register their church.	No legal basis for the refusal to issue document required for registering applicants' denomination.	EUR 5,000 jointly
Association Les Témoins de Jéhovah v. France no. 8916/05 5 July 2012	Taxation of manual gifts received by association, which represented the main source of its funding.	Interference not prescribed by law.	Finding of a violation was sufficient.

Case	Principal issue(s)	Violation(s) found	Award
Bayatyan v. Armenia no. 23459/03 7 July 2011	Applicant – a Jehovah's Witness – denounced his conviction given for refusing to serve in the army.	Interference not necessary in a democratic society.	EUR 6,000
Jakóbski v. Poland no. 18429/06 7 December 2010	Refusal of a meat-free diet in prison, contrary to requirements of applicant's faith.	No fair balance between interests of the prison authorities and those of applicant to manifest his religion.	EUR 3,000
Ahmet Arslan and Others v. Turkey no. 41135/98 23 February 2010	Conviction under criminal law for manifesting religion through clothing.	No sufficient reasons for interference with applicants' right of freedom to manifest their convictions.	Finding of a violation was sufficient.
Miroļubovs and Others v. Latvia no. 798/05 15 September 2009	Three applicants complained that authorities had intervened in an internal dispute within their religious community.	The courts failed to examine the case on the merits and to afford redress for damage sustained.	EUR 4,000 to each
Soltész v. Slovakia no. 11867/09 22 October 2013	Applicant complained that he had been ordered to pay damages in connection with publication of an article of which he was author.	Defective legal protection received by applicant at domestic level.	EUR 5,850

Ricci v. Italy no. 30210/06 8 October 2013	Conviction and sentence for disclosing confidential images recorded for internal use of a television station.	No exceptional circumstance justifying recourse to sanctioning of such harshness.	Finding of a violation was sufficient.
Nagla v. Latvia no. 73469/10 16 July 2013	Applicant alleged that she had been compelled to disclose information that had enabled a journalistic source to be identified.	No sufficient reasons were given for overriding the public interest in protection of journalist's freedom of expression.	EUR 10,000
Belek and Özkurt v. Turkey no. 1544/07 16 July 2013	Two applicants, owner and editor-in-chief of a daily newspaper, complained about their criminal conviction.	No sufficient grounds for justifying conviction.	EUR 3,000 to each
Eon v. France no. 26118/10 14 March 2013	Applicant was found guilty of insulting the French President and received a suspended fine of EUR 30.	Recourse to criminal penalty was disproportionate and unnecessary.	Finding of a violation was sufficient.
Bugan v. Romania no. 13824/06 12 February 2013	Applicant was ordered to pay damages to the director of a public hospital because of article he had written about him.	The courts failed to give relevant and sufficient reasons for interference.	EUR 4,500

Case	Principal issue(s)	Violation(s) found	Award
Tatár and Fáber v. Hungary nos. 26005/08 and 26160/08 12 June 2012	Prosecution conducted against applicants for having organized a political 'performance'.	No relevant and sufficient arguments for justifying necessity to sanction applicants.	EUR 1,500 to each
Martin and Others v. France no. 30002/08 12 April 2012	Search of premises of a daily newspaper to determine how journalists obtained a copy of a confidential draft report.	No sufficient arguments for justifying search, thus measure was disproportionate.	EUR 5,000 to each
Kaperzyński v. Poland no. 43206/07 3 April 2012	Applicant – editor-in-chief of a local newspaper – complained about his criminal conviction.	Interference not necessary in a democratic society.	EUR 3,000
Tuşalp v. Turkey nos. 32131/08 and 41617/08 21 February 2012	Judgments given in civil cases against applicant breached his right to freedom of expression.	No pressing social need for putting Prime Minister's personality rights above applicant's rights.	EUR 5,000
Lahtonen v. Finland no. 29576/09 17 January 2012	Conviction and sentence not proportionate to accepted aims of limiting freedom of expression.	No fair balance between competing interests at stake.	EUR 2,000

Case	Principal issue(s)	Violation(s) found	Award
John Anthony Mizzi v. Malta no. 17320/10 22 November 2011	Judgments finding applicant guilty of defamation and ordering him to pay civil damages were in breach of his right to freedom of expression.	The courts upheld the right of reputation without explaining why this outweighed applicant's freedom of expression.	EUR 4,000
Fratanoló v. Hungary no. 29459/10 3 November 2011	Prosecution for having worn a red star.	The government did not prove that restriction corresponded to a 'pressing social need'.	EUR 4,000
Gün and Others v. Turkey no. 8029/07 18 June 2013	Prison sentence and fine imposed for taking part in an illegal demonstration.	Criminal conviction did not correspond to a 'pressing social need'.	EUR 7,500 to each
Sáska v. Hungary no. 58050/08 27 November 2012	Refusal of plaintiff's application to organize a demonstration.	Prohibition of demonstration did not respond to a 'pressing social need'.	Finding of a violation was sufficient.
Disk and Kesk v. Turkey no. 38676/08 27 November 2012	Police intervention in the Labour Day Celebrations.	Forceful intervention was disproportionate and was not necessary for prevention of disorder.	Finding of a violation was sufficient.

Case	Principal issue(s)	Violation(s) found	Award
Aşıcı v. Turkey (no. 2) no. 26656/04 31 January 2012	Police intervention hindered applicant's freedom of association.	No reasons to justify 'pressing social need' requiring police intervention.	EUR 1,800
Szerdahelyi v. Hungary no. 30385/07 17 January 2012	Police intervention and subsequent measures prevented applicant from exercising his right to peaceful assembly.	Ban on a peaceful protest was devoid of basis in domestic law and could not be regarded as 'prescribed by law'.	EUR 4,000
Patyi v. Hungary no. 35127/08 17 January 2012	Police measure prevented applicant from exercising his right to peaceful assembly.	Ban at material time was devoid of basis in domestic law.	EUR 2,400
Singartiyski and Others v. Bulgaria no. 48284/07 18 October 2011	Five applicants were banned from holding a meeting.	Regional Governor relied on grounds which, at the time that the Governor made his decision, the Court had already found deficient.	EUR 9,000 jointly

Compensation for non-pecuniary damage for violations of Article 1 of Protocol No. 1

Case	Principal issue(s)	Violation(s) found	Award
Benenati and Scillamà v. Italy no. 33312/03 4 February 2014	Three applicants, owners of a piece of land, complained about constructive expropriation.	Unlawful interference.	EUR 10,000 jointly
Giannitto v. Italy no. 1780/04 28 January 2014	Constructive expropriation.	Unlawful interference.	EUR 5,000
Pascucci v. Italy no. 1537/04 14 January 2014	Constructive expropriation.	Unlawful interference.	EUR 10,000
Danielyan and Others v. Armenia no. 25825/05 9 October 2012	Expropriation of applicants' house.	Unlawful interference.	EUR 1,500 to each

Case	Principal issue(s)	Violation(s) found	Award
Catholic Archdiocese of Alba Iulia v. Romania no. 33003/03 25 September 2012	Failure to return to religious community one of the richest collections of ancient books in Romania which had been confiscated during communist period.	No legitimate justification for the state's failure to act for fourteen years.	EUR 15,000
Herrmann v. Germany no. 9300/07 26 June 2012	Applicant denounced compulsory membership of a hunting association and obligation for him to tolerate hunting on his property.	Obligation to tolerate hunting imposed disproportionate burden on applicant, who was opposed to hunting for ethical reasons.	EUR 5,000
Kostadimas and Others v. Greece nos. 20299/09 and 27307/09 26 June 2012	Applicants complained about retrospective adjustment of their retirement pensions.	No fair balance between interests at stake.	Finding of a violation was sufficient.
Milosavljev v. Serbia no. 15112/07 12 June 2012	Applicant complained about confiscation of his vehicle.	Confiscation was disproportionate and it imposed an excessive burden on applicant.	EUR 7,500

Andreyeva v. Russia no. 73659/10 10 April 2012	Applicant alleged that she had been unable to obtain any payment from the state on Soviet bonds of a 1982 issue belonging to her.	No fair balance between applicant's interests and public interest in the area of state finances.	EUR 4,300
Gubiyev v. Russia no. 29309/03 19 July 2011	Applicant complained about destruction of his company's property and refusal of compensation.	Unlawful interference.	EUR 6,000
Yıldırır v. Turkey no. 21482/03 5 April 2011	Applicant denounced demolition of his house without payment of compensation.	Failure to award any compensation.	EUR 2,500
Tarnawczyk v. Poland no. 27480/02 7 December 2010	Land designated for expropriation and unsuccessful attempts to secure compensation.	Applicant had to bear an excessive individual burden.	EUR 1,000
Consorts Richet and Le Ber v. France nos. 18990/07 and 23905/07 18 November 2010	The state has not honoured its contractual agreements entered into with applicants.	Applicants had to bear excessive individual burden.	EUR 10,000 to one of them EUR 3,000 to the other four

Case	Principal issue(s)	Violation(s) found	Award
Schembri and Others v. Malta no. 42583/06 28 September 2010	Compensation awarded for land expropriation was not fair and adequate.	Compensation reflected values applicable decades earlier, although its payment had been deferred for at least twenty years.	EUR 2,500 to each
Đokić v. Bosnia and Herzegovina no. 6518/04 27 May 2010	Applicant failed, despite legally valid purchase contract, to repossess his pre-war flat and to register his title.	Inadequate legal framework for compensation.	EUR 5,000
Kasyanchuk v. Ukraine no. 4187/05 10 December 2009	Impossibility to recover debt from state-owned company for a long period of time.	Delay in payment exceeded five years.	EUR 2,100
Naydenov v. Bulgaria no. 17353/03 26 November 2009	No restitution or compensation for property because of deficiencies in domestic legislation.	Failure to provide adequate and effective framework for restitution.	EUR 500
Kök and Others v. Turkey no. 20868/04 24 November 2009	Deprivation of property, designated as forest area, without compensation.	Lack of compensation.	Finding of a violation was sufficient.

Suljagić v. Bosnia and Herzegovina no. 27912/02 3 November 2009	Domestic legislation on old foreign-currency savings failed to strike fair balance between relevant interests.	Deficient implementation of domestic legislation on old foreign-currency savings.	EUR 5,000
Jenisová v. Slovakia no. 58764/00 3 November 2009	Compulsory lease of applicant's land.	Applicant received low compensation for the letting out of her land.	EUR 1,000
Šefčíková v. Slovakia no. 6284/02 3 November 2009	Compulsory lease of applicant's land.	Applicant received low compensation for the letting out of her land.	EUR 2,000
Bohnenschuh v. Romania no. 14427/05 27 October 2009	Two applicants alleged an inability to obtain compensation for property illegally nationalized.	Lack of compensation.	EUR 2,000 jointly
Efendioğlu v. Turkey no. 3869/04 27 October 2009	Deprivation of land without payment of compensation.	Annulment of title deed without compensation.	Finding of a violation was sufficient.
Rukas v. Ukraine no. 15879/06 15 October 2009	Non-enforcement of judgment regarding salary arrears.	Applicant was prevented from receiving the money to which he was entitled.	EUR 1,800

Case	Principal issue(s)	Violation(s) found	Award
Adzhigovich v. Russia no. 23202/05 8 October 2009	Confiscation of applicant's money did not have sufficient and clear basis in domestic law.	Impugned interference with applicant's property rights was not lawful.	EUR 1,000
Amato Gauci v. Malta no. 47045/06 15 September 2009	New law imposed on applicant a unilateral lease relationship for an indeterminate time without providing him with fair and adequate rent.	No fair balance between general and individual interests.	EUR 1,500
Trgo v. Croatia no. 35298/04 11 June 2009	The courts refused to acknowledge applicant's ownership, which he had acquired by adverse possession.	Applicant should not bear consequences of the state's own mistake committed by enacting unconstitutional legislation.	Finding of a violation was sufficient.
Buczkiewicz v. Poland no. 10446/03 26 February 2008	Land which two applicants owned was designated for expropriation and they were not entitled to any compensation.	Inadequacies of land development plan and absence of any reasonable timeframe.	EUR 5,000 jointly
Cazacu v. Moldova no. 40117/02 23 October 2007	Applicant's employer refused to pay his redundancy payments and the courts accepted this refusal, despite clearly contrary legal provisions.	Unlawful refusal of the domestic courts to allow applicant's claims.	EUR 2,000

BIBLIOGRAPHY

Books

Bates, E., *The Evolution of the European Convention on Human Rights: From Its Inception to the Creation of a Permanent Court of Human Rights*, Oxford University Press, 2010

Burgorgue-Larsen, L., and Úbeda de Torres, A., *Les grandes décisions de la Cour interaméricaine des droits de l'homme*, Brussels: Bruylant, 2008

The Inter-American Court of Human Rights: Case Law and Commentary, Oxford University Press, 2011

Burnett, J., et al. (eds.), *Guidelines for the Assessment of General Damages in Personal Injury Cases*, Oxford University Press, 2012

Clements, L. J., Mole, N., and Simmons, A., *European Human Rights: Taking a Case under the Convention*, London: Sweet & Maxwell, 1999

Council of Europe, *Collected Edition of the 'Travaux Préparatoires' of the European Convention on Human Rights*, 8 vols., The Hague: Martinus Nijhoff Publishers, 1975–85

Crawford, J., *The International Law Commission's Articles on State Responsibility: Introduction, Text, and Commentaries*, Cambridge University Press, 2002

D'Argent, P., *Les réparations de guerre en droit international public: la responsabilité internationale des États à l'épreuve de la guerre*, Brussels: Bruylant, 2002

Dailler, P., Forteau, M., and Pellet, A., *Droit international public*, Paris: LGDJ, 2009

Delzangles, B., *Activisme et Autolimitation de la Cour européenne des droits de l'homme*, Clermont-Ferrand: Fondation Varenne, 2009

Dwertmann, E., *The Reparation System of the International Criminal Court*, Leiden: Martinus Nijhoff Publishers, 2010

Emberland, M., *The Human Rights of Companies: Exploring the Structure of ECHR Protection*, Oxford University Press, 2006

Fawcett, J. E. S., *The Application of the European Convention on Human Rights*, Oxford: Clarendon Press, 1987

Franck, T. M., *Fairness in International Law and Institutions*, Oxford: Clarendon Press, 1995

Gray, C., *Judicial Remedies in International Law*, Oxford: Clarendon Press, 1990

Harris, D. J., et al., *Law of the European Convention on Human Rights*, Oxford University Press, 2009

Horton Rogers, W. V. (ed.), *Damages for Non-Pecuniary Loss in a Comparative Perspective*, Vienna: Springer, 2001

Keller, H., Forowicz, M., and Engi, L., *Friendly Settlements before the European Court of Human Rights: Theory and Practice*, Oxford University Press, 2010

Kilkelly, U., *The Child and the European Convention on Human Rights*, Aldershot: Ashgate, 1999

Koskenniemi, M., *From Apology to Utopia: The Structure of International Legal Argument*, Cambridge University Press, 2005

Koziol, H., and Wilcox, V. (eds.), *Punitive Damages: Common Law and Civil Law Perspectives*, Vienna: Springer, 2009

Lambert Abdelgawad, E. (ed.), *Preventing and Sanctioning Hindrances to the Right of Individual Petition before the European Court of Human Rights*, Cambridge: Intersentia, 2011

Leach, P., *Taking a Case to the European Court of Human Rights*, Oxford University Press, 2011

Lemmens, P., and Vandenhole, W. (eds.), *Protocol No. 14 and the Reform of the European Court of Human Rights*, Antwerp: Intersentia, 2005

Pasqualucci, J. M., *The Practice and Procedure of the Inter-American Court of Human Rights*, Cambridge University Press, 2013

Reid, K., *A Practitioner's Guide to the European Convention on Human Rights*, London: Sweet & Maxwell, 2011

Rivière, F., *Les opinions séparées des juges à la Cour européenne des droits de l'homme*, Brussels: Bruylant, 2004

Rossi, C. R., *Equity and International Law: A Legal Realist Approach to International Decisionmaking*, New York: Transnational Publishers, 1993

Schachter, O., *International Law in Theory and Practice*, Dordrecht: Martinus Nijhoff Publishers, 1991

Shelton, D., *Remedies in International Human Rights Law*, Oxford University Press, 2005

Van Dijk, P., et al., *Theory and Practice of the European Convention on Human Rights*, Antwerp: Intersentia, 2006

White, R., and Ovey, C., *The European Convention on Human Rights*, Oxford University Press, 2010

Articles, book chapters and reports

Alkema, E. A., 'The European Convention as a Constitution and Its Court as a Constitutional Court', in P. Mahoney et al. (eds.), *Protection des droits de l'homme: la perspective européenne, mélanges à la mémoire de Rolv Ryssdal*

= *Protecting Human Rights: The European Perspective, Studies in Memory of Rolv Ryssdal*, Cologne: Carl Heymanns Verlag, 2000, 41–63

Ang, F., and Berghmans, E., 'Friendly Settlements and Striking Out of Applications', in P. Lemmens and W. Vandenhole (eds.), *Protocol No. 14 and the Reform of the European Court of Human Rights*, Antwerp: Intersentia, 2005, 89–104

Antkowiak, T. M., 'An Emerging Mandate for International Courts: Victim-Centered Remedies and Restorative Justice', *Stanford Journal of International Law* 47 (2011), 279–332

Barbier, S., 'Assurances and Guarantees of Non-Repetition', in J. Crawford, A. Pellet and S. Olleson (eds.), *The Law of International Responsibility*, Oxford University Press, 2010, 551–61

Barthe-Gay, C., 'Réflexions sur la satisfaction en droit international', *Annuaire français de droit international* 49 (2003), 105–28

Baudoin, M.-E., 'Consonances et dissonances dans le discours européen des droits de l'homme – Violationnistes et étatistes: la définition du rôle du juge européen', in S. Hennette-Vauchez and J.-M. Sorel (eds.), *Les droits de l'homme ont-ils constitutionnalisé le monde?*, Brussels: Bruylant, 2011, 65–92

Becue, E., et al., 'The Administrative, Tax, Financial and Cost Hindrances against NGOs and Lawyers', in E. Lambert Abdelgawad (ed.), *Preventing and Sanctioning Hindrances to the Right of Individual Petition before the European Court of Human Rights*, Cambridge: Intersentia, 2011, 136–47

Berger, V., 'Le règlement amiable devant la Cour', in L.-E. Pettiti, E. Decaux and P.-H. Imbert (eds.), *La Convention européenne des droits de l'homme. Commentaire article par article*, Paris: Economica, 1999, 783–92

'Le "préjudice important" selon le Protocole n° 14 à la Convention européenne des droits de l'homme: questions et réflexions', in M. G. Kohen (ed.), *Promoting Justice, Human Rights and Conflict Resolution through International Law = La promotion de la justice, des droits de l'homme et du règlement des conflits par le droit international: Liber Amicorum Lucius Caflisch*, Leiden: Martinus Nijhoff Publishers, 2007, 81–91

Bernhardt, R., 'Human Rights and Judicial Review: The European Court of Human Rights', in D. M. Beatty (ed.), *Human Rights and Judicial Review: A Comparative Perspective*, Dordrecht: Martinus Nijhoff Publishers, 1994, 297–319

Birsan, C., 'Les aspects nouveaux de l'application des articles 41 et 46 de la Convention dans la jurisprudence de la Cour européenne des droits de l'homme', in H. Hartig (ed.), *Trente ans de droit européen des droits de l'homme: études à la mémoire de Wolfgang Strasser*, Brussels: Bruylant, 2007, 19–44

Cabral Barreto, I., 'Le règlement amiable devant la Cour européenne des droits de l'homme', *Bulletin des droits de l'homme* 10 (2002), 27–54

Caflisch, L., 'The *Pellegrin* Ruling: Origins and Consequences', in L. C. Vohrah et al. (eds.), *Man's Inhumanity to Man: Essays on International Law in Honour of Antonio Cassese*, The Hague: Kluwer Law International, 2003, 183–209

'L'efficacité du système européen de protection des droits de l'homme', in L. Caflisch et al. (eds.), *El derecho internacional: normas, hechos y valores: Liber Amicorum José Antonio Pastor Ridruejo*, Madrid: Universidad Complutense, 2005, 43–58

'La mise en oeuvre des arrêts de la Cour: nouvelles tendances', in F. Salerno (ed.), *La nouvelle procédure devant la Cour européenne des droits de l'homme après le Protocole n° 14: actes du colloque tenu à Ferrara les 29 et 30 avril 2005*, Brussels: Bruylant, 2007, 157–74

'Waivers in International and European Human Rights Law', in M. H. Arsanjani et al. (eds.), *Looking to the Future: Essays on International Law in Honor of W. Michael Reisman*, Leiden: Martinus Nijhoff Publishers, 2011, 407–31

Cameron, I., 'Damages for Violations of ECHR Rights: The Swedish Example', *Swedish Studies in European Law* 1 (2006), 97–128

Cohen-Jonathan, G., and Flauss, J.-F., 'Cour européenne des droits de l'homme et droit international général', *Annuaire français de droit international* 48 (2002), 675–93

Colandrea, V., 'On the Power of the European Court of Human Rights to Order Specific Non-Monetary Measures: Some Remarks in Light of the *Assanidze*, *Broniowski* and *Sejdovic* Cases', *Human Rights Law Review* 7, no. 2 (2007), 396–411

Costa, J.-P., 'The Provision of Compensation under Article 41 of the European Convention on Human Rights', in D. Fairgrieve, M. Andenas and J. Bell (eds.), *Tort Liability of Public Authorities in Comparative Perspective*, London: British Institute of International and Comparative Law, 2002, 3–16

Coufoudakis, V., 'Cyprus and the European Convention on Human Rights: The Law and Politics of *Cyprus v. Turkey*, Applications 6780/74 and 6950/75', *Human Rights Quarterly* 4, no. 4 (1982), 450–73

De Salvia, M., 'La satisfaction équitable au titre des mesures individuelles et la pratique des organes de la Convention européenne des droits de l'homme: qu'en est-il du principe de sécurité juridique?', in H. Hartig (ed.), *Trente ans de droit européen des droits de l'homme: études à la mémoire de Wolfgang Strasser*, Brussels: Bruylant, 2007, 45–53

'Le principe de l'octroi subsidiaire des dommages-intérêts: d'une morale des droits de l'homme à une morale simplement indemnitaire?', in J.-F. Flauss and E. Lambert Abdelgawad (eds.), *La pratique d'indemnisation par la Cour européenne des droits de l'homme*, Brussels: Bruylant, 2011, 9–26

De Schutter, O., 'Le règlement amiable dans la Convention européenne des droits de l'homme: entre théorie de la fonction de juger et théorie de la négociation', in *Les droits de l'homme au seuil du troisième millénaire: mélanges en hommage à Pierre Lambert*, Brussels: Bruylant, 2000, 225–61

'L'accès des personnes morales à la Cour européenne des droits de l'homme', in *Avancées et confins actuels des droits de l'homme aux niveaux international, européen et national: mélanges offerts à Silvio Marcus Helmons*, Brussels: Bruylant, 2003, 83–108

'La protection juridictionnelle provisoire devant la Cour européenne des droits de l'homme', in H. Ruiz Fabri and J.-M. Sorel (eds.), *Le contentieux de l'urgence et l'urgence dans le contentieux devant les juridictions internationales: regards croisés*, Paris: Pedone, 2003, 105–48

Dembour, M.-B., 'What It Takes to Have a Case: The Backstage Story of *Muskhadzhiyeva v. Belgium* (Illegality of Children's Immigration Detention)', in E. Lambert Abdelgawad (ed.), *Preventing and Sanctioning Hindrances to the Right of Individual Petition before the European Court of Human Rights*, Cambridge: Intersentia, 2011, 75–104

Drzemczewski, A., 'Decision on the Merits: By the Committee of Ministers', in R. St. J. Macdonald, F. Matscher and H. Petzold (eds.), *The European System for the Protection of Human Rights*, Dordrecht: Martinus Nijhoff Publishers, 1993, 733–54

'The European Human Rights Convention: Protocol No. 11 – Entry into Force and First Year of Application', *Human Rights Law Journal* 21, nos. 1–3 (2000), 1–17

Dubout, E., 'Les "nouvelles" frontières des droits de l'homme et la définition du rôle de juge européen', in S. Hennette-Vauchez and J.-M. Sorel (eds.), *Les droits de l'homme ont-ils constitutionnalisé le monde?*, Brussels: Bruylant, 2011, 37–63

Emberland, M., 'Compensating Companies for Non-Pecuniary Damage: *Comingersoll S.A. v. Portugal* and the Ambivalent Expansion of the ECHR Scope', *British Yearbook of International Law* 74, no. 1 (2003), 409–32

Enrich Mas, M., 'Right to Compensation under Article 50', in R. St. J. Macdonald, F. Matscher and H. Petzold (eds.), *The European System for the Protection of Human Rights*, Dordrecht: Martinus Nijhoff Publishers, 1993, 775–90

Feldman, T., 'Indirect Victims, Direct Injury: Recognising Relatives as Victims under the European Human Rights System', *European Human Rights Law Review*, no. 1 (2009), 50–69

Fiss, O., 'Against Settlement', *Yale Law Journal* 93, no. 6 (1984), 1073–90

Flauss, J.-F., 'La pratique du Comité des ministres du Conseil de l'Europe au titre de l'article 32 de la Convention européenne des droits de l'homme (1985–1987)', *Annuaire français de droit international* 33 (1987), 728–48

'La "satisfaction équitable" devant les organes de la Convention européenne des droits de l'homme: développements récents', *Juris-Classeur Europe* 2, no. 6 (1992), 1–4

'Convention européenne des droits de l'homme: une nouvelle interlocutrice pour le juriste d'affaires', *Revue de jurisprudence de droit des affaires* 6 (1995), 524–45

'La réparation due en cas de violation de la Convention européenne des droits de l'homme', *Journal des Tribunaux* 4, no. 25 (1996), 8–15

Frowein, J. A., 'La notion de victime dans la Convention européenne des droits de l'homme', in *Studi in onore di Giuseppe Sperduti*, Milan: Giuffrè, 1984, 587–99

Gardbaum, S., 'Human Rights and International Constitutionalism', in J. L. Dunoff and J. P. Trachtman (eds.), *Ruling the World? Constitutionalism, International Law, and Global Governance*, Cambridge University Press, 2009, 233–57

Garin, A., 'La perte de chance, un préjudice indemnisable: contribution à une problématique de l'indemnisation du dommage par la Cour européenne des droits de l'homme', in J.-F. Flauss and E. Lambert Abdelgawad (eds.), *La pratique d'indemnisation par la Cour européenne des droits de l'homme*, Brussels: Bruylant, 2011, 155–85

Gassama, C., 'Le principe de *restitutio in integrum* dans le contentieux international des droits de l'homme', *Mediterranean Journal of Human Rights* 9 (2005), 121–62

Golsong, H., 'The European Court of Human Rights and the National Law-Maker: Some General Reflections', in F. Matscher and H. Petzold (eds.), *Protecting Human Rights: The European Dimension – Studies in Honour of G. J. Wiarda = Protection des droits de l'homme: la dimension européenne – Mélanges en l'honneur de G. J. Wiarda*, Cologne: Carl Heymanns Verlag, 1988, 239–44

Greer, S., 'Reforming the European Convention on Human Rights: Towards Protocol 14', *Public Law* (2003), 663–73

Heiskanen, V., 'The United Nations Compensation Commission', *Collected Courses of the Hague Academy of International Law* 296 (2002), 255–398

Hondius, F. W., 'The Other Forum', in F. Matscher and H. Petzold (eds.), *Protecting Human Rights: The European Dimension – Studies in Honour of G. J. Wiarda = Protection des droits de l'homme: la dimension européenne – Mélanges en l'honneur de G. J. Wiarda*, Cologne: Carl Heymanns Verlag, 1988, 245–51

Jennings, R. Y., 'Equity and Equitable Principles', *Annuaire suisse de droit international* 42 (1986), 27–38

'The Judicial Function and the Rule of Law in International Relations', in *International Law at the Time of Its Codification: Essays in Honour of Roberto Ago*, Vol. III, Milan: Giuffrè, 1987, 139–51

Jorgensen, N., 'A Reappraisal of Punitive Damages in International Law', *British Yearbook of International Law* 68 (1997), 247–66

Keller, H., Fischer, A. and Kühne, D., 'Debating the Future of the European Court of Human Rights after the Interlaken Conference: Two Innovative Proposals', *European Journal of International Law* 21, no. 4 (2010), 1025–48

Kerbrat, Y., 'Interaction between the Forms of Reparation', in J. Crawford, A. Pellet and S. Olleson (eds.), *The Law of International Responsibility*, Oxford University Press, 2010, 573–87

Kiss, A., 'Conciliation', in R. St. J. Macdonald, F. Matscher and H. Petzold (eds.), *The European System for the Protection of Human Rights*, Dordrecht: Martinus Nijhoff Publishers, 1993, 703–11

Krüger, H.-C., 'Reflections on Some Aspects of Just Satisfaction under the European Convention on Human Rights', in G. Cohen-Jonathan, J.-F. Flauss and P. Lambert (eds.), *Liber Amicorum Marc-André Eissen*, Brussels: Bruylant, 1995, 255–69

Lambert Abdelgawad, E., 'La saisine de la Cour européenne des droits de l'-homme', in H. Ruiz Fabri and J. M. Sorel (eds.), *La saisine des juridictions internationales*, Paris: Pedone, 2006, 211–49

Lapidoth, R., 'Equity in International Law', *Proceedings of the Annual Meeting (American Society of International Law)* 81 (1987), 138–47

Leckie, S., 'The Inter-State Complaint Procedure in International Human Rights Law: Hopeful Prospects or Wishful Thinking?', *Human Rights Quarterly* 10, no. 2 (1988), 249–303

Lester, A., 'The European Court of Human Rights after 50 Years', in J. Christoffersen and M. R. Madsen (eds.), *The European Court of Human Rights between Law and Politics*, Oxford University Press, 2011, 98–118

Leuprecht, P., 'The Protection of Human Rights by Political Bodies: The Example of the Committee of Ministers of the Council of Europe = Der Schutz der Menschenrechte durch politische Organe: das Beispiel des Ministerkomitees des Europarates', in M. Nowak et al. (eds.), *Fortschritt im Bewusstsein der Grund- und Menschenrechte: Festschrift für Felix Ermacora = Progress in the Spirit of Human Rights*, Kehl: N. P. Engel, 1988, 95–108

'Article 32', in L.-E. Pettiti, E. Decaux and P.-H. Imbert (eds.), *La Convention européenne des droits de l'homme. Commentaire article par article*, Paris: Economica, 1999, 699–710

Loucaides, L. G., 'Reparation for Violations of Human Rights under the European Convention and *Restitutio in Integrum*', *European Human Rights Law Review*, no. 2 (2008), 182–92

Mowbray, A. R., 'The European Court of Human Rights' Approach to Just Satisfaction', *Public Law* (1997), 647–59

Myjer, E., 'Article 1 Protocol 1 and the Entitlement of Just Satisfaction', in H. Vandenberghe, M. Muylle and T. Viaene (eds.), *Propriété et droits de l'homme = Property and Human Rights*, Bruges: Die Keure/La Charte; Bruylant, 2006, 99–128

Myjer, E., and Kempees, P., 'Notes on Reparations under the European Human Rights System', *Inter-American and European Human Rights Journal* 2, nos. 1–2 (2009), 81–98

Nascimbene, B., 'Violation "structurelle", violation "grave" et exigences interprétatives de la Convention européenne des droits de l'homme', in F. Salerno (ed.), *La nouvelle procédure devant la Cour européenne des droits de l'homme après le Protocole n° 14: actes du colloque tenu à Ferrara les 29 et 30 avril 2005*, Brussels: Bruylant, 2007, 135–48

Nicolaou, G., 'The New Perspective of the European Court of Human Rights on the Effectiveness of Its Judgments', in C. Hohmann-Dennhardt, P. Masuch and M. Villiger (eds.), *Grundrechte und Solidarität: Durchsetzung und Verfahren: Festschrift für Renate Jaeger*, Kehl: N. P. Engel, 2011, 163–78

Nørgaard, C. A., and Krüger, H. C., 'Article 28-1-b et Article 28-2', in L.-E. Pettiti, E. Decaux and P.-H. Imbert (eds.), *La Convention européenne des droits de l'homme. Commentaire article par article*, Paris: Economica, 1999, 661–79

Nowicki, M. A., 'Non-Governmental Organisations (NGOs) before the European Commission of Human Rights', in M. De Salvia and M. Villiger (eds.), *The Birth of European Human Rights Law = L'éclosion du droit européen des droits de l'homme: Liber Amicorum Carl Aage Norgaard*, Baden-Baden: Nomos, 1998, 267–73

Orrego-Vicuña, F., 'Individuals and Non-State Entities before International Courts and Tribunals', *Max Planck Yearbook of United Nations Law* 5 (2001), 53–66

Padelletti, M. L., 'Les nouvelles conditions de recevabilité matérielles d'une requête individuelle: l'entité du préjudice invoqué par la victime', in F. Salerno (ed.), *La nouvelle procédure devant la Cour européenne des droits de l'homme après le Protocole n° 14: actes du colloque tenu à Ferrara les 29 et 30 avril 2005*, Brussels: Bruylant, 2007, 85–105

Palmisano, G., 'La garantie de non-répétition entre codification et réalisation juridictionnelle du droit: à propos de l'affaire *LaGrand*', *Revue generale de droit international public* 106 (2002), 753–89

Pettiti, L.-E., 'Le système de Strasbourg. Les recours interétatiques dans le système de la Convention européenne des droits de l'homme', in D. Bardonnet (ed.), *The Peaceful Settlement of International Disputes in Europe: Future Prospects*, Dordrecht: Martinus Nijhoff Publishers, 1991, 331–95

'Réflexions sur les principes et les mécanismes de la Convention. De l'idéal de 1950 à l'humble réalité d'aujourd'hui', in L.-E. Pettiti, E. Decaux and P.-H.

Imbert (eds.), *La Convention européenne des droits de l'homme. Commentaire article par article*, Paris: Economica, 1999, 27–40

Piacentini de Andrade, I., 'L'affaire *Loayza Tamayo c/ Pérou* et ses suites', in E. Lambert Abdelgawad and K. Martin-Chenut (eds.), *Réparer les violations graves et massives des droits de l'homme: la Cour interaméricaine, pionnière et modèle?*, Paris: Société de législation comparée, 2010, 111–33

Popovic, D., 'Pilot Judgments of the European Court of Human Rights', in Steering Committee for Human Rights (ed.), *Reforming the European Convention on Human Rights: A Work in Progress*, Strasbourg: Council of Europe, 2009, 352–62

Prebensen, S. C., 'Inter-State Complaints under Treaty Provisions – The Experience under the European Convention on Human Rights', in G. Alfredsson et al. (eds.), *International Human Rights Monitoring Mechanisms: Essays in Honour of Jakob Th. Möller*, The Hague: Martinus Nijhoff Publishers, 2001, 533–59

Reffi, G. B., and Bultrini, A., 'Le décès de la partie requérante dans la procédure devant les organes de la Convention européenne des droits de l'homme', in M. De Salvia and M. Villiger (eds.), *The Birth of European Human Rights Law = L'éclosion du droit européen des droits de l'homme: Liber Amicorum Carl Aage Norgaard*, Baden-Baden: Nomos, 1998, 291–300

Reid, K., 'Article 25 of the Convention: Application by Children', in M. De Salvia and M. Villiger (eds.), *The Birth of European Human Rights Law = L'éclosion du droit européen des droits de l'homme: Liber Amicorum Carl Aage Norgaard*, Baden-Baden: Nomos, 1998, 301–7

Ress, G., 'Reflections on the Protection of Property under the European Convention on Human Rights', in S. Breitenmoser et al. (eds.), *Human Rights, Democracy and the Rule of Law = Menschenrechte, Demokratie und Rechtsstaat = Droits de l'homme, démocratie et état de droit: Liber Amicorum Luzius Wildhaber*, Zurich: Dike, 2007, 625–45

Rigaux, F., 'International Responsibility and the Principle of Causality', in M. Ragazzi (ed.), *International Responsibility Today: Essays in Memory of Oscar Schachter*, Leiden: Martinus Nijhoff Publishers, 2005, 81–91

Rogge, K., 'The "Victim" Requirement in Article 25 of the European Convention on Human Rights', in F. Matscher and H. Petzold (eds.), *Protecting Human Rights: The European Dimension – Studies in Honour of G. J. Wiarda = Protection des droits de l'homme: la dimension européenne – Mélanges en l'honneur de G. J. Wiarda*, Cologne: Carl Heymanns Verlag, 1988, 539–45

'Inter-State Cases under Article 33 of the European Convention on Human Rights', in H. Hartig (ed.), *Trente ans de droit européen des droits de l'homme: études à la mémoire de Wolfgang Strasser*, Brussels: Bruylant, 2007, 289–306

Rozakis, C., 'Unilateral Declarations as Means of Settling Human Rights Disputes: A New Tool for the Resolution of Disputes in the ECHR's Procedure', in M. G. Kohen (ed.), *Promoting Justice, Human Rights and Conflict Resolution through International Law = La promotion de la justice, des droits de l'homme et du règlement des conflits par le droit international: Liber Amicorum Lucius Caflisch*, Leiden: Martinus Nijhoff Publishers, 2007, 1003–14

Sansonetis, N., 'Costs and Expenses', in R. St. J. Macdonald, F. Matscher and H. Petzold (eds.), *The European System for the Protection of Human Rights*, Dordrecht: Martinus Nijhoff Publishers, 1993, 755–73

Sardaro, P., '*Jus Non Dicere* for Allegations of Serious Violations of Human Rights: Questionable Trends in the Recent Case Law of the Strasbourg Court', *European Human Rights Law Review*, no. 6 (2003), 601–30

Schwaighofer, C., 'Legal Persons, Organisations, Shareholders as Applicants: Article 25 of the Convention', in M. De Salvia and M. Villiger (eds.), *The Birth of European Human Rights Law = L'éclosion du droit européen des droits de l'homme: Liber Amicorum Carl Aage Norgaard*, Baden-Baden: Nomos, 1998, 321–31

Sharpe, J. L., 'Awards of Costs and Expenses under Article 50 of the European Convention on Human Rights', *Law Society's Gazette* (1984), 905–7

Sørensen, M., 'Lost Opportunity: When Human Rights Were Sacrificed', reproduced in English by the Consultative Assembly in AS/Inf (70) 10, Strasbourg: Council of Europe, 1970

Stern, B., 'The Elements of an Internationally Wrongful Act', in J. Crawford, A. Pellet and S. Olleson (eds.), *The Law of International Responsibility*, Oxford University Press, 2010, 193–220

Stone Sweet, A., 'On the Constitutionalisation of the Convention: The European Court of Human Rights as a Constitutional Court', *Faculty Scholarship Series* 71 (2009), 1–14

Sudre, F., 'Existe-t-il un ordre public européen?', in P. Tavernier (ed.), *Quelle Europe pour les droits de l'homme? La Cour de Strasbourg et la réalisation d'une 'Union plus étroite' (35 années de jurisprudence: 1959–1994)*, Brussels: Bruylant, 1996, 39–80

Tanzi, A., 'Is Damage a Distinct Condition for the Existence of an Internationally Wrongful Act?', in M. Spinedi and B. Simma (eds.), *United Nations Codification of State Responsibility*, New York: Oceana, 1987, 1–33

Tavernier, P., 'La contribution de la jurisprudence de la Cour européenne des droits de l'homme relative au droit de la responsabilité internationale en matière de réparation – Une remise en cause nécessaire', *Revue trimestrielle des droits de l'homme* 72 (2007), 945–66

Tomuschat, C., '*Quo Vadis, Argentoratum*? The Success Story of the European Convention on Human Rights – and a Few Dark Stains', *Human Rights Law Journal* 13, nos. 11–12 (1992), 401–6

'Just Satisfaction under Article 50 of the European Convention on Human Rights', in P. Mahoney et al. (eds.), *Protection des droits de l'homme: la perspective européenne, mélanges à la mémoire de Rolv Ryssdal = Protecting Human Rights: The European Perspective, Studies in Memory of Rolv Ryssdal*, Cologne: Carl Heymanns Verlag, 2000, 1409–30

Touzé, S., 'Les limites de l'indemnisation devant la Cour européenne des droits de l'homme: le constat de violation comme satisfaction equitable suffisante', in J.-F. Flauss and E. Lambert Abdelgawad (eds.), *La pratique d'indemnisation par la Cour européenne des droits de l'homme*, Brussels: Bruylant, 2011, 127–53

Trechsel, S., 'Article 27', in L.-E. Pettiti, E. Decaux and P.-H. Imbert (eds.), *La Convention européenne des droits de l'homme. Commentaire article par article*, Paris: Economica, 1999, 621–47

'Article 31', in L.-E. Pettiti, E. Decaux and P.-H. Imbert (eds.), *La Convention européenne des droits de l'homme. Commentaire article par article*, Paris: Economica, 1999, 691–8

Turgis, S., 'Le recours aux expertises', in J.-F. Flauss and E. Lambert Abdelgawad (eds.), *La pratique d'indemnisation par la Cour européenne des droits de l'homme*, Brussels: Bruylant, 2011, 113–25

Van Brustem, M., and van Brustem, E., 'Les hésitations de la Cour européenne des droits de l'homme: à propos du revirement de jurisprudence en matière de satisfaction équitable applicable aux expropriations illicites: note sous CEDH, 21 octobre 2008, *Guiso-Gallisay c. Italie*, req. no. 58858/00', *Revue française de droit administratif* 2 (2009), 285–93

Vanneste, F., 'A New Inadmissibility Ground', in P. Lemmens and W. Vandenhole (eds.), *Protocol No. 14 and the Reform of the European Court of Human Rights*, Antwerp: Intersentia, 2005, 69–88

Vegleris, P., 'Modes de redressement des violations de la Convention européenne des droits de l'homme: esquisse d'une classification', in *Mélanges offerts à Polys Modinos: problèmes des droits de l'homme et de l'unification européenne*, Paris: Pédone, 1968, 369–88

Velu, J., 'Report on "Responsibilities for States Parties to the European Convention"', in *Proceedings of the Sixth International Colloquy about the European Convention on Human Rights (13–16 November 1985) = Actes du sixième Colloque international sur la Convention européenne des droits de l'homme (13–16 novembre 1985)*, Dordrecht: Martinus Nijhoff Publishers, 1988, 532–705

Virally, M., 'L'équité dans le droit. A propos des problèmes de délimitation maritime', in *International Law at the Time of Its Codification: Essays in Honour of Roberto Ago*, Vol. II, Milan: Giuffrè, 1987, 523–34

Voeten, E., 'Politics, Judicial Behaviour, and Institutional Design', in J. Christoffersen and M. R. Madsen (eds.), *The European Court of Human Rights between Law and Politics*, Oxford University Press, 2011, 61–76

Waldock, C. H. M., 'The European Convention for the Protection of Human Rights and Fundamental Freedoms', *British Yearbook of International Law* 34 (1958), 356–63

White, R. C. A., and Boussiakou, I., 'Separate Opinions in the European Court of Human Rights', *Human Rights Law Review* 9, no. 1 (2009), 37–60

Wildhaber, L., 'A Constitutional Future for the European Court of Human Rights?', *Human Rights Law Journal* 23, nos. 5–7 (2002), 161–5

'"Constitutionnalisation" et "juridiction constitutionnelle": le point de vue de Strasbourg', in S. Hennette-Vauchez and J.-M. Sorel (eds.), *Les droits de l'homme ont-ils constitutionnalisé le monde?*, Bruxelles: Bruylant, 2011, 93–103

'Rethinking the European Court of Human Rights', in J. Christoffersen and M. R. Madsen (eds.), *The European Court of Human Rights between Law and Politics*, Oxford University Press, 2011, 204–29

Wittich, S., 'Awe of the Gods and Fear of the Priests: Punitive Damages in the Law of State Responsibility', *Austrian Review of International and European Law* 3 (1998), 101–57

'Punitive Damages', in J. Crawford, A. Pellet and S. Olleson (eds.), *The Law of International Responsibility*, Oxford University Press, 2010, 667–75

Zagrebelsky, V., 'Violations structurelles et jurisprudence de la Cour européenne des droits de l'homme', in F. Salerno (ed.), *La nouvelle procédure devant la Cour européenne des droits de l'homme après le Protocole n° 14: actes du colloque tenu à Ferrara les 29 et 30 avril 2005*, Brussels: Bruylant, 2007, 149–56

Zwaak, L. F., 'The Interstate Complaint under the European Convention on Human Rights and Fundamental Freedoms: The Five Complaints against Turkey', *SIM Newsletter* 0 (1982), 13–16

'The Five Inter-State Complaints versus Turkey under the European Convention on Human Rights', *SIM Newsletter* 6 (1984), 14–22

'A Friendly Settlement in the European Inter-State Complaints against Turkey', *SIM Newsletter* 13 (1986), 44–8

Documents

Council of Europe

Rules of procedure adopted by the Committee of Ministers relating to the application of Article 32 of the Convention, *Yearbook of the European Convention on Human Rights* 4 (1961), p. 14

Protocols 1 to 16 to the European Convention on Human Rights, available on the Council of Europe's website (http://conventions.coe.int/Treaty/Commun/ListeTraites.asp?MA=3&26CM=7&26CL=ENG)

Explanatory Report to Protocol No. 9, ETS No. 140, available on the Council of Europe's website (http://conventions.coe.int/treaty/en/Reports/Html/140.htm)

Explanatory Report to Protocol No. 14, CETS No. 194, available on the Council of Europe's website (http://conventions.coe.int/Treaty/EN/Reports/Html/194.htm)

Recommendation R(2000)2 of 19 January 2000 on the re-examination or reopening of certain cases at domestic level following judgments of the European Court of Human Rights, available on the Council of Europe's website (https://wcd.coe.int/ViewDoc.jsp?id=334147)

Rules adopted on 10 January 2001 by the Committee of Ministers for the application of Article 46, paragraph 2, of the European Convention on Human Rights (available at https://wcd.coe.int/ViewDoc.jsp?id=744279&BackColorInternet=9999CC&BackColorIntranet=FFBB55&BackColorLogged=FFAC75)

Report of the Evaluation Group to the Committee of Ministers on the European Court of Human Rights, EG Court(2001)1, 27 September 2001, available on the Council of Europe's website (https://wcd.coe.int/ViewDoc.jsp?id=226195&Lang=fr)

Human rights working methods – Improved effectiveness of the Committee of Ministers' supervision of execution of judgments, Information document, CM/Inf(2004)8 final, 7 April 2004 (available at https://wcd.coe.int/ViewDoc.jsp?Ref=CM/Inf(2004)8&Language=lanEnglish&Ver=final)

Resolution Res(2004)3 of 12 May 2004 on judgments revealing an underlying systemic problem, available on the Council of Europe's website (https://wcd.coe.int/ViewDoc.jsp?id=743257)

Recommendation Rec(2004)5 of the Committee of Ministers to member states on the verification of the compatibility of draft laws, existing laws and administrative practice with the standards laid down in the European Convention on Human Rights, 12 May 2004, available on the Council of Europe's website (https://wcd.coe.int/ViewDoc.jsp?id=743297)

Recommendation Rec(2004)6 of the Committee of Ministers to member states on the improvement of domestic remedies, 12 May 2004, available on the Council of Europe's website (https://wcd.coe.int/ViewDoc.jsp?id=743317)

Rules of the Committee of Ministers for the supervision of the execution of judgments and of the terms of friendly settlements, adopted on 10 May 2006 (available at https://wcd.coe.int/ViewDoc.jsp?id=999329)

Report of the Group of Wise Persons to the Committee of Ministers, CM(2006) 203, 15 November 2006, available on the Council of Europe's website (https://wcd.coe.int/ViewDoc.jsp?id=1063779&Site=CM)

Practice Direction for just satisfaction claims, issued by the President of the Court on 28 March 2007, available on the Court's website (www.echr.coe.int/Pages/home.aspx?p=basictexts/rules&c=)

Monitoring of the payment of sums awarded by way of just satisfaction: an overview of the Committee of Ministers' present practice, CM/Inf/DH

(2008)7 final, 15 January 2009 (available at https://wcd.coe.int/ViewDoc.jsp?id=1393941&Site=CM)

Preliminary opinion of the Court in preparation for the Brighton Conference (adopted by the Plenary Court on 20 February 2012), available on the Court's website (www.echr.coe.int/Pages/home.aspx?p=court/reform&c=)

Rules of Court, entered into force on 1 January 2014, available on the Court's website (www.echr.coe.int/Pages/home.aspx?p=basictexts/rules&c=)

United Nations

Decision 8: Determination of Ceilings for Compensation for Mental Pain and Anguish (UN Doc. S/AC.26/1992/8, 27 January 1992), taken by the Governing Council of the United Nations Compensation Commission during its Fourth Session, at the 22nd meeting, held on 24 January 1992

ILC Articles on the Responsibility of States for Internationally Wrongful Acts, UN Doc. A/56/10 (2001)

Basic Principles and Guidelines on the Right to a Remedy and Reparation for Victims of Gross Violations of International Human Rights Law and Serious Violations of International Humanitarian Law, 19 April 2005, UN Doc. E/CN.4/2005/L.10/Add.11

Organization of American States

Rules of Procedure of the Inter-American Court of Human Rights, approved in December 2009, available on the Inter-American Court's website (www.corteidh.or.cr/index.php/en/about-us/reglamento/reglamento-vigente)

Annual Report of the Inter-American Court of Human Rights, 2012, available on the Inter-American Court's website (www.corteidh.or.cr/index.php/en/court-today/publicaciones)

Websites

Council of Europe: www.coe.int

European Court of Human Rights: www.echr.coe.int

Inter-American Court of Human Rights: www.corteidh.or.cr

United Nations: www.un.org

INDEX

For EU product safety concerns, contact us at Calle de José Abascal, 56–1°, 28003 Madrid, Spain or eugpsr@cambridge.org.

www.ingramcontent.com/pod-product-compliance
Lightning Source LLC
LaVergne TN
LVHW011530200926
848484LV00001B/219
* 9 7 8 1 1 0 7 0 7 2 3 6 7 *